A MANUAL GRAMMAR
of the
GREEK NEW TESTAMENT

BY

H. E. DANA, Th.D.

*Professor of New Testament Interpretation
in the Southwestern Baptist Theological
Seminary in Fort Worth, Texas*

AND

JULIUS R. MANTEY, Th.D., D.D.

*Professor of New Testament Interpretation
in the Northern Baptist Theological
Seminary in Chicago, Illinois*

*MACMILLAN PUBLISHING CO., INC.
New York*

Printing   54 55   Year   0

Printed with new index to Scripture References, 1957

ISBN   0-02-327070-5

Library of Congress catalog card number: 57-9544

The Macmillan Company
Collier-Macmillan Canada, Ltd., Toronto, Ontario

Printed in the United States of America

PREFACE

The need most keenly felt by present-day teachers of the Greek New Testament is for an accurate and comprehensive compendium of grammar which is adaptable to the average student. This need we have attempted to supply in the following pages. The book is not offered as an exhaustive treatment of the grammatical phenomena of the Greek New Testament, for its scope and design would not permit it to be such. It is intended to give to the student a comprehensive survey of the chief features of the grammar of the Greek New Testament in simple outline form, as an introduction to a more detailed and inductive study. Our chief effort has been to bring the best Greek scholarship within reach of the average student, and produce a textbook which, while being easy to comprehend, would adequately meet his needs. To this end we have made the method of presentation largely deductive, but the conclusions offered have been based upon more than a decade of careful inductive effort. In all our work of preparation we have sought to keep before us the average Greek student rather than the technical Greek scholar, at the same time endeavoring to make the book sufficiently accurate and thorough to stand the most severe tests of technical scholarship.

The primary consideration which induced the authors to undertake the production of this manual was their own experience in seeking to find among the number of great treatises already in existence on the grammar of the Greek New Testament a work readily adapted to class-room use. That we need at this time another exhaustive treatise on the grammar of the Greek Testament is doubtful; that we need a practical and adaptable textbook is beyond question. Just here is where we have sought to make a worthwhile contribution.

The foundation of scholarship, upon which it has been our privilege to build, is immense. The grammatical phenomena of the Greek New Testament have been attracting scientific attention for nearly, if not quite, three centuries. We have been able to trace the history of definite effort in this field back as far as 1650, when Caspian Wyss published the results of his investigations. Antedating his work was that of Salamanda Glass, but his accomplishments seem to have been of but slight consequence. The honor of the first published work to which we could at all accommodate the term grammar belongs to George Pasor, whose work appeared in 1655, though prepared much earlier. From Pasor we must skip a period of one hundred and sixty years to 1815, when P. H. Haab published at Tübingen his *Hebrew-Greek Grammar of the New Testament.*

The title of the last-mentioned book is indicative of the type of work which up to this time had been done on the Greek of the New Testament. It was largely an attempt— and of course a vain attempt—to conform the linguistic phenomena of the New Testament to the vague principles of Semitic grammar. The true light, in the full glow of which we now labor, dawned in 1824. Its earliest gleams found entrance through the mind and work of Johann Winer, whose *Grammar* first appeared in 1824. Winer's work was epoch-making in the highest degree. A grateful multitude of New Testament students are ready to join A. T. Robertson in his admiring declaration that "in a true sense he was a pathfinder" (*Grammar*, p. 4). He introduced a revolution into the study of the Greek New Testament by adopting and substantiating the premise that

Biblical Greek, and particularly that of the New Testament, was not a special "Holy Ghost" language, nor a conglomerate of Greek words and Semitic grammar, but the ordinary colloquial tongue of the day, spoken throughout the Graeco-Roman world. This idea has remained since his day an axiom in the study of the Greek New Testament.

As one scans the history of the period he gains the impression that progress after Winer's day was strangely slow. Much work was done here and there, the greater part of it based on Winer's fundamental premise, but none of it developed into any very definite production. It was 1860 before another conspicuous publication appeared. At about this date Buttmann's *Grammar* came from the press. A short while afterward (1864) there was published a work which has not received considerable attention, but which unquestionably has some real merit. It was a brief treatment of the *Syntax and Synonyms of the New Testament*, by William Webster, a Cambridge scholar. Further progress was made by Blass, whose *Grammar* was published in 1896, and S. G. Green, whose *Handbook to the Grammar of the Greek Testament* has served many classes well as a text-book, but is rather too elaborate and detailed for the most effective class-room use. E. D. Burton's *New Testament Moods and Tenses*, which first appeared in pamphlet form in 1888, then in book form in 1893, was a notable contribution to one phase of the study.

The greatest and most fruitful field for investigation which Greek New Testament scholarship has ever known is found in the Greek papyri. Chief honor for the effective exploration of this vast source of information on behalf of the Greek Testament belongs to Adolf Deissmann and J. H. Moulton. The earliest work of Moulton was his *Introduction to the Study of New Testament Greek*, which was first published in 1896. His *Prolegomena* appeared ten years later, and his *Grammar* (vols. ii and iii, the *Prol.* being vol. i) is now in process of publication. It is a posthumous publication, for Moulton met a tragic and premature death during the early years of the World War. For the enormous and delicate task of editing Moulton's *Grammar* from the notes which he left, the world of New Testament scholarship owes a great debt of gratitude to W. F. Howard, M.A., B.D. Deissmann's *Bible Studies* and *Philology of the Greek Bible* are his works of greatest linguistic interest.

A chapter of incalculable import in the history of the grammar of the Greek New Testament transpired when Gessner Harrison had in his Greek classes in the University of Virginia the young ministerial student John A. Broadus. Harrison was a highly accomplished Greek scholar, and far advanced beyond his own era in the understanding and use of the modern linguistic method, as is evidenced by his great work on *Greek Prepositions and Cases*. From him young Broadus acquired an incentive and equipment which made of him a mighty teacher and peerless scholar in the Greek New Testament. It was possibly regrettable that he published no work of his own on the Greek Testament, but the fruit of his labor has ripened into a most glorious yield in spite of that fact. The priceless heritage of his vast scholarship fell into worthy and competent hands in the person of his student and son-in-law, A. T. Robertson, that towering genius and masterful scholar who stands today without a rival at the forefront of the Greek scholarship of the world. In 1908 he first attracted the attention of New Testament students with his *Short Grammar of the Greek New Testament,* and then in 1914 appeared that stupendous work, so far superior to every preceding effort in the entire field, *A Grammar of the Greek New Testament in the Light of Historical Research.* This book is, and is probably for a long time to remain, the unrivaled standard in its realm.

To this colossal work the authors of this book are indebted more than to all their other sources combined. What a benediction it would be to all the coming generations of New Testament students if this great scholar could yet find it possible to give us a translation of the New Testament, and what a loss it will be if we must be deprived of it!

Among works on elementary Greek devoted to the New Testament, two of the earliest to hold the field in America were those by Harper and Weidner, and Huddilston. In recent years an elementary Greek text and brief work on syntax have been contributed by H. P. V. Nunn, a Cambridge scholar. The best textbooks on elementary Greek at present in the field are those by W. H. Davis and J. G. Machen.

This brief historical review makes it quite obvious that extensive and highly efficient efforts have already been bestowed upon the grammar of the Greek New Testament —and a considerable number of minor works have not been mentioned. Major works may also have been omitted through oversight or ignorance. But in all this aggregation of scholarly treatises there is no work satisfactorily adapted to class-room use. It is our hope that we offer here a book which will fill that need. We have sought to select and present with the greatest possible clearness the matters essential to a working knowledge of the language of the New Testament. The primary principles we have set out in large type and plain language. Matters of detail and the comparison of the opinions of leading scholars we have presented in smaller type, hoping that instructors and students will not regard the smaller type as a suggestion to skip anything, or an intimation that the matters so presented are of minor importance. As a matter of fact, the material in the small type represents the authors' widest research and most diligent effort.

We have adopted the simplest language possible in an adequate statement of grammatical principles. As far as could be done in conformity with our own judgment we have followed the terminology of Robertson and Moulton, in the firm belief that they come most nearly offering to English-speaking students a terminology which can become standard. Where the two have differed we have usually given the preference to Robertson, though not invariably. Of course, we have found instances in which we believed there were sufficient reasons for differing from them both, in which cases we have in honesty followed our own best judgment. We have had a fundamental principle in selecting terminology: to use terms which are simple and expressive, and easily apprehended by the average student. It has been our policy to avoid coining new terms. Those already familiar in Greek grammatical usage have been employed as far as possible.

In our discussion on Cases we have taken the advanced position that the cases should be approached from the viewpoint of function rather than of form, and that there were in reality eight cases in Greek. From the time that we began with the eight-case hypothesis we have found no evidence in Greek literature to confute it, while we have found ample evidence to confirm it. A decade of patient and wide research has established for us a conviction on this matter which is inescapable. We invite any who think it gratuitous to treat the cases from this viewpoint to ascertain whether it harmonizes with the original Aryan case divisions, and whether it contributes to simplicity and accuracy. It is our conviction that it does.

In the sections on Prepositions, Conjunctions, and Particles, which deal with the extensive and elusive field of connectives, several new meanings illustrated by various and vivid examples are set forth. An inductive study of these connectives was begun several years ago. An unusual use of a connective was carefully noted and its apparent meaning was written into a notebook or on the margin of whatever document was being studied. Later on these connectives were reëxamined, and their meanings were classified in the light of the inductive evidence thus derived. The papyri proved to be most helpful in this study. The discoveries of new meanings for οὖν, in particular, are of exceptional interest and value. It was a coincidence that in our independent research we arrived at the same conclusions that Professor Moulton did as to ἄν having the force of *ever* in most passages.

The illustrations have in the main been taken from the actual text of the Greek New Testament, but have been in some cases slightly altered for purposes of brevity and greater clearness. The discussion throughout has been based on the WH. text, and kept free from technical problems of textual criticism, with which the student at the stage of training contemplated by this book is rarely acquainted. We have sought to put the material in convenient outline form, and if we have made a distinctive contribution to this important field of science, it is chiefly a better organization of the material already produced.

To be used for study supplementary to the textbook, we have provided at the beginning of each section a list of references to Robertson's *Grammar* and *Short Grammar*, and Moulton's *Prolegomena*. The instructor would do well to assign one reference in each section as required parallel reading. Every student should be urged to own a copy of Robertson's *Grammar of the Greek New Testament in the Light of Historical Research*.

This book is in an unusual degree a coöperative product. The names of the two chief contributors appear on the title page, but many other proficient hands have wrought faithfully upon it—too many to mention by name. Nevertheless, for every aid received we record our most hearty thanks. It is but just that we should acknowledge here our constant use of the unpublished grammar notes of Professor C. B. Williams, Union University, Jackson, Tennessee, who, while in the chair of Greek New Testament in the Southwestern Seminary, was the honored preceptor of both authors. The fact that this material was not in published form has prevented any very definite reference in the text of the book. At the cost of great labor and painstaking care, the paradigms of conjugation were prepared by Professor L. R. Elliott, Librarian and Instructor in Biblical Greek in the Southwestern Seminary. Mr. John W. Patterson has rendered most valuable aid in the preparation of the vocabulary. To Mr. C. W. Koller, Fellow in the New Testament department of the Southwestern Seminary, we are grateful for valuable suggestions and assistance, while to Messrs. W. L. Moore and J. R. Branton we record our thanks for careful and effective proof reading. A large part of the typing of the manuscript has been done by Mr. E. P. Baker, who brought to the task a personal knowledge of the Greek language which in the nature of the case was indispensable.

This work is a successor to a former edition, published as a private enterprise by the authors chiefly for their own classes, under the title, *A Manual for the Study of the Greek New Testament*. Several of our friends, however, have kindly adopted it and used it as a textbook; and for words of commendation and suggestion from them we are deeply grateful.

A task which has been sometimes tedious but ever intensely interesting is at last completed. We would place the book in the hands of the average student of the Greek

New Testament, with the hope and prayer that it may secure for him access to the rich treasures of scholarship, and thereby to the deep mines of religious truth and inspiration which lie imbedded in the original text.

H. E. DANA,
    Seminary Hill, Tex.

J. R. MANTEY,
    Chicago, Ill.

KEY TO ABBREVIATIONS

We give here a list of the principal works cited in this volume. The books here listed would make a fairly complete working library on the grammar of the Greek New Testament for the average student. For such purpose there should be added, however, Moulton and Geden's *Concordance to the Greek Testament*. One who wishes a beginner's book for elementary Greek may secure Machen: *New Testament Greek for Beginners* (Macmillan) or Davis: *Beginner's Grammar of the Greek New Testament* (Doran). If an extensive bibliography is desired, Robertson provides in his *Grammar* one which will serve all ordinary purposes.

The method of citation in this book is to insert the adopted abbreviation for the name of the author or for the title of his book (as indicated below), followed by the page numbers. The abbreviations used are as follows:

ASV ....American Standard Version.

AV ....Authorized Version.

Bl. ....Blass: *Grammar of New Testament Greek* (2d ed.).

Br. ....Burton: *New Testament Moods and Tenses.*

Bt. ....Buttmann: *Grammar of New Testament Greek.*

D. ....Deissmann: *Philology of the Greek Bible* (*P. G. B.*) and *Bible Studies* (*B. S.*).

G. ....Green: *Handbook to the Grammar of the Greek New Testament.*

LXX ....Septuagint (Greek Old Testament).

M. ....Moulton: *Prolegomena to the Grammar of New Testament Greek.*

M-II. ....Moulton: *Grammar of New Testament Greek,* vol. ii.

R. ....Robertson: *A Grammar of the Greek New Testament in the Light of Historical Research.*

R-S. ....Robertson: *A Short Grammar of the Greek New Testament.*

RV ....Revised Version.

T. ....Thumb: *Handbook of the Modern Greek Vernacular.*

W. ....Thayer's translation of Luneman's revision of Winer: *Grammar of the Idiom of the New Testament* (7th ed.).

WH. ....Westcott and Hort: *Greek Text of the New Testament.*

Wr. ....Wright: *Comparative Grammar of the Greek Language.*

All cross references in the book are made by paragraph numbers. For instance, 120, (3), ii would refer to paragraph 120, subhead (3), the second paragraph in small type. We have tried so to enumerate the materials in the book as to make reference easy and accurate.

CONTENTS

APPENDIX

A MANUAL GRAMMAR OF THE GREEK NEW TESTAMENT

INTRODUCTION

References: R. 76–83; R.-S. 3, 4; M. 22–34.*

1. The modern historical method as applied to all phases of linguistic science is to investigate a language in the light of all the periods of its own history, and its relationship to all kindred languages. This investigation of linguistic kinship and development is known as the science of comparative philology. No really informed student now attempts the study of any language without the use of this comparative method. Consequently we should approach the study of New Testament Greek by considering its relation to the other representatives of human speech, and the stages of its own development. It will be of value to the student to become acquainted especially with the relation of the Greek to those languages nearest it in kinship, and in general with the entire scope of linguistic development.

The Indo-European Languages.

2. The languages of mankind may be divided into families, the families into branches, and the branches into dialects. However, it will be necessary here to offer complete analysis only of the family to which the Greek belongs. And indeed, the family to which the Greek belongs submits itself most readily to thorough analysis, for it is the most highly developed, and at the same time the most clearly defined of all languages. Besides its designation as Indo-

* For key to abbreviations see pp. xvii and xviii.

European, it is sometimes called Indo-Germanic, or Aryan. Of these three designations the last is the most convenient, but may be confusing because so often restricted to the Asiatic dialects of the family; the second is undesirable because it gives an exaggerated prominence to the German language; the one here used, though rather clumsy, is by far the most accurately descriptive.

3. The Indo-European was the original tongue of those tribes which in prehistoric times are believed to have inhabited a region somewhere about east-central Asia or west-central Europe. The earliest historical evidences of them appear in western Europe, though at some extremely ancient period a large remnant of the race moved southward and settled in Persia and India—hence the name Indo-European. There have developed seven branches of this family, each branch being represented in several dialects. Only the chief dialects will be mentioned here. For a fuller discussion the student is referred to Whitney's *Life and Growth of Language* and Sweet's *History of Languages*.

4. The oldest representative of the family is the *Indian* branch, of which the chief known dialect is the *Sanskrit*, which is of special interest to the student of the Greek New Testament because of its close relation to the Greek, of which it may be described as an elder sister. The preservation of Sanskrit was largely due to its use in the Vedic hymns, the sacred literature of the Hindus. Later remains of it may be found in laws, epic writings, etc. Its inflection of the noun is the most highly developed of all the languages, there being eight inflectional endings, with occasional traces of a ninth.

A later stage of the Indian branch is represented in the Prakrit.

5. The second oldest branch of the Indo-European is the *Greek*. Its dialects belong to antiquity, the language

having become unified and universalized several centuries before the Christian era. This matter will receive fuller attention later. Greek is the most literary of all the ancient languages, having produced a veritable stream of literature, beginning with Homer about 900 B.C.

6. Next in age to the Greek is the *Italic,* of which the Latin was the chief dialect. Other ancient dialects of the Italic were the Umbrian of northern Italy and the Oscan of southern Italy. Only scant remains of these dialects have come down to us. The Latin is witnessed by an abundance of ancient literature, and survives, though greatly modified, in the Romanic (or Romance) languages, which include the Italian, French, Spanish, Portugese, and Roumanian.

7. From this point on the question of comparative age must be waived for want of sufficient evidence. If we follow the order of historical prominence we are brought next to the *Teutonic* branch, of which our own English is the most widely distributed dialect. It, with the Dutch and German, seems to have come to us from a sister dialect of the ancient Gothic (if the German be not a direct successor of the Gothic), of which the only surviving literary remains are fragments of the Bible translated by Ulfilas, the great Christian missionary to the Goths. Of ancient origin also is the Scandinavian, the chief literary remains of which are the Eddas and Sagas of Iceland, its surviving dialects being the language of Denmark, Sweden, Norway, and Iceland. "The oldest records of this branch are the runic inscriptions, some of which date as far back as the third or fourth century" (Wr. 2).

8. The *Slavic* is the branch of the Indo-European tongue now distributed in eastern and southern Europe. It survives chiefly in Russia, Poland, and some of the Balkan states. It is also usually regarded as embracing the Lettic

languages, unless these last be placed in a separate class as the Baltic branch (cf. Sweet: *op. cit.*, p. 98). The Bulgarian has the oldest literature, but the Russian is the most widely distributed.

9. The *Celtic* is the ancient language of western Europe, represented chiefly by the Gauls and Britons. The Irish, Scotch, and Welch also belong to this branch.

10. The *Iranian* branch is represented mainly in the Persian language. It also includes the Zend dialect, preserved in the Avesta, the sacred book of the Zoroastrian religion.

The foregoing outline will furnish the student with a fair working analysis of the family of language to which the Greek belongs. Beyond this even greater brevity may be adopted, but a comprehensive sketch of the entire field of linguistic research is of value as giving the student a proper appreciation of the modern approach to the science of language. There is one other family fairly well defined, but the remaining six are difficult of classification, and appear to be the result of combining elements of one family or dialect with those of another.

11. The *Semitic* family is almost as well defined as the Indo-European. Its geographical origin was probably southern Asia. To it belong the Assyrian, the Hebrew, the Phoenician, the Aramaic, the Syriac, the Arabic, and the Abyssinian. It is the second family in the degree of its development.

12. After leaving the Indo-European and Semitic families we face a bewildering conglomerate. We turn from forms of speech which present orderly and intelligible inflection, and hence are subject to systematic analysis, and approach a mode of expression which is monosyllabic, or agglutinative, or both. One is immediately seized with the impression that they all belong to a single family, but philologists have been unable to reduce the matter to any such simple solution. On the contrary, they have discovered sufficient lines of distinction to divide these mongrel tongues into six different families.

The *Scythian* family has dialects in Asia and Europe, being represented by the Turkish, Finnish, and Hungarian. The *Mongolian* or Monosyllabic family has its home in southeastern Asia with the Himalayan tribes, the Mongols, the Manchus, and the Chinese. Japanese is also probably a kindred tongue. The *Malay-Polynesian* family belongs to the islands of the southern Asiatic seas. The *Caucasian* is spoken by the tribes dwelling among the Caucasus Mountains in south-central Asia. The *Hamitic* is represented by the Egyptian, Libyan, and Ethiopian, with possible kinship to the lower African dialects. The languages of the savage tribes of Africa practically defy classification. The *American* family includes the languages of the Indians of our own continent. But comparative philologists are not entirely agreed that the Indian languages belong to a single family. In fact, several of the conclusions adopted in the foregoing discussion are but tentative. The science of comparative philology is still in its infancy, and offers a wide and important field of investigation. Much may be learned about the antiquity of the race by searching in the origins of linguistic expression.

13. Robertson (R. 37) classifies language as *isolating, agglutinative,* and *inflectional.* The isolating languages are those without inflection, employing other devices, such as word-order, for variety in expression. They include Chinese, Burmese, etc. Agglutinative languages make use of separable prefixes, infixes, and suffixes, such as may be seen in the Turkish. The inflectional languages vary expression by means of endings, stems, and prefixes. This type of language is represented in the Indo-European and Semitic families. Some languages, e.g., modern English, employ to a greater or less extent all these methods. Sweet adds one other class to these three, which he calls the *incorporative* languages. These gather into a single word several elements of the sentence, such as subject, verb, and object (cf. Sweet: *op. cit.,* pp. 65ff.). For a splendid brief discussion of the Indo-European languages the student may refer to Wr. 1-4.

The Greek Language

14. The history of the Greek language extends back to about 1500 B.C. Previous to Homer, however, the history of the language is wrapped in great obscurity. The development of the language may be divided into five periods:

(1) *The Formative Period.* This period extends from the prehistoric origin of the race to Homer (c. 900 B.C.).

The primitive tribes from which the Greek nation arose were members of the great Aryan family which had its original home somewhere in west-central Asia. In prehistoric times a group of tribes from this original stock migrated into the little peninsula of southern Europe now known as Greece. The topographical character of this country is exceedingly irregular. Numerous mountain ranges and the inland penetration of arms of the sea cut the country up into many divisions. As a result of this irregular topography the original tribes were practically barred from intercourse with one another, and hence were slow in developing unity of life and language. There grew a number of different dialects, the chief of which were the Attic, Boeotian, Northwestern, Thessalian, and Arcadian. These probably developed from three original dialects: the Doric, Aeolic, and Ionic. The most vigorous and attractive of these was the Ionic, which, therefore, exerted the greatest influence upon subsequent linguistic developments among the Greeks.

(2) *The Classical Period.* This period embraces the centuries from Homer to the Alexandrian conquests (c. 330 B.C.). In this period the Attic dialect, based chiefly on the old Ionic, with the best elements of the Doric and Aeolic, secured supremacy. The ancient Greek literature which has come down to us is predominantly Attic. Any general grammar of classical Greek deals primarily with the Attic speech, noting the elements from other dialects as irregularities and exceptions. The Attic was the molding force in all the subsequent developments of the Greek language. It constituted the chief basis of New Testament Greek.

(3) *The Koiné Period.* This period extends from 330 B.C. to A.D. 330. It is the period of the common or universal Greek. During this period the Greek language was freely used and understood throughout the civilized world,

being spoken as freely on the streets of Rome, Alexandria, and Jerusalem as in Athens. There were four main causes bringing about the development of the Koiné Greek.

a. Extensive Colonization. The Greeks were a very aggressive people, and early learned seafaring from the Phoenicians, and vied with the latter in the extent of maritime activities. As a result Greek colonies were planted on nearly all the shores of the Mediterranean. One of the strongest of these colonies was on the eastern coast of Italy, not far from the center of the Latin world.

b. Close Political and Commercial Affiliation of the Separate Greek Tribes. The broadening of the life of the people by extensive colonization, and more especially the common peril of eastern conquerors, brought the several tribes of Greece into closer touch, and developed a sense of racial homogeneity. Doubtless no single cause contributed more to this result than the long struggle with the Persians. The campaign of Cyrus, recounted for us by Xenophon in his *Anabasis* and *Katabasis*, brought together Greeks of all tribes and dialects into one great army, and hence did much to develop a common tongue. There are foretokens of a Koiné language to be found even in so astutely Attic a document as Xenophon's *Anabasis*.

c. Religious Interrelations. Though each Greek tribe had its own tribal god or gods, yet there was a sense of religious unity in the race. This exhibited itself in the common reverence of all the tribes for certain preëminent deities of the pantheon, especially Zeus. These leading deities which we might speak of as racial gods, served to promote the unity of the race. This was particularly true after the establishment of the great national festivities at such religious centers as Olympia, Delos, and Delphi. Inscriptions upon the statues and memorials of various kinds erected at these centers were in all the leading dialects, and led to the acquaintance of one tribe with the language of another. As the people from all the different localities of widely distributed Hellas mingled together at these periodical celebrations, there arose a natural tendency toward a common speech. This factor was certainly very potent in the creation of the Koiné.

d. The Alexandrian Conquests. The climax of this merging process in the growth of the Greek language was reached in the Alexandrian conquests (334 to 320 B.C.). The mingling of representatives from all the Greek tribes in Alexander's army matured the development of a common Greek, and the wide introduction of Greek culture under his direction distributed the common tongue throughout the Macedonian empire. When Rome conquered this Hellenized territory, she in turn was Hellenized, and thereby the civilized world adopted the Koiné Greek. Hence Paul could write his doctrinal masterpiece to the political center of the Latin world in the Greek language, and Augustus, emperor of Rome, must needs inscribe his official seal in Greek (cf. D., *B. S.* 243).

The remaining two periods of development in the Greek language will need but bare mention.

(4) *The Byzantine Period* extends from A.D. 330 to 1453. It begins with the division of the Roman empire, and its progress is largely affected by the uncertain fortunes of the throne at Constantinople.

(5) *The Modern Period* is from 1453 to the present. We have in this period the development of the language now spoken on the streets of Athens. The remarkable fact is that it bears a closer kinship to the New Testament language than do the writings of Euripides and Plato.

15. Robertson discusses the essential and obvious unity of the Greek language. While it consists of a variety of dialects, and presents several successive stages of growth, yet all its various mem-

bers are so related as to compose a single language. Therefore, no one phase of the language or its history should be set up as the final standard (cf. also D., *P.G.B.*). The classical Attic is in no sense to be regarded as the standard Greek, any more than we are to make Homer the criterion. Both are dialectic variations of the one Greek language. Greek is one whether we consider it at 1000 B.C. or A.D. 1000; whether used by the Attic poet, the Koiné letter-writer, or the resident of modern Athens. "It is one language whether we read the Epic Homer, the Doric Pindar, the Ionic Herodotus, the Attic Xenophon, the Aeolic Sappho, the Atticistic Plutarch, Paul the exponent of Christ, an inscription in Pergamus, a papyrus letter in Egypt, Tricouphis or Vlachos in the modern times" (R. 42). Robertson outlines the history of the Greek language as follows: The Mycenaean Age, 1500 B.C. to 1000 B.C.; the Age of Dialects, 1000 B.C. to 300 B.C.; the Age of the Koiné, 300 B.C. to A.D. 330; the Byzantine Greek, A.D. 330 to 1453; the Modern Greek, 1453 to the present. He remarks with great truth, "As a matter of fact, any division is arbitrary, for the language has had an unbroken history, though there are three general epochs in that history" (R. 41-43).

The Greek of the New Testament

16. There was a time when the scholars who dealt with the original text of the New Testament regarded its Greek as a special Holy Ghost language, prepared under divine direction for the Scripture writers. When the fallacy of this conception began to grow evident, two opposing schools developed. The Hebraists contended that the Septuagint and the New Testament were written in a Biblical Greek, dominated largely by Hebrew or Aramaic modes of expression; the Purists contended that they represented variations of the classical Attic. But beginning with Winer in 1825 there came a revolution in the views of New Testament scholarship relative to this matter. As a result of the labors of Deissmann in Germany, Moulton in England, and Robertson in America all question has been removed from the conclusion that New Testament Greek is simply a

sample of the colloquial Greek of the first century; i.e., the Koiné Greek. The inspired writers of the New Testament wrote in the ordinary language of the masses, as might have been expected.

17. Robertson shows that the progress of opinion among New Testament Greek scholars has been for more than half a century toward the conclusion now universally accepted that the Greek of the New Testament is but a specimen of the vernacular Koiné of the first century. He deals extensively with the witness of the inscriptions and papyri to this fact. The evidence of inscriptions was employed as early as 1887. Two pioneers in this new field were E. L. Hicks and W. M. Ramsay. But the complete establishment of the new method is an accomplishment of the twentieth century. Deissmann has doubtless done the most extensive work in this particular field. The future will countenance no other view of the Greek New Testament (cf. R. 31–48).

Literary Witnesses to the Koiné

18. Since the Greek of the New Testament is the current language of the period in which it was written, it is of interest to the New Testament student to learn what other literary monuments this language has left to us, from which he may obtain additional light on the Greek New Testament. There are six of these sources of light on the Koiné.

(1) *Biblical Greek.* Not because it is a separate language, or even dialect, but because it exhibits certain characteristics and possesses an interest all its own, we may still speak of the language of the New Testament and Septuagint as "Biblical Greek." When one has read the epoch-making works of Deissmann, he is just a little shy of the term, but still it is true that there is a place in philological science for the term "Biblical Greek." This would be true for the one fact alone of the distinctive literature of transcendant interest which composes it. It is also true that the New Testament and Septuagint present a distinc-

tive type of the Koiné. They are superior in literary quality to the average presented by the papyri, and yet do not exhibit the classical aim of the Atticistic writers. So while heeding and properly applying the warning of Deissmann, at the same time we need to preserve a serviceable distinction.

(2) *Literary Koiné.* There was formal literary effort of considerable extent during the Koiné period which much more readily approaches the classical nature of the Attic than does our New Testament. To this class belong the writings of Plutarch, Polybius, Josephus, Strabo, Philo, etc. (cf. M. 25–26).

(3) *Papyri.* This ancient writing material was made from the papyrus reed, an Egyptian water plant. Its use dates back to extreme antiquity, and extends down to the Byzantine period. Papyri are now discovered in Egypt, where climatic conditions have favored their preservation. They are especially valuable to the student of the Greek New Testament, both because of the wide range of their literary quality and their exhibition of the typical Koiné. They represent every kind of general literature, from the casual correspondence of friends to the technicalities of a legal contract. There is, however, little formal literature— such as poem or treatise—to be found among them. They consist in the main of private letters, contracts, wills, court records, government documents, etc. They represent the ordinary language of the people, and it was in this type of language that our New Testament was written (cf. D., *P. G. B.* 23–33; M. 27–28; especially Goodspeed in Mathews-Smith, *Dictionary of Religion and Ethics,* p. 324).

(4) *Inscriptions.* These are more widely distributed than the papyri, being found in abundance on several sites of important centers of Mediterranean civilization. They are found "either in their original positions or lying under

ruins and mounds of rubbish" (D., *P. G. B.* **17f.**). They are usually epigraphs or notices, carved upon slabs of stone for official, civic, and memorial purposes. They are of a more formally literary character than the papyri. Their value has been not only literary but historical. The great works of Sir William Ramsay on the historical criticism of the New Testament have secured a rich contribution of evidence from the inscriptions (cf. D., *P. G. B.* 17–23; M. 28–29).

(5) *Ostraca.* The *ostraca* were potsherds—fragments of broken jugs or other earthen vessels—used by the poorer classes for memoranda, receipts, and the like. "As linguistic memorials of the lower classes these humble potsherd texts shed light on many a detail of the linguistic character of our sacred book—that book which was written, not by learned men but by simple folk, by men who themselves confessed that they had their treasure in earthen vessels (2 Cor. 4:7). And thus the modest ostraca rank as of equal value with the papyri and inscriptions" (D., *P. G. B.* 35). It would be well here to add the observation of Moulton that "it must not be inferred . . . that the New Testament writers are at all comparable to these scribes in lack of education" (M. 28; cf. D., *P. G. B.* 17–23; R. 21).

(6) *Modern Greek.* The important relation of Modern Greek to the Koiné is a discovery of the nineteenth century, dating back only to 1834. The connection is simply that the Modern Greek is an outgrowth of the Koiné rather than of the Attic, which, of course, was to be expected. Vernacular is always the chief factor of change in the growth of a language. Hence the real basis of the Greek now spoken in Athens is that represented in our New Testament, and not the classic tongue of Aeschylus, or even the Atticistic attempts of Polybius. Moulton quotes Hatzidakis, the Modern Greek grammarian, as saying that

"the language generally spoken today in the towns differs less from the common language of Polybius than this last differs from the language of Homer" (cf. M. 29f.).

19. Deissmann assigns to the inscriptions the chief place as evidence on the Greek of the New Testament. To the papyri he gives a high but secondary place (*B. S.* 80f.). Moulton contends that the private letters discovered among the papyri are the most important source of light on New Testament Greek (M. 27f.). Biblical Greek could not be understood until their evidence was brought to light. Robertson cites one hundred and eighty-six words formerly supposed to be peculiar to Biblical Greek which the papyri and inscriptions have shown were in common use (R. 65f.). Deissmann offers a list of seventeen merely as examples (*B. S.* 83), and later presents an extended discussion of scores of others which he has found current in the first-century world (*B. S.* 86ff.). On the whole, Moulton is probably correct in maintaining that the papyri offer the most important source of light on the Greek of the New Testament.

Types of the Koiné

20. As is true of any language which develops a literature, Koiné Greek presents characteristic differences between the spoken and written language. This fact presents the two types of Koiné.

(1) The *literary* Koiné is represented by extra-Biblical literature, by most of the inscriptions, and by a few papyri.

(2) The *vernacular* Koiné is represented by most of the papyri and ostraca, and by nearly all Biblical Greek. Luke and the author of Hebrews approximate the literary type.

Moulton says of the literary Koiné: "The post-classical writers wrote Attic according to their lights, tempered generally with a plentiful admixture of grammatical and lexical elements drawn from the vernacular, for which they had too hearty a contempt even to give it a name," and he further observes with reference to their censure of the vernacular as "bad Greek" that they were "thus incidentally providing us with information concerning a Greek which interests us more than the artificial Attic which they prized so highly" (cf. M. 24–26). Most of the literary Koiné represents a clumsy and unsuccessful effort to restore the classical type and idiom of the Attic. Hence it is neither good Attic nor good Koiné.

Other Elements in New Testament Greek

21. The life out of which the New Testament came was affected by a variety of historical currents. The one which most deeply influenced the language was Hellenistic culture. But this is not the only factor reflected in the language. The writers of the New Testament were Jews (with the probable exception of Luke), which would lead us quite naturally to expect traces of their native tongue. The political regime under which the New Testament was written was controlled by Rome, the center of the Latin language. It is, therefore, quite natural that we find effects of Hebrew and Latin influence in the Greek of the New Testament.

(1) *Hebraisms.* There are in the New Testament unquestionably some traces of Hebrew idiom. They result chiefly from the influence of the Hebrew Old Testament and the LXX. Since Aramaic was the native vernacular of Palestine, it is probable that the New Testament was affected to some extent by it. It is thought by many that Luke had literary sources of his gospel which were in Aramaic. In view of these several means of Hebraic influence upon the New Testament the amount of Hebraisms in it has been overestimated. There are really but few. Examples may be found in Mt. 19:5; Lu. 1:34, 42; 20:12.

Moulton finds three results of Semitic influence in the New Testament: (1) words which reflect Semitic idiom; (2) Semitic influence upon syntax; (3) Semitisms which result from the translation of Hebrew or Aramaic into Greek. He discusses at length the prevalence of Semitic peculiarities in Luke's writings, and accounts for it in two ways: (1) the use of rough Greek translations from

Semitic originals; (2) the literary adaptation of the style of the LXX. He cites the paratactic construction with καί as a probable result of Semitic influence, paralleling the *waw-consecutive* of the Hebrew. The introduction of a narrative with καὶ ἐγένετο is likely a reflection of ויהי (M. 10-18). Deissmann regards such Semitisms in the New Testament as a matter of religious technicality, "like that of our sermons and Sunday magazines" (cited M. 18). He considers the general Semitic influence upon the New Testament as a very potent factor, and describes the LXX as "the mother of the Greek New Testament" (cf. *P. G. B.* 8-15). As a matter of fact, however, the LXX is not as intensely Semitic as has formerly been supposed. Of eighty-one varieties of grammatical usage discussed by Conybeare and Stock *(Selections from the Septuagint)*, a careful examination in the light of the present knowledge of the Koiné reveals that fifty-three of them are typical Greek, and the remaining twenty-eight would likely be considerably reduced by further knowledge of the Koiné. That is, at least sixty-five per cent of the Septuagint represents Greek of the age in which it was made. "We have come to recognize that we had greatly overestimated the number of Hebraisms and Aramaisms in the Greek Bible" (*P. G. B.* 52; cf. also R. 88-108).

(2) *Latinisms.* These are from Roman influence, being chiefly names of persons, offices, institutions, etc. The number is small, even in comparison with the Hebraisms.

Moulton thinks that Latin can scarcely be said to have influenced the language of the New Testament. He admits there are terms derived from Latin, but as to grammar—the really vital point in language—the Latinisms of the New Testament present a vanishing quantity. "Apart from lexical matters, we may be content with a general negative" (M. 21). Robertson presents an exhaustive list of the Latin terms in the New Testament, the total number being thirty-two—with one in question. He finds four Latin phrases (cf. R. 108-111). So while we must follow Moulton in regarding New Testament grammar as free from Latin influence, yet it is still true that there are Latinisms, and a thorough review must in justice recognize them.

PART I

ACCIDENCE

I. ORTHOGRAPHY

References: R. 177-181, 206-208, 221-222, 236-238; R.-S. 11-16; M. 44-47.

22. Orthography comes from two Greek words, ὄρθος meaning *straight*, and γράφειν meaning *to write*. Hence it means the correct or accepted forms of writing. The term is employed in grammatical science to embrace all those matters which have to do with the mechanical structure of words. In the Greek of the New Testament it covers a field about which there is much uncertainty. We will discuss here only the more important matters.

The Alphabet

23. There were twenty-four letters in the Greek alphabet of the Koiné period. The Greek alphabet was originally derived from the Phoenecian, several additions and modifications having been made, as for instance the invention of the vowels. The alphabet underwent several changes in preclassical times, such as the loss of digamma and the change of *h* (derived from the Semitic *heth*) to η. The forms of the characters as they became fixed in the Attic continued in the Koiné. But as to phonetic value, there were probably numerous changes.

Four different types of letters have developed in the history of the language. (1) Probably the oldest were the *capitals* which appear in the inscriptions, being practically the same as the forms now used for capitals. (2) The rapid formation of these capitals in the writing of manuscripts after the use of papyri and vellum were introduced developed what is known as the *uncial* type. (3) The effort to join together in writing these uncial letters resulted in what we call the *cursive* ("running") or *minuscule* type. (4) When print-

ing was invented, a "printer's type" of small characters was derived
from the minuscules (cf. M-II. 37ff.).

Alphabet

Name	Capitals	Small Letters	Uncials
Alpha............	A	α	ᴀ
Beta.............	B	β	ʙ
Gamma..........	Γ	γ	ᴦ
Delta............	Δ	δ	ᴧ
Epsilon..........	E	ε	ε
Zeta.............	Z	ζ	ᴢ
Eta..............	H	η	ʜ
Theta...........	Θ	θ	θ
Iota.............	I	ι	ɩ
Kappa..........	K	κ	κ
Lambda.........	Λ	λ	λ
Mu.............	M	μ	ᴍ
Nu.............	N	ν	ɴ
Xi..............	Ξ	ξ	ᴣ
Omicron.........	O	ο	ο
Pi..............	Π	π	ᴨ
Rho............	P	ρ	ᴘ
Sigma...........	Σ	σ ς	ᴄ
Tau.............	T	τ	ᴛ
Upsilon.........	Υ	υ	ʏ
Phi.............	Φ	φ	φ
Chi.............	X	χ	χ
Psi.............	Ψ	ψ	ψ
Omega..........	Ω	ω	ω

24. Language was originally spoken, so that letters are
but arbitrary symbols invented to represent sounds. Vocal
sounds are made by contracting the vocal cords so that they
vibrate as the breath passes through. The varieties of
enunciation are secured by varying the positions of the

organs of the mouth. These variations may be separated into two principal classes, those made by obstructed breath and those made by unobstructed breath. Consequently there are, in the nature of the case, only two classes of letters. The consonants are those made by obstructed breath. The vowels are those made by unobstructed breath.

(1) The *consonants* may be classified as follows:

a. Liquids:	λ, μ, ν, ρ.		
b. Mutes:	*Smooth*	*Middle*	*Rough*
Gutturals...........	κ	γ	χ
Labials.............	π	β	φ
Dentals............	τ	δ	θ
c. Sibilants:	ζ, ξ, σ, ψ.		

(2) The *vowels* are α, ε, η, ι, ο, υ, ω. The pronunciation of these vowels in the past history of the Greek language is a problem practically impossible to solve. The interchange in the papyri of vowels for dipthongs and vice versa, and of vowels for one another shows that there was much duplication in sound, but just what the sounds were we are unable to tell. As a matter of fact, we may be sure "that considerable difference existed between the Greek of Rome and Asia, Hellas and Egypt" so far as pronunciation was concerned (cf. M–II 41f.). Adopting for these vowels the pronunciation of Modern Greek would not "compensate in accuracy for the inconvenience it would cause" (*ibid.* 42). Robertson is undoubtedly correct in his opinion that the Greek of the New Testament was pronounced much more like the vernacular Greek of Demosthenes' times than like the Modern Greek (R-S. 15). The matter must be left an open question.

25. Sometimes two vowels are united and blended into a single sound. Such a combination is called a *diphthong*. The Greek dipthongs are αι, αυ, ει, οι, ου, ευ, ηυ, υι. The

iota subscript with α, η, and ω is a sort of diphthong, though it in no way modifies the sound. Like the vowels, the pronunciation of the diphthongs is a problem for which there can be no final solution.

Spelling

26. At no other point of mechanical structure does so much uncertainty obscure the Koiné as we find here. / The oldest known MSS. of the New Testament were written more than two and a half centuries after the original autographs, / and so widely do these MSS. differ in spelling that we may be sure that the copyists were least faithful at this point. In this matter the papyri offer us but little aid, as they, too, present a chaos of variations. But these differences in spelling really have little weight in exegesis. We may accept without fear of being led astray in interpretation the spelling of the WH. text.

Especially does difficulty arise from a tendency in transcription known as *itacism*. This is the modification of other vowels and diphthongs in the direction of the short *i* sound. This feature appears even as early as the Sinaitic MS. Such confusion in sound naturally led to a confusion in transcription. Two other tendencies need mention. One was an inclination to suppress the distinction between the long and short vowels. Length of vowels was assiduously observed in the classical Attic, but the differentiation began to disappear in the Koiné, and has continued to fade until Modern Greek makes no distinction at all (cf. T. 7). In line with the itacistic tendency we find a disposition to replace diphthongs by simple sounds (cf. M-II. 42f.). And yet the reverse of this frequently occurs in the papyri, where we find ι and ε replaced by ει and αι. In fact, these vowels and diphthongs are used interchangeably in the papyri. Such tendencies meant inevitable confusion in the MSS., for it is obvious that "the scribe is under the constant temptation to correct the spelling in his document by the spelling of his day" (R-S. 11).

Elision

27. If a final vowel is short, it may be omitted before a word beginning with a vowel. The omission is indicated by an apostrophe. Elision is seen chiefly in prepositions and particles, as δι' αὐτοῦ, κατ' οἶκον, οὐδ' ἄν.

Elision is not so extensively used in the New Testament as in classical Greek. It is comparatively infrequent in modern Greek. In the New Testament its use "takes place habitually and without variation before pronouns and particles; also before nouns in combinations of frequent occurrence, as ἀπ' ἀρχῆς κατ' οἶκον, In other cases there is much diversity and occasional variation" (M–II. 61).

Crasis

28. Crasis is the merging of a word into the one following by the omission and contraction of vowels. It affects the conjunction καί and the article, and is marked by the retention of the breathing of the second word, which is called the *coronis;* e.g., κἀγώ for καὶ ἐγώ; τοὔνομα for τὸ ὄνομα.

Crasis is rare in the New Testament. In fact, "except for τοὔνομα in Mt. 27:57, τοὐναντίον ter, and ταῦτά in Luke, crasis is confined to combinations with καί which retains the same tendency in Modern Greek more conspicuously. . . . Papyri of culture low enough to admit phonetic spelling show us that crasis was practiced sometimes when unaccented words were capable of being fused with the preceding word" (M–II. 63).

Movable Consonants

29. The final s of οὕτως is used in classical Greek only before vowels, but in the New Testament it is used prevailingly before consonants as well. WH. admit only ten exceptions.

30. The omission of s from ἄχρι and μέχρι is observed in the New Testament with but few exceptions, if we accept the WH. text.

31. Movable ν is added to the third person singular ending in ε, to words ending in σι and to ἐστί; as ἔλαβεν, πᾶσιν, ἐστίν. In classical Greek it is used only before words beginning with a vowel, or at the end of a sentence or clause, but in the New Testament—as also in the papyri—it occurs frequently before consonants. So we may say that the rule of the Koiné was to use the ν *movable* irrespective of what followed.

Breathings

32. *Kinds of Breathings.* The Koiné Greek like the classical has two breathings, rough (') and smooth ('). The indication of these breathings is a device of later Greek. Moulton finds that "literary documents have begun to insert them at a date not much later than ℵ and B" (M–II, 97ff.).

33. *Aspiration.* In classical Greek when a preposition preceded a word with a rough breathing and the final vowel of the preposition elided, if the consonant thus left final had an aspirate form, it was aspirated, but in the New Testament, aspiration sometimes occurs where there is no rough breathing; as ἀφοράω for ἀπό and ὁράω, but ἀφίδω for ἀπό and ἴδω.

Contraction

34. When two vowels or a vowel and diphthong come together in adjoining syllables they usually blend into a single syllable. Thus γένε-ος becomes γένους; ἐφίλε-ε becomes ἐφίλει.

i. Contraction in verbs with vowel stems presents a uniform system in general, with rarely an exception. In other parts of speech there are many variations, which must be learned by observation. The following scheme of vowel contractions will be found to apply in most cases, especially with verbs.

To locate a contract form in the following table, find the stem vowel in the first vertical column, and the connecting vowel in the top line, follow the columns to their intersection and there the regular contraction will be found.

	ε	η	ο	ω	ει	ῃ	ου	οι
α	ᾱ	ᾱ	ω	ω	ᾳ	ᾳ	ω	ῳ
ε	ει	η	ου	ω	ει	ῃ	ου	οι
ο	ου	ω	ου	ω	οι	οι	ου	οι

ii. The formation of infinitives in contract verbs presents some exceptions which should be noted. Verbs with α as their stem vowel have their present infinitive active form in -ᾱν instead of -ᾷν, as it would be with the regular contraction of -άειν. The present infinitive active of verbs with ο stem contract -όειν to -οῦν instead of -οῖν. The verb ζάω has as its present active infinitive ζῆν instead of ζᾷν.

iii. In word formation, stem formation and inflection the combination of consonants occasions frequent changes and contractions. We offer the following table as an aid to the student in tracing these variations.

Liquids.

Submit easily to transposition.

Sometimes λ is doubled to compensate for the loss of a vowel.

Regularly ρ is doubled when preceded by a vowel.

As to ν: before liquids it becomes the same liquid.

        before gutturals it becomes γ (nasal).

        before labials it becomes μ.

        before dentals it remains unchanged.

        before σ it is dropped, and the preceding vowel lengthened.

Mutes.

Gutturals: before μ become γ; before σ become ξ;
           before τ become κ; before θ become χ.

Labials: before μ become μ; before σ become ψ;
           before τ become π; before θ become φ.

Dentals: before μ become σ; before σ are dropped;
           before τ become σ; before θ become σ;
           before κ are dropped.

Sibilants.

ζ is a combination of a dental and σ.

ξ is a combination of a guttural and σ.

ψ is a combination of a labial and σ.

σ between two consonants or vowels is usually dropped.

σ at the beginning of a word usually appears as a rough breathing.

Accent

35. The matter of accent is regarded with but slight concern by many Greek teachers, but in this neglect such teachers betray their own lack of appreciation for the genius and history of the language. If one wishes with finished accuracy to learn the Greek language, it is important that he should master the principles and practice of accenting. We present here a brief statement of the principles and the resulting methods for the help and guidance of the student. He cannot master Greek accent by memorizing rules; he should comprehend the principles and discern the application of these in the methods, and thus obtain a real working knowledge of the system.

36. We begin by summarizing briefly the *principles of accentuation.* "The limits of the position of an accent depend on the 'three syllable law,' by which the rising inflexion cannot stand further back than on the third syllable from the end of a word" (M-II. 53). That is, accent is governed by principles of intonation. These principles were very thoroughly developed and rigidly observed by those who produced the Greek classics. The "acute" represents the rising inflection of the voice, while the "grave" represents the falling inflection. Every syllable has an accent, either grave or acute, though the grave is not indicated except on the last syllable of a word which has no acute. A word which in continuous composition has no acute accent must receive an acute if standing alone (as in the lexicon) or at a pause (at the end of a clause or

sentence). Thus we say that an acute on the last syllable changes to a grave in continuous composition. If a single syllable is treated with both a rising and falling inflection, it carries a combination of the acute and grave accents, which we call "circumflex." Thus ἡ βασιλεία τοῦ Θεοῦ when the accents are analyzed and all represented would be written ἤ βάσἰλεἰὰ τοῦ Θεοῦ.

37. The degree of stress is modified by the length of the syllable. Though the long syllable need not be the accentuated syllable, it greatly affects the accent. Hence a word with a long ultima cannot have the accent farther back than the penult.

38. The acute accent will sustain the tone for three syllables; hence, the antepenult may have an acute if the ultima is short. The word needs no additional accent before a monosyllabic enclitic if the acute is on the penult, or before a dissyllabic enclitic if the acute is on the ultima. But a dissyllabic enclitic must take its own accent if preceded by a word with the acute on the penult, or if the acute is on the antepenult there must be before a dissyllabic enclitic an additional accent on the ultima. Note that when this additional accent is placed on the ultima, it and the two syllables of the enclitic make the three syllables which it is possible for the acute to carry.

39. The circumflex will sustain the tone for only two syllables, for the obvious reason that the circumflex represents the accentual equivalent of two syllables, since it is a combination of both the rising and falling inflection. For this reason the circumflex can stand no farther back than the penult, and cannot furnish the accent for a dissyllabic enclitic, or for a monosyllabic enclitic if it is on the penult.

40. We will now review the application of these principles in more systematic form as classified in a summary of the *methods of accentuation*. It is important that the

student should keep in mind that these are not mere arbitrary "rules," but methods which represent the application of fundamental principles of intonation.

(1) *Acute* (').

a. May stand on one of the last three syllables; e.g., ἄνθρωπος, ἀγάπη, ἀδελφός.

b. Cannot stand farther back than the penult if the ultima is long; e.g., ἄνθρωπος, but ἀνθρώπου.

c. Cannot stand on the ultima when immediately followed by another word; that is, without intervening punctuation marks; e.g., ὁ Χριστὸς ἀγαθός.

(2) *Circumflex* (˜).

a. May stand on one of the last two syllables; e.g., δοῦλος, θεῷ.

b. Must stand on the penult if a long penult is accented before a short ultima; e.g., δῶρον.

c. Cannot stand on the penult if the ultima is long; e.g., δῶρον, but δώρου.

d. Cannot stand on a short syllable; e.g., δῶρον, but λόγος.

(3) *Grave* (`).

a. May stand on the last syllable; e.g., ὁ θεὸς φιλεῖ.

b. Occurs only when immediately followed by another word; e.g., ἡ καλὴ γυνή.

(4) *Accent in Conjugation.*

a. In conjugation accent is *recessive;* i.e., it stands as far back as the ultima will allow; e.g., ἀκούω, ἤκουον.

Moulton regards this method of accenting verbs as "a consequence of their primitive enclitic condition" (M–II. 55).

b. There are several irregularities in the accent of verbs. In the regular ω verbs the aorist active infinitive, the perfect active infinitive, the perfect middle-passive participle, and the aorist passive infinitive accent the penult, while the perfect active and aorist passive participle accent the ultima. The irregular verbs present still other irregularities in accent; e.g., ἀκοῦσαι, λελυκέναι, λελυμένος, λυθῆναι, λελυκώς, λυθείς, λαβών.

It will be noticed that the exceptions to the principle of recessive accent are in every case infinitives and participles. Moulton considers that since these are essentially nouns and adjectives, rather than properly verbs, they are not really exceptions to the recessive principle in verbal accent (M–II. 55).

c. In compound verbs (those combined with a preposition) the accent regularly does not rest on the preposition. Several exceptions to this rule occur; e.g., ἐξῆλθεν, ἔξεστιν.

d. In contract verbs, if the accent on the uncontracted form occurs on the first of the two contracted syllables, it becomes a circumflex; e.g., φιλέει becomes φιλεῖ. If the accent of the original form is on the second of the two contracted syllables, it remains acute; e.g., φιλεέτω, becomes φιλείτω. If the original accent is on neither of the contracted syllables, it is governed by the regular rule of recessive accent; e.g., ἐφίλεε becomes ἐφίλει.

(5) *Accent in Declension.*

In declension the accent remains as in the nominative singular, as nearly as the general rules for accent will permit. The accent of the nominative must be learned by observation. There are in declension, however, three special rules which we should notice.

a. All nouns and participles of the first declension have the circumflex on the ultima in the genitive plural; e.g., ἡμερῶν, προφητῶν.

b. Any word declined in the first or second declension which has its accent on the ultima takes the circumflex in the genitive and dative, singular and plural; e.g., singular: ἀρχή, ἀρχῆς, ἀρχῇ, ἀρχήν; plural, ἀρχαί, ἀρχῶν, ἀρχαῖς ἀρχάς.

c. Monosyllabic nouns of the third declension accent the ultima in the genitive and dative, singular and plural; e.g., singular: νύξ, νυκτός, νυκτί, νύκτα; plural: νύκτες, νυκτῶν, νυξί, νύκτας.

(6) Proclitics and Enclitics.

a. A *proclitic* is a word which has no accent, and is pronounced with the word following; as, ἐκ θεοῦ. The New Testament examples are the forms of the article ὀ, ἠ, οἰ, αἰ; the prepositions, εἰς, ἐκ, ἐν; the conjunctions εἰ, ὡς; and the negative οὐ.

b. An *enclitic* is a word which, whenever possible, loses its accent and is pronounced with the word preceding; as as ὀ θεός ἐστιν ἀγαθός. The enclitics found in the New Testament are the pronoun forms μοῦ, μοί, μέ, σοῦ, σοί, σέ; the indefinite pronoun τìς; the indefinite adverbs πού, ποτέ, πώ, πώς; the particles γέ, τέ; all the present indicative forms of εἰμί, except the second person singular εῖ, and φημί, φησί.

It is to be noted that μοῦ and σοῦ "throw an acute upon the preceding word, and receive it from a following enclitic; e.g., σύνδουλός σού εἰμι (Rev. 19:10"; cf. M-II. 54).

The following methods of accent for enclitics may be observed.

(*a*) An acute accent on the ultima is retained before an enclitic; e.g., ὀ θεός ἐστιν ἀγαθός.

(*b*) If the word preceding has an acute on the penult or a circumflex on the ultima, a dissyllabic enclitic retains its accent, while a monosyllabic enclitic loses its accent; e.g., ὀ λόγος ἐστìν ἀληθής, ὀ λόγος τοῦ θεοῦ ἐστìν ἀληθής, τήν χώραν μου εἰσῆλθεν, ὀ θεòς φιλεῖ με.

(*c*) An enclitic at the beginning of a sentence retains its accent; e.g., ἐσμὲν μακάριοι.

(*d*) If a word preceding an enclitic has an acute on the

antepenult, it takes an additional acute on the ultima; e.g., ὁ Χριστὸς ἄνθρωπός ἐστιν, οὗτος ἐγένετο ὁ ἀπόστολός μου.

(e) If a word preceding a dissyllabic enclitic has a circumflex on the penult, it takes an additional acute on the ultima; e.g., τὸ δῶρόν ἐστιν ἐκ τοῦ θεοῦ.

(f) A monosyllabic enclitic takes its own accent if the word preceding has a circumflex on the penult; e.g., ὁ οἶκος μοῦ.

(g) A dissyllabic enclitic takes its own accent when preceded by a word with the circumflex on the ultima, e.g., τέκνον θεοῦ εἰμί.

(h) A proclitic or an enclitic followed by an enclitic receives an accent; e.g., εἴ τίς ἐστιν δίκαιος.

i. Let it be observed that enclitics which consist of long syllables are, for purposes of accent, regarded as short syllables when added to a preceding word; οὗτος ὁ λόγος μου ἦν.

ii. There are three situations in which ἐστί becomes ἔστι:

(1) At the beginning of a sentence, e.g., ἔστιν ἀγαθὸς ἄνθρωπος.

(2) When it signifies existence or possibility, e.g., ὁ θεὸς ἔστιν.

(3) When it follows οὐκ, εἰ, ὡς, καί, τοῦτο, e.g., οὐκ ἔστιν καλόν.

(7) *Special Rules.*

a. On a diphthong the accent and breathing must stand over the second vowel; e.g., οὗτος.

b. The diphthongs αι and οι when final (except in the optative mood) are regarded as short when accenting; e.g., ἄνθρωποι, χῶραι.

We have not sought to relate every method of accent to the general principles, but the student can readily discern the connection in most instances. A few of the methods are simply facts of the language for which no logical explanation appears. It is well always to keep in mind the three-syllable law (see §36) and to observe that: (1) the antepenult may have only the acute; (2) the penult may have the acute or circumflex; (3) the ultima may have the acute, circumflex, or grave. In all these variations the situation of the accent is to be decided in consideration of the length of the ultima, with the exception of enclitics and a very few other cases which can be learned by observation. An excellent discussion of the principles of accentuation, based upon a wide induction, may be found in M–II. 51–56. When this is compared with R. 226–236, the matter has been seen from every important angle.

II. Declension

References: R. 246–254; R–S. 17–31; M. 48–49.

41. Declension is the inflection of a substantive (noun, adjective, pronoun, or participle) for the purpose of indicating its relation to the rest of the sentence. In the primitive stages of the Indo-European language it is probable that case was indicated almost exclusively by inflection. Though "comparative philology has nothing to say as to the origin of the case suffixes" (R. 250), it seems most likely that they originated from pronouns and adverbs (Wr. 144f.). This question, however, must remain largely in the realm of subjective speculation, the only point of objective probability being that inflection was originally the sole means of expressing case relations. Later the preposition began to do service in this capacity, and gradually encroached upon the inflectional endings until in modern speech declension has almost disappeared.

Relation of Declension and Case

42. Let it be remembered that inflection did not arise as determining case, but for the purpose of indicating case. The case was determined by considerations of use. *Declension, then, is a matter of form; case is a matter of function.* Case is determined by the relations of the substantive in the grammatical structure of the sentence. Declension was developed as a means of indicating such substantive relations. Hence it may be seen that, without question, the

case of a noun is to be decided, not by its inflectional form, but by the grammatical relations which it sustains. The importance of this fact will appear more clearly when we come to the study of case in the part on Syntax. Our interest in the matter here is to note that it is not really accurate to speak of the various forms in declension as cases, for their relation to case is not essential but modal. It tends toward confusion even to speak of them as case endings, the better plan being to refer to them as inflectional endings.

The above consideration will enable the student to understand why we may speak of more cases than a noun has inflectional endings.

43. A single inflectional ending may do service for several cases. This is already a familiar phenomenon to the Greek student; as, for instance, the nominative, vocative, and accusative of neuter nouns, where we have three cases represented by one inflectional ending. Therefore, it is not possible to deny that there may be more than one case represented by a single inflectional ending in other instances. The new historico-scientific method by which Greek has been studied in recent years has discovered that the language has eight cases: nominative, vocative, genitive, ablative, dative, locative, instrumental, and accusative. Ordinarily we find only four inflectional endings. The first usually embraces the nominative and vocative; the second, the genitive and ablative; the third, the dative, locative, and instrumental; the fourth, the accusative. The student should be careful to bear in mind that these inflectional endings do not decide the question of case.

Wright believes that "the parent Indogermanic language had eight cases—probably more—if we call the vocative a case" (Wr. 144). Robertson finds eight clearly defined cases in Greek (R. 247-250). Moulton is in general agreement with him (cf. M. 60ff.), and Nunn follows their lead—omitting the instrumental (H. P. V. Nunn, *Syntax of N. T. Gr.*, p. 38). Full discussion of this question belongs to Syntax.

Number in Substantives

44. In classical Greek we meet with three numbers: singular, dual, and plural; but in the Koiné the dual has disappeared. The details of the history of the dual and its final decadence cannot be recited here, it being necessary to the present purpose only to call attention to the fact. The singular and plural are usually employed in the normal way. The nature of some nouns requires that they be used in the singular only or the plural only, as the case may be. The irregularities cannot be reduced to systematic statement, but are best learned by observation.

Moulton finds that many Greek dialects—"Ionic conspicuously"—had lost the dual before the advent of the Koiné. He thinks it arose by reason of a limitation in primitive speech and inevitably decayed after this limitation was removed (M. 57). Robertson suggests that it might have arisen from a desire to emphasize pairs, such as hands and eyes (R. 251). A combination of the suggestions given by Moulton and Robertson would likely come nearest to the facts.

Gender in Substantives

45. We meet in the Koiné the familiar three genders of the Attic Greek; masculine, feminine, and neuter. Where there are no facts of sex to decide the matter, the gender of a noun must be learned by observation. The distinctions of gender are strictly adhered to in the Greek New Testament.

Robertson and Green think that distinctions in gender grew out of the fact of sex and became applied to inanimate objects by poetic personification (R. 252; G 17). Sweet, however, dissents from this opinion (*Hist. of Lang.*, p. 38). Moulton regards it as a rather remarkable fact that Modern Greek "is nearly as much under the domination of this outworn excrescence on language as was its classical ancestor" (M. 59). But, however we may regard the importance of gender, as students of the Greek New Testament we must adapt ourselves to the fact. It is to be carefully observed that there is not only "sense gender"—that which is relative to actual sex—but "grammatical gender"—that which is determined purely by grammatical usage.

The Greek Declensions

46. It is best to divide the Greek language into three declensions, on the basis of the ending of the noun stem. Nouns which have α as their characteristic stem ending are assigned to the first declension. Those with ο as the characteristic stem ending are in the second declension. The third declension includes nouns whose stems end in a consonant, or in ι, υ, or ευ. The third declension is to be determined by observing both the stem ending and the inflectional endings, which are distinctive for this declension. The variation in the stem ending of third-declension nouns has occasioned some difference of opinion as to the number of Greek declensions, but there is general agreement upon the three we have mentioned.

Robertson believes that it is not possible with final precision to draw fixed limits for the declensions. This may most naturally be expected when we remember that declensions had no rules by which to develop, but came with the spontaneous growth of the language. With this fact in view there is no wonder that there is mixing and overlapping. In the earliest grammatical effort they tried to make an exhaustive classification of all variations, which resulted in division into ten or more declensions. Whitney has divided noun inflection in the Sanskrit into five declensions, but the difference is not pronounced. In Modern Greek there has been a blending of the first and third declensions (cf. R. 246–247).

47. *The First Declension.* The nouns of this declension are usually feminine, though a few are masculine. The stem ends in α, but this α is frequently found in contract or

modified form. The forms vary with different kinds of stems. These variations are seen in the singular only, the plural being the same for all nouns of this declension (see Paradigm 1).

(1) When the stem ending is preceded by ϵ, ι, or ρ, the a is retained throughout.

But in the New Testament we sometimes find ¨ης and η following ι and ρ (cf. M-II. 118).

(2) When the stem ending is preceded by $\sigma, \lambda, \lambda\lambda$, or a double consonant, the vowel is generally short a, which becomes η in the genitive and dative singular.

(3) After other consonants the stem ending is usually η (see Paradigm 1).

(4) The regular masculine ending for nouns of this declension is ηs.

(5) After ϵ, ι, or ρ masculine nouns have -as after the analogy of feminine nouns

It should be carefully observed that there are also nouns of the third declension which end in a, as, and ηs. The difference of declension is to be noted in the genitive singular. A few masculine nouns of the first declension have a in the genitive singular; e.g., $\mathrm{B}o\rho\rho\tilde{a}s$, -$a$, $\mu a\mu\omega\nu\tilde{a}s$, -$a$, $\mathrm{K}\eta\varphi\tilde{a}s$, -$a$. Some nouns in ρa have their genitive and dative in -ηs, -η; e.g., $\sigma\pi\epsilon\tilde{\iota}\rho a$, -$\eta s$, $\mu\acute{a}\chi a\iota\rho a$, -$\eta s$.

48. *The Second Declension.* The nouns in this declension are masculine and neuter, with a few feminines. There are two sets of terminations, one for masculine and feminine and another for neuter. The genitive and dative endings correspond in both numbers for all three genders (see Paradigm 2).

In this declension there are a few nouns with nominative in ωs and some in $\epsilon o s$ and oos which appear in contract forms.

49. *The Third Declension.* This declension presents the greatest variety and at the same time the greatest difficulty

of the three. The important element of variation is the stem ending. The stem may be found by omitting the ending of the genitive form. The nouns of the third declension are of all three genders. No classification can be accomplished which would hold absolutely without variation, and an exhaustive analysis would require treatment of greater length than is possible here. The simplest analysis we can secure which approximates accuracy is to divide the declension into the following five classes (see Paradigm 3).

(1) *Mute Stems.* Here we have masculine and feminine nouns whose stems end in a mute, mostly the dental mutes τ and δ, with one in θ. There are several in κ, some in γ and χ, four in π, and one in β. Some New Testament nouns of this class are χάρις, -τος; ἐλπίς, -δος; ὄρνις, -θος; ἄνθραξ, -κος; φλόξ, -γος.

(2) *Liquid Stems.* These nouns are chiefly masculine, though a few are feminine. Some representatives in the New Testament are ἅλς, ἅλος; αἰών, -ωνος; ἡγεμών, -ονος, ποιμήν, -ενος; ῥήτωρ, -ορος; μήν, μῆνος.

(3) *Syncopated Stems.* In this class we have those nouns of the third declension which lose the vowel from the final syllable of the stem in the second and third forms singular and in the third plural; as ἀνήρ, stem ἀνερ-, gen. ἀνδρός. They are masculine and feminine in gender, and are represented in the New Testament by such words as πατήρ, -τρος; μήτηρ, -τρος; θυγάτηρ, -τρος.

(4) *Vowel Stems.* These are masculines in ευ, feminines in ι, and masculines and feminines and one neuter (δάκρυ) in υ. The masculines in ευ have their genitive ending in εως. The same is true of the feminine stems in ι. The υ stems have ος for the genitive. Nouns of this class are ἁλιεύς, Βασιλεύς, πόλις, στάσις, ἰχθύς, στάχυς.

(5) *Stems in* ατ *and* εσ. These are all neuter nouns. Those in ατ are the second largest third-declension group, the largest being the feminines in ι. Some of the ατ stems form their nominative by changing the τ of the stem to s, but generally the nominative is formed by dropping the τ. The εσ nouns lose their distinctive stem ending in the nominative and terminate in os. In inflection the σ of the stem is dropped and the ε contracts with the vowel of the termination. Some New Testament nouns of this class are κέρας, -ατος; σῶμα, -ατος; γένος, γένους (contraction of γένεος from γένεσος); ἔτος, ἔτους (contraction of ἔτεος from ἔτεσος). The masculine noun συγγενής apparently belongs to this class, since it has its genitive in συγγενοῦς (cf. M-II.138), but it was originally an adjective declined like ἀληθής.

(6) Besides these nouns which may be classified with more or less distinctness, there are a good many third-declension nouns in the New Testament which are so irregular as to preclude definite classification. For irregular nouns of all three declensions see Paradigm 4.

i. An exhaustive treatment of the third-declension nouns which occur in the New Testament may be found in M-II. 128–143.

ii. It will be helpful to the student to observe that there are certain forms which are common to all three declensions.

(1) Neuters have but three forms for all the cases, one embracing nominative, vocative, and accusative, another the genitive, and ablative, and a third the dative, locative, and instrumental. (2) The neuter plural always has α for its nominative, vocative, and accusative ending. However, this α sometimes appears in contract form, as γένη for γενε-α. (3) The dative singular always ends in ι, which becomes subscript when it follows a long vowel, as in the first and second declensions. (4) The genitive plural always has -ων for its ending. (5) Masculine and neuter nouns always have their ending alike in the genitive and dative (cf. G. 16).

iii. Several New Testament nouns, borrowed from Hebrew, are indeclinable; such e.g., ῥαββεί, Ἰερουσαλήμ, μάννα, Ἀββά. This is probably the explanation of the phrase in Rev. 1:4, ὁ ὢν καὶ ὁ ἦν καὶ ὁ

ἐρχόμενος, which is likely treated as an indeclinable noun for the
Hebrew *Yahweh* (Jehovah).

iv. There are a few cases in the New Testament of mixed declension.
A word is found sometimes in one declension, and again in another: with
one case expressed by one declension, and another by another. Thus
σάββατον has σαββάτῳ in the singular, but σάββασι in the plural.
A complete review of the matter is offered by Moulton (M-II. 124-128).

The Article

50. The Greek article is, strictly speaking, a pronoun,
but its entirely distinctive function makes it best that it
should receive distinct treatment both in accidence and
syntax. As to inflectional form, it is declined after the
analogy of the first and second declensions. It is to be
observed that the article is an unfailing means for determining the gender of substantives (see Paradigm 5).

The Adjective

51. *Declension of Adjectives.* In declension adjectives
follow the analogy of nouns. When the masculine and
feminine differ, they are usually declined in the first and
second declensions, though sometimes in the first and third.
When the masculine and feminine are the same, they are
declined in the second or third declension only (see Paradigm 6).

52. *Comparison of Adjectives.* In comparison the Koiné
adjective does not differ greatly from the classical method,
the chief difference being that the superlative form rarely
occurs in the Koiné. There are two regular forms of comparison, besides a number of irregular forms.

(1) The prevalent method of comparison is the addition
of -τερος and -τατος to the stem; e. g. πιστός, πιστότερος,
πιστότατος. If the penultimate syllable ends in a short
vowel, the connecting -o- is regularly lengthened to -ω-;
e. g., σόφος, σοφώτερος, σοφώτατος. Adjectives of the third

declension whose stems end in εσ add the comparative suffixes to the stem; e.g., ἀληθής, ἀληθέστερος, ἀληθέστατος. Those in ων add εσ to the stem; e.g., σώφρων, σωφρωνέστερος, σωφρωνέστατος.

(2) There are frequent comparatives in -ιων, with a few superlatives in -ιστος; e.g., καλός, καλλίων, κάλλιστος.

(3) Some adjectives present irregular forms of comparison; e.g., μικρός, ἐλάσσων, ἐλάχιστος.

i. For declension of comparative and superlative adjectives and a list of the principal irregular comparisons see Paradigm 6.

ii. Adverbs are formed from adjectives by adding ως to the stem of the positive, using the neuter accusative singular for the comparative, and the neuter accusative plural for the superlative; e.g., καλῶς, κάλλιον, κάλλιστα.

The Pronoun

53. Since the pronoun was introduced into language as a helper to the noun, it quite naturally follows the noun in inflection (see Paradigm 7).

(1) The great majority of the Greek pronouns are found in the first and second declensions.

(2) The interrogative, indefinite, and indefinite relative are declined in the third declension.

Participles

54. Participles present five inflectional types. Four of them are in the first and third declensions, and the other in the first and second (see Paradigm 8).

(1) Present and future active; λύων, -οντος; -ουσα, -ουσης; -ον, -οντος; λύσων in the same way.

(2) Aorist active: λύσας, -σαντος; -σασα, -σάσης; -σαν, σαντος.

(3) Perfect active: λελυκώς, -κότος; -κυῖα, -κυίας; -κός, -κότος.

(4) Aorist passive: λυθείς, -θέντος; -θεῖσα, -θείσης; -θέν, -θέντος.

(5) The remaining passives and all the middle participles are declined in the first and second declensions; e.g., λυόμενος, -η, -ον.

Proper Names

55. Proper names in the New Testament derived from the Hebrew, or the transliteration of Hebrew names, are usually indeclinable. Some of them have been Hellenized and inflected like a Greek noun. Greek and Latin names are regularly declined. Proper names are found in all three of the declensions. For a detailed treatment of this matter see M–II. 143ff.

Numerals

56 In the nature of the case the first numeral εἷς is declined in the singular only, and the others in the plural only. Many of them are indeclinable. It is not difficult to discern just which do submit to inflection. Εἷς is declined after the analogy of the first and third declensions; δύο, τρεῖς, and τέσσαρες, the third only. The ordinals and the cardinals in -οι are declined in the first and second declension, like καλός (see Paradigm 9).

III. CONJUGATION

References: R. 303–306, 330–343; R–S. 32–47; M. 51–56.

57. In Greek the verb reaches the acme of its development in the history of language. In no other branch of human speech are the structural phenomena of the verb so extensively elaborated, or organized with such "architectural skill" (R–S. 33). To analyze the Greek verb in all its varied modifications is an extended and minute process which can be presented here only in brief outline. A com-

plete system of verbal inflection is presented in Paradigm 10.

Moulton observes that the Koiné verb has moved considerably in
the direction of simplification, as compared with the complexity of
the Attic verb. This tendency has continued into Modern Greek,
which lacks the optative and infinitive, and has but few survivals of
the middle voice and -μι forms. "These and other tendencies, the
issue of which is seen in Modern Greek, were all at work early in
Hellenistic; but they have not travelled far enough to relieve the
accidence of much grammatical lumber, once significant but now
outworn" (M-II. 182).

Classes of Greek Verbs

58. *The Regular Verbs.* These are the verbs whose
present indicative active first person singular ends in ω,
which retain the same verb stem throughout, and whose
tense stems occasion no irregularities in inflection. They
may be defined as *omega* verbs with regular inflection.
They present the typical form of the Greek verb; e.g., λύω,
λύσω, ἔλυσα, λέλυκα, etc.

59. *The Irregular Verbs.* These are the verbs which
present variations in the structure of the stem.

(1) This variation is sometimes caused by changes made
in the formation of tense stems as ἀγγέλλω, aorist ἤγγειλα.

(2) Many verbs present two or more different verb
stems from entirely different roots. These roots appear to
be the survival of several different original verbs; e.g.,
ἔρχομαι, stem ἐρχ-; ἐλεύσομαι, stem ἐλευ-; ἦλθον, stem ἐλθ-.

60. *The Contract Verbs.* Here we have verbs whose stems
end in a vowel, which vowel occasions certain changes in
termination or in the formation of tense stems. There
are three classes of these verbs: those ending in α, as ἀγαπάω;
those ending in ε, as φιλέω; those ending in ο, as δηλόω.
In the terminations of the present and imperfect the final
vowel combines with the vowel of the ending and gives a

contract form (for table of contractions, see §34). In the formation of the stems for the other tenses the final vowel is lengthened; α and ε become η, and ο becomes ω; e.g., ἀγαπάω contract form ἀγαπῶ, future ἀγαπήσω; φιλέω, contract form φιλῶ, future φιλήσω; δηλόω, δηλῶ, δηλώσω.

61. *The Mι Verbs.* This class is composed of the verbs which retain the primitive Greek endings. They are the oldest of the Greek verbs. Quite a number of μι forms are found in Homer, but they are much fewer in the classical Greek, and continue to diminish through the Koiné and Byzantine periods, and disappear entirely from Modern Greek vernacular—though still surviving to a slight extent in the more formal or literary use. The verbs in most constant use appear in this form, which fact gives evidence of its primitive character; e.g., εἰμί, ἵστημι, τίθημι.

The Structure of the Greek Verb

The typical Greek verb is composed of four parts.

62. *The Verb Stem,* which is the simple basal form of the verb, and constitutes the foundation of its inflection. It is not accurate to call this part of the verb the "root," because the root may be a still more remote element of the verb stem, which may be "a derivative stem like τιμα" (R-S. 33), of which the root is τιμ. As has been shown above, many verbs have more than one stem. The verb stem may usually be found by removing the affixes of the aorist, though there are exceptions; e.g., ἄγω, aorist ἤγ -αγ -ον, stem αγ; λείπω, aorist ἐ -λιπ -ον, stem λιπ; but στέλλω, perfect ἐ -σταλ -κα, stem σταλ.

63. *The Tense Stem.* This is the form of the verb employed to distinguish the tense; e.g., ἄγω, aorist stem ἀγαγ-; τίθημι, present stem τιθε-; λείπω, perfect stem λελοιπ-.

64. *The Connecting Vowel.* This is used in uniting the terminations with the tense stem, and generally distinguishes

the mood; e.g., ἀγάγ-η-τε, where -η- suggests the subjunc‚ tive mood.

65. *The Verbal Suffix.* This is the termination proper, and serves to distinguish voice, person, and number. Thus in λύ-ε-σθε the termination -σθε indicates the middle voice, second person, plural number.

With these facts in view we may analyze λύσωμεν thus:

Verb stem,	λυ-
Tense stem,	λυσ-
Connecting vowel,	-ω-
Verbal suffix,	-μεν.

Tense Stems

66. Considering the verb stem under the figure of the foundation of the verb system, we may aptly describe the tense stem as the ground floor. It must always appear as the basis to which the terminations are affixed.

67. *Formation of Tense Stems.* In the normal, regular tense stem the primary distinguishing element is an affixed consonant which we call a *stem ending.* The two other features employed in distinguishing tense functions are *augment* and *reduplication.*

(1) *Stem Endings.* The ordinary Greek verb presents four characteristic stem endings.

a. The future has σ, with the connecting vowels ο/ε; e.g., λύσω, λύσομεν, λύσετε.

b. The aorist active and middle has σ, with the connect‚ ing vowel α; e.g., ἔλυσα, ἐλύσαμεν, ἐλύσατε.

c. The passive has θε, which in actual inflection usually appears as θη; e.g., ἐλύθην, λυθήσομαι.

d. The perfect active has κα; e.g., λέλυκα.

e. The perfect middle and passive has no distinctive end‚ ing, but attaches the verbal suffix (personal ending) directly to the reduplicated stem; e.g., λέλυμαι, λέλυσαι, λέλυται, etc.

Verb stems which end in a consonant present important changes in their combination with the stem ending. As an aid to the student in constructing verb forms we insert here a table of these consonant changes. Compare with this table the one given under §34, iii.

(1) *Future and Aorist Stems.*   Before σ:

As to *liquids.*

The future inserts ε and elides σ: ἀγγέλλω, ἀγγελέσω, becomes ἀγγελέω, contracted to ἀγγελῶ (cf. §68, (3), *b*). The aorist omits σ and lengthens the stem vowel: μένω, ἔμεινα, (cf. §68, (1), *a*, (*b*)).

As to *mutes.*

Gutturals become ξ: ἄγω, ἄξω, ἦξα.
Labials become ψ: τρίβω, τρίψω, ἔτριψα.
Dentals are dropped: πείθω, πείσω, ἔπεισα.

As to *sibilants.*

Sibilants are dropped: σώζω, σώσω, ἔσωσα.

(2) *Passive Stem.*   Before θ:

As to *liquids.*

ν is dropped: κρίνω, ἐκρίθην.
λ, ρ are retained: ἀγγέλλω, ἠγγέλθην; αἴρω, ἤρθην.
μ inserts ε, lengthened to η: νέμω, ἐνεμήθην. (These are the only μ stem forms in the New Testament.)

As to *mutes.*

Gutturals.

κ, γ are changed to χ: διώκω, ἐδιώχθην; ἄγω, ἤχθην, χ is retained: διδάσκω (διδαχ-), ἐδιδάχθην.

Labials.

π, β are changed to φ: πέμπω, ἐπέμφθην; τρίβω, ἐτρίφην.
φ elides θ, producing a second aorist: γράφω, ἐγράφην; or is retained: ἀλείφω, ἠλείφθην.

Dentals are changed to σ: πείθω, ἐπείσθην.

As to *sibilants.*

Sibilants are changed to σ: κτίζω, ἐκτίσθην. (But σώζω becomes ἐσώθην.)

(3) *Perfect Active Stem.* Before κ:

As to *liquids.*

λ, ρ are retained: ἀγγέλλω, ἤγγελκα; αἴρω, ἦρκα.
ν is dropped: κρίνω, κέκρικα.
  or inserts ε lengthened to η: μένω, μεμένηκα.
  or forms a second perfect: φαίνω, πέφηνα.

As to *mutes.*

Gutturals.

κ changes to χ and elides κ of stem ending: διώκω, δεδίωχα.
γ changes to χ and elides κ of stem ending: ἄγω, ἦχα.
  ǀor is retained and elides κ of stem ending: ἀνοίγω, ἀνέῳγα.
χ is retained and elides κ of stem ending: τυγχάνω (τυχ-), τέτυχα.

Labials are changed to φ and elide κ: τρίβω, τέτριφα.
Dentals are dropped: πείθω, πέπεικα.

As to *sibilants.*

Sibilants are dropped: ἁρπάζω, ἥρπακα.

(4) *Perfect Middle Stem.*

Before μ:
As to *liquids.*

ν is changed to σ: φαίνω, πέφασμαι;
  or is dropped: κρίνω, κέκριμαι.
λ, ρ are retained: ἀγγέλλω, ἤγγελμαι; αἴρω, ἦρμαι.

As to *mutes.*

Gutturals.

κ, χ are changed to γ: διώκω, δεδίωγμαι; διδάσκω, δεδίδαγμαι.
γ is retained: ἄγω, ἦγμαι.
Labials are changed to μ: γράφω, γέγραμμαι.
Dentals are changed to σ: πείθω, πέπεισμαι.

As to *sibilants.*

Sibilants are changed to σ: κτίζω, ἔκτισμαι.

Before σ :-

As to *liquids.*

Liquids remain as before μ: πέφα(σ)σαι, κέκρισαι, ἤγγελσαι, ἦρσαι.

As to *mutes*.

Gutturals are changed to ξ: δεδίωξαι, ἦξαι.
Labials are changed to ψ: γέγραψαι.
Dentals are elided: πέπεισαι.

As to *sibilants*.

Sibilants are elided: ἔκτισαι.

Before τ:-
As to *liquids*.

Liquids remain as before μ: πέφασται, ἤγγελται, etc.

As to *mutes*.

Gutturals.

γ, χ are changed to κ: ἦκται, δεδίδακται.
κ is retained: δεδίωκται.

Labials.

β, φ are changed to π: γέγραπται.
π is retained: πέπεμπται.

Dentals remain as before μ: πέπεισται.

As to *sibilants*.

Sibilants remain as before μ: ἔκτισται.

The indicative second person plural of the perfect middle elides σ and combines θ with the stem according to the praxis indicated under the passive stem: ἔκριθε, ἤγγελθε, ἦχθε, etc.

The indicative third person plural of the perfect middle is formed by the perfect middle participle and the third person plural of εἰμί: λείπω, λελειμμένοι εἰσί; ἄγω, ἠγμένοι εἰσί, πείθω, πεπεισμένοι εἰσί.

With these suggestions the student will be able to work out the other changes.

(2) *Augment*. In the indicative the tenses which refer to past time have an augment, and are called secondary tenses. There are two kinds of augment.

a. Syllabic augment is the prefixing of ε to the verbs beginning with a consonant: e.g., ἔλυον.

b. Temporal augment is used in the case of verbs beginning with a vowel, and is the lengthening of the initial vowel; e.g., ἀκουω, ἤκουον.

If the initial vowel is ε, it is regularly changed to η, but occasionally to ει as ἔχω, imperfect εἶχον. Α is changed to η, ο to ω. Since ι and υ have no corresponding long vowel, the augment is not indicated unless marked ῑ, ῡ. If the initial vowel is already long, it of necessity remains unchanged. Diphthongs which have ι as the second vowel lengthen the first vowel, and the ι becomes subscript; e.g., ῃ for αι and ει; ῳ for οι.

In other diphthongs the first vowel is lengthened and the second remains unchanged; e.g., ηυ for ευ and αυ.

c. A few verbs appear with both the temporal and syllabic augments, as μέλλω, ἤμελλον; ἀνοίγω, ἀνέῳξα.

i. When a verb is compounded with a preposition, the augment is placed between the preposition and the verb stem; e.g., ἐνδύω, ἐνέδυσα. If the preposition has a final vowel, it is elided before the augment; e.g., διαπορεύομαι, διεπορευόμην. Before the augment ἐκ changes to ἐξ; e.g., ἐκβάλλω, ἐξέβαλον.

ii. Sometimes traces of a primitive initial consonant appear in the form of syllabic augment where we should normally expect temporal augment; e.g., εἶχον for ἐ-εχον, which is from ἔσεχον, the σ having been lost.

(3) *Reduplication.* This appears in the perfect stem as a part of its regular formation. As in augment, the method varies in accordance with the initial letter.

a. When a verb begins with a consonant, the initial consonant is doubled with ε inserted to form a syllable: e.g., λέλυκα.

If the initial consonant is a rough mute, it is reduplicated with the corresponding smooth mute; e.g., θαυμάζω, τεθαύμακα. When a verb begins with two consonants (unless it be a mute followed by a liquid) or a double consonant, it follows the analogy of syllabic augment, and takes only ε; e.g., στεφανόω, ἐστεφάνωκα; ξηραίνω, ἐξήραμμαι; γινώσκω (verb stem γνο-), ἔγνωκα (cf. G. 99).

b. When a verb begins with a vowel, the vowel is lengthened, as in the case of the temporal augment; e.g., ἀγαπάω, ἠγάπηκα. In a few instances the entire first syllable is reduplicated; e.g., ἀκούω, ἀκήκοα.

c. Sometimes a verb with an initial vowel appears with both forms of augment for reduplication; e.g., ὁράω, ἑώρακα.

68. *Classification of Tense Stems.* The Greek verb presents five distinctive tense stems; viz., aorist, present, future, perfect, and passive. It is well to treat the aorist first as it is the basic and most prevalent tense.

(1) *The Aorist Stem.* On this stem are formed the aorist active and middle. It appears in two varieties, known as first and second aorist.

a. The first-aorist stem is formed in three ways.

(a) It is usually formed by adding σ (a) to the verb stem; e.g., λύω, verb stem λυ-, first-aorist stem λυσ(a)-.

(b) Liquid verbs form the aorist by lengthening the stem vowel; e.g., ἀγγέλλω, stem ἀγγελ-, aorist ἤγγειλα.

(c) A few first aorists are formed by adding κ to the verb stem; e.g., δίδωμι, stem δο-, aorist ἔδωκα.

b. The second aorist usually lies closest to the root of the word, and forms the basal verb stem. It is formed in three ways.

(a) Some second aorists merely add the endings to the simple verb stem, prefixing the augment in the indicative and adding the secondary endings; e.g., λαμβάνω, stem λαβ-, aorist ἔλαβον.

(b) A few lengthen the vowel of the verb stem; e.g., γινώσκω, stem γνο-, aorist ἔγνων.

(c) Still fewer reduplicate the verb stem; e.g., ἄγω, stem αγ-, aorist ἤγαγον.

(2) *The Present Stem.* On the present stem are formed the present and imperfect—active, middle, and passive. It presents the greatest variation in form and is the most difficult of classification. These various forms likely had functional significance in prehistoric times, but the distinctions had largely become obsolete even in the classical

period (cf. M-II. 183). A simple working analysis of the structure of the present tense may be made as follows:

a. Simple present stems. Sometimes the simple verb stem is employed for the present stem; e.g., λύω, stem λυ-.

b. Lengthened stems. Some verbs form the present stem by lengthening the stem vowel, usually to a diphthong. Most of these verbs have stems which end in a mute; e.g., φεύγω, stem φυγ-.

c. Reduplicated stems. Sometimes in the formation of the present stem reduplication is used, after the analogy of the perfect; e.g., δίδωμι, stem δο-.

d. Tau stems. Many verbs whose stem ends in a labial mute add τ to form the present; e.g., κρύπτω, stem κρυπ-.

e. Iota stems. Some verbs add ι to the verb stem in form-ing the present. This ι unites:

(a) With κ, γ, χ and forms σσ; e.g., φυλάσσω, verb stem φυλακ-, present stem φυλακι-.

(b) With δ and occasionally γ, to form ζ; e.g., σώζω, stem σωδ-, present stem σωδι-.

(c) With λ to form λλ; e.g., ἀγγέλλω, stem ἀγγελ-, present stem ἀγγελι-.

(d) With ν and ρ, and is transposed and becomes part of the stem, usually becoming a diphthong; e.g., αἴρω, stem ἀρ-, present stem ἀρι-.

f. Nasal stems. These are of two kinds.

(a) Sometimes a nasal consonant is added to the verb stem; e.g., πίνω, stem πι-, present stem πιν-.

(b) A nasal consonant (or consonants) is sometimes in-serted in the verb stem; e.g., λαμβάνω, stem λαβ-.

g. Inceptive stems. These are present stems in -σκω- and are called inceptive because verbs of this class usually denote the initiation of a state or action; e.g., μιμνήσκω, stem μνη-.

In μιμνῄσκω, as is frequently the case, we have a combination of two characteristics of the present stem, reduplication and the addition of -σκω-.

h. Vowel stems. These verbs add a vowel—generally—to the verb stem to form the present; e.g., δοκέω, stem δοκ-; γαμέω, stem γαμ-.

i. Irregular stems. Here belong a large number of irregular verbs whose present stem offers no characteristic for classification; e.g., γίνομαι.

For a more detailed and technical analysis of the present stem see M-II. 184f.

(3) *The Future Stem.* This stem has fallen heir to some primitive uses of the present, and hence usually shares stem characteristics with the present. However, it presents distinctive stems with sufficient frequency to justify separate classification. The future stem exhibits four methods of formation.

a. Regularly it is formed by adding σ to the simple verb stem; e.g., λύω, stem λυ-, future λύσω.

b. In liquid verbs considerations of euphony prevent the addition of σ, so the future is formed by affixing ε, which regularly appears in contract form; e.g., ἐγείρω, stem ἐγερ-, future ἐγερέω, contracted to ἐγερῶ.

c. A few futures are built on the unaltered verb stem; e.g., φάγομαι, future of ἐσθίω, the verb stem being φαγ- (aorist ἔφαγον).

d. Frequently when the vowel of the final stem syllable is ι, the σ is displacd by ε; e.g., ἐλπίζω, regular future ἐλπίσω, but ἐλπιῶ is the form actually found, being a contraction of ἐλπιέω.

(4) *The Perfect Stem.* On the perfect stem are formed the perfect and pluperfect, active, and middle, and the

future perfect passive (with the addition of σ). The perfect stem presents three variations.

a. The first perfect is formed by reduplicating the simple stem and adding κ as a stem ending. On it are formed the first perfect and pluperfect active; e.g., λέλυκα, (ἐ)λελύκειν.

The formation of the perfect in liquid verbs frequently changes the stem vowel to α; e.g., στέλλω, ἔσταλκα. Observe also that in reduplication an initial σ is usually dropped or changed to the rough breathing. In some verbs a final consonant is dropped before the stem ending; e.g., πείθω, πέπεικα.

b. The second-perfect stem is formed by reduplicating the simple stem, lengthening the stem vowel, and adding α. On it are formed the second perfect and pluperfect active; e.g., λείπω, root λιπ-, perfect λέλοιπα, pluperfect (ἐ)λελοίπειν.

c. The perfect-middle stem is formed by reduplicating the simple stem and adding the verbal suffixes directly to this reduplicated stem, without any stem ending or connecting vowel. On this stem are built the perfect and pluperfect middle and passive. In the case of the future-perfect passive the characteristic σ of the future stem is added to the reduplicated stem and the connecting vowels are used; e.g., λέλυμαι. (ἐ)λελύμην, λελύσομαι.

(5) *The Passive Stem.* On this stem are built the aorist and future passive. It is formed in two ways.

a. The first-passive stem is formed by adding -θε- to the simple stem, the ε usually appearing lengthened to η; e.g., ἐλύθην, λυθήσομαι.

b. The second-passive stem is formed by adding ε, lengthened to η, to the verb stem; e.g., ἐλίπην, λιπήσομαι.

Connecting Vowels

69. Between the tense stem and the verbal suffix a vowel is ordinarily inserted, called a connecting vowel. It

usually appears in combination with some other vowel, though in the first and second person plural it is regularly found unchanged. These connecting vowels vary with the moods, and hence by some grammarians are called "mood suffixes." But this designation is not wholly accurate, because they also vary with different tenses of the same mood. It is true, however, that each mood has its distinctive set of connecting vowels, and it is by this means that we differentiate the moods. It seems most nearly accurate to call them simply connecting vowels (or variable vowels), and to classify them according to moods.

(1) *In the Indicative.*

a. The present, imperfect, and future have *o* before μ and ν, and ϵ elsewhere; e.g., λύ-o-μεν, λύ-ε-τε.

b. The aorist and perfect have *a*; e.g., ἐλύσ-α-μεν, λελύκ-α-τε.

c. The pluperfect has $\epsilon\iota$; e.g., (ἐ)λελύκ-ει-μεν.

(2) *In the Subjunctive.*

Here we find ω before μ and ν, and η elsewhere in all tenses; e.g., λύ-η-s, λύσ-ω-μεν.

(3) *In the Optative.*

Though but few of these are found in the New Testament, we must present here the scheme of connecting vowels for the sake of completeness.

a. The present active and middle, future active and middle, perfect active, and future-perfect passive have $o\iota$; e.g. λύ-οι-μι, λυ-οί-μην, λύσ-οι-μι, λυσ-οί-μην, λελύκ-οι-μι, λυθησ-οί-μην.

b. The aorist active and middle have $a\iota$; e.g., λύσ -αι-μι, λυσ -αί -μην.

c. The aorist passive and perfect middle have $\epsilon\iota$: e.g., λιθ-εί-ην, λελυμένος εἴ-ην.

(4) *In the Imperative.*

This follows the analogy of the indicative, except that in the perfect there is ε instead of α; e.g., λέλυκ-ε, λελυκ-έ-τω, etc.

(5) *In the Participle.*

The middle and passive participle ending μενος takes ο as a connecting vowel, except the perfect;} e.g., λυ-ό-μενος, but λελυ-μένος.

The Verbal Suffixes

70. These vary with tense and voice, number and person. They furnish the chief means for distinguishing voice, number, and person. The most convenient classification, however, is to present them according to tense and voice.

(1) *The Primary Suffixes.*

These are used with unaugmented or primary tenses.

a. In the active voice they are: singular μι, σι, τι; plural μεν, τε, νσι. These suffer great change when used in actual inflection; e.g., ο-μι becomes ω; ε-σι becomes εις; ε-τι becomes ει; and ο-νσι becomes ουσι.

b. In the middle and passive they are: singular μαι, σαι, ται; plural μεθα, σθε, νται. In actual inflection σαι usually becomes η.

(2) *The Secondary Suffixes.*

These are used with the augmented tenses of the indicative and with the optative middle.

a. In the active voice they are ν, s, —; μεν, τε, ν or σαν. These are also used in the aorist passive indicative.

b. In the middle and passive they are μην, σο, το; μεθα, σθε, ντο.

Terminations of Infinitive and Participle

71. It is helpful to the student in grasping in broad perspective the inflectional phenomena of the verb to get before

him in a single view the characteristic endings of the Greek infinitive and participle.

(1) *The Infinitive.*

a. The present, future, and second aorist active have -ειν; e.g., λύειν, λύσειν, λαβεῖν.

b. The first-aorist active has -αι; e.g., λῦσαι.

c. The perfect active and aorist passive have -ναι; e.g., λελυκέναι, λυθῆναι.

d. The middle and remaining passives have -σθαι; e.g., λύεσθαι, λύσεσθαι, λύσασθαι, etc.

(2) *The Participle.*

a. The present, future, and second aorist active have -ων, -ουσα, -ον; e.g., λύων, λύσων, λαβών.

b. The first-aorist active has -ας, -ασα, -αν; e.g., λύσας.

c. The perfect active has -ως, -υια, -ος; e.g., λελυκώς.

d. The aorist passive has -εις, -εισα, -εν; e.g., λυθείς.

e. The middle and remaining passives have -μενος, -η, -ον; e.g., λυόμενος, λυσόμενος, λυσάμενος, etc.

A splendid aid to the student in constructing various verb forms is offered in a table in Moulton's *Introduction to the Study of New Testament Greek*, p. 98, which we take the liberty of adopting, with abridgment. The scheme indicates the modifications of the verb stem in forming tense stems. With this scheme compare §67

Pres. Act.	Fut. Act.	1st-Aor. Act.	Past-Perf. Act.	Perf. Mid.	1st-Aor. Pas.
-αω -εω }	-ησω	-ησα	-ηκα	-ημαι	-ηθηρ
-οω	-ωσω	-ωσα	-ωκα	-ωμαι	-ωθην
-βω, -πω, -φω, -πτω }	-ψω	-ψα	-φα	-μμαι	-φθην
-γω, -κω, -ξω -σσω, ττω }	-ξω	-ξα	-χα	-γμαι	-χθην
-δω, -θω, -ζω	-σω	-σα	-κα	-σμαι	-σθην
-νω	-νῶ	-να	-γκα	-μμαι	-νθην

PART II
SYNTAX

Introductory

References: R. 379–389; R–S. 63, 64.

72. We have been studying accidence; we now turn to the study of syntax. It is well that we should just here distinguish between the two. Accidence deals with the structural form of words. Syntax deals with the grammatical relations between words. Accidence deals with the facts which result from incidental development, while syntax deals with the rational principles of thought expression. Accidence differs with every different dialect, while syntax is largely the same for all human speech.

73. Nothing is more important in the study of syntax than securing an adequate idea of its scope and nature. This is a point which has been hurtfully neglected. Too often in the study of the grammar of a language the student has gone into the field of syntax with no consciousness more than that he has passed to a new heading of the general subject under consideration. And as he proceeded he has known only that he was reviewing an array of facts—or "rules"—with varying significance. He has not thought sufficiently about the fundamental reasons for these facts, and their consequent relations to one another. His task is too often thought of as memorizing a list or arbitrary "rules of grammar." This attitude totally misapprehends the true nature of syntax.

74. The idea that syntax is a formulation of rules for correct speech is an erroneous notion. *Syntax is the process of analyzing and classifying the modes of expression presented by a language.* It does not govern language; it deals with the facts of language as they are found. **Hence**

we are now to study the history and aspects of linguistic phenomena as they appear in the Greek text of the New Testament. "The scientific grammar is at bottom a grammatical history, and not a linguistic law-book. The seat of authority in language is therefore not in the books about language, but the people who use the language" (R. 31).

75. Logically the next question for consideration is: What is language? It is the means by which thought is communicated from one mind to another, or, from the converse viewpoint, the means by which one mind is enabled to think with another. "Language may be defined as the expression of thought by means of speech-sounds" (Sweet: *Hist. of Lang.*, p. 1). The term "speech-sounds" can be made to include both spoken and written language, for written language is but a system of symbols which represent spoken sounds. But there is another type of thought-expression which we know as sign-language. This is produced by gesture, and while not nearly so accurate or convenient as speech-language, it is nevertheless language, for it expresses thought. Consequently a more adequate definition is that of Whitney: "Language . . . signifies . . . certain instrumentalities whereby men consciously and with intention represent their thought, to the end, chiefly, of making it known to other men: it is expression for the sake of communication" (*Life and Growth of Lang.*, p. 1). Then, essentially, language is a system of symbols which represent thought.

76. We have thus far observed that syntax deals with the facts of language, and that language is a medium for the conveyance of thought. This brings us to the final and fundamental fact that syntax deals essentially with the forms which thought may take in the process of expression. So we discover that grammar and psychology are twin sciences. Therefore, for a study of syntax to be adequate,

"its account of the facts of speech should first of all reflect the ascertained facts of conceptual thinking," for which reason the best of modern grammarians "follow the ideas they work with into their background of psychology and logic" (Sheffield: *Grammar and Thinking,* pp. vi, 3). Syntax deals primarily with modes of thought. Thought is the action of the mind upon the phenomena of environment or experience. A phenomenon presents itself in consciousness, perception takes account of its occurrence, and judgment defines and relates it. For example, I glance across the landscape from my window, and an object occurs in the line of my vision. Perception presents it as a fact in consciousness. Judgment, through the faculties of memory, imagination, and reason, defines it—it belongs to a known class of things which I have learned under the word *tree.* Hence the bare concept occurring in consciousness is *tree.* But judgment enlarges the limits of thought beyond that. It not only discerns that the concept in consciousness belongs to a known class of things, but it also determines that there is existing yonder on the landscape the occasion of that concept—hence, *tree is.* But judgment also distinguishes a feature in the character of that concept—*tree is green.* Furthermore, this concept appears as a particular member of its class—*the tree is green.* Thus through the activity of perception and judgment there is offered as the material of thought a complete idea. This complete idea is the starting point of syntax.

We have observed that the thought created in consciousness is expressed with a group of words—*the tree is green.* This group of words we call a *sentence.* Notice that this typical expression of thought contains two elements: the designation of an object—*the tree,* and an assertion about that object—*is green.* The first element we call the *subject,* and the second the *predicate.* But the basis of this com-

plete expression of thought consisted of only two words—
tree is. Hence the basal element in the subject is the *noun*,
and the basal element in the predicate is the *verb*. Thus
we conclude that the sentence lies at the foundation of
syntax, and its essential parts, the noun and the verb, constitute the fundamental elements in syntax. We will build
our study of New Testament syntax around these two
fundamental elements.

We have called our example *the tree is green* a typical sentence
for the reason that it contains the two normal elements of a complete idea, designation and assertion—subject and predicate. But
there may be sentences which do not present this typical form, and
yet they are truly sentences, for they express a complete idea, as
the exclamation, "What a beautiful rose!" or the reply, "Why, of
course." These, however, are not to be regarded as the typical sentence with which syntax deals. For a thorough scientific discussion
of the nature of the sentence see R. 390–445, or for a brief summary
of the more important points see R–S. 63, 64. A very illuminating
discussion of the sentence from the viewpoint of psychology and
logic may be found in Sheffield: *op. cit.*, pp. 18–29.

I. The Noun

77. A noun is a vocal sound by which one designates a
fact of consciousness. This vocal sound may be mediately
represented by written symbols. As utilized in processes
of thought the noun may be employed and qualified in
various ways. This group of contextual relations gives to
us the subjects to be treated under the syntax of the noun.

(1) As used in the expression of a thought the noun may
bear various relations to the rest of the sentence. It may
be the subject proper, or it may qualify the subject, or it
may function in various ways in the predicate. This variety
in the fundamental relations of the noun we call CASE.

(2) It may be desired to make the functional relation of
the noun to its context more vivid than can be done by

the devices of inflection. This purpose is served by the PREPOSITION.

(3) Often one wishes to qualify the noun by some attribute. For this he uses the ADJECTIVE.

(4) The object before consciousness may be referred to frequently in the same context. To avoid the monotony of repetition the processes of linguistic development have produced the PRONOUN.

(5) If it is desired to represent the thing designated by the noun as particular or known, we may use the ARTICLE.

Therefore, the study of the syntax of the noun includes *cases, prepositions, adjectives, pronouns,* and the *article.*

II. The Verb

78. A verb is a vocal sound by which one makes an assertion relative to a fact of consciousness. Like the noun, it may be represented by written symbols. The relations which condition the assertion determine variations in the function of the verb.

(1) The subject is varied in accordance with its relation to the speaker, as to whether the speaker indicates himself, the one addressed, or an object referred to; hence, PERSON.

(2) The subject may include one or many; hence, NUMBER.

(3) If the assertion relative to the person is an act, it may be viewed as either performed or received by the subject; hence, VOICE.

(4) The assertion must reflect the speaker's attitude of mind in making it; hence, MOOD.

(5) The assertion represents a certain character of the fact asserted, and may be related to a certain time; hence, TENSE.

(6) An assertion may be subjoined as auxiliary to an-

other, so partaking of the nature of both noun and verb, for which one may use the INFINITIVE or PARTICIPLE.

(7) If the force of the assertion is to be varied by certain qualifications, we may use the ADVERB.

(8) In subjoining one assertion to another a connecting word may be used, which we call a CONJUNCTION.

(9) The speaker's attitude or concern in the assertion is frequently expressed by a word which we call a PARTICLE.

These variations in verbal function thus include under the syntax of the verb a consideration of *person, number, voice, mood, tense, infinitive, participle, adverb, conjunction,* and *particle.* The last three may be used with nouns or adjectives as well as verbs, though it is doubtless more logical to treat them in connection with the verb.

i. Robertson regrets that greater advance has not been made in the scientific study of syntax, especially such as recognizes the results of comparative philology. The work in this field which has been done was inadequate because based upon too restricted an induction from the facts of language. The need is syntax which is historically and inductively exhaustive. The dawn of a better day, however, is indicated in the work of Delbrück, who in conjunction with Brugmann has made encouraging advancement along this line.

ii. There is difficulty in keeping the province of syntax distinct Form and meaning of form are very intimately related. Syntax, however, has its distinct place. It is indicating and interpreting the facts with regard to usage in a language. Such a process is essentially historical and not philosophical. Hence we are not to construct theories and arbitrary rules which we seek to illustrate by a few facts selected from the language, but we are to take all the facts of the language, with the irregularities and personal peculiarities, and seek the best possible classification and interpretation of these facts (cf. R. 379–389).

DIVISION I

THE NOUN

I. The Cases

References: R. 441–456; R–S. 86–90; M. 60–70.

79. There were certainly at least eight cases in the primitive Indo-European tongue—with the associative case in addition as a sort of auxiliary to the instrumental. In support of this statement we have, along with many others, the very pointed and emphatic testimony of Professor Joseph Wright of Oxford: "The present Indogermanic language had at least eight cases—probably more—if we call the vocative a case" (Wr. 144).

80. There are two reasons for concluding that we properly have eight cases in Greek. The first intimation of the fact was obtained from investigation of the Sanskrit, which exhibits eight case forms. When the Greek cases were studied in the light of these eight Sanskrit cases, it was discovered that the same general distinctions prevailed. This sound method of comparative philology has brought the twentieth century Greek grammarian to recognize that there are eight cases in Greek instead of five.

81. In addition to the process of comparative investigation, this conclusion is also based upon the very obvious fact that case is a matter of function rather than of form. The case of the Greek noun is to be determined by its relation to the rest of the sentence. "Every case, as such, stands in a necessary connection, according to its nature, with the structure of the sentence in which it occurs" (W. 181). We have seen above that the fundamental elements

of a sentence are a noun and verb. In the simplest typical sentence the noun is the subject, and, therefore, in the nominative case. It is absurd to think of turning this statement around, and saying that the noun is in the nominative case, and, therefore, the subject. Hence it may easily be seen that function rather than form determines case, and is consequently the fundamental consideration.

82. Then as we attempt to analyze the cases of the Greek noun, we must seek to discover the functions which it performed in the structure of a sentence. As a noun is commonly employed in Greek it exhibits the following uses: (1) Its primary and typical use is to designate an object of consciousness, concerning which the assertion contained in the predicate is made; i.e., the function of subject. This function we call the *Nominative* case. (2) A noun is sometimes used without specific grammatical relations, simply as the object of address, which use we call the *Vocative* case. (3) One noun may be used to define the character or relations of another, which function we describe as the *Genitive* case. (4) A noun may be used to denote the point of departure, in a thought of removal or derivation, for which the *Ablative* case is used. (5) A noun may be used to indicate an object of interest or reference, which function we call the *Dative* case. (6) A noun may be used to indicate the position of an object or action, for which the *Locative* case is used. (7) Sometimes a noun denotes the means described in an expression of thought. Such use we call the *Instrumental* case. (8) A noun may be used in some way to limit an assertion, which function we describe as the *Accusative* case. These eight functions define the root idea of the eight cases. For the eight cases we ordinarily find only four inflectional endings, with occasionally a separate form for the Vocative. The matter may be graphically presented thus:

Inflectional Form	Case	Root Idea
First	Nominative Vocative	Designation Address
Second	Genitive Ablative	Definition Separation
Third	Dative Locative Instrumental	Interest Position Means
Fourth	Accusative	Limitation

i. Robertson takes a positive stand for eight cases in the Greek language, and shows the trend of present-day linguistic scholarship in that direction (R. 247–250; 446–449). Sheffield says, "Indo-European languages have as oblique cases, the genitive, dative, accusative, ablative, instrumental and locative. Over against these cases stand the nominative for noun-function, and the vocative as a kind of noun-imperative" (op cit., p. 147). This statement reflects what is now the prevailing judgment of comparative philologists. Those who do not admit the eight cases as entirely distinct, at least recognize some distinction by the use of such terms as ablatival genitive, instrumental dative, and the like. Robertson calls the coalescing of several cases into one form the "Syncretism of Cases" (R. 448). This merging in form rarely causes ambiguity, though Robertson notes a few instances in which the case is difficult to determine. These exceptions, of course, are not to be regarded as destroying the fundamental distinctions existing between the cases. Every case had its original root idea, which has persisted in the history of the case, and may be discerned by sufficient study (R. 453–456).

ii. Moulton is not positive in his recognition of the eight cases in Greek. He characterizes the evidence for the ablative, instrumental, and locative as "a few moribund traces" (M. 60). He discusses at considerable length the decay of cases before the encroachment of prepositions, clearly having in mind inflectional forms rather than case function. But he does deny that the "old distinctions of case meaning have vanished," and in pursuing his discussion of cases admits the historical distinctions. He takes issue with Winer in defining the genitive as "unquestionably the *whence*-case," remarking in this connection that "the ablative . . . is responsible for a part of the uses of the genitive in which it has merged." But he does injustice to his great scholarship and linguistic insight by referring to the *locative* dative and *instrumental* dative. If locative or instrumental, then why dative at all? We seriously doubt the wisdom of thus confusing terms (cf. M. 60–76). Blass falls into the same inconsistency when he devotes considerable space to discussing the "instrumental dative" (Bl. 116ff.). Winer refers to the dative's doing service for the ablative (W. 208), wherein he misses the case function utterly, and falls into a confusion doubtless induced by inflectional phenomena of the Latin. Buttmann, in his discussion of cases, follows Winer very closely, adopting, for instance, his definition of the genitive as the whence-case (Bt. 157). Yet, in spite of their confusion of terms, Winer, Buttmann, and Blass give abundant evidence of their recognition of the fundamental distinctions. The dawn of the nineteenth century found so many misapprehensions befogging the atmosphere of the Greek New Testament that we could not expect of these pioneers that they should clear up all of the confusions—especially when we recall that comparative philology is but an infant science. Especially in the latter half of the century, progress was steadily being made toward the light. Gessner Harrison, in a treatise published in 1858, recognizes that there are more than five cases in Greek (cf. *Greek Prepositions and Cases,* pp. 70ff.). His renowned student, John A. Broadus, blazed a way in the new method for that prince of modern Greek grammarians, A. T. Robertson (cf. R. viii). The twentieth century will unquestionably see the full and final victory of this far more logical and historical interpretation of the cases in Greek, as well as in other Indo-European languages.

The Nominative Case

References: R. 456–461; R–S. 90–91; M. 69–70.

83. Taking up the treatment of the cases in the familiar order we approach the nominative first, "though it is not the first in the order of time" (R–S. 90). The original func-

tion of the nominative was to lend more specific identification to the subject of a finite verb. In Greek the verb
expresses its own subject, as ἐκήρυξε means *he preached*.
Consequently when we express a noun subject of the verb,
it is in apposition with the subject implied in the verb
itself. Thus ὁ Παῦλος ἐκήρυξεν really means, *he preached*,
that is, *Paul*. Therefore, the nominative is more than
the case of the subject: it is the case of specific *designation*,
and is in appositional relationship.

(1) *The Subject Nominative.* Though the nominative
cannot be strictly defined as the case of the subject, yet its
chief use is to specify that which produces the action or
presents the state expressed by a finite verb. This is really
the *appositional* use of the nominative (cf. 2 Cor. 10:1),
and hence includes what is usually termed the nominative
of apposition.

ὁ πατὴρ ἀγαπᾷ τὸν υἱόν.

The Father loves the Son. Jn. 3:35.

(2) *The Predicate Nominative.* A further example of
the appositional aspect of the nominative is seen in its use
as predicate. Here its significance of designation is
strengthened by making it the thing emphatically defined
by the sentence, as when we say, ὁ κηρύσσων ἐστὶ Παῦλος,
the one preaching is Paul.

ὑμεῖς γάρ ἐστε ἡ δόξα ἡμῶν.

For ye are our glory. 1 Ths. 2:20.
See also: Eph. 2:14; 1 Jn. 4:8.

(3) *The Nominative of Appellation.* Since the nominative is by nature the naming-case, it is not strange that
there should be a tendency to put proper names in this
case irrespective of contextual relations. So we often find
a proper name in the nominative in such connection as to

leave an awkward grammatical structure. Such instances yield to the genius of the case rather than the demands of the context.

ἤγγισεν πρὸς τὸ ὄρος τὸ καλούμενον Ἐλαιῶν.

He drew near to the mount called Olivet. Lk. 19:29.
See also: Lk. 21:37; Jn. 1:6; 3:1; Ac. 7:40; 2 Cor. 12:18; Rev. 9:11.

This use of the nominative is a possible explanation of the grammatical difficulty in Rev. 1:4. It is also frequently seen in the New Testament with the passive of καλέω, as in Lk. 2:21 and 19:2.

(4) *The Independent Nominative.* When an idea is conceived independent of any particular verbal relations, the expression of it may be left standing alone in the nominative, with some descriptive or explanatory phrase added. Thus employed the nominative names an *idea* rather than an *object.* This includes what is sometimes called the parenthetic nominative and nominative absolute.

ταῦτα ἃ θεωρεῖτε, ἐλεύσονται ἡμέραι.

These things which ye see, the days shall come. Lk. 21:6.
See also: Mk. 8:2; Eph. 4:15.

The nominative as used in salutations is an example of this use of the case (cf. 1 Cor. 1:1). We also find the independent nominative used as a sort of "nominative absolute" in proverbial expressions and quotations (cf. 2 Pt. 2:22; 1 Cor. 3:19).

(5) *The Nominative of Exclamation.* When it is desired to stress a thought with great distinctness, the nominative is used without a verb. The function of designation, serving ordinarily as a helper to the verb, thus stands alone and thereby receives greater emphasis. It is as when a child in joyous surprise points his finger at a friend who approaches with fruit, and cries, "Apples!" It would quite obviously weaken the expression to say, "There are apples!" The nominative is the pointing case, and its pointer capacity is strengthened when unencumbered by a verb.

ταλαίπωρος ἐγὼ ἄνθρωπος.

Wretched man that I am! Rm. 7:24.

See also: Mk. 3:34; Rm. 11:33.

We have omitted in our analysis that use of the nominative which the grammarians generally describe as "the nominative used as vocative" for we agree with Robertson that the true situation in this use is not one case used for another, but one case ending serving for two cases. Wherever the idea of address is present, the case is vocative, regardless of the inflectional form (cf. R. 461). The remark of Blass that "the nominative has a tendency to usurp the place of the vocative" is based upon the erroneous idea that the ending determines the case (cf. Bl. 86).   The same confusion as to the significance of case influenced Moulton when he concluded that, "The *anarthrous* nominative should probably be regarded as a mere substitute for the vocative" (M. 71). Moulton is here, as in many places, yielding to established modes of expression. He falls into the same error when in an earlier work he says that in Jn. 17:25 "we find a vocative adjective with a nominative noun" (*Introd. to the Study of N. T. Gr.*, p. 168). Adjectives must agree with the nouns they modify in case, but not in inflectional form, as is clear from such an instance as ἡ ἄδικος γυνή, *the unjust woman.*

The Vocative Case

References: R. 461–466; R–S. 91–92; M. 71.

84. The vocative has but a single use, and that is as the case of direct address—if, indeed, the vocative may properly be called a case (see below). When address is intended to carry special force, the inflectional particle ὦ is used, as in Mt. 15:28. Otherwise the simple vocative is used, as in Ac. 17:22. Where it is desired to ascribe to the object of address special definiteness, the article is used; and since it is necessary to use the nominative form of the article—there being no distinct vocative form—this influences the use of the nominative ending for the noun, but the vocative function is there just the same (cf. Lk. 8:54).

θάρσει, θύγατερ.

Be of good cheer, daughter. Mt. 9:22.

The vocative is hardly to be regarded as a case. Where it has a distinctive form it is usually the root of the word, as ἰχθύ, βασιλεῦ, δαῖμον. We may safely follow Robertson in his conclusion that "in reality it is not a case at all. Practically it has to be treated as a case, though technically it is not (Farrar: *Gr. Syntax,* p. 69). It is wholly outside of syntax in that the word is isolated and has no word relations" (R. 461). The distinctive vocative form is falling into disuse in the Koiné period, and has entirely disappeared from Modern Greek. A trace of its classical use may be seen in Lk. 1:3.

The Genitive Case

(The Pure Genitive)

References: R. 491–514; R–S. 98–104; M. 72–74.

85. The genitive is the case of definition or description. It "is in function adjectival" (R-S. 98), and usually limits a substantive or substantival construction, though its use is not infrequent with verbs, adjectives, and adverbs. Its adjectival nature is very pronounced and quite obvious. To say "a flower of beauty" is not very different from saying "a beautiful flower." So καρδία ἀπιστίας, *a heart of unbelief,* is practically the same in sense as ἄπιστος καρδία, *an unbelieving heart.* But the qualifying force of the genitive is more emphatic than that of the adjective.

Many examples of nouns in the genitive case functioning as adjectives can be cited. A recognition of this usage is necessary to avoid translating certain sentences as if they were stilted or clumsy in form. Thus in Acts 9:15 σκεῦος ἐκλογῆς ἐστίν μοι is rightly translated, *he is a chosen vessel to me.* So, ἐν πυρὶ φλογός (2 Ths. 1:7) reads best, *in a flaming fire.* And τῆς δόξης in Col. 1:27 means *glorious*—τὸ πλοῦτος τῆς δόξης τοῦ μυστηρίου τούτου. In I Ths. 1:3 τῆς πίστεως, τῆς ἀγάπης, and τῆς ἐλπίδος may fittingly be translated as adjectives, respectively, *faithful, loving,* and *hopeful.* Our common versions give a vague and awkward rendering of Heb. 4:2, ὁ λόγος τῆς ἀκοῆς, by translating it *the word of hearing.* It is literally *the heard*

word; that is, *the word of their hearing,* or *the word which they heard.*
So Moffatt, Weymouth, Broadus, et al.

86. There is marked penetration in the statement of
Gessner Harrison that the genitive "is employed to qualify
the meaning of a preceding noun, and to show in what
more definite sense it is to be taken" (*op. cit.,* p. 15). Thus
the basal function of the genitive is to define. In this it
quite clearly carries with it an idea of limitation, and thus
shows kinship with the accusative, which also has the idea
of limitation. But the genitive limits as to kind, while the
accusative limits as to extent. Εἰργάσατο τὴν ἡμέραν means
he worked through a portion of or *throughout the day,* while
εἰργάσατο τῆς ἡμέρας means *he worked in day time,* and
not *in night time.* The genitive reduces the range of reference possible to an idea, and confines its application within
specific limits. Thus βασιλεία denotes an idea of a wide
variety of possible meanings. Kingdoms are of many kinds,
when we consider both the literal and metaphorical use of
the term. But ἡ βασιλεία θεοῦ denotes but a single kingdom, and a particular *kind* of kingdom. Thus by the use
of the genitive the implications of an idea are brought
within a definite scope.

87. Then it would appear that the basal function of the
genitive is to set more definitely the limits of an idea as to
its class or kind. "It simply marks attributive nouns,
expressing almost any relation with which they may enter
into complex concepts" (Sheffield: *op. cit.,* p. 152). We
may, however, carry the investigation of its root meaning
a step farther. Upon the basis of what general principle
does the genitive thus define? It by no means sets arbitrary limits; nor does it set incidental limits, as does the
accusative. The genitive signifies essential limits, presenting that which has "some obvious point of affinity with the
term defined" (Harrison: *op. cit.,* p. 16). Thus βασιλεία

requires a certain nature on the part of its limiting genitive:
it must express an idea which may be consistently associated with the thought of a realm of organized and regu-
lated activity. Hence it is because of God's essential
sovereignty that we may construct the phrase ἡ βασιλεία
θεοῦ. The genitive θεοῦ ascribes to βασιλεία a rational
attribute. So the use of the genitive is to ascribe a rational
attribute to the idea defined. To denote by the genitive
that which is not a rational attribute results in an ab-
surdity; as, "the humidity of the desert," "the heat of the
ice," ἡ βασιλεία δούλου, etc. So the genitive qualifies the
noun by the attribution of some essential relation or characteristic.

88. So we may say that the root meaning of the genitive
is *attribution*. This attribution may be in either of two
ways. It may employ an essential relationship. Thus
ἡ βασιλεία θεοῦ is the kingdom which has as its distinguishing attribute its relationship to God. It may employ an
essential quality. Thus καρδία ἀπιστίας is a heart which
has as its distinguishing attribute the quality of unbelief.
Therefore, the genitive defines by attributing a quality or
relationship to the noun which it modifies.

89. When the idea of relationship receives a physical
application, it becomes *contact*. The "roof of the house"
is the roof on the house, and the "grass of the field" is the
grass on the field. This significance is seen in the fact that
verbs which imply the idea of taking hold of or attaining
are regularly used with the genitive. It is even more clearly
seen with prepositions. Thus ἐπί with the locative signifies
general position, while with the genitive it signifies actual
contact. In Mt. 9:2 the use of ἐπί κλίνης, *upon a bed*,
places emphasis upon the fact that the man was actually
confined to his bed, while in Lk. 21:6 λίθος ἐπί λίθῳ, *stone
upon stone*, contemplates a general situation when the

Temple stones will no longer be in their proper position. This idea applies with remarkable precision throughout the prepositions used with the genitive.

Present-day grammarians justly express their respectful disapproval of Winer's dictum that "the Genitive is acknowledged to be the *whence*-case" (W. 184). In this erroneous definition many later scholars have followed Winer. He manifests much greater insight into the basal significance of the genitive when he calls it "the case of dependence" (W. 190). This may readily be seen to be in line with its significance of definition or attribution. Webster follows Winer in confusing the root meaning of the genitive with the ablative, declaring that "its primary meaning appears to denote an object *from which something proceeds*," but he shows progress toward a more accurate view when he says, at the close of the same paragraph, "Thus the genitive in Greek answers to the Latin genitive and ablative" *(Syntax and Synon. of the Gr. Test.,* pp. 63, 66). Robertson shows his characteristic apprehension of the genius of the language when he defines the genitive as the specifying case, the case expressive of *genus* or kind (R. 493). A similar definition is offered by Dr. C. B. Williams of Union University in his unpublished grammar notes. He proposes as the root meaning the idea of classification. We may combine these two suggestions and obtain a very appropriate definition of the genitive as the case which specifies with reference to class or kind. This is the same as saying that it specifies by the ascription of a rational attribute.

90. For the use of the genitive in the New Testament we offer the following analysis, which we have sought to make accurate and plain, if not exhaustive.

(1) *The Genitive of Description.* This is clearly the use of the genitive which lies closest to its root meaning. To denote a rational attribute is to describe. In fact, this usage is so very near the root meaning of the case, that we find difficulty in fixing exact limits. All genitives are more or less descriptive. Blass correctly observes that this is the most extensive use of the genitive (Bl. 95). When a genitive stands out boldly in its typical significance, with-

out shading off into combination with some contextual idea, we then classify it as a descriptive genitive. Many examples may be found which are perfectly distinct.

> ἐγένετο Ἰωάνης κηρύσσων βάπτισμα μετανοίας.
> John came preaching a baptism of repentance. Mk. 1:4.
> See also: Rom. 6:6; Col. 1:22.

The adjective force of the genitive is most clearly seen when the descriptive genitive is used in the predicate, in identically the same relation as a predicate adjective, as in Heb. 10:39, ἡμεῖς δὲ οὐκ ἐσμὲν ὑποστολῆς, *but we are not of a shrinking back* (cf. Rom. 9:9).

(2) *The Genitive of Possession.* Attribution quite easily blends with the idea of ownership. To denote ownership is to make one noun the attribute of another in the relation of privilege of prerogative. To say ἡ βίβλος, *the book,* is to assign a thing to a class of indefinite limits, but to say ἡ βίβλος τοῦ Ἰωάνου, *John's book,* is to immediately specify it in a particular way by attributing to it a certain relationship—it is the particular book owned by John. This is one of the most prevalent uses of the genitive, especially with personal pronouns.

> ἐν τῶν πλοίων, ὃ ἦν Σίμωνος.
> One of the boats, which was Simon's. Lk. 5:3.
> See also: Mt. 26:51.

(3) *The Genitive of Relationship.* In this use of the genitive a person is defined by the attribution of some genital or marital relationship. It is closely akin to the previous use, being really "the possessive genitive of a special application" (R. 501). The usual construction simply presents the article in the proper gender with the genitive of the person related, omitting the noun which indicates the relationship. It is assumed that the relationship is known or has been made sufficiently clear by the

context. Thus, should we find in the gospels Ἰησοῦς ὁ Μαρίας, we would unhesitatingly supply υἱός after ὁ. Sometimes, however, the relationship is obscure to the modern reader (cf. Ἰούδας Ἰακώβου, Ac. 1:13). This construction was abundantly used in colloquial Greek of the Koiné period, as is evidenced by its frequent occurrence in the papyri.

Δαυεὶδ τὸν τοῦ Ἰεσσαί.

David, the (son) of Jesse. Ac. 13:22.

See also: Mt. 4:21; Jn. 6:71; 21:15.

(4) *The Adverbial Genitive.* The genitive is sometimes used to define a verbal idea by attributing local or temporal relations, or as qualifying an adjective. Here its attributive function is still clearly present, for it is kind of action which is being emphasized. Thus action νυκτός does not mean action *at night* (point of time) or *during* the night (limit of time), but action *within* the night (kind of time), or, to put it literally, *night-time action.* The adverbial force of this construction is obvious, as attributes of time and place normally modify a verbal idea, and adjectives are regularly limited by adverbs. This adverbial use includes:

a. The Genitive of *Time.* As already indicated, the significance here is distinction of time rather than point of time (locative) or duration of time (accusative). It is "this rather than some other time" (R-S. 100).

οὗτος ἦλθεν πρὸς αὐτὸν νυκτός.

This one came to him in the night. Jn. 3:2.

See also: Mt. 25:6; Lk. 18:7; Jn. 19:39.

b. The Genitive of *Place.* In this use the sense of contact is prominent. But attribution is still the emphatic point. When ἐκείνης is used in Lk. 19:4 it is that way rather than any other way that Jesus is expected to come. Homer uses λούεσθαι ποταμοῖο to indicate bathing in a river rather than anywhere else; i.e., he defines the bathing by attributing in the genitive the place at which it occurs, and distinguishes it as *river bathing*. It is clear that the idea of bathing has kinship with the thought of a river, and therefore ποταμοῖο is a *rational* attribute.

ἵνα βάψῃ τὸ ἄκρον τοῦ δακτύλου αὐτοῦ ὕδατος.

That he might dip the tip of his finger in water. Lk. 16:24.

See also: Lk. 19:4; Ac. 19:26.

c. The Genitive of *Reference.* The genitive is sometimes used with adjectives to refer their qualifying force to certain definite limits. Thus ἰσχυρὸς πίστεως means *strong with reference to the matter of faith,* and might be rendered *faithly strong.* The adverbial force is obvious.

καρδία πονηρὰ ἀπιστίας.

A heart evil with reference to unbelief. Heb. 3:12.

See also: Heb. 5:13; Jas. 1:13.

(5) *The Genitive with Nouns of Action.* Sometimes the noun defined by the genitive signifies action. In this construction the noun in the genitive indicates the thing to which the action is referred, either as subject or object of the verbal idea.

a. The *Subjective* Genitive. We have the subjective genitive when the noun in the genitive *produces* the action, being therefore related *as subject* to the verbal idea of the noun modified.

τὸ κήρυγμα ᾽Ιησοῦ Χριστοῦ.

The preaching of Jesus Christ. Rom. 16:25.

See also: Rom. 8:35; 2 Cor. 5:14.

b. The *Objective* Genitive. We have this construction when the noun in the genitive *receives* the action, being thus related *as object* to the verbal idea contained in the noun modified.

ἡ δὲ τοῦ πνεύματος βλασφημία οὐκ ἀφεθήσεται.

But the blasphemy of the Spirit shall not be forgiven. Mt. 12:31.
See also: 1 Cor. 1:6; 1 Pt. 3:21.

(6) *The Genitive of Apposition.* A noun which designates an object in an individual or particular sense may be used in the genitive with another noun which designates the same thing in a general sense. In this construction a thing denoted as a representative of a class is more specifically defined by attributing to it in the genitive a particular designation. Here the genitive stands in exact apposition with the noun it modifies. Thus in ἡ πόλις Ἐφέσου the noun πόλις denotes a member of a class and Ἐφέσου specifies this same member in an individual and particular sense.

ἔλεγεν περὶ τοῦ ναοῦ τοῦ σώματος αὐτοῦ.

He spoke concerning the temple of his body. Jn. 2:21.
See also: Rm. 4:11; 2 Cor. 5:1.

(7) *The Partitive Genitive.* A noun may be defined by indicating in the genitive the whole of which it is a part. The sense of attribution is remote here, but nevertheless present. If it is said, ὁ Πέτρος ἦν εἷς τῶν ἀποστόλων, *Peter was one of the apostles,* Peter is thereby defined by attributing to him a relation to a group. Hence we have in this construction the typical genitive function.

δώσω σοι ἕως ἡμίσους τῆς βασιλείας μου.

I will give you as much as a half of my kingdom. Mk. 6:23
See also: Mt. 15:24; Rev. 8:7.

It is altogether possible to interpret this construction as an ablative, for it is easy to conceive of the whole as the source from which the part is taken (cf. G. 215). In construing it as an ablative we would be sup-

ported by the fact that the partitive idea is sometimes expressed in the
New Testament by ἀπό (Mt. 27:21) and ἐκ (Mt. 27:48) with the
ablative. This construction is found also in the papyri; e.g., P. Petr.
II, 11:5: ἀπὸ τούτου τὸ μὲν ἥμισυ, *the half of this.* This view is further strengthened by the use in Modern Greek of ἀπό as the regular partitive construction. There is no doubt that these indications forcibly
point toward the partitive as ablative rather than genitive, yet the very
fact that the Koiné writers had ready at hand a construction for the
exact expression of the idea of source would make it all the more probable that they used the genitive to stress character rather than source.
Reference to that from which a thing is taken may be either with a view
to stressing derivation or definition—source or character. To emphasize the former the ablative with a preposition exactly serves the purpose; to emphasize the latter would require the use of the genitive, since
the ablative has no such significance. Therefore, we had best regard
the partitive construction without the preposition as a genitive.

(8) *The Genitive Absolute.* A noun and participle in
the genitive case not grammatically connected with the rest
of the sentence are called a genitive absolute. It is possible to construe this as an ablative absolute, after the
analogy of Latin, but the variety of usage as to case in
this construction exhibited by the Indo-European languages
prevents any positive conclusion. In Sanskrit we have
genitive, locative, and instrumental absolute (Whitney:
Sansk. Gram., pp. 98, 100, 102), while Modern Greek has a
nominative absolute (T. 32). There is no particular reason
against calling the construction here a genitive absolute.

καὶ ἐκβληθέντος τοῦ δαιμονίου ἐλάλησεν ὁ κωφός.
And the demon having been cast out, the dumb man spoke. Mt. 9:33.
See also: Mt. 25:5; Mk. 9:28.

The genitive is used with adjectives and adverbs where the idea
implied needs some specific definition to make complete sense. Thus
κοινωνοί ἐστε would leave the thought in suspense, but κοινωνοί
ἐστε τῶν παθημάτων, *ye are partakers of the sufferings* (2 Cor. 1:7),
presents the thought complete and definite. The genitive is also frequently found with verbs where the verb "relates itself to the root-idea

of the genitive" (R. 507). Some of the chief classes of verbs taking the genitive are those of:

a. Sensation. Lk. 15:25 (cf. English "smell of," "taste of," "hear of," etc.).

b. Emotion. Ac. 20:33 (cf. English "to be careful of," "forgetful of," "desirous of," etc.).

c. Sharing. 1 Cor. 10:21 (cf. English "partake of"). This construction contains the partitive idea.

d. Ruling. Mt. 2:22 (cf. English "to have charge of," "to get possession of," etc.).

The Ablative Case

(The Ablatival Genitive)

References: R. 514–520; R–S. 104, 105; M. 72.

91. This case has seldom occurred in Indo-European languages with a distinctive ending of its own, but it does have quite a distinct function. The name suggests the basal significance of the case: *ablativus,* that which is borne away, or separated. Its basal significance is point of departure. This idea may be elemental in various conceptions. It is involved not only in the literal removal of one object from the vicinity of another, but in any idea which implies departure from antecedent relations, such as derivation, cause, origin, and the like. It contemplates an alteration in state from the viewpoint of the original situation, as when we say ἡ σωτηρία τῆς ἁμαρτίας, we are considering salvation from the standpoint of man's original condition of bondage in sin. The use of the ablative comprehends an original situation from which the idea expressed is in some way removed. Hence, in simplest terms we may say that its root idea is *separation.*

(1) *The Ablative of Separation.* This use is where the ablative presents its simple basal significance, unaffected by any associated idea.

ἀπηλλοτριωμένοι τῆς πολιτείας τοῦ Ἰσραήλ.

Having been alienated from the commonwealth of Israel. Eph. 2:12.
See also: Heb. 13:7; 2 Pt. 1:14; Rev. 21:2.

(2) *The Ablative of Source.* The idea of separation may
be accompanied by the implication that the original situation contributed in some way to the present character or
state. That which is named in the noun modified by the
ablative owes its existence in some way to that which is
denoted in the ablative.

διὰ τῆς παρακλήσεως τῶν γραφῶν.

Through the consolation from the Scriptures. Rm .15:4.
See also: Ac. 1:4; 2 Cor. 4:7.

(3) *The Ablative of Means.* The ablative is not the
regular case used in expressing means, but may be used
when the expression of means is accompanied by an implication of origin or source.

ἱκανὸς δὲ κλαυθμὸς ἐγένετο πάντων.

There was great lamentation by all. Ac. 20:37.
See also: Lk. 2:18; Ac. 20:3.

It may readily be seen in the example given that the sense would
still be preserved if πάντων were rendered *from all.* The means or
agency is at the same time the source. By far the greatest number
of the occurrences of this construction in the New Testament are with
the preposition ὑπό. The so-called "genitive of material or measure-
ment" belongs in this class (cf. Rom. 15:13; Lk. 2:44).

(4) *The Ablative of Comparison.* It is immediately evident that what has usually been defined as a genitive of
comparison is really an ablative. Comparison obviously
implies separation in degree. Thus μείζων τοῦ δεῖνος
means *advanced in a position beyond,* consequently *away
from, some one.* The thought of separation is obvious. The
ablative of comparison may also be used with the superlative degree (cf. Mk. 12:28).

οὐκ ἔστιν δοῦλος μείζων τοῦ κυρίου αὐτοῦ.

A servant is not greater than his lord. Jn. 13:16.

See also: Mt. 3:11; Mk. 4:31.

i. The ablative is quite frequently used with verbs, though not so frequently as the genitive, dative, and accusative. Of course, the ablative with verbs must be distinguished by sense rather than form. Verbs compounded with ἀπό, ἐκ, and παρά in the very nature of the case take the ablative where these prepositions bring to the verb the idea of separation. Verbs of ceasing, abstaining, missing, lacking, despairing, or kindred ideas take the ablative. Where a verb contains a comparative or partitive idea, it naturally takes the ablative. It may be seen that verbs take the ablative when their sense is akin to the root idea of the ablative (cf. R. 517-519).

ii. The ablative and genitive have been confused by nearly all Greek grammarians, both classical and New Testament. A few have realized the underlying distinction, and given separate treatment to the "ablatival genitive," but this characterization "is only true as to form, not as to sense, and causes some confusion" (R. 514). Robertson takes a positive stand for the ablative as a distinct case. Moulton recognizes the distinction, but gives little prominence to it. Nunn acknowledges that the ablative is a distinct case from the genitive, but does not distinguish its uses, because he wishes "to avoid conflicting with established usage" (*Syntax of N. T. Greek*, p. 42). Most other New Testament grammarians follow Winer in regarding the genitive as the "whence-case."

The Dative Case

(The Pure Dative)

References: R. 535-543; R-S. 111-114; M. 62-64.

92. The dative, locative, and instrumental cases are all represented by the same inflectional form, but the distinction in function is very clear—much more so than the distinction between the ablative and genitive. Recent grammarians nearly all recognize this distinction, and even those of the previous century have discerned it. Blass observes that "a distinction must be made between the pure dative, which expresses the person more remotely concerned, the

instrumental dative (and dative of accompaniment), and, thirdly, the local dative" (Bl. 109). Even Gessner Harrison, as far back as 1858, observed the distinction of the instrumental and locative from the dative, though he erroneously confounded these cases with the ablative, influenced, of course, by the Latin (*op. cit.*, p. 53). If case is determined by function, then there can be no question that the third inflectional form of the Greek noun includes three cases, the dative, locative, and instrumental.

93. The observation of Blass, quoted above, that the dative "expresses the person more remotely concerned," is, without doubt, in line with the root meaning of the case. The dative deals very largely with the personal idea. "It is sometimes used of things, but of things personified," having "a distinctive personal touch" (R. 576). It is primarily a case of personal relations, and it is with this in view that we must interpret it when applied to things. We adopt Robertson's view of the root idea as *personal interest*. The idea of interest as applied to things becomes *reference*.

(1) *The Dative of Indirect Object*. This use lies nearest the simple root idea. It indicates the one for whom or in whose interest an act is performed. Thus it carries the basal significance of the dative.

πάντα ἀποδώσω σοι.

I will give you all things. Mt. 18:26.
See also: Mt. 13:3; 1 Cor. 5:9.

(2) *The Dative of Advantage or Disadvantage*. Growing out of the use of the dative of indirect object we have the dative used in a more specific expression of personal interest. If I say ἔδωκεν τὸ βιβλίον μοι, it is clear that the giving of the book was in my interest, and the sense is not materially changed if it be said that τὸ βιβλίον μοι ἠγοράσθη, *the book was bought for me*, only making the idea of personal

interest more emphatic. The negative aspect of the same idea is the dative of disadvantage.

ἔκρινα ἐμαυτῷ τοῦτο.

I determined this for myself. 2 Cor. 2:1.
See also: Mt. 23:31; Rev. 21:2.

(3) *The Dative of Possession.* This is an idiom for which we have no exact equivalent in English. It is personal interest particularized to the point of ownership. There is in it manifest kinship with the dative of indirect object. Thus ἔδωκεν τὸ βιβλίον μοι is obviously closely related in sense to τὸ βιβλίον ἐστί μοι.

καὶ οὐκ ἦν αὐτοῖς τέκνον.

And they had no child. Lk. 1:7.
See also: Lk. 4:16; Jn. 1:6.

(4) *The Dative of Reference.* The force of interest in the dative may be diminished to the idea of mere reference. Thus in ἔδωκεν τὸ βιβλίον μοι οἰκοδομῇ, *for edification*, the idea of interest is quite emphatic in μοι but is remote in οἰκοδομῇ, though still present, for the word might with good sense be rendered, *in the interest of edification*, which, however, is a personification of οἰκοδομῇ. This use of the dative occurs mostly with things, though it may also be used with persons.

ἀπεθάνομεν τῇ ἁμαρτίᾳ.

We died with reference to sin. Rm. 6:2.
See also: Rm. 8:12; 2 Cor. 5:13.

i. A special application of the dative of reference is found in its use with intransitive and impersonal verbs (cf. 1 Cor. 6:12).

ii. On the question of the syncretism of the dative case with the locative and instrumental, Robertson observes that the distinction is much more pronounced than that between the genitive and ablative. He quotes Monro as saying that "distinct forms for these three cases survived down to a comparatively late period in

Greek itself" (R. 535). Buttmann shares the confusion about the dative and ablative in Greek, influenced by the analogy of the Latin (Bt. 171). This shows to what extent grammarians have allowed themselves to be affected by the matter of form in their conclusions with reference to syntax. Buttmann inherits his opinion from Winer (cf. W. 208). There seems to have been a general tendency of former grammarians to confuse the dative with the ablative. Moulton correctly defines the distinction in the three cases of the third inflectional form, but employs the compound terms locative dative and instrumental dative (M. 75). Let it be admitted, however, that this procedure is not wholly unjustifiable, for we cannot ignore form entirely while we are in the realm of syntax, for it often happens that we would be utterly unable to determine what the intended function is except for the form. The matter for caution is not to give form the preëminence in our analysis of syntax.

iii. The dative is used most frequently with verbs. It occurs with verbs implying personal interest, help, etc. It is also widely used with substantives and adjectives. It rarely occurs with adverbs, and it is very doubtful whether we ever find it used with a preposition (cf. R. 536–538, 541).

The Locative Case

(The Local Dative)

References: R. 520–525; R–S. 105–108.

94. There is no case in Greek more clearly marked in its use than the locative. Its root idea is quite distinct, and the application of the root idea in its various uses is readily discernible. Certainly we could be on no surer ground than when we are treating the locative as a distinct case. "The significance of the locative is very simple. In Sanskrit Whitney calls it the *in* case, and so it is in Greek. It indicates a point within limits and corresponds in idea with the English *in, on, among, at, by,* the resultant conception varying according to the meaning of the words and the context. In every instance it is not hard to see the simple

root idea of the case, a point with limits set by the word
and context" (R-S. 106). So in simplest terms we may
define the locative as the case of *position*. Its varieties in
use are few and plain.

(1) *The Locative of Place.* When the limits indicated
by the locative are *spatial*, we call it the locative of place.
We may regard this use as lying nearest the simple root
idea. It is most frequent in the New Testament with prepositions, but sometimes occurs without.

οἱ μαθηταὶ τῷ πλοιαρίῳ ἦλθον.
The disciples came in the little boat. Jn. 21:8.
See also: Acts 21:21; 1 Ths. 3:1.

(2) *The Locative of Time.* The limits indicated by the
locative may be *temporal*, in which case we call it the locative of time. The idea of position is quite clear in this
use: it signifies the time *at which;* i.e., point of time.

καὶ τῇ τρίτῃ ἡμέρᾳ ἐγερθήσεται.
And on the third day he will be raised up. Mt. 20:19.
See also: Mk. 14:30; Ac. 21:16.

(3) *The Locative of Sphere.* We have here a metaphorical use of the locative, but still exhibiting the root
idea. The limits suggested are *logical* rather than spatial
or temporal, confining one idea within the bounds of another, thus indicating the sphere within which the former
idea is to be applied. This use may occur with nouns,
verbs or adjectives.

a. With *nouns.*

νωθροὶ γεγόνατε ταῖς ἀκοαῖς.
Ye have become babes in hearing. Heb. 5:11.
See also: 1 Cor. 14:20.

b. With *verbs.*

ἐνεδυναμώθη τῇ πίστει.

He was made strong in faith. Rom. 4:20.

See also: Ac. 18:5; Heb. 3:10.

c. With *adjectives.*

μακάριοι οἱ καθαροὶ τῇ καρδίᾳ.

Blessed are the pure in heart. Mt. 5:8.

See also: Mt. 11:29; Heb. 3:5.

i. Sometimes ἐν with the locative is used with expressions of motion, where we would expect to find εἰς with the accusative. This is called the *pregnant* use of the locative.

ii. The unqualified statement of Blass that "there is no trace of a local dative in the New Testament" (Bl. 119) appears very strange when we examine the convincing examples cited by Robertson (R. 521). We are compelled to accept the latter's conclusion that "it is overstating it to assert that the locative of place has entirely disappeared from the New Testament" (*ibid.*).

iii. The locative is used with quite a number of adjectives and verbs, and with a few substantives, but the predominant use is with prepositions.

The Instrumental Case

(The Instrumental Dative)

References: R. 525–535; R–S. 108–111.

95. This case was likely preceded historically by the old associative case, of which traces remain in the Sanskrit. The idea of association and instrumentality are really much more closely related than might appear at first thought. One is in a sense associated with the means by which he accomplishes an objective, and in personal association the second person supplies the means of fellowship. The connection between the two ideas appears in the use of our word *with* in the expression, "I walked down the road *with* my friend, who was walking *with* a cane." The simpler and cruder idea of the implement used in a task being associated with the one using it developed into the more advanced notion of its being the instrument. The function of the instrumental case is quite distinct. Its root idea is manifestly *means*.

i. The significance of the instrumental sometimes approaches, much more closely than one would think, that of the locative. For instance, in Jas. 2:25, where it is said that Rahab sent the Israelitish messengers out ἐτέρᾳ ὁδῷ, *by another way*, Robertson concludes that "we probably have the locative, though the instrumental is possible" (R. 527). But the emphatic idea is not the *place* by which they went out, but the *method* of their departure. Hence it is most easily explained as an instrumental of manner. We can generally decide such a question by looking for the emphatic idea.

ii. A distinct inflectional ending for the instrumental survives in historical Greek in the Cyprian dialect. It also appears in the form of several adverbs (cf. R. 525).

(1) *The Instrumental of Means.* Quite obviously this is the use lying closest to the root meaning of the case. It is the most prevalent use of the case in the New Testament. It is the method for expressing impersonal means, while personal agent is usually expressed by ὑπό with the ablative.

ἐξέβαλεν τὰ πνεύματα λόγῳ.

He cast out the spirits with a word. Mt. 8:16.
See also: Mk. 5:4; Lk. 6:1.

(2) *The Instrumental of Cause.* It is an easy transition from the intermediary means by which a result is produced to the original factor producing it. Thus when we say, "He was destroyed by an earthquake," the mode of expression is but slightly different from saying, "He was destroyed by an assassin's dagger." In the former construction agency is referred to the original cause. This is clearly instrumental, and could not be elsewhere classified.

φόβῳ θανάτου ἔνοχοι ἦσαν δουλείας.

Because of fear of death they were subjects of bondage. Heb. 2:15

See also: Rom. 11:30; 2 Cor. 2:7.

(3) *The Instrumental of Manner.* This is one of the most obvious uses of the instrumental. It is expressive of the *method by means of which* an act is performed or an end achieved. It is seen frequently in adverbs of the instrumental form, such as δημοσίᾳ, *publicly* (Ac. 16:37). "But the usage is abundant outside of adverbs, chiefly with verbs, but also with adjectives and even with substantives" (R. 530).

προφητεύουσα ἀκατακαλύπτῳ τῇ κεφαλῇ.

Prophesying with the head unveiled. 1 Cor. 11:5.

See also: Ac. 11:23; 1 Cor. 10:30.

(4) *The Instrumental of Measure.* The idea of instrumentality in measure is not difficult to see. Two points of time or space are separated *by means of* an intervening distance. In the New Testament it is used chiefly with reference to time. Indeed, Robertson classifies this use as instrumental of time (R. 527). It may also be used to express the degree of difference (cf. Heb. 1:4).

ἱκανῷ χρόνῳ ταῖς μαγίαις ἐξεστακέναι αὐτούς.

For a long time he had amazed them by his sorceries. Ac. 8:11.

See also: Lk. 8:27; Rom. 16:25.

(5) *The Instrumental of Association.* The instrumental idea contained in association has been discussed above. To have association, a second party must furnish the means of that association. However, association is not necessarily personal, though predominantly so. In Rom. 15:27, τοῖς πνευματικοῖς ἐκοινώνησαν means literally *they had fellowship (with you) by means of your spiritual benefits.* This is clearly an example of association, though the means of

association is not personal. This use of the instrumental is quite extensive in the New Testament. Robertson gives seventy-eight examples.

νεανίσκος τις συνηκολούθει αὐτῷ.

A certain young man followed with him. Mk. 14:51.

See also: Rom. 11:2; 1 Cor. 4:8.

(6) *The Instrumental of Agency.* Agency is expressed occasionally in the New Testament by the instrumental case without the use of any preposition. At such times the verb is always in the passive or middle voice.

ὅσοι γὰρ πνεύματι θεοῦ ἄγονται, οὗτοι υἱοὶ θεοῦ εἰσίν.

For as many as are led by the Spirit of God, these are the sons of God. Rom. 8:14.

See also: Gal. 5:18; Col. 1:16.

The Accusative Case

96. The accusative is probably the oldest, and is certainly the most widely used of all the Greek cases. Its function is more general than that of any other case. Truly it is "the normal oblique case for a noun unless there is some reason for it to be used in some other case" (R-S. 29). It must originally have had a great variety of uses, as a result of which its root idea is not easy to discern. It certainly belongs in a particular way to the verb, even as the genitive is especially allied with the substantive. It relates primarily to action, and indicates the direction, extent, or end of action. "The accusative signifies that the object referred to is considered as the point toward which something is proceeding: that it is the end of the action or motion described, or the space traversed in such motion or direction" (Webster: *Syntax and Synon. of the Greek Testament*, p. 63). So the root meaning of the accusative really

embraces three ideas: the end, or direction, or extent of motion or action. But either of these ideas is employed to indicate the limit of the action, and hence we may define the root meaning of the accusative as *limitation*. If one say, ὁ ἄνθρωπος ἔπεμψεν, *the man sent*, the act of sending is left without a boundary, and has no definite meaning; but to say, ὁ ἄνθρωπος ἔπεμψε τὸν δοῦλον, *the man sent the servant*, immediately *limits* the action by the specification of its object. Or to say, ὁ ἄνθρωπος ἦλθεν τὴν χώραν, *the man went to the country*, limits the motion by specifying its destination. Likewise, to say, ὁ ἄνθρωπος ἐπορεύετο μακρὰν ὁδόν, *the man traveled a long journey*, limits the action by indicating its extent. So, in either case, limitation appears as the ultimate function. This basal function is more or less evident in the various uses of the accusative.

(1) *The Accusative of Direct Object*. The idea of limitation is most clearly seen when a noun receives the action expressed by a transitive verb. Blass calls this use the complement of transitive verbs (Bl. 87). It refers the action of the verb to some object which is necessary to the completion of its meaning. Of course, any number of examples occur in the New Testament.

ἀλήθειαν λέγω.

I speak truth. Jn. 8:46.

See also: Mt. 4:21; Jn. 1:14.

It must be kept in mind in determining the accusative of direct object in Greek that many verbs which in English are intransitive are treated as transitive in Greek. Such verbs are those which mean to speak well or ill of one, to abstain, to have mercy, etc. Occasionally we find such verbs connecting their object by means of a preposition, just as in our own idiom (cf. Bt. 146ff.).

(2) *The Adverbial Accusative*. Sometimes in performing its limiting function the accusative does not directly

complement the verb, but qualifies it in an indirect way. It is an "accusative employed to denote a material object only in a mediate or remote way" (W. 229). It limits by indicating a fact indirectly related to the action rather than an object directly affected by the action. Many words came to be so frequently employed in this indirect use of the accusative that they became essentially adverbs, some disappearing entirely from use in the other cases and becoming exclusively adverbs; e.g., πρότερον, πλεῖστον, μᾶλλον, σχεδόν. The adverbial accusative may be used in three senses.

a. Of *Measure*.

ἀπεσπάσθη ἀπ' αὐτῶν ὡσεὶ λίθου βολήν.

He was separated from them about a stone's throw. Lk. 22:41.
See also: Mt. 20:6; Jn. 6:19.

To this adverbial accusative of measure belongs the accusative of the time during which (Mt. 20:6). Sometimes the accusative is used to indicate point of time, much as the locative (Ac. 20:16), but with a sense of duration or extension not possible for the locative. When the accusative is used to indicate a point of time, it is part of a continuous period implied in the context (cf. Jn. 4:52; Ac. 27:33; 1 Cor. 15:30). This implication is not possible for the locative.

b. Of *Manner*.

δωρεὰν ἐλάβετε, δωρεὰν δότε.

Freely ye have received, freely give. Mt. 10:8.
See also: I Cor. 14:27; 1 Pt. 3:21.

c. Of *Reference*.

ἥτις πολλὰ ἐκοπίασεν εἰς ὑμᾶς.

Who labored for you with reference to many things. Rom. 16:6.
See also: I Cor. 9:25; Eph. 4:15.

i. The accusative used with the infinitive is not properly the "subject" of the infinitive, but is an accusative of reference used to describe "the person connected with the action" (R–S. 97).

ii. The adverbial accusative is used widely in the papyri (cf. B. G. U. 22:5).

(3) *The Cognate Accusative.* When an accusative of the direct object contains the same idea signified by the verb, it is called a cognate accusative. Here the limits set by the accusative are coextensive with the significance of the verb, the use being for emphasis.

τὸν καλὸν ἀγῶνα ἠγώνισμαι.

I have fought the good fight. 2 Tim. 4:7.

See also: Mk. 4:41; 1 Pt. 5:2.

(4) *The Double Accusative.* Some verbs require more than one object to complete their meaning. Such are those which take:

a. A personal and impersonal object.

ἐκεῖνος ὑμᾶς διδάξει πάντα.

He will teach you all things. Jn. 14:26.

See also: Mk. 6:34; Heb. 5:12.

b. A direct and predicate object.

οὐκέτι λέγω ὑμᾶς δούλους.

No longer do I call you servants. Jn. 15:15.

See also: Jn. 6:15; Lk. 1:59.

i. We have followed here substantially Blass's outline of the double accusative (cf. Bl. 91f.). Winer divides it into the "accusative of the person and thing" (Jn. 19:2), and the "accusative of subject and predicate" (Jn. 6:15; cf. W. 226–228). It will be noticed that the basal lines of analysis are the same in both authors. Webster analyzes the construction in practically the same way (*op. cit.*, p. 64).

ii. Many verbs which occur with some other construction in English take a double accusative in Greek; e.g., ἐνέδυσαν αὐτὸν τὰ ἱμάτια αὐτοῦ, *they clothed him with his own garments* (Mk. 15:20). On the other hand, when we would sometimes expect a second accusative, we find instead εἰς with the accusative, a probable Hebraism, influenced by the Hebrew construction with ? (cf. Ac. 7:21 and Gen. 12:2 of the

LXX; cf. Bt. 150). Robertson shows that we may even have three accusatives with one verb, as in Mk. 10:18 (R. 479). Where the double accusative occurs with the active of a verb, when changed to the passive it ordinarily retains the accusative of the thing (Ac. 18:25), though sometimes, especially with καλέω, both nouns are changed to the nominative (Luke 2:21; cf. W. 229).

(5) *The Accusative Absolute.* Sometimes an accusative, with or without a participle, is set off in a sort of explanatory way grammatically independent of the rest of the sentence. This use is very rare in the New Testament. Robertson gives Ac. 26:3 as the clearest example. There are a few other possible instances.

γνώστην ὄντα σε.
Since thou art expert. Ac. 26:3.
See also: 1 Cor. 16:6; Eph. 1:18; Rm. 8:3.

One cannot be positive that any of these constructions is an accusative absolute. Each of them may be otherwise explained. Winer regards Ac. 26:3 as an *anacoluthon,* a construction of frequent occurrence in the New Testament. He expresses doubt about there being any instance of the accusative absolute in the New Testament, giving it as his opinion that "on close examination the grammatical reason for the Accusative can be discovered in the structure of the sentence" (W. 231). It is used in classical Greek (Goodwin: *Greek Moods and Tenses,* p. 338), and in the inscriptions (Buck: *Gr. Dialects,* p. 125), but is very doubtful in the papyri (M. 74). Webster quite pertinently defines this usage as "the accusative in apposition to the whole sentence" (*op. cit.,* p. 66). An appositive use of the accusative it undoubtedly is.

(6) *The Accusative with Oaths.* In the New Testament ὁρκίζω, *I adjure,* is regularly followed by two accusatives.

ὁρκίζω σε τὸν Θεόν, μή με βασανίσῃς.
I adjure thee by God, torment me not. Mk. 5:7.
See also: Ac. 19:13; 1 Ths. 5:27.

This construction is really a double accusative, and is placed by Robertson in that class (R. 483f.), but the peculiarity of the idiom justifies distinctive treatment.

II. Prepositions

References: R. 571–636; R–S. 115–126; M. 98–107.

97. A preposition is a word used as an aid in the expression of substantive relations. This is its chief function, though, as explained below, it has other uses as well. It is called "preposition" because in its use it is regularly placed before the noun. Beginning merely as an auxiliary to noun inflection, it has progressively encroached upon the inflectional endings until they have been almost entirely displaced. Modern Greek, like most other modern languages, uses the preposition as the chief device for representing case distinctions.

Origin

98. Originally prepositions were adverbs. That is, they were at first adjuncts to verbs rather than substantives. They gradually became more closely associated with the noun, until custom finally fixed their use with particular cases. "It is not difficult . . . to infer that the Aryan prepositions were originally adverbs, which at first were adjuncts not to the noun but to the accompanying verbs. . . . By degrees these old adverbs came to be more and more closely connected in thought with the inflected nouns they now served to define, till at last the original meanings of the cases were subordinated to those of the accompanying prepositions and in some cases forgotten" (Sweet: *op. cit.*, p. 54).

99. Most of the prepositions found in Homer are used also as adverbs. There are instances in the New Testament of prepositions used as adverbs, which indicate that at one time they were pure adverbs. Note for example 2 Cor. 11:23, διάκονοι Χριστοῦ εἰσίν; ὑπὲρ ἐγώ. *Are they ministers of Christ? I more.* Here ὑπέρ functions as a regular adverb; also εἰς in Lk. 21:4, ἔβαλον εἰς τὰ δῶρα, *they cast in their gifts.* In Rev. 21:21 ἀνὰ εἷς and in Mk. 14:19 κατὰ εἷς are used distributively: *one by one,* or *each.* (Note that εἷς is in the nominative case.) We also find indications of how prepositions were formed from adverbs; e.g., ἀνά from ἄνω, *upwards;* κατά from κάτω, *downwards;* εἰς from ἔσω, *within;* and ἐκ from ἔξω, *outside.*

100. In addition there are many adverbial prepositions, which some have unwittingly termed "improper" prepositions, that function in one passage as an adverb and in another as a preposition. A list of them follows: ἅμα, *together with;* ἄντικρυς, ἀπέναντι, κατέναντι, *opposite;* ἄνευ, ἄτερ, *without;* ἄχρι(ς), *up to;* ἔγγυς, *near;* ἔκτος, ἔξω, *outside;* ἔμπροσθεν, ἐνώπιον, *before;* ἕνεκεν, *for the sake of;* ἔνοχος, *guilty of;* ἐντός, ἔσω, *within;* ἐπάνω, ὑπεράνω, *above;* ἐπέκεινα, ὑπερέκεινα, *beyond;* ἕως, *up to;* μέσον, *in the midst of;* μεταξύ, *between;* ὀψέ, *after;* πλήν, *besides;* ὑποκάτω, *under;* χωρίς, *apart from.*

Function

101. While adverbs qualify the action, motion, or state of verbs as to manner, place, time, and extent, prepositions do also; but, in addition to this, they mark the direction and relative position of the action, motion, or state expressed by the verb. Prepositions then attend upon verbs to help them express more specifically their relation to substantives. Thus in ἠκούσατε ἀπ' ἀρχῆς, *you heard from the beginning,* the hearing is qualified by being localized in time; in ἦλθεν εἰς τὸ ἱερόν, *he went into the temple,* the going is limited as to place. It is incorrect in view of the above to say that prepositions govern cases. Neither is the opposite true, that cases govern prepositions. But it is true that as cases limit and define the relations of verbs to substantives, so also prepositions help to express

more exactly and effectively the very distinctions for which cases were created. They are also used to express the case relations of substantive with substantive, as Eph. 6:23, ἀγάπη μετὰ πίστεως ἀπὸ θεοῦ, *love with faith from God.* Thus from being purely an adjunct of the verb in function, prepositions were transferred to more intimate association with the noun, to define more closely its relation to the rest of the sentence. Some came to have case endings according to the case with which they were first used. Thus to understand the full significance of a preposition one needs to know the function of the case with which it is used in each instance, the meaning of the preposition absolutely, and, what is most difficult, learn what it means relatively in each context.

Significance

102. Nearly every preposition may be prefixed to a word and thus add a new idea to the word or modify or even intensify the meaning of that particular word. A very frequent use of prepositions is in composition with words for the purpose of expressing emphasis or intensity. Grammarians term this the "perfective" use of the preposition. One can often detect shades of meaning from this usage that are otherwise impossible to discern. All the prepositions except ἀμφί, περί, and πρό drop a final vowel before a word beginning with a vowel.

103. Some prepositions are used with only one case; e.g., ἀνά, ἀντί, ἀπό, ἐκ, and εἰς; some with two, and the others with three cases.

104. A very important fact to remember in studying prepositions is that each one, unlike the English use, may be used to express one or several either kindred or diversified ideas. The best way to determine the meanings of a preposition is to study it in its various contexts and note its

various uses. References are given to facilitate this. This is the inductive method. Each preposition originally had, very likely, only one meaning. We cannot know definitely what that was, but we have ventured a guess for each preposition and term it the *root* meaning. Additional meanings were accumulated in succeeding years, most of them kindred to the root meaning, but some not. These we call *resultant* meanings. They are by far the more numerous and are the meanings to which the student should confine himself in his prose composition. Then there is a special, rare use of prepositions whose meanings we term *remote*, because they are remote from the root idea and because they are seldom used. A knowledge of them will be of great help in interpreting difficult passages of Scripture.

’Aνά

105. Root meaning: *up.*

In composition: *up, back, again.* Rom. 12:2, ἀνα-καινώσει, *new again* or *renewal.*

Resultant meaning: it is rarely used out of composition, and only with the accusative case. It means *to the number of* in Rev. 4:8, ἔχων ἀνὰ πτέρυγας ἕξ, *having wings to the number of six.* See also Jn. 2:6. In Mt. 20:9, ἀνὰ δηνάριον means *at the rate of a denarius.* It is most frequently used in the distributive sense: Lk. 10:1, ἀνὰ δύο, *by twos;* 1 Cor. 14:27, ἀνὰ μέρος, *by turns.* See also Mt. 10:9, 10; Rev. 21:21. The expression ἀνὰ μέσον in Mt. 13:25, Mk. 7:21 and Rev. 7:17 means *in the midst of;* but in 1 Cor. 6:5 it means *between.*

’Aντί

106. Root meaning: *face to face.*

In composition: *face to face.* Lk. 24:17, ἀντι-βάλλετε, *throwing into each other's face,* or *against;* Jn. 19:12, ἀντιλέγει, *speaks against.* It is used with the ablative case only. One of its regular meanings in classical Greek was *in exchange for,* and this translation fits Heb. 12:16 perfectly, *who in exchange for (ἀντί) one meal gave away his birth-right.* So Kühner and Winer translate it. In Mt. 5:38 and Rom. 12:17 *for* is a good translation, *eye for an eye, evil for evil.* See also Mt. 17:27; Jn. 6:16. The phrase ἀνθ᾽ ὧν occurs five times with the sense of *because* (cf. Lk. 1:20; 12:3).

107. There is conclusive proof now that the dominant meaning for ἀντί in the first century was *instead of.* "By far the commonest meaning of ἀντί, is the simple *instead of*" (Moulton-Milligan: *Voc. of the Gr. N. T.*). This statement refers to the papyri usage. Professor Whitesell (Chicago) made a study of ἀντί in the Septuagint and found thirty-eight passages where it is rightly translated *instead of* in the RV. Since ἀντί is used in two atonement passages in the New Testament, such a translation needs careful consideration. Notice the following: Gen. 22:13, *and offered him up for a burnt offering instead of (ἀντί) his son;* Gen. 44:33, *Let thy servant, I pray thee, abide instead of (ἀντί) the lad a bondman to my lord;* Num. 3:12, *I have the Levites from among the children of Israel instead of (ἀντί) all the first-born.* These three sentences unmistakably deal with substitution. This translation applies especially to the following: Mt. 2:22, *Archelaus was reigning over Judea instead of (ἀντί) his father Herod;* Lk. 11:11, *and he instead of (ἀντί) a fish give him a serpent;* 1 Cor. 11:15, *for her hair is given her instead of (ἀντί) a covering;* Heb. 12:2, *Jesus . . . who instead of (ἀντί) the joy that was set before him endured the cross.* But does it mean *instead of* in Mt. 20:28 and Mk. 10:45, δοῦναι τὴν ψυχὴν αὐτοῦ λύτρον ἀντὶ πολλῶν ? Either that, or else it means *in exchange for,* and each implies substitution. The obscurity of this passage is not the result of linguistic ambiguity, but of theological controversy.

Ἀπό

108. Root meanings: *off*, *away from*.

In composition: *off*, *back*. Jn. 18:26, ἀπέκοψεν, *cut off*; Mt. 16:27, ἀποδώσει, *give back*. This preposition is very common. It implies separation, and is, therefore, used only with the ablative case.

Resultant meaning: *from*. Mt. 3:16, ἀνέβη ἀπὸ τοῦ ὕδατος, *he went up from the water*. But Mark is more descriptive and adds further details by using a present participle and ἐκ, *out of:* 1:10, ἀναβαίνων ἐκ τοῦ ὕδατος, *going up out of the water*.

Remote meanings: (1) *by*: Jas. 1:13, ἀπὸ θεοῦ πειράζομαι, *I am tempted by God* (cf. Ac. 15:4; 2 Cor. 7:13; Rev. 12:6). These all emphasize source. (2) *On account of:* Heb. 5:7. ἀκουσθεὶς ἀπὸ τῆς εὐλαβείας, *heard on account of his devotion;* cf. Jn. 21:6; Ac. 28:3. This usage is supported by the papyri. Fayum CXI: 4, *I blame you greatly for having lost two little pigs* ἀπὸ τοῦ σκυλμοῦ τῆς ὁδοῦ, *on account of the fatigue of the journey*. Ἀφ' ἧς or οὖ means *since*.

Ἀπό may include the idea expressed in ἐκ, but its usual significance is *from the edge of*, while ἐκ has the idea *from within*. Παρά with the ablative emphasizes source and is used only with persons; as in Jn. 9:16, οὐκ ἔστιν οὗτος παρὰ θεοῦ, *this one is not from God*.

Διά

109. Root meaning: *two;* from δύο. Jas. 1:8, δί-ψυχος, *double-lived*.

In composition: *two, between, through*. It is also frequently used in the "perfective" sense. Heb. 1:11, σὺ δὲ διαμένεις, *but thou abidest through*, or *endlessly*.

Resultant meanings: (1) with the genitive case; *through*. Jn. 3:17, ἵνα σωθῇ ὁ κόσμος δι' αὐτοῦ, *that the world might be saved through him*. This usage is very common. (2) With the accusative case: (a) *because of*. Mt. 6:25, διὰ τοῦτο λέγω ὑμῖν, *because of this I say to you.* This usage is also very common. (b) *For the sake of, for.* Mk. 2:27, τὸ σάββατον διὰ τὸν ἄνθρωπον ἐγένετο, *the sabbath was made for the sake of man* (cf. Mt. 19:12; Rom. 4:23, 24; 11:28; Rev. 1:9; 2:3).

Remote meanings: (1) *by, through* (agency). 2 Cor. 1:19, Ἰησοῦς ὁ ἐν ὑμῖν δι' ἡμῶν κηρυχθείς, *Jesus, who was preached among you by us* (cf. 1 Cor. 11:12; Gal. 1:1). (2) *By means of.* Lk. 8:4, εἶπεν διὰ παραβολῆς, *he spoke by means of a parable* (cf. Ac. 15:23; 18:9). The phrase διὰ τί regularly means *why* (cf. Mt. 21:25; Mk. 11:31).

In G. Milligan's *Greek Papyri*, pp. 39, 40, there are four places where διά means *by*. A writer says he is sending two letters, διὰ Νηδύμου μίαν, διὰ Κρονίου ... μίαν, and he states that an inclosed document is to be signed διὰ Διοδώρου ... ἢ διὰ τῆς γυναικός. Although διά is occasionally used to express agency, it does not approximate the full strength of ὑπό. This distinction throws light on Jesus' relation to the creation, implying that Jesus was not the absolute, independent creator, but rather the intermediate agent in creation. See Jn. 1:3, πάντα δι' αὐτοῦ ἐγένετο; Heb. 1:2, δι' οὗ καὶ ἐποίησεν τοὺς αἰῶνας; Mt. 1:22, ἵνα πληρωθῇ τὸ ῥηθὲν ὑπὸ κυρίου διὰ τοῦ προφήτου (cf. Mk. 1:5; Lk. 2:18; Jn.1:10).

Ἐκ

110. Root meanings: *out of, from within.*

In composition: *out of, away*—emphasis. 2 Cor. 4:8 furnishes a striking example of the perfective use, ἀπορούμενοι ἀλλ' οὐκ ἐξαπορούμενοι, *perplexed, but not completely perplexed.*

Resultant meanings: with the ablative case, the only case it occurs with: *out of, from within.* Ac. 8:39, ὅτε δὲ ἀνέβησαν ἐκ τοῦ ὕδατος, *and when they came up out of the water.*

Remote meanings: (1) *on.* Mt. 20:21, 23, εἷς ἐκ δεξιῶν καὶ εἷς ἐξ εὐωνύμων, *one on the right hand, and one on the left.* So also Lk. 20:42. The papyri substantiate such a translation: οὐλὴ καστροκνημίῳ ἐκ δεξιῶν, *a scar on the calf of the leg on the right* (B.G.U. 975:15). But ἐκ is so used

only when it occurs with the words "right" or "left." (2)
By means of. Rom. 1:17, πίστεως ζήσεται, *saved by means
of faith.* In Rom. 3:30 we have *who will justify* ἐκ πίστεως.
(cf. Jas. 2:18, 22; 1 Jn. 4:6). (3) *Because of.* Jn. 6:66,
ἐκ τούτου πολλοὶ . . . ἀπῆλθον, *because of this many
went away.*

Εἰς

111. Root meanings: *within, in.* It was derived from ἐν
and gradually took over its functions, so much so that in
Modern Greek ἐν does not occur.

In composition: *into, in;* as εἰσελθεῖν, *to go into.*

Resultant meanings: with the accusative case: *into, unto,
to, for.* These meanings are very common. Εἰς is used
more than seventeen hundred times in the New Testament,
and it occurs only with the accusative case. Ac. 11:26,
ἐξῆλθεν δὲ εἰς Ταρσόν, *but he went forth to Tarsus;* 16:19,
εἵλκυσαν εἰς τὴν ἀγοράν, *they dragged them into the market-
place;* Rom. 1:5, ἀποστολὴν εἰς ὑπακοὴν πίστεως, *apostleship
unto the obedience of faith;* 1 Cor. 14:22, αἱ γλῶσσαι εἰς
σημεῖόν εἰσιν, *tongues are for a sign.*

Remote meanings: (1) *in.* Lk. 8:48, πορεύου εἰς εἰρήνην,
go in peace (cf. Jn. 1:18; Ac. 2:27, 31; 19:22). (2) *Upon.*
Mk. 1:10, καταβαῖνον εἰς αὐτόν, *coming down upon him*
(cf. Ac. 27:26). This use is common in the papyri. (3)
Against. Lk. 12:10, ὃς ἐρεῖ λόγον εἰς τὸν υἱόν, *who will
speak a word against the Son* (cf. Lk. 15:18; Ac. 6:11). (4)
Among. Lk. 10:36, ἐμπεσόντος εἰς τοὺς λῃστάς, *fell
among thieves* (cf. Jn. 21:23; Ac. 4:17). (5) *With respect to,
with reference to.* Ac. 2:25, Δαυεὶδ γὰρ λέγει εἰς αὐτόν,
for David says with reference to him (cf. Rom. 10:4; 15:2; 16:19).
(6) *As,* expressing equivalence. Heb. 1:15, ἐγὼ ἔσομαι αὐτῷ
εἰς πατέρα, *I will be to him as a father* (cf. Mk. 10:8; Ac. 7:53;
13:22). (7) *Because of.* Rom. 4:20, εἰς δὲ τὴν ἐπαγγελίαν

τοῦ θεοῦ οὐ διεκρίθη τῇ ἀπιστίᾳ, *but because of the promise of God he did not waver in unbelief* (cf. Mt. 3:11; Mk. 2:18; Rom. 11:32; Tit. 3:14). (8) *For the purpose of*, regularly when used with the infinitive, but a few times also without. Mt. 8:34, ἡ πόλις ἐξῆλθεν εἰς ὑπάντησιν τῷ Ἰησοῦ, *the city went out for the purpose of meeting Jesus* (cf. Mt. 8:4; 1 Cor. 11:24; 2 Cor. 2:12).

i. The following is a quotation from J. R. Mantey's article in the *Expositor* (London), June, 1923, "Unusual Meanings for Prepositions in the Greek New Testament":

When one considers in Ac. 2:38 repentance as self-renunciation and baptism as a public expression of self-surrender and self-dedication to Christ, which significance it certainly had in the first century, the expression εἰς ἄφεσιν τῶν ἁμαρτιῶν ὑμῶν may mean *for the purpose of the remission of sins.* But if one stresses baptism, without its early Christian import, as a ceremonial means of salvation, he does violence to Christianity as a whole, for one of its striking distinctions from Judaism and Paganism is that it is a religion of salvation by faith while all others teach salvation by works.

The sentence μετανόησεν εἰς τὸ κήρυγμα Ἰωνᾶ in Mt. 12:41 and Lk. 12:32 is forceful evidence for a causal use of this preposition. What led to their repentance? Of course, it was Jonah's preaching. Mt. 3:11 furnishes further evidence: ἐγὼ μὲν ὑμᾶς βαπτίζω ἐν ὕδατι εἰς μετανοίαν. Did John baptize that they might repent, or because of repentance? If the former, we have no further Scriptural confirmation of it. If the latter, his practice was confirmed and followed by the apostles, and is in full harmony with Christ's demand for inward, genuine righteousness. In connection with this verse we have the testimony of a first-century writer to the effect that John the Baptist baptized people only after they had repented. Josephus, *Antiquities of the Jews*, book 18, chapter 5, section 2: "Who (John) was a good man, and commanded the Jews to exercise virtue, both as to righteousness towards one another and piety towards God, and so to come to baptism; for that the washing (with water) would be acceptable to him, if they made use of it, not in order to the putting away of some sins, but for the purification of the body; supposing still that the soul was thoroughly purified beforehand by righteousness."

ii. Deissmann in *Light From the Ancient East* gives several convincing quotations from the papyri to prove that πιστεύειν εἰς αὐτόν meant *surrender* or *submission to.* A slave was sold *into the name of the god of a temple;* i.e., to be a temple servant. G. Milligan agrees with Deissmann that this papyri usage of εἰς αὐτόν, is also found regularly in the New Testament. Thus to believe on or to be baptized into the name of Jesus means to renounce self and to consider oneself the lifetime servant of Jesus.

'Ἐν

112. Root meaning: *within.*

In composition: *within, in;* as ἐνεργέω, *work in; on;* as, ἐνδύω, *put on.*

Resultant meanings: (1) with the locative case; *in, on, at, within, among.* Mt. 2:5, ἐν 'Βηθλεέμ, *in Bethlehem;* Ac. 1:17, ἐν ὑμῖν, *among us.* With the locative case it is used mostly with words of place, but it also occurs with words of time (cf. Ac. 1:15). (2) With the instrumental case: *with, by means of.* 1 Cor. 4:21, ἐν ῥάβδῳ ἔλθω πρὸς ὑμᾶς; *should I come to you with a rod?* Rev. 6:8, ἀποκτεῖναι ἐν ῥομφαίᾳ καὶ ἐν λιμῷ καὶ ἐν θανάτῳ, *to kill by means of sword, famine and death.* See also Lk. 1:51; Rom. 1:18; Heb. 9:25; Rev. 13:10. To introduce temporal clauses ἐν τῷ, *while,* is frequently used, both with infinitives and finite verbs; e.g., Mt. 13:4, ἐν τῷ σπείρειν αὐτόν, *while he was sowing* (cf. Lk. 5:34).

Remote meanings: (1) *besides,* used only once. Lk. 16:26, καὶ ἐν πᾶσι τούτοις μεταξὺ ἡμῶν καὶ ὑμῶν, *and besides all these things, between us and you,* etc. (2) *Into.* Jn. 3:35, πάντα δέδωκεν ἐν τῇ χειρὶ αὐτοῦ, *he has given all things into his hand* (cf. Mt. 26:23; Rom. 2:5). (3) *Because of.* Gal. 1:24, ἐδόξαζον ἐν ἐμοὶ τὸν θεόν, *they were glorifying God because of me* (cf. Rom. 1:24; Col. 1:21; 1 Pt. 2:3.)

i. "Prof. H. A. A. Kennedy has collected a number of instances of this use of ἐν—*because of, on account of*—from the LXX and from the Pauline Epistles" (cf. M. and M.: *op. cit.*).

ii. On the expression ἐν Χριστῷ, which occurs one hundred and sixty-four times in Paul's letters, Deissmann says, "There cannot be any doubt that 'Christ in me' means the exalted Christ living in Paul . . . and Paul is in Christ. Christ, the exalted Christ, is Spirit. Therefore, He can live in Paul and Paul in Him." This mystic relation is likened to the air that is in us and yet we are in it.

iii. Ἐν is used in Heb. 1:1, 2 with about the same force that διά with the genitive has, ὁ θεός λαλήσας τοῖς πατράσιν ἐν τοῖς προφήταις ἐπ᾽ ἐσχάτου τῶν ἡμερῶν τούτων ἐλάλησεν ὑμῖν ἐν υἱῷ, *God spoke through prophets then, but now through a son* (cf. Mt. 12:27, 28).

Ἐπί

113. Root meaning: *upon.*

In composition: *upon,* and also for emphasis, as ἐπιγινώσκω, *know thoroughly.*

Resultant meanings: (1) with the genitive case: *upon, on, at, by, before,* emphasizing contact. Lk. 2:14, ἐπὶ γῆς εἰρήνη, *peace upon earth.* (2) With the locative case: *upon, on, at, over, before,* emphasizing position. Mt. 18:13, χαίρει ἐπ᾽ αὐτῷ, *he rejoices over it.* (3) With the accusative case: *upon, on, up to, to, over,* emphasizing motion or direction. Mk. 16:2, ἔρχονται ἐπὶ τὸ μνημεῖον, *they came to the tomb.*

Remote meanings: (1) *in.* Ex. 2:5, λούσασθαι ἐπὶ τὸν ποταμόν, *to bathe in the river;* Rom. 1:10; 6:21; Tit. 1:1. (2) *Against.* Mk. 14:48, ὡς ἐπὶ λῃστὴν ἐξήλθατε, *you came out as against a thief* (cf. Lk. 12:53; Ac. 13:50). (3) *For.* Mt. 3:7, ἐρχομένους ἐπὶ τὸ βάπτισμα, *coming for baptism,* Lk. 7:44; 18:4; Ac. 19:10, 34. (4) *After.* Lk. 1:59, ἐκάλουν αὐτὸ ἐπὶ τ̄ ὀνόματι τοῦ πατρός, *they were going to call it after the name of his father* (cf. Lk. 14:34; Rom. 5:14; Rev. 1:7). (5) *On account of.* Ac. 4:21, ἐδόξαζον τὸν θεὸν ἐπὶ τῷ γεγονότι, *they were glorifying God on account of the event* (cf. Lk. 1:47; Rom. 5:12; 1 Cor. 1:4). The phrase ἐφ᾽ ᾧ in Rom. 5:12 and 2 Cor. 5:4 means *because.* (6) *In the time of.* Ac. 11:28, ἥτις ἐγένετο ἐπὶ Κλαυδίου, *which really happened*

in the time of Claudius (cf. Mt. 1:11; Mk. 2:26; Lk. 3:2). (7)
In addition to. 2 Cor. 7:13, ἐπὶ τῇ παρακλήσει ἡμῶν, *in
addition to our comfort.* This was a common usage in classical Greek.

Κατά

114. Root meaning: *down.*

In composition: *down.* Rom. 1:18, τὴν ἀλήθειαν . . .
κατεχόντων, *holding down* (*hindering*) *the truth.* At times it
is emphatic; as Mt. 3:12, τὸ δὲ ἄχυρον κατακαύσει, *and he
will burn completely the chaff.*

Resultant meanings: (1) with the ablative case: *down from.*
Mk. 5:13, ὥρμησεν ἡ ἀγέλη κατὰ τοῦ κρημνοῦ, *the herd
rushed down from the cliff.* (2) With the genitive case:
down upon, down, against, throughout, by. Ac. 9:42, γνωστὸν
δὲ ἐγένετο καθ᾽ ὅλης Ἰόππης, *and it became known throughout all Joppa.* (3) With the accusative case: *along, at, according to.* Lk. 10:4, μηδένα κατὰ τὴν ὁδὸν ἀσπάσησθε,
salute no one along the road. Also in the distributive sense:
Ac. 2:46, κατ᾽ οἶκον, *from house to house;* Lk. 2:41, κατ᾽ ἔτος,
from year to year; 1 Cor. 14:27, κατὰ δύο, *by twos;* see also
Lk. 8:1; 13:32.

Remote meanings: (1) *with reference to, with respect to, pertaining to,* etc. Phs. 4.11, οὐχ ὅτι καθ᾽ ὑστέρησιν λέγω,
not that I speak with reference to lack; Rom. 14:22; 2 Cor.7:11;
Eph. 6:21. (2) *In.* Ac. 11:1, οἱ ὄντες κατὰ τὴν Ἰουδαίαν,
those in Judea (cf. Ac. 13:1; 15:23; 24:12; Heb. 11:13). (3)
Before. Lk. 2:31, κατὰ πρόσωπον πάντων, *before the face of all*
(cf. Ac. 2:10; Gal. 2:11; 3:1).

Μετά

115. Root meaning; *in the midst of.* Mt. 1:23, μεθ᾽ ἡμῶν
ὁ θεός, *God in the midst of us.*

In composition: three clearly defined meanings. (1) *With.*
Lk. 5:7, μετόχος, from μετά and ἔχω, *one who holds with;*

hence a *partner*. (2) *After*. Ac. 10:5. μετάπεμψαι Σίμωνα, send after (*summon*) *Simon*. (3) It is frequently used to express the idea of change or difference; as μετανοέω, *think differently;* μεταμορφοῦσθε, *transform yourselves;* μετατίθημι, *translate.*

Resultant meanings: (1) with the genitive: *with*. Mk. 1:13, ἦν μετὰ τῶν θηρίων, *he was with the wild animals;* see also Mk. 1:20, 29, 36. (2) With the accusative: *after*. Lk 5:27, μετὰ ταῦτα ἐξῆλθεν, *after these things he went out;* see also Lk. 9:28; 10:1; 12:4.

Παρά

116. Root meaning: *beside*.

In composition: *beside*. Mt. 4:13, Καφαρναοὺμ τὴν παραθαλασσίαν, *Capernaum beside the sea.* Closely akin to this are the meanings *by* and *along*. It also signifies emphasis at times. Mt. 8:5, παρακαλῶν αὐτόν, *calling earnestly;* i.e.. *beseeching him* (cf. Ac. 17:16; Heb. 3:16; Gal. 4:10).

Resultant meanings: (1) with the ablative case: *from*. Jn. 4:9, παρ᾽ ἐμοῦ πεῖν αἰτεῖς, *ask a drink* (infinitive used as object) *from me.* (2) With the locative case: *by the side of, in the presence of, with, before.* Lk. 1:30, εὗρες χάριν παρὰ τῷ θεῷ, *you have found favor with God;* Rom. 2:13, δίκαιοι παρὰ θεῷ, *just before God.* Παρά is used only with words denoting person in the ablative and locative cases, but it is just the reverse with the accusative case, with a few exceptions. (3) With the accusative case: *to the side of, beside, along, beyond.* Mt. 18:35, παρὰ τὴν ὁδὸν ἐπαιτῶν, *begging beside the road;* Lk. 13:4, ὀφειλέται ἐγένοντο παρὰ πάντας, *became debtors beyond all*(cf. Rom. 1:25; Heb. 1:9). In comparisons its sense is best translated by *than*. Heb. 1:4; 2:7, ἠλάττωσας αὐτὸν . . . παρ᾽ ἀγγέλλους, *having made him lower than angels.* A few times it means *contrary to*. Rom. 1:26, τὴν φυσικὴν χρῆσιν εἰς τὴν παρὰ φύσιν, *the natural use into that contrary to nature* (cf. Ac. 18:13; Rom. 11:24).

Περί

117. Root meaning: *around.*

In composition: *around.* Ac. 13:11, περιάγων ἐζήτει χειραγωγούς, *going around he was seeking guides.* It is used in the perfective sense, implying emphasis, occasionally. Heb. 10:11, περιελεῖν ἁμαρτίας, *to take away sins completely* (cf. Ac. 27:20; Mt. 26:38).

Resultant meanings: (1) with the genitive case: *about, concerning.* Mt. 16:11, οὐ περὶ ἄρτων εἶπον, *I did not speak concerning loaves* (cf. Mt. 17:16; 18:19; 19:17). (2) With the accusative case: *around, about.* Mt. 8:18, ὄχλον περὶ αὐτόν, *a crowd around him* (cf. Mt. 20:3, 5, 6, 9). In the accusative case περί implies position around, whereas in the genitive case it implies general relationship, as in the statement, "He was talking *about* him."

Remote meanings: (1) *in behalf of.* Mt. 26:28, τὸ αἷμά μου . . . περὶ πολλῶν, *my blood in behalf of many* (cf. Mk. 1:44; Jn. 16:26; Heb. 5:3; Ex. 14:14, 25). (2) In Ac. 13:13 it may best be rendered *with*; οἱ περὶ Παῦλον, *those with Paul.* (3) In Tit. 2:7 περὶ πάντα may well be translated *in everything.*

Πρό

118. Root meaning: *before.*

In composition: *before.* Mt. 2:9, ὁ ἀστὴρ . . . προῆγεν αὐτούς, *the star went before them.*

Resultant meaning, with the ablative case: *before.* Jn. 5:7, ἄλλος πρὸ ἐμοῦ καταβαίνει, *another goes down before me.*

Remote meanings: πρό deviates only twice in the New Testament from its regular meaning *before.* (1) In Jn. 10:8, πάντες ὅσοι ἦλθον πρὸ ἐμοῦ κλέπται εἰσὶν καὶ λῃσταί, this preposition is translated *before,* but the context favors *in the room of,* or *in the name of,* which are recognized translations for πρό. In Gessner Harrison's *Greek Prepositions and Cases* (p. 408) are quoted examples of such a use. He there says, "whence comes the idea of occupying the place of another, or becoming his substitute." (2) The expression πρὸ πάντων in Jas. 5:12 and 1 Pt. 4:8 means *above all.*

Πρός

119. Root meaning: *near, facing.*

In composition: *near* (Mt. 15:32); *toward* (Lk. 9:41); *for* (Mt. 13:21). Its significance is emphasis occasionally. Ac. 10:10, πρόσπεινος, *very hungry;* Ac. 2:42, προσκαρτηρέω, *continue steadfastly.*

Resultant meanings: (1) with the locative case: *at.* Jn. 20:12, ἕνα πρὸς τῇ κεφαλῇ 'καὶ ἕνα πρὸς τοῖς ποσίν, *one at the head and one at the feet* (cf. Lk. 19:37; Jn. 18:16; Rev. 1:13). (2) With the accusative case. (*a*) *To, towards.* Mt. 2:12, μὴ ἀνακάμψαι πρὸς Ἡρῴδην, *to not return to Herod.* (*b*) *Beside.* Mk. 4:1, ὁ ὄχλος πρὸς τὴν θάλασσαν, *the crowd beside the sea.* (*c*) *Against.* Ac. 6:1, πρὸς τοὺς Ἑβραίους, against *the Hebrews.* (*d*) *With.* Jn. 1:1, ὁ λόγος ἦν πρὸς τὸν θεόν, *the word was with God.* (*e*) *At.* Mk. 7:25, προσέπεσεν πρὸς τοὺς πόδας αὐτοῦ, *she fell at his feet.*

Remote meanings: (1) *for.* Ac. 27:34 (its only occurrence with the ablative case); Jn. 5:35; Rom.15: 2; Tit. 1:16; 2 Tim. 3:17, πρὸς πᾶν ἔργον ἀγαθὸν ἐξηρτισμένος, *thoroughly prepared for every good work.* (2) *With reference to, pertaining to.* Heb. 5:1, τὰ πρὸς τὸν θεόν, *things pertaining to God* (cf. Lk. 12:47; Rom. 10:21; Heb. 1:7). (3) *On.* Mk. 5:11, ἦν δὲ ἐκεῖ πρὸς τῷ ὄρει ἀγέλη χοίρων, *and there was there on the mountain a herd of swine.* (4) *On account of.* Mk. 10:5, πρὸς τὴν σκληροκαρδίαν ὑμῶν, κτλ., *on account of your hardheartedness he wrote you this command* (cf. Mt. 19:8). (5) It is used with the infinitive to express purpose. Mt. 6:1, πρὸς τὸ θεαθῆναι αὐτοῖς, *in order to be seen by them.*

Σύν

120. Root meaning: *together with.*

In composition: (1) *with.* Mk. 14:51, νεανίσκος τις συνηκο-
λεύθει αὐτῷ, *a certain young man followed with him.* (2)
Together. 1 Cor. 14:26, ὅταν συνέρχησθε, *when you come together.* (3) At times it intensifies the meaning of the word
to which it is joined. Lk. 2:19, συνετήρει, *carefully kept*
(cf. Lk. 12:2; 13:11; Rom. 11:32).

Resultant meaning, with the instrumental case: *together
with, with.* Jn. 12:2, ὁ Λάζαρος ἦν . . . σὺν αὐτῷ, *Lazarus
was with him* (cf. Lk. 1:56; 5:9; 9:32). It is used almost exclusively with persons, and implies close fellowship or co-
öperation.

Remote meaning: *besides.* Lk. 24:21, σὺν πᾶσιν τούτοις,
besides all these things. It may be so translated also in Ac.
17:34.

Ὑπέρ

121. Root meaning: *over.*

In composition: (1) *over.* Heb. 9:5, ὑπεράνω, *over above.*
(2) *More than.* 1 Ths. 3:10, ὑπερεκπερισσοῦ δεόμενοι,
praying more than abundantly (cf. 2 Cor. 12:7; Phs. 4:7).
(3) *Beyond.* 1 Ths. 4:6, ὑπερβαίνειν, *go beyond, defraud.*
(4) It is "perfective" or intensive at times. Phs. 2:9,
ὁ θεὸς αὐτὸν ὑπερύψωσεν, *God has highly exalted him* (cf. 1
Tim. 1:14).

Resultant meanings: (1) with the ablative case. (*a*) *For,
for the sake of, in behalf of.* Tit. 2:14, ἔδωκεν ἑαυτὸν ὑπὲρ
ἡμῶν, *he gave himself in behalf of us* (cf. Mk. 4:24; Lk. 22:19,
20; Heb. 2:9). (*b*) *Instead of.* Jn. 11:50, "it is expedient
for you that one man should die *instead of the people*, ὑπὲρ τοῦ
λαοῦ, and not that the whole nation perish"; Gal. 3:13,
"Christ redeemed us from the curse of the law, having
become a curse *instead of us, ὑπὲρ ἡμῶν.* In both of these

passages the context clearly indicates that substitution is meant (cf. 2 Cor. 5:14, 15); *Cat. of Gr. Papyri*, 94:15. (2) With the accusative case. (*a*) *Over, above.* Mt. 10:24, οὐκ ἔστιν μαθητὴς ὑπὲρ τὸν διδάσκαλον, *a disciple is not above his teacher.* (*b*) *Beyond.* Ac. 26:13, ὑπὲρ τὴν λαμπρότητα τοῦ ἡλίου, *beyond the brightness of the sun.* (*c*) *More than.* Mt. 10:37, ὁ φιλῶν πατέρα ἢ μητέρα ὑπὲρ ἐμέ, *he who loves father or mother more than me.*

Remote meanings. (1) *Concerning, with reference to.* Jn. 1:30, οὗτός ἐστιν ὑπὲρ οὗ ἐγὼ εἶπον, *this is he concerning whom I spoke* (cf. 2 Cor. 8:23; 2 Ths. 2:1). (2) After a comparative adjective it may be translated *than.* Heb. 4:12, τομώτερας ὑπὲρ μάχαιραν, *sharper than a sword* (cf. Lk. 16:8; Jn. 12:43).

Ὑπό

122. Root meaning: *under.*

In composition: *under.* Mt. 5:35, ὑποπόδιον, *under-foot;* i.e., *foot-stool.*

Resultant meanings: (1) with the accusative case: *under.* Mt. 8:9, ἄνθρωπός εἰμι ὑπὸ ἐξουσίαν, *I am a man under authority.* (2) With the ablative case: *by* (agency). Mt. 1:22, ῥηθὲν ὑπὸ κυρίου, *spoken by the Lord.*

Ὑπό is most frequently used for expressing agency. In fact, agency is expressed with the aid of ὑπό more frequently than it is by all the other methods combined. The instrumental case without a preposition is used frequently. Rom. 8:14, ὅσοι γὰρ πνεύματι θεοῦ ἄγονται, *for as many as are led by the Spirit of God.* Four other prepositions are used rarely for expressing agency: ἐκ (Gal. 4:4), παρά (Jn. 17:7), ἀπό (1 Cor. 3:18), and διά (Mt. 1:22). In our discussion of διά we have given examples of its use in expressing intermediate agency.

Prepositional Phrases

123. Prepositions may be used in conjunction with adjectives, nouns, pronouns, and adverbs in forming phrases. The resultant meaning of such a phrase is idiomatic at times.

For instance, the following phrases serve as conjunctions:
Lk. 21:24, ἄχρι οὗ, *until;* Rev. 16:18, ἀφ' οὗ, *since;* Lk. 12:3,
ἀνθ' ὧν, *because;* Rom. 5:12, ἐφ' ᾧ, *because;* Mt. 25:40, 45, ἐφ'
ὅσον, *inasmuch as,* but in Mt. 9:15 and 2 Pt. 1:13, *as long as;*
Heb. 3:3; 9:27, καθ' ὅσον, *inasmuch as, since;* Mt. 21:25, διὰ
τί, *why;* Mt. 14:31, εἰς τί, *why;* Lk. 5:34, ἐν ᾧ, *while.*

Diagram of the Directive and Local Functions of Prepositions

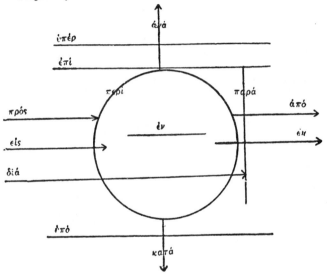

124. The following phrases function chiefly as **adverbs:**
2 Cor. 1:14, ἀπὸ μέρους, *in part;* Mt. 4:17, ἀπὸ πότε, *from
that time on;* Mt. 23:39, ἀπ' ἄρτι, *henceforth;* Mt. 18:10, διὰ
παντός, *always;* Heb. 7:25, εἰς τὸ παντελές, *completely;*
2 Cor. 13:13, εἰς τὸ πάλιν, *again;* Jn. 6:51, εἰς τὸν αἰῶνα,
forever; Ac. 12:7, ἐν τάχει, *quickly;* Jn. 4:31, ἐν τῷ μεταξύ,
meanwhile; 3 Jn. 1, ἐν ἀληθείᾳ, *sincerely* or *genuinely;* 2 Cor.
9:6, ἐπ' εὐλογίαις, *bountifully;* Ac. 23:19, κατ' ἰδίαν, *pri-
vately;* Ac. 3:17, κατ' ἄγνοιαν, *ignorantly.*

PREPOSITIONAL MEANINGS CLASSIFIED

	Direction	Position	Relation	Agency	Means	Cause	Association	Purpose
ἀνά	up	in, by						
ἀντί			in exchange for, instead of, for			because of		
ἀπό	from		for	by		on account of		
διά	through		for	by	through, by means of	because of		for the sake of
ἐκ	out of	on			by means of	because of		
ἐν	into	in, on, at, among, within	besides	in	with, by means of	because of	with	
εἰς	into, unto, to	in, among, upon	as, for, against, in respect to			because of		for the purpose of
ἐπί	up to, to	upon, at, on, in, by, before, over	against, after, in the time of			on account of		for
κατά	along, down, upon, through-out	down, from, upon, at, in, by, before	according to, with reference to					
μετά			after				with	
παρά	beyond, to the side of, from	beside, before	contrary to				with	
περί	around, about		in behalf of, concerning, about				with	
πρό		before						
πρός	to, toward	at, on, beside	against, for, pertaining to		by means of	on account of	with	for
σύν			besides				with	
ὑπέρ	beyond	over, above	concerning, for, instead of, on behalf of					for the sake of
ὑπό		under		by				

125. Occasionally prepositional phrases may be translated as adjectives. G. Milligan in his *Greek Papyri* (p. 47) translates ἐξ ὑγιοῦς καὶ ἐπ' ἀληθείας, *sound and true*, and in the *Voc. of the Gr. Test.* (p. 59), he translates ἀπὸ δημίας, *blameless*. In 2 Cor. 8:2 the phrase κατὰ βάθους means *deep*. When prepositional phrases occur in the attributive position, i.e., follow the article, they are adjectival in function: Ac. 7:13, οἱ ἀπὸ τῆς Θεσσαλονίκης 'Ιουδαῖοι, *the from-Thessalonica Jews;* Ac. 18:25, ἐδίδασκεν ἀκριβῶς τὰ περὶ τοῦ 'Ιησοῦ, *he was teaching accurately the concerning-Jesus things;* Rom. 4:12, τῆς ἐν ἀκροβυστία πίστεως, *the in-uncircumcision faith.*

126. In a similar way a noun in the descriptive genitive may be translated as an adjective sometimes. In Col. 1:27 and Tit. 2:13 τῆς δόξης means *glorious*, and in Lk. 16:8 τῆς ἀδικίας is rightly translated *unjust*. Notice this in Ac. 9:15, σκεῦος ἐκ λογῆς ἐστίν μοι, *he is a chosen vessel to me.*

III. THE ADJECTIVE

References: R. 650–675; R–S. 65–66; M. 77.

127. We approach here a neglected point in the treat ment of Greek grammar. Since the character of the adjec‧ tive is so close to that of the substantive few grammarians give it separate treatment. Those who do, devote relatively little space to its discussion. Yet there has never been a language which, in its use of the adjective, presented greater wealth or variety than the Greek. Hence it is highly neces- sary that the student of the Greek New Testament should be familiar with at least the more characteristic features of the Greek use of the adjective.

The Origin of the Adjective

128. The adjective is simply a use of the substantive highly specialized. Of its derivation from the substantive

there can be no reasonable doubt. Three evidences of this fact may be mentioned here, and others will appear in the further development of the subject. There is first the close kinship between the noun and the adjective in root and inflection. In the second place, the Sanskrit makes much less distinction between the noun and adjective than does the Greek. The third and perhaps the strongest evidence is the employment of an appositional substantive in the exact relation of an adjective, which has persisted even down to the present time. Note for instance such expressions as "a city home," "a treasure house," etc. An example of this adjective use of the noun in the New Testament may be seen in Mt. 3:6, ἐν τῷ Ἰορδάνῃ ποταμῷ, *in the Jordan river.* These indications point unquestionably to the origin of the adjective in the substantive. But its highly developed use in the Greek language justifies separate treatment.

Winer observes that there are "two sorts of nouns, substantive and adjective," and that, though they are "distinct from each other in thought, yet the latter (including participles) enters the sphere of substantives far more abundantly in Greek than, for instance, in Latin" (W. 234).

The Agreement of the Adjective

129. The close relation of the adjective to the substantive is further exhibited in the fact that the substantive regularly governs its form. The adjective agrees with the noun it qualifies in gender, number, and case.

ἐγώ εἰμι ὁ ποιμὴν ὁ καλός.

I am the good shepherd. Jn. 10:11.

See also: Mt. 7:24; Heb. 8:2.

A collective noun may take a plural adjective (Ac. 21:36), in which case the agreement is determined by sense rather than form. This agreement in sense may apply also to gender (1 Cor. 7:19).

The Function of the Adjective

130. The genius of the adjective is description. It denotes some fact which distinguishes or qualifies a noun. Thus in the expression "beautiful garden" the adjective simply points to the fact of *beauty* as it relates to the garden. But note that the adjective designates a state of being, *beauty*, just as the noun designates an object, *garden*. So the fundamental sense of the expression might be represented "beauty-garden" (a garden of beauty). Thus, in its function, we see that the adjective is at heart a substantive, being the outgrowth of a noun used in qualifying relationship with another noun.

i. While the genius of the adjective is description, it is not the only idiom in Greek whose distinctive character it is to perform this function. The same force belongs to the genitive, especially the genitive of description and apposition. When the article is absent from the genitive construction, the adjectival relation is strengthened. It is possible that historically the noun in the descriptive genitive preceded the adjective, and constituted its immediate origin. There would be, then, three steps in the development of the adjective: (1) *a beauty garden,* (2) *a garden of beauty,* (3) *a beautiful garden.* We also find appositional nouns in the genitive case (cf. § 90 (6)).

ii. All these qualifying devices fill their distinctive purposes. It is a mistake to say that any one of them is used "for" another. Robertson justly differs from Winer in the statement that a certain idiom "should naturally be expressed by an adjective" (R. 651; cf. W. 236). The writer "should" use the idiom that he does use, for we must assume that it most accurately represents his thought.

131. The adjective is abundant in the variations of its use in Greek, but for the practical purposes of the average student the following analysis will prove sufficient.

(1) *The Adjective Used as a Modifier.* The primary and most characteristic use of the adjective is to limit or describe a noun. In the performance of this function it

exhibits a twofold relation. It may be either *attributive* or *predicate*.

a. An adjective is in the attributive relation when it ascribes a quality to the noun which it modifies; e.g., ὁ ἄδικος κριτής, *the unjust judge.*

πρῶτον τὸν καλὸν οἶνον τίθησιν.

He first sets forth the good wine. Jn. 2:10.

b. An adjective is in the predicate relation when it *makes an assertion* concerning the noun which it modifies; e.g., ὁ κριτὴς ἄδικος, *the judge is unjust.*

ἕστηκεν ἐν τῇ καρδίᾳ ἑδραῖος.

He stands stedfast in heart. 1 Cor. 7:37.

While attribution is an adjectival function, it may also be true of other parts of speech, such as nouns, pronouns, participles, infinitives, adverbs, and clauses. We should be careful to distinguish the attributive and predicate adjective from the attributive and predicate position of the article. An attributive adjective usually has the article, but may not (Jn. 1:18). The predicate adjective occurs invariably without the article. The article, however, does not determine the relation of the adjective to the noun. This is determined by the mode of description by which the adjective presents the noun—whether the adjective is incidental or principal in the statement. Robertson sums the matter up well by saying that "the predicate presents an additional statement, is indeed the main point, while the attributive is an incidental description of the substantive about which the statement is made" (R. 656).

(2) *The Adjective Used as a Noun.* Sometimes the adjective so far recovers its original substantive character as to perform the full function of a noun. In this use the three genders present variation.

a. It is so used in the *masculine* gender when the noun is *concrete.*

σὺ εἶ ὁ ἅγιος τοῦ θεοῦ.

Thou are the Holy One of God. Jn. 6:69.

b. The *feminine* gender is generally in agreement with a feminine substantive *understood.*

ἐπορεύθη εἰς τὴν ὀρινήν.
She went into the mountain. Lk. 1:39.

This is, literally rendered, *She went into the mountainous,* with *country,* χώραν, understood.

c. The *neuter* singular is ordinarily used as an *abstract* noun.

τὸ χρηστὸν τοῦ θεοῦ.
The goodness of God. Rom. 2:4.

Frequently a neuter substantive is implied (Mt. 10:42). Sometimes the adjective in the neuter plural refers to definite classes of things, and is to that extent concrete, as in Rom. 1:20 (cf. W. 235).

(3) *The Adjective Used as an Adverb.* The adverb bears a very close relation to the adjective, which was "probably the earliest and simplest adverb" (R–S. 66). This primitive connection is demonstrated in the use of the adjective in direct relation to the verbal idea of the sentence. The case of the adjective in this construction is usually accusative (of reference), though the other oblique cases may be used (cf. πολλῷ in Rom. 5:9).

τὸ λοιπόν, χαίρετε ἐν κυρίῳ.
Finally, rejoice in the Lord. Phs. 3:1.
See also: Mk. 1:19; Jn. 10:40.

Frequently an adjective is used in its pure adjectival relation when English idiom would require an adverb (Mk. 4:28; cf. G. 269). Care should be taken to distinguish these instances from the true adverbial use of the adjective. The distinction is sometimes obscure between the predicate adjective and the adverbial adjective. The question is to be determined by whether the relation of the adjective is more intimate with the noun or the verb. Thus ὅπου ἦν Ἰωάνης τὸ πρῶτον βαπτίζων in Jn. 10:40 means, not *where John was the first to baptize,* but *where John first entered upon the process of baptizing;* while in Mk. 4:28

ἡ γῆ καρποφορεῖ πρῶτον χόρτον means *the land bears a blade first* and not *the first thing the land does is to bear a blade.* That is, in the latter instance πρῶτον is more closely related to χόρτον than it is to καρποφορεῖ, while in Jn. 10:40 πρῶτον clearly modifies βαπτίζων rather than Ἰωάνης, and, therefore, functions as an adverb. In that fact lies the distinction (cf. R. 657).⏐

The Comparison of the Adjective

132. The comparison of adjectives in Koiné Greek presents many distinctive peculiarities. It is imperative that the English student discard his own idiom in approaching the study of the Greek usage, if he is really to comprehend these peculiarities. Several differences from the classical Greek are to be observed in the New Testament, especially the infrequency of the superlative, which when it does occur is usually for emphasis, rarely in its normal function.

(1) *The Comparative Degree.* This is expressed in the New Testament in five ways.

a. By the positive adjective with a prepositional phrase.

ἀμαρτωλοὶ παρὰ πάντας τοὺς Γαλιλαίους.

Greater sinners than all the other Galileans. Lk. 13:2.

See also: Rom. 8:18; Heb. 4:12.

b. By the positive adjective followed by ἤ.

καλόν σοί ἐστιν ἢ βληθῆναι εἰς τὸ πῦρ.

It is better for thee than to be cast into the fire. Mt. 18:8.

c. By the positive adjective with μᾶλλον.

καλόν ἐστιν αὐτῷ μᾶλλον εἰ βέβληται εἰς τὴν θάλασσαν.

It were better for him had he been cast into the sea. Mk. 9:42.

d. By the comparative adjective followed by ἤ.

μείζων ὁ προφητεύων ἢ ὁ λαλῶν γλώσσαις.

Greater is the one prophesying than the one speaking with tongues.
1 Cor. 14:5.

e. By the comparative adjective followed by the ablative.

τὸ μωρὸν τοῦ θεοῦ σοφώτερον τῶν ἀνθρώπων ἐστίν.

The foolishness of God is wiser than men. 1 Cor. 1:25.

It will be observed that the New Testament presents several devices for expressing comparison by the use of the positive form of the adjective with adjuncts. This unquestionably exhibits Hebraistic influence, being analogous to the use of the positive adjective with מִן. Occasionally we find a double comparison where μᾶλλον or πολλῷ is used with the comparative form of the adjective (Mk. 7:36; Lk. 18:39). Sometimes the comparative is used as a means of emphasis when the relative object is only implied, sometimes clearly, often very remotely. (Jn. 13:27).

(2) *The Superlative Degree.* The superlative idea as employed in Koiné Greek presents three variations.

a. The comparative form is sometimes used for a superlative function.

μείζων δὲ τούτων ἡ ἀγάπη.

But the greatest of these is love. 1 Cor. 13:13.

b. Rarely the regular superlative adjective is used in its normal function.

ἐγὼ γάρ εἰμι ὁ ἐλάχιστος τῶν ἀποστόλων.

For I am the least of the apostles. 1 Cor. 15:9.

See also: Mk. 5:7; Ac. 17:15.

c. The majority of the superlatives in the New Testament are used for emphasis, in the sense of *very* or *exceedingly.* These are called *elative* superlatives.

τὰ τίμια καὶ μέγιστα ἡμῖν ἐπαγγέλματα δεδώρηται.

He has given unto us the precious and exceeding great promises.
2 Pt. 1:4.

The use of the comparative for the superlative is one of the distinguishing idioms of the Koiné (cf. R. 667; Bl. 108: M. 78). This tendency continued until in Modern Greek we have no distinctive superlative form, the superlative idea being expressed by the use of the article

with the comparative form: e.g., ὁ μικρότερος, *the smallest* (cf. T. 73).
This extension of the comparative to include more than two was probably influenced by the disuse of the dual. So Moulton says, "Of
course the first step was taken ages ago in the extinction of the dual"
(M. 77). Blass accounts for this change by "the absorption of the
category of duality into that of plurality" (Bl. 33). The use of the
superlative in the Koiné, however, is not fairly represented in the New
Testament, for while the New Testament presents but few occurrences
of the true superlative, "there are scores of them in the papyri" (M.
78).

IV. The Pronoun

References: R. 676–753; R–S. 78–85; M. 84–98.

133. The pronoun is a device of language employed to
prevent the monotony which would necessarily result from
the indefinite multiplication of the noun. That is, it is
used "to avoid the repetition of the substantive" (R. 676).
The word is derived from the Latin *pro* and *nomen*, meaning "for a noun." The name is appropriate, as it is quite
obviously suggestive of the function. There are nine classes
of pronouns in the New Testament whose grammatical
phenomena require orderly treatment. They are the personal, relative, demonstrative, intensive, possessive, reflexive, reciprocal, interrogative, and indefinite pronouns.

There are three other classes, alternative, distributive, and negative
pronouns, which we do not discuss in this treatment. They hold
no very important grammatical place in the New Testament as
pronouns, their significance being chiefly lexical. The matters of
grammatical interest connected with them may be found fully
discussed in R. 744–753.

Personal Pronoun

134. The personal pronouns are ἐγώ, ἡμεῖς, σύ, ὑμεῖς.
The Attic third-personal pronouns οὗ and σφεῖς are not
used in the New Testament, the third person being expressed by the intensive pronoun αὐτός. We also occasion-

ally find the article used as a third-personal pronoun (cf. Lk. 1:29).

(1) *The Personal Pronoun for Emphasis.* The pronominal subject of a finite verb is ordinarily not expressed, the person and number of the subject being indicated by the verbal ending. When the personal pronoun is used, it is for emphasis.

τί οὖν βαπτίζεις εἰ σὺ οὐκ εἶ ὁ Χριστός;

Why then dost thou baptize, if thou are not the Christ? Jn. 1:25.
See also: Mt. 3:11; Jn. 1:42.

Winer declares that the personal pronoun "nowhere occurs without emphasis" (W. 153). Robertson, however, thinks that "this is not quite true of all examples," and cites Gildersleeve in support of his position (R. 676). Moulton concurs in this opinion (M. 85). As a matter of fact, there appear varying degrees of emphasis, being sometimes perfectly obvious, but shading off to where it is very obscure (cf. Jn. 3:10 and Lk. 19:2). On the whole, Winer is likely correct, because the simple fact that the personal pronoun is a repetition of the subject expressed in the verb lends at least some degree of emphasis. The emphasis is generally antithetical (Mt. 5:28), though it may be used merely to give prominence to a thought (Col. 1:7).

(2) *The Objective Uses of the Personal Pronoun.* It is in the oblique cases that we find the abundance of personal pronouns in the New Testament. As a natural characteristic of vernacular speech, and probably as influenced to some extent by Semitic usage, the personal pronouns occur in the New Testament with marked frequency (cf. R. 682f.). They appear in practically all the various uses of the oblique cases. Two of the objective uses of the personal pronoun deserve special attention.

a. It may be used as a *possessive.* Pronominal possession is expressed in the New Testament far more often by the genitive of the personal pronoun than by the possessive pronoun.

πάτερ ἡμῶν ὁ ἐν τοῖς οὐρανοῖς.

Our Father who art in heaven. Mt. 6:9.

See also: Lk. 21:19; 2 Cor. 4:16.

b. It may be used as a *reflexive.* There are at least two clear instances in the New Testament—with possibly others —in which the personal pronoun is used with a reflexive force.

μὴ θησαυρίζετε ὑμῖν θησαυροὺς ἐπὶ τῆς γῆς.

Lay not up for yourselves treasures on earth. Mt. 6:19.

See also Mt. 6:20; Eph. 1:9 (?).

i. Frequently the personal pronoun appears in a context in which its use makes the impression of unnecessary repetition (cf. Mt. 8:1; Ac. 7:21; Rev. 3:12). Moulton declares that this "redundancy of the personal pronoun is just what we should expect in the colloquial style, to judge from what we have in our own vernacular" (M. 85). Robertson regards it as "also a Hebrew idiom" (R. 683). It is a tendency of the vernacular Greek which yields readily to the influence of a similar Hebrew idiom. Hence both elements are present in it.

ii. The frequency of personal pronouns in the New Testament is regarded by Winer as due to Hebraistic influence (W. 143). Blass also observes that this fact is to be accounted for by "the dependence of the language on Semitic speech" (Bl. 164). Moulton dissents from this view upon the evidence of the papyri, and thinks the cause is to be found in the vernacular character of the New Testament language rather than Semitic influence (M. 85), but Robertson thinks that we need not "go as far as Moulton does and deny that there is any Semitic influence in the New Testament on this point" (R. 683). The fact is that the vernacular and Hebrew coincided at many points in the use of the pronouns, and both became factors to the product in the New Testament.

The Relative Pronoun

135. A relative pronoun is used to connect a substantive with a clause which in some way qualifies its meaning. For example, in the sentence, "The eunuch was converted," we might qualify the noun "eunuch" by the addition of two explanatory clauses, thus: "The eunuch, *who* had been to Jerusalem to worship, and *who* was returning in his chariot, was converted." It will be seen that the connection of these clauses with the substantive is expressed by the relative pronoun *who*. So Robertson declares that the relative is "the chief bond of connection between clauses" (R. 711). The principal relative pronouns of the New Testament are ὅς, ὅστις, οἷος, ὁποῖος and ὅσος (cf. R. 710).

The relative was originally identical with the demonstrative. It is Whitney's opinion that in Sanskrit the relative *yas* was originally a demonstrative, though "from the earliest period of the language," as known to grammarians, it "has lost all trace of the demonstrative meaning" (*op. cit.*, p. 195). The survival of the demonstrative force has been much more persistent in Greek. As the relative appears in the earliest literature of the language, its distinction is unsettled. In Homer ὅς is used alternately as demonstrative and relative. In classical Greek the function and form of the relative have become definite and fixed, though in the best Attic prose it sometimes retains its demonstrative force. This usage continues into the Koiné, and is found in the New Testament. The Greek article shares with the relative its lineage from the demonstrative. They are but specialized functions of the demonstrative pronoun (cf. R. 695, 711).

(1) *Agreement of the Relative Pronoun.* The substantive with which the relative pronoun connects the qualifying clause is called the *antecedent*. The relative pronoun agrees with its antecedent in gender and number, but *not* in case. Its case is determined by its relation to the clause with which it occurs.

> ἐν αὐτῷ, ὅς ἐστιν ἡ κεφαλή.
> *In him, who is the head.* Col. 2:10.
> See also: Mt. 2:9; Rom. 2:6.

The person of the verb in the relative clause is determined by the antecedent; e.g., ἐγώ εἰμι ὅς τοῦτο ἐποίησα, *I am the one who did this.*

The relative may sometimes agree with the predicate of an explanatory clause in which it is used (Eph. 3:13).

(2) *Attraction.* The antecedent and the relative quite naturally react upon one another in the determination of case. This interchange of case is called *attraction.* It may be the relative drawn to the case of the antecedent, or, less frequently, the antecedent to the case of the relative.

a. When the relative is attracted to the case of the antecedent it is called *direct attraction.*

ὅς δ' ἂν πίῃ ἐκ τοῦ ὕδατος οὗ ἐγὼ δώσω αὐτῷ.
Whosoever shall drink of the water which I shall give him. Jn. 4:14.
See also: Lk. 1:4; Ac. 1:1.

b. When the antecedent is attracted to the case of the relative it is called *indirect attraction.*

ὅν ἐγὼ ἀπεκεφάλισα Ἰωάνην οὗτος ἠγέρθη.
This John whom I beheaded is risen. Mk. 6:16.
See also: Ac. 21:16; Rom. 6:17.

Other irregularities occasionally presented in the agreement of the relative are its assimilation to the gender of a predicate substantive when the predicate substantive "is viewed as the principal subject" (W. 166; cf. Mk. 15:16), or to the natural gender of the antecedent (Ac. 15:17), or to the neuter gender under the influence of an abstract idea implied in the entire statement (Jn. 2:8; cf. R. 712f.). Frequently the antecedent is incorporated in the relative clause, both appearing in the same case (Jn. 6:14).

(3) *Omission of the Antecedent.* When the antecedent is made clear by the context it may be omitted.

ὅν ἔχεις οὐκ ἔστιν σου ἀνήρ.
(He) whom thou hast is not thy husband. Jn. 4:18.
See also: Lk. 9:36; Heb. 5:8.

Sometimes an antecedent is introduced which from the viewpoint of the English idiom seems superfluous (Mk. 1:7). It is, however, perfectly good Greek, as may be seen from the history of the matter presented by R. 722. While "in ancient Greek it was a very rare usage" (*ibid.*), yet it was used there, and all the way down through all the periods of the Greek language, and has "in modern Greek become very common" (R. 723). So this *pleonastic antecedent* is perfectly normal Greek, though awkward to English eyes (cf. further Rev. 7:2).

(4) *The Indefinite Relative.* In classical Greek ὅς is used as the definite relative, and ὅστις as indefinite, but this distinction has almost disappeared in the Koiné. However, it is the distinctive use of ὅστις which is fading out, for ὅς is still used in accord with Attic practice.

ὅστις δ'ἂν ἀρνήσηταί με.

Whosoever shall deny me. Mt. 10:33.

See also: Jn. 14:13; Col. 3:5.

It should be observed that ὅς used with ἂν has the indefinite force and may be rendered "whoever" (cf. Mt. 5:22). The indefinite pronoun τὶς may be used with ἂν in the sense of "anything whatever" (cf. Jn. 16:23). It is usually clear from the context whether a relative construction is to be regarded as definite or indefinite (cf. Bl. 172; R. 712, 727).

The Demonstrative Pronoun

136. Sometimes it is desired to call attention with special emphasis to a designated object, whether in the physical vicinity of the speaker or the literary context of the writer. For this purpose the demonstrative construction is used. It may take any one of several forms.

(1) Ordinarily the regular *demonstrative pronouns* are used.

a. For that which is relatively near in actuality or thought the *immediate* demonstrative is used.

οὗτος γὰρ ὁ Μελχισεδὲκ μένει ἱερεύς.

For this Melchizedek remains a priest. Heb. 7:1.

See also: Mt. 3:3; Rom. 9:9.

b. For that which is relatively distant in actuality or thought the *remote* demonstrative is used.

> ἐσώθη ἡ γυνὴ ἀπὸ τῆς ὥρας ἐκείνης.
> *The woman was saved from that hour.* Mt. 9:22.
> See also: Jn. 10:1; Ac. 2:16.

(2) The *article* sometimes retains its original demonstrative force, being used with μέν or δέ.

> οἱ μὲν οὖν συνελθόντες ἠρώτων αὐτόν.
> *These, therefore, having come, asked him.* Ac. 1:6.
> See also: Ac. 8:4; Mt. 26:67.

Sometimes ὁ μέν and ὁ δέ are set over against each other in contrast (cf. 1 Cor. 7:7; Ac. 14:4).

(3) Occasionally the *relative* is restored to its demonstrative force, employing like the article the particles μέν and δέ.

> ὃς μὲν πεινᾷ, ὃς δὲ μεθύει.
> *One is hungry, and another is drunken.* 1 Cor. 11:21.
> See also: Mk. 15:23; 2 Tim. 2:20.

(4) Ten times the New Testament uses the pronouns ὅδε, ἥδε, τόδε.

> σήμερον ἢ αὔριον πορευσόμεθα εἰς τήνδε τὴν πόλιν.
> *Today or tomorrow we will go into this city.* Jas. 4:13.
> See also: Lk. 10:39; Rev. 2:1.

The use of these pronouns is characteristic of Revelation, where we find seven of the ten occurrences. The infrequency of them in the New Testament is typical of the Koiné in general, for they occur but rarely in the papyri. There are but faint traces of them left in Modern Greek. The force of ὅδε in Attic Greek as a sort of subsequent demonstrative (referring to something which follows), Robertson says "amounts to little in the New Testament, since ὅδε is so rare" (R. 702).

(5) The *intensive* pronoun is sometimes used with demonstrative force in Luke's writings.

διδάξει ὑμᾶς ἐν αὐτῇ τῇ ὥρᾳ.
He will teach you in that hour. Lk. 12:12.
See also: Lk. 10:7, 20:19.

The distinction between the demonstratives which we have denomi-
nated "immediate" and "remote" is not always evident in the New
Testament, though ordinarily it may be discerned. Οὖτος may sometimes refer "not to the noun locally nearest, but the one more remote,"
but it will generally be found upon close scrutiny that the antecedent of
οὖτος "was *mentally* the nearest, the most present to the writer's
thought" (W. 157). Thus it does not necessarily denote that which is
physically adjacent, but that which is immediately present to the thinking of the writer. So ἐκεῖνος need not denote that which is physically
distant, but may be only that which is mentally remote. Hence we have
termed them immediate and remote demonstratives.

The Intensive Pronoun

137. The intensive pronoun is αὐτός. It is the most frequently used of all the pronouns in the New Testament,
and is the most varied in use, being employed as personal,
possessive, and demonstrative, as well as intensive pronoun.
It is its distinctive use as intensive pronoun which we consider here.

138. The function of the intensive pronoun is to emphasize identity. It is the demonstrative force intensified.
There are two uses of the intensive pronoun, distinguished
by the attributive and predicate position.

(1) *The Attributive Use.* When αὐτός is used in the
attributive position it means *the same.*

ἔχοντες δὲ τὸ αὐτὸ πνεῦμα τῆς πίστεως.
Having the same spirit of faith. 2 Cor. 4:13.
See also: Mt. 26:44; Rom. 2:1.

(2) *The Predicate Use.* When αὐτός is used in the
predicate position it means *self.*

αὐτὸ τὸ πνεῦμα συνμαρτυρεῖ τῷ πνεύματι ἡμῶν.

The Spirit Himself beareth witness with our spirit. Rom. 8:16.
See also: Rom. 8:26; 1 Ths. 4:9.

The use of αὐτός as a demonstrative calls for special attention. That Luke uses it in this sense is certain, and it is possibly to be so construed in other authors (cf. Mt. 3:4). Thus in Lk. 13:1 we are forced by the context to translate ἐν αὐτῷ τῷ καιρῷ "in that very season" rather than "in the season itself." The use is probably to secure an emphatic demonstrative (*that very*) without the employment of two pronouns. It may be readily seen that ἐν ἐκείνῳ τῷ αὐτῷ καιρῷ would make a bunglesome construction (cf. R. 686). This demonstrative use of αὐτός is characteristic of the Koiné in general. "There is an apparent weakening of αὐτὸς ὁ in Hellenistic, which tends to blunt the distinction between this and ἐκεῖνος ὁ" (M. 91). Abundant evidence of this change appears in the papyri (cf. Moulton and Milligan: *op. cit.*, p. 94). Αὐτός is used as a regular demonstrative in Modern Greek, right alongside of τοῦτος (οὗτος) and ἐκεῖνος, appearing as such in its normal form, and also in the altered form αὐτόνος (T. 90).

The Possessive Pronoun

139. The possessive pronouns are ἐμός, σός, ἡμέτερος and ὑμέτερος. The Koiné Greek offers no possessive pronoun for the third person, but uses the genitive of αὐτός instead. The article and ἴδιος are also used to denote possession. So we find pronominal possession expressed in the New Testament in four ways.

(1) *By the Possessive Pronouns.*

ἡ κρίσις ἡ ἐμὴ δικαία ἐστίν.

My judgment is righteous. Jn. 5:30.
See also: Rom. 10:1; Phs. 3:9.

(2) *By the Genitive of the Personal Pronoun.* This is decidedly the most prevalent mode employed in Koiné Greek.

τὸ πάσχα ἡμῶν ἐτύθη Χριστός.

Christ as our passover was sacrificed. 1 Cor. 5:8.
See also: Mt. 7:3; Rom. 1:4.

(3) *By the Article.* The article is used when the one to whom possession is referred is made clear by the context.

καὶ ἐκτείνας τὴν χεῖρα ἥψατο αὐτοῦ.

And putting forth his hand he touched him. Mt. 8:3.

See also: Heb. 7:24; 1 Pt. 4:8.

(4) *By* ἴδιος. Where the idea of possession is emphatic ἴδιος is used.

ἦλθεν εἰς τὴν ἰδίαν πόλιν.

He went into his own city. Mt. 9:1.

See also: Lk. 6:41; Jn. 4:44.

The Reflexive Pronoun

140. When the action expressed by the verb is referred back to its own subject, the construction is called *reflexive.* There are two usual ways of expressing this reflexive idea in the New Testament.

(1) By the regular *reflexive pronouns* ἐμαυτοῦ, σεαυτοῦ ἑαυτοῦ, and ἑαυτῶν. In the New Testament ἑαυτῶν is used for all three persons in the plural.

μηδὲν πράξῃς σεαυτῷ κακόν.

Do thyself no harm. Ac. 16:28.

See also: Lk. 12:1; 2 Cor. 3:1.

(2) By an oblique case of the *personal pronoun,* as discussed above, § 134 (2), *b* (cf. Mt. 6:19).

The Reciprocal Pronoun

141. When a plural subject is represented as affected by an interchange of the action signified in the verb, it is called a reciprocal construction; e.g., οὗτοι οἱ ἄνθρωποι ἀδικοῦσιν ἀλλήλους, *these men are injuring one another.* The New Testament uses three methods for the expression of this idiom.

(1) *The Regular Reciprocal Pronoun.*

ἀγαπητοί, ἀγαπῶμεν ἀλλήλους.
Beloved, let us love one another. 1 Jn. 4:7.
See also: Rom. 12:5; 1 Cor. 16:20.

(2) *The Reflexive Pronoun.*

κρίματα ἔχετε μεθ' ἑαυτῶν.
Ye have lawsuits with one another. 1 Cor. 6:7.
See also: Eph. 5:19; Col. 3:16.

(3) *The Middle Voice.*

καὶ συνεβουλεύσαντο.
And they took counsel with one another. Mt. 26:4.
See also: Lk. 14:7; Jn. 9:22.

The Interrogative Pronoun

142. The interrogative pronoun is τίς. It is used to intro duce both dependent and independent questions. As em· ployed in the New Testament it presents five fairly distinct uses.

(1) *The Interrogative Use.* It is the regular pronoun for introducing questions.

οὐκ οἴδατε τί αἰτεῖσθε.
Ye know not what ye ask. Mt. 20:22.
See also: Mt. 3:7; Lk. 12:14.

(2) *The Adverbial Use.* When τίς is used in the ad· verbial sense it means *why.*

τί δὲ βλέπεις τὸ κάρφος;
Why seest thou the mote? Mt. 7:3.
See also: Mt. 6:28; Ac. 5:4.

(3) *The Exclamatory Use.* The adverbial use of τίς sometimes has the force of exclamation rather than interrogation.

καὶ τί θέλω εἰ ἤδη ἀνήφθη.

And how I wish it were already kindled! **Lk. 12:49.**

See also: Lk. 22:45.

(4) *The Relative Use.* τίς sometimes adds to its interrogative function a distinct relative force, the construction presenting a shading off of the indirect question toward the relative clause.

ἀλλ' οὐ τί ἐγὼ θέλω ἀλλὰ τί σύ.

Nevertheless, not what I will, but what thou wilt. **Mk. 14:36.**

See also: Mt. 10:19; Lk. 17:8.

This construction presents a vernacular tendency of the Koiné Greek toward "a confusion much further developed in our own language" (M. 94). The confusion arises from a common ground lying between the relative clause and the indirect question. Thus, "I know what you are doing," presents the blending of a relative sense ("that which you are doing") and an interrogative sense ("What are you doing?").

(5) *The Alternative Use.* Instead of the classical πότερος *which of two*, the Koiné Greek uses τίς to introduce alternative questions.

τί γάρ ἐστιν εὐκοπώτερον;

For which (of the two) is easier? **Mt. 9:5.**

See also: 1 Cor. 4:21; Phs. 1:22.

Moulton regards the disappearance of πότερος from the Koiné as resulting directly from the decadence of the dual. He finds but a single occurrence in the papyri. He says, "I have twelve papyrus collections by me, with *one* occurrence of πότερος in the indices, and that is nearly illegible and (to me, at least) quite unintelligible" **(M. 77).**

The Indefinite Pronoun

143. Frequently the occasion arises for the expression ot a substantive idea in a general sense, as representative of a category. For example, we might wish to mention an act performed by one who was a disciple of Jesus, without caring to specify his exact identity. The mode of expression employed for this purpose would be the indefinite pronoun (τὶς, τὶ), thus μαθητής τις, *a certain disciple.* Thus the indefinite pronoun provides a means of general reference. It presents five forms of construction.

(1) *The Pronominal Use.* Τὶς may be used independently when it functions as a pronoun.

μή τινος ὑστερήσατε;
Did ye lack anything? Lk. 22:35.
See also: Ac. 3:5; Phs. 3:15.

(2) *The Adjective Use.* When associated with a noun, τὶς functions as an adjective.

ἐγένετο ἱερεύς τις.
There was a certain priest. Lk. 1:5.
See also: Ac. 15:36; Jas. 1:18.

(3) *The Emphatic Use.* Τὶς is sometimes used as a reflection of a sense of distinction or importance (cf. Bt. 114).

λέγων εἶναί τινα ἑαυτόν.
Saying that he was somebody. Ac. 5:36.
See also: 1 Cor. 3:7; Gal. 2:6.

(4) *The Numerical Use.* Τὶς may be employed with a number to convey the idea of approximation.

προσκαλεσάμενος δύο τινὰς τῶν μαθητῶν.
Having called some two of his disciples. Lk. 7:18.
See also: Ac. 15:36.

(5) *The Alternative Use.* We sometimes find τινες . . . τινες, or τὶς . . . ἕτερος, employed in alternative expressions.

ἐλέγοντο ὑπὸ τινῶν ὅτι Ἰωάνης ἠγέρθη ἐκ νεκρῶν, ὑπὸ τινῶν δὲ ὅτι Ἠλείας ἐφάνη.

It was being said by some that John had risen from the dead, but by others that Elijah had appeared. Lk. 9:7.

See also: Phs. 1:15; 1 Cor. 3:4.

i. Regularly pronouns take their grammatical form from a substantive antecedent expressed or understood. Sometimes, instead of direct agreement with the grammatical form of an expressed antecedent, we have logical agreement, in some instances with actual or assumed sex rather than grammatical gender (Mt. 28:19), in others with the plural sense of a collective noun rather than its grammatical number (Eph. 5:12).

ii. The use of the pronoun is becoming more extended in the Koiné period, and continues to increase down to the modern period. In the main the pronouns in the New Testament are nearer to Attic usage than the adjectives. There are many instances "where the pronouns are used carefully according to classical precedent" (M. 79). Winer observes that in the use of the pronoun, the New Testament differs from Attic Greek at two main points: "First, it multiplies the personal and demonstrative pronouns for the sake of greater perspicuity. . . . Secondly, it neglects . . . many forms which ranked rather among luxuries of the language" (W. 140).

V. The Article

References: R. 754–796; R–S. 68–77; M. 81–84.

144. Nothing is more indigenous to the Greek language than its use of the article. Moulton finds that in the New Testament "its use is in agreement with Attic," a feature in which the New Testament is more literary than the papyri (M. 80f.). We are, therefore, upon a broad historical basis when we are studying this important element of the Greek language. It is also true that we are entering one of the most fascinating fields of linguistic research, for, without doubt, "the development of the Greek article is one of the most interesting things in human speech" (R. 754). Scholars have not accorded it sufficient attention, nor sought with proper diligence to apprehend the real genius underlying its various uses. We do not claim that the discussion here offered is conclusive, but hope that it may prove suggestive of the directions in which an adequate comprehension of the article lies. An exhaustive treatment of the question would require more space than is covered by this entire volume. One who wishes to pursue the study further could not do better than consult the discussions by Gildersleeve (*Syntax*, pp. 215–332) and Robertson (R. 754–796).

The Origin of the Article

145. The article was originally derived from the demonstrative pronoun ὁ, ἡ, τό, and is clearly akin to the relative pronoun ὅς, ἥ, ὅ. It always retained some of the demonstrative force. This fact is evidenced by its frequent use in the papyri purely as a demonstrative pronoun (e.g., *P. Elph.* 1:15). Robertson says, "Hence ὁ is originally a demonstrative that was gradually weakened to the article or heightened to the relative" (R-S. 68).

τοῦ γὰρ καὶ γένος ἐσμέν.
For, indeed, of him are we the offering. Ac. 17:28.
See also: Rm. 8:24; Gal. 4:25.

Like the pronoun, the article ordinarily agrees with its noun in gender, number, and case, though it sometimes agrees with an implied gender (cf. Rev. 3:14; ὁ ἀμήν, where ὁ is governed by the reference to Jesus. The Greek had no indefinite article, though τὶς and εἷς sometimes approximated this idiom (cf. Lk. 10:25; Mt. 8:19).

The Function of the Article

146. The function of the article is to point out an object, or to draw attention to it. Its use with a word makes the word stand out distinctly. "Whenever the article occurs the object is certainly definite. When it is not used the object may or may not be" (R. 756). The use of prepositions, possessive and demonstrative pronouns, and the genitive case also tends to make a word definite. At such times, even if the article is not used, the object is already distinctly indicated.

i. The basal function of the Greek article is to point out *individual identity*. It does more than mark "the object as one definitely conceived" (W. 105), for a substantive in Greek is definite without the article. In this respect the Greek substantive shares character with the Latin. "The function of the article, which was originally a demonstrative, and always has more or less demonstrative force, is to fix a floating adjective or substantive" (Gildersleeve; *op. cit.*, § 514). Gildersleeve goes on to show that the Greek noun has an intrinsic definiteness, an "implicit article." Therefore, the explicit article does more than merely ascribe definiteness. Green is touching its genius when he says that it is used "to mark a specific object of thought" (G. 170). It should be kept in mind that the Greek article retained much of its original demonstrative significance. "The vital thing is to see the matter from the Greek point of view and find the reason for the use of the article" (R. 756).

ii. A suggestion of the essential function of the article is to be seen in the fact that it is used regularly with the pronouns οὗτος and ἐκεῖνος, "inasmuch as they distinguish some individual from the mass" (W. 110). The stress on individual identity is here perfectly evident. It may be further observed that in Homer "the article marks contrast and not mere definiteness" (R. 755).

iii. The genius of the article is nowhere more clearly revealed than in its use with infinitives, adverbs, phrases, clauses, or even whole sentences (cf. Gal. 5:14). We have an advantage here in the fact that we are not bothered with having to divest ourselves of any confusing associations arising from our English idiom. There is no English usage even remotely akin to this, for in English we never use an article with anything other than a substantive. and then to mark definiteness.

When we begin to find the article used with phrases, clauses, and entire sentences, we are, so to speak, "swamped in Greek." The use of the article with the phrase, clause, or sentence specifies in a particular way the *fact* expressed: marks it out as a single identity. So in Mt. 13:4, καὶ ἐν τῷ σπείρειν αὐτόν, *and as he sowed*, points to the *fact* of that particular sowing, while in Mt. 12:10, τοῖς σάββασιν θεραπεύειν, *to heal on the Sabbath*, emphasizes the *character* of the deed (a Sabbath healing). Note that the former infinitive has the article, while the latter has not. The articular infinitive singles out the act as a particular occurrence, while the anarthrous infinitive employs the act as descriptive.

iv. In Mt. 2:3 we have ὁ βασιλεὺς Ἡρῴδης because the emphasis is upon the fact of Herod's being king (Herod and no other), while in Lk. 1:5 ἐν ταῖς ἡμέραις Ἡρῴδου βασιλέως, *in the days of king Herod*, defines a certain period of time (Herod-days), and βασιλεῦ Ἀγρίππα in Ac. 25:26 defines the rank of Agrippa (Agrippa, a king). In the first example the purpose is identification, in the other two it is definition. When identity is prominent, we find the article; and when quality or character is stressed, the construction is anarthrous. Note that in all three of the cases just given the noun is definite. In Ac. 7:30 τοῦ ὄρους Σινᾶ means the wilderness of Mt. Sinai as distinguished from any other wilderness, while in Gal. 4:24 ὄρους Σινᾶ means the Mt. Sinai sort of covenant. In Rev. 14:1 τὸ ὄρος Σιών points out the distinct position of the Lamb, while in Heb. 12:22 Σιὼν ὄρει argues that the Christian is not, like the Israelite of old, approaching a destiny like unto Mt. Sinai, but is approaching a Mt. Zion destiny. We may read the passage, "But ye have not come to a Mt. Sinai, but to a Mt. Zion" (cf. R. 760). In Rom. 9:28 ποιήσει κύριος ἐπὶ τῆς γῆς, *the Lord will work upon the earth*, identifies the field of divine operation, while Heb. 6:7 γῆ γὰρ ἡ πιοῦσα τὸν ὑετόν, *the earth which drinketh in the rain*, characterizes the ground which is made fruitful by the refreshing showers. Observe that in both cases the noun is equally definite, and normally takes the article in English (cf. ASV). In Mt. 14:3 τὴν γυναῖκα Φιλίππου particularizes Herodias as the wife of Philip, while ἑνὸς ἀνδρὸς γυνή in 1 Tim. 5:9 means *a one-husband sort of wife*. Ordinarily English renders the first *the wife of Philip*, and the second *the wife of one husband*, treating the noun as definite in both instances. The difference is particular specification in the first example and a required qualification in the second. Examples might be multiplied *ad infinitum*.

v. In determining the function of the Greek article, an exceedingly important consideration is its demonstrative origin. The danger is that we will approach the matter from the wrong side; that we will view it from the standpoint of the force of our modern English article rather than consider it in the light of its own origin and history. We must take our stand at Homer and look down toward the New Testament, and must not, from our present English idiom, look back toward the New Testament. "In Homer ὁ, ἡ, τό is the commonest of the demonstrative pronouns" (Milden: *The Predicative Position in Greek*, p. 7), and constantly oscillates between pronoun and article. Thus in *Iliad* 1:11, 12,

> ...τὸν Χρύσην ἠτίμησ᾽ ἀρητῆρα
> Ἀτρείδης ὁ γὰρ ἦλθε θοὰς ἐπὶ νῆας Ἀχαιῶν.

Atreides dishonored the priest Chryses, for he came to the swift ships of the Achaeans, τόν is used in the first clause as an article and ὁ in the second as a personal pronoun. In *Iliad* 1:125,

> ἀλλὰ τὰ μὲν πολίων ἐξεπράθομεν, τὰ δέδασται,

but the spoil which we took from the cities, that has been divided, τά in the first clause is used as a relative pronoun and in the second clause as a demonstrative pronoun. "In the *Iliad* ὁ, ἡ, τό occurs as a pronoun 3000 times and as an article 218 times, or in a ratio of 14 to 1; in the *Odyssey* it is used as a pronoun 2178 times and as an article 171 times, or in a ratio of 13 to 1" (Milden: *op. cit.*, p. 8). The prevalence of the pronominal use ὁ, ἡ, τό persists in the inscriptions, especially as a demonstrative. The relative use occurs frequently in the Lesbian, Thessalian, Arcado-Cyprian, and the older Boeotian inscriptions (cf. Buck: *Greek Dialects*, pp. 92f.). Frequency as an article increases during the classical period and, at the zenith of the Attic dominance, ὁ, ἡ, τό is typically article and exceptionally pronoun. At this point the New Testament is more classical than the papyri, which incline more toward the Homeric use (M. 81). Occasionally we find in the papyri, the old Homeric forms τοί, ταί (cf. P. El. 1:15), which is a result of Western Greek influence (cf. Buck: *op. cit.*, p. 92). Thus we see that the article in the New Testament carries with it a pronounced heritage from its demonstrative origin, and one would make a serious blunder to ignore this fact.

vi. The use of the articular and anarthrous constructions of θεός is highly instructive. A study of the uses of the term as given in Moulton and Geden's *Concordance* convinces one that without the article θεός signifies divine essence, while with the article divine personality is chiefly in view. There is keen discernment in Webster's statement, published as far back as 1864:

> Θεός occurs without the article (1) where the Deity is contrasted with what is human, or with the universe as distinct from its Creator, or with the nature and acts of evil spirits, (2) when the essential attributes of Deity are spoken of, (3) when operations proceeding from God are appropriated to one of the three Divine Persons, (4) when the Deity is spoken of as heathens would speak, or a Jew who denied the existence of the Son and of the Holy Spirit. But the article seems to be used (1) when the Deity is spoken of in the Christian point of view, (2) when the First Person of the blessed Trinity is specially designated, unless its insertion is unnecessary by the addition of πατήρ, or some distinctive epithet (*op. cit.*, p. 29).

This analysis is doubtless more exact and detailed than the facts will support, but it certainly shows admirable discrimination. Surely when Robertson says that θεός, as to the article, "is treated like a proper name and may have it or not have it" (R. 761), he does not mean to intimate that the presence or absence of the article with θεός has no special significance. We construe him to mean that there is no definite rule governing the use of the article with θεός, so that sometimes the writer's viewpoint is difficult to detect, which is entirely true. But in the great majority of instances the reason for the distinction is clear. The use of θεός in Jn. 1:1 is a good example. Πρὸς τὸν θεόν points to Christ's fellowship with the person of the Father; θεὸς ἦν ὁ λόγος emphasizes Christ's participation in the essence of the divine nature. The former clearly applies to personality, while the latter applies to character. This distinction is in line with the general force of the article. It may be seen even in the papyri, as ὁ φῶς ἐκ φωτός, θεὸς ἀληθινός, *O Light of light, true God*, where the emphasis is clearly on God's character rather than His personality (Milligan: *op. cit.*, p. 134).

vii. The articular construction emphasizes *identity;* the anarthrous construction emphasizes *character.* If the student will turn to Rom. 8:1ff. and apply this principle, he will find how illuminating it becomes in actual interpretation. It is certain that one engaged in exegesis cannot afford to disregard the article. The New Testament justifies the observation of Buttmann that "the use of the article has everywhere its positive reason" (Bt. 88).

THE GREEK NEW TESTAMENT 141

The Regular Uses of the Article

147. In harmony with its basal significance there are certain constructions in which the article is normally used. We employ the term "regular" here in the sense of ordinary, and not as implying use in keeping with any fixed rules. There are no "rules" for the use of the article in Greek, but there is a fundamental principle underlying its significance —as we have seen in the foregoing section—and this gives rise to a normal usage. Deviation from this normal usage may occur at the will of the writer.

(1) *To Denote Individuals.* Nearest to the real genius of its function is the use of the article to point out a particular object.

ἡ βασιλεία τῶν οὐρανῶν.
The kingdom of Heaven. Mt. 3:3.

(2) *To Denote Previous Reference.* The article may be used to point out an object the identity of which is defined by some previous reference made to it in the context.

πόθεν οὖν ἔχεις τὸ ὕδωρ τὸ ζῶν;
Whence hast thou the living water? Jn. 4:11.

That is, "the living water" to which Christ had just made reference. See also: Mt. 2:1, 7; Rev. 15:1, 6.

(3) *With Abstract Nouns.* Abstract nouns are ordinarily general in their character and application, and therefore indefinite. But in Greek, when it is desired to apply the sense of an abstract noun in some special and distinct way the article accompanies it. Thus ἀλήθεια, *truth,* means anything in general which presents a character of reality and genuineness, but ἡ ἀλήθεια as used in the New Testament means that which may be relied upon as really in accord with God's revelation in Christ. The general sense of the abstract noun is restricted, and given a particular

application: the particular truth which is revealed in Christ.

> τῇ γὰρ χάριτί ἐστε σεσωσμένοι.
> *For by grace are ye saved.* Eph. 2:8.

That is, grace in its particular application in securing man's salvation. It is not grace as an abstract attitude, nor yet the gracious attitude of God in general; but *"the* grace" of God which operated through the atonement in providing human redemption. Grace is a quality which may characterize various objects; but here it is particularized as an attribute of God, exercised in a particular realm. See also: 1 Cor. 13:4; 15:21.

(4) *With Proper Names.* Frequently the article is used with the name of some person whose identity is made clear by the context, or assumed as well known by the reader. Thus in the New Testament, which was written for those already acquainted with the historical facts of the Christian religion, when we find ὁ Ἰησοῦς, we know immediately that it is the particular Jesus who was the Messiah and Savior. In Col. 4:11, when Paul refers to a member of the Colossian congregation who bears the name of Jesus, he significantly omits the article with Ἰησοῦς and adds the explanatory phrase ὁ λεγόμενος Ἰοῦστος. The entire phrase means, "a man named Jesus, but who is distinguished by being called Justus." It is a general custom with New Testament writers to leave off the article when an explanatory phrase is added to the name; as, Σαῦλος δέ, ὁ καὶ Παῦλος (Ac. 13:9); Σίμων ὁ λεγόμενος Πέτρος (Mt. 10:2). In such a construction the emphasis is upon the name as a designation rather than the identity of the individual indicated by the name.

> ὁρκίζω ὑμᾶς τὸν Ἰησοῦν ὃν Παῦλος κηρύσσει.
> *I adjure you by Jesus whom Paul preaches.* Ac. 19:13.

i. That is, "by the particular Jesus whom one by the name of Paul preaches." The thought of definite identity belongs to Ἰησοῦς, but not to Παῦλος. This is to put special stress upon the designation of Jesus. See also: Ac. 15:19; 19:1.

ii. Gildersleeve says that proper names, "being in their nature particular do not require the explicit article, and when the article is used with them, it retains much of its original demonstrative force" (*op. cit.*, 215). It is the particularizing force of the article which is employed in this idiom. Ἰωάνης as a proper name may denote any number of individuals, but ὁ Ἰωάνης is a particular individual bearing this name. Hence, when ὁ Ἰωάνης is used, it means a particular John assumed as known by the reader. This distinction seems in general to lie at the basis of the idiom, though it is not invariably observed in actual use. In fact, it is difficult to find a principle which will apply with uniformity to this use of the article. Winer is undoubtedly correct in his opinion that "the use of the article with names of persons . . . can hardly be reduced to rule" (W. 112). Moulton concurs by saying that "scholarship has not yet solved completely the problem of the article with proper names" (M. 83). Thus far we are compelled to yield to Robertson's conclusion that "no satisfactory principle can be laid down for the use or non-use of the article with proper names" (R. 761). This is not to assume that the writer had no reason for using the article with a proper name, or not using it, but that frequently we are unable to discover his reason. It is precarious to suppose in any instance that a writer is employing an idiom at random, though in rare cases this is possibly true.

iii. It is instructive in dealing with this problem to observe the use of the article with Ἰησοῦς. The word occurs nine hundred and nine times in the New Testament (according to Moulton and Geden: *op. cit.*). It is used three hundred and fifty-nine times without the article (WH). In one hundred and seventy-five of these instances the emphasis is on the Messianic significance of the name, which means "a deliverer"; forty-one times the emphasis is upon the name as a designation rather than upon the identification of the person—approximating the force of our expression "a man named"; ten times it is used in the vocative without the article. In several instances these anarthrous uses are in salutations, where the absence of the article is doubtless due to the general custom in the New Testament and the papyri of not using the article in salutations. But there are one hundred and thirty-three times that Ἰησοῦς occurs without the article, for which we can find no evident reason. Though this is but fifteen per cent of the occurrences of the word and thirty-four per cent of the anarthrous constructions, yet it is sufficient to prove that we are as yet unable to lay down any rigid principle according to which we can explain the use of the article with proper names. The anarthrous constructions of Ἰησοῦς prevail in John, Hebrews, and Revelation. In John they are mostly in the phrases "Jesus said" or "Jesus answered." Most of the anarthrous constructions in Luke are in the expression "Jesus said." This is probably in line with the custom of not using the article in stereotyped or technicalized expressions.

(5) *The Generic Use.* This is the use of the article with a noun which is to be regarded as representing a class or group. Gildersleeve says, "The principle of the generic article is the selection of a representative or normal individual" (*op. cit.,* 255). It comprehends a class as a single whole and sets it off in distinction from all other classes. It individualizes a group rather than a single object, and points out that group as identified by certain characteristics.

αἱ ἀλώπεκες φωλεοὺς ἔχουσιν.

Foxes have dens. Mt. 8:20.

The thought of the entire passage here is that a thing even as lowly and insignificant as the fox has shelter of a kind, but the Son of man is humbled even beneath that lowly estate. The meaning is, "The foxes, mere little beasts though they are, have dens." Thus the noun is used to represent a class rather than a group of individuals. See also: Lk. 10:7; 1 Tim. 3:2.

(6) *With Pronouns.* Since a pronoun ordinarily conveys the force of identification, it is quite naturally associated with the article. Thus the article regularly occurs when the pronouns οὗτος and ἐκεῖνος are used with a noun (Lk. 14:30). It is used with possessive pronouns except when they are predicate (Mt. 7:22; Jn. 17:10). It is ordinarily used with the genitive of the personal pronoun (Mt. 26:25; cf. Mt. 27:46). Its use with αὐτός has been discussed sufficiently under pronouns. The use of the article with πᾶς presents important variations. In the singular, anarthrous πᾶς means *every* (Rom. 3:19). Ὁ πᾶς means *the whole* (Gal. 5:14) and πᾶς ὁ means *all* with a substantive

(Ac. 10:2), though it is ordinarily to be rendered *every* with a participle (Mt. 5:28). The plural πάντες is rare without the article, though it is found occasionally meaning *all* (Eph. 3:8). Οἱ πάντες likewise means *all*, as does πάντες οἱ, but in the former the collective idea is stronger (Mt. 1:17). These are the ordinary changes in the meaning of πᾶς as affected by the article, though variations from the common practice are often indicated by the context (cf. R. 771ff.).

(7) *With Other Parts of Speech.* In keeping with the genius of the article, whenever a sense of individuality is sought in any form of expression, the article is used. In such a construction, the article functions as a sort of bracket, to gather the expression into a single whole and point it out in a particular way. Thus in Lk. 5:10, ἀπὸ τοῦ νῦν signifies more than would be expressed by *from the present.* It means from the present as distinguished within itself—as defined by a new set of circumstances: the entrance of Jesus into the experience of those addressed. It is not just *from now*, but *from the now* defined and particularized by a new relation to Jesus. In Lk. 19:48 καὶ οὐχ ηὕρισκον τὸ τί ποιήσωσιν, *they could not find what they might do,* means, freely rendered, *they could not find the effective course which they might take.* (The chief priests and scribes were seeking to destroy Jesus, and found it difficult because of his popularity.) It is not that they could not find *anything* to do, but they could not find *the particular thing* which would accomplish their purpose. This principle may apply to adjectives, adverbs, participles, infinitives, prepositional phrases, clauses, and even entire sentences.

τὸ εἰ δύνῃ, πάντα δυνατὰ τῷ πιστεύοντι.

"*If thou canst!*" *All things are possible to him who believes.* Mk. 9:23

i. Freely rendered τὸ εἰ δύνῃ means *beware of the lack of faith implied in that remark,* "*If thou canst.*" See also Mt. 5:3, 4; Ac. 15:11; Rom. 13:10; Gal. 5:14; Heb. 13:24.

ii. Gildersleeve undoubtedly misses the point here when he speaks of the article as "substantivizing these various parts of speech; that is, altering their nature in the direction of the noun" (op. cit., 262f). He is here influenced by the almost inseparable association of the article with the noun in English idiom. But such is not true of the Greek article. It is of a nature which enables it to lend itself naturally to the essential force of these various parts of speech. In Mk. 1:24, ὁ ἅγιος is not a substantive construction by reason of the article: the nature of the adjective itself makes it such (cf. § 131,(2), a). We have already seen the reason for the article in τοῦ νῦν (Lk. 5:10); it does not change the adverb into a noun, but defines more particularly its reference. Since participles and infinitives are of their own nature verbal nouns, the article in no way affects their substantive character. In such phrases as οἱ μετ᾽ αὐτοῦ, those with him, the article, instead of modifying the prepositional phrase in the direction of a substantive, is itself returning to its original demonstrative force. In Lk. 11:3, δίδου ἡμῖν τὸ καθ᾽ ἡμέραν is more difficult for English eyes to perceive. In this case τό is an adverbial accusative of reference. Give us our ἐπιούσιον bread with reference to that which comes in the regular order of the day; i.e., our need of physical sustenance. So it is again the demonstrative force of the article blending with the unaltered significance of the prepositional phrase. In clauses and sentences it is the particularizing function of the article which is employed. In Rom. 8:26 we have a clear example: τὸ γὰρ τί προσευξώμεθα καθὸ δεῖ οὐκ οἴδαμεν, we know not what we should pray for as we ought. Paul's point here is: "that problem of praying as we ought we do not know about." The article converges the clause into a single point and presents the problem as a particular issue, more rigidly defined than any device of English can render it. This is what we might call "the bracket force" of the article. The fact that we find difficulty in translating these constructions without using substantival expressions in English is due to the character of the English idiom and not of the Greek. It is vitally important in exegesis to see the matter from the Greek point of view. Compare further Rom. 1.26; 4:16.

The Special Uses of the Article

148. Some phenomena presented by the article are but remotely related to its basal function, and consequently may be treated as special uses.

(1) *With Nouns Connected by* καί. The following rule by Granville Sharp of a century back still proves to be true: "When the copulative καί connects two nouns of the same case, if the article ὁ or any of its cases precedes the first of the said nouns or participles, and is not repeated before the second noun or participle, the latter always relates to the same person that is expressed or described by the first noun or participle; i.e., it denotes a farther description of the first-named person."

τοῦ κυρίου καὶ σωτῆρος Ἰησοῦ Χριστοῦ.
Of our Lord and Savior Jesus Christ. 2 Pt. 2:20.

The article here indicates that Jesus is both Lord and Savior. So in 2 Pt. 1:1 τοῦ θεοῦ ἡμῶν καὶ σωτῆρος Ἰησοῦ Χριστοῦ means that Jesus is our God and Savior. After the same manner Tit. 2:13, τοῦ μεγάλου θεοῦ καὶ σωτῆρος Ἰησοῦ Χριστοῦ, asserts that Jesus is the great God and Savior.

(2) *As a Pronoun.* The original pronominal nature of the article survives in many of its uses. In such a construction it is not strictly speaking an article, but is restored to its use as a pronoun. This is a standard Attic characteristic. Gildersleeve, under what he terms the "Substantive Use" of the article, gives a multitude of examples from a number of classical authors (*op. cit.*, 216ff.).

a. The article may sometimes have the full force of a *demonstrative* pronoun.

οἱ τοῦ Χριστοῦ.
Those who belong to Christ. Gal. 5:24.
See also: Mt. 13:29; Heb. 13:24.

b. The article may be used with μέν and δέ as an *alternative* pronoun.

οἱ μὲν ἐχλεύαζον, οἱ δὲ εἶπον, ἀκουσόμεθά σου.
Some began mocking, but others said, "We will hear thee." Ac. 17:32.
See also: Mt. 21:35; Ac. 14:4.

c. The article is frequently used practically as a *posses-sive* pronoun.

ἐκτείνας τὴν χεῖρα ἥψατο αὐτοῦ.

Stretching forth his hand he touched him. Mt. 8:3.

See also: Ac. 5:19; 2 Cor. 8:18.

This use of the article is abundant in the papyri, as *P. Oxy.* 294:31. Δωρίωνα τὸν πατέρα, *Dorion our father,* and *P. Oxy.* 292:6: Ἑρμίαν τὸν ἀδελφόν, *Hermias my brother.* It is not, however, distinctively Koiné, but is a typical classical Greek usage; e.g., *Thuc.* 1:69. οὐ τῇ δυνάμει ἀλλὰ τῇ μελλήσει ἀμυνόμενοι, *defending yourselves, not by your power, but by your threatening aspect.*

d. The repetition of the article with some word or phrase which modifies the noun is a device employed for emphasis, in which the article functions with more than its ordinary force, and appears as a mild *relative* pronoun.

ὁ λόγος ὁ τοῦ σταυροῦ.

The word which is of the cross. 1 Cor. 1:18.

See also: Mt. 26:28; 1 Tim. 3:13.

This use of the article is to lend greater emphasis and prominence to a clause which in some particular way defines. It is a prevalent construction in Attic Greek. The emphasis is really a matter of contrast. This contrast may be specific, as in Rom. 2:14, ἔθνη τὰ μὴ νόμον ἔχοντα, where *Gentiles who have no law* are contrasted with Jews who do have law; or it may be general, as in Ac. 20:21, πίστιν τὴν εἰς τὸν κύριον ἡμῶν Ἰησοῦν Χριστόν (TR), where *faith which is in our Lord Jesus Christ* is contrasted with any other sort of faith. When the article is not used, no contrast is intended (cf. 2 Ths. 3:14).

(3) *With the Subject in a Copulative Sentence.* The article sometimes distinguishes the subject from the predicate in a copulative sentence. In Xenophon's *Anabasis,* 1:4:6, ἐμπόριον δ' ἦν τὸ χωρίον, *and the place was a market,* we have a parallel case to what we have in John 1:1, καὶ θεὸς ἦν ὁ λόγος, *and the word was deity.* The article points out the subject in these examples. Neither was *the place* the

only market, nor was *the word* all of God, as it would mean if the article were also used with θεός. As it stands, the other persons of the Trinity may be implied in θεός.

> μάρτυς γάρ μού ἐστιν ὁ θεός.
>
> *God is my witness.* Rom. 1:9.
>
> See also: Mk. 6:35; 1 Jn. 4:8.

In a convertible proposition, where the subject and predicate are regarded as interchangeable, both have the article (cf. 1 Cor. 15:56). If the subject is a proper name, or a personal or demonstrative pronoun, it may be anarthrous while the predicate has the article (cf. Jn. 6:51; Ac. 4:11; 1 Jn. 4:15).

The Absence of the Article

149. Sometimes with a noun which the context proves to be definite the article is not used. This places stress upon the qualitative aspect of the noun rather than its mere identity. An object of thought may be conceived of from two points of view: as to *identity* or *quality*. To convey the first point of view the Greek uses the article; for the second the anarthrous construction is used. Also in expressions which have become technicalized or stereotyped, and in salutations, the article is not used. This is due to the tendency toward abbreviation of frequent or customary phraseology, such as our expressions "at home," "down town," etc.

> τοῦτο γὰρ ὑμῖν λέγομεν ἐν λόγῳ κυρίου.
>
> *For this we say to you by the word of the Lord.* 1 Ths. 4:15.

i. That is, by a word of that character which comes from one who is a Lord. It is the divine authority of the teaching which is being stressed. See also: Jn. 4:27; 1 Ths. 5:5; Heb. 6:7.

ii. We adopt Robertson's conclusion that it is more accurate to speak of the "absence" of the article than the "omission" of the article. When we use "omission," we imply "that the article ought to be present" (R. 790), while as a matter of fact it ought not to be, because the writer was seeking to convey an idea which the use of the article would not have properly represented. To say "omitted" is too much like measuring Greek idiom with an English yardstick. Winer (W. 119) discusses the "omission of the article," and falls into the common error of supposing that where the article is not used it is merely because the substantive is sufficiently definite without it. Rigid caution should be exercised in viewing the article from its Greek character and history and not from English usage. Buttmann is making for the point when he says that "the omission of the article is very common in cases where we employ it," but utterly ruins matters by adding, "and where in strictness it ought to stand in Greek also" (Bt. 88). By what standard of judgment are we to conclude that "it ought to stand in Greek?" The ancient Greek writer is arraigned at the bar of modern German and English idiom!

iii. It is instructive to observe that the anarthrous noun occurs in many prepositional phrases. This is no mere accident, for there are no accidents in the growth of a language: each idiom has its reason. Nor is it because the noun is sufficiently definite without the article, which is true, as Greek nouns have an intrinsic definiteness. But that is not the reason for not using the article. A prepositional phrase usually implies some idea of quality or kind. Ἐν ἀρχῇ in Jn. 1:1 characterizes Christ as preëxistent, thus defining the nature of his person. When, in Col. 2:20, Paul says, "If ye died with Christ from the rudiments of the world, why, as if living ἐν κόσμῳ, *in the world*, do ye subject yourselves to decrees?" it is clear that ἐν κόσμῳ defines a kind of life: an "in-the-world life." So we might present innumerable instances in proof of the fact that in a prepositional phrase it is the qualitative aspect of the noun which is prominent, rather than its identity (cf. ἐν νόμῳ, Rom. 2:23; πρός ἐντροπήν, 1 Cor. 15:34; κατὰ θεόν, Eph. 4:24). Anarthrous nouns without a preposition present the same stress upon character or quality (cf. τέκνα φωτός, Eph. 5:9).

iv. Robertson gives but slight attention to this phase of the question, though he does say that qualitative force "is best brought out in anarthrous nouns" (R. 794). Moulton recognizes the importance of this point in saying that "for exegesis, there are few of the finer points of Greek which need more constant attention than this omission of the article when the writer would lay stress on the quality or character of the object" (M. 83).

v. It is important to bear in mind that we cannot determine the English translation by the presence or absence of the article in

Greek. Sometimes we should use the article in the English translation when it is not used in the Greek, and sometimes the idiomatic
force of the Greek article may best be rendered by an anarthrous
noun in English. The best guide in this matter is well-informed
common sense, exercised in keeping with the principle of exegesis
proposed long ago by William Webster: "The reason then for the
insertion or omission of the article will not be evident, unless we
can look at the matter from the same point of view as that in which
the writer regarded it" (*op. cit.*, p. 27).

The Position of the Article

150. The use of the article with the adjective, participle,
and demonstrative pronoun calls for special attention.

(1) When the article precedes the adjective it is said to
be in the *attributive position*.

ὅταν τὸ ἀκάθαρτον πνεῦμα ἐξέλθῃ.

When the unclean spirit came forth. Mt. 12:43.

See also: Mk. 12:37; Jn. 10:11.

The attributive relation is not essentially affected by the article,
but arises from other considerations which were discussed under
adjectives (§ 131, (1)). But when the article is used with an
adjective in the attributive relation it does occupy regularly the
attributive position. Sometimes the attributive relation must be
discovered from the context, there being no article to indicate it
(Eph. 2:10). We must remember that the use or absence of the
article in an attributive construction "depends on the point of
view of the speaker or writer" (R. 787), but also that the author
had a reason for the form used, hence it is not to be regarded as
a matter of accident. Entire phrases or clauses are sometimes found
in the attributive position (1 Pt. 1:11).

(2) When the article does not precede the adjective it is
called the *predicate position*.

οὐ καλὸν τὸ καύχημα ὑμῶν.

Your glorying is not good. 1 Cor. 5:6.

See also: Heb. 7:24; 1 Pt. 4:8.

i. A noun in the predicate relation never takes an article unless there is some very special reason for it. It is obvious that a predicate noun ordinarily emphasizes quality, and should, therefore, naturally be anarthrous. In the above example καλόν manifestly describes the kind of boasting. When the article is used with the predicate, it marks its essential identity with the subject. Thus ἡ ἁμαρτία ἐστὶν ἡ ἀνομία (1 Jn. 3:4) makes sin identical with lawlessness. The use of the article with the noun but not with the adjective determines the adjective as predicate, though the idiom may seem awkward in English (cf. 1 Cor. 11:5).

ii. Care should be taken to distinguish between the attributive and predicate *relation*, which has to do with the essential connection of the adjective with its context, and the attributive and predicate *position*, which has to do with the use of the article with the adjective.

(3) When the article is repeated with an adjective which follows the noun, it distributes the emphasis equally between the adjective and noun, and causes the adjective to function as an appositive. Here the particularizing force of the article is operative.

ἐγώ εἰμι ὁ ποιμὴν ὁ καλός.

I am the good shepherd. Jn. 10:11.

i. The real idiomatic force of this construction is, *I am the shepherd*—or, more particularly defined—*the good one.* See also: Mt. 17:5; Heb. 13:20.

ii. Robertson explains the significance of the attributive's being placed before or after the noun. Before the noun the attributive receives primary emphasis, while following the noun the emphasis is more equally distributed, the adjective being "added as a sort of climax in apposition with a separate article" (R. 776). Sometimes when the noun is indefinite and the attributive defines it in some particular relation, the noun is anarthrous while the attribute has an article. Frequently other attributes besides the adjective follow the noun with the article repeated (cf. 1 Cor. 1:18; Mk. 4:31) though such attributes may follow the noun without the article. The article may occur in the attributive position when it is translated by a relative pronoun in English (Rom. 8:39).

iii. When several adjectives modify one noun, if differentiation is emphasized, the article is repeated with each adjective (Rev. 1:17); but if simple qualification is intended, only one article is used (Rev. 3:17). When the article is repeated in the enumeration of a series of items, it blends them into a single object of consideration (Eph. 2:20). In this matter, however, we need to note the observation of Gildersleeve: "Theoretically the repetition compels a separate consideration while the omission suggests unity. Practically the Greeks were almost as loose as we are prone to be, and a sharp difference cannot be made" (op. cit., 277).

iv. The repetition of the article with a modifying phrase or clause for emphasis, with the approximate force of a relative pronoun, has been mentioned above. It is closely akin to the usage under consideration here.

(4) When a participle has the article, it is thereby attached to the noun as a qualifying phrase, as a sort of attribute; without the article the participle functions as a predicate. Thus ὁ ἄνθρωπος ὁ ἐλθὼν εἰς τὴν πόλιν means *the man who came into the city*, but ὁ ἄνθρωπος ἐλθὼν εἰς τὴν πόλιν means *the man having come into the city*. The attributive participle may come between the article and noun, just as the attributive adjective. The demonstrative force of the article lends itself naturally to the participle, and hence we find the article with the participle more often than with ordinary adjectives.

ἀλλὰ λαλοῦμεν θεοῦ σοφίαν τὴν ἀποκεκρυμμένην.

But we speak a wisdom of God which is hidden. 1 Cor. 2:7.

See also: Ac. 9:39; 1 Ths. 2:15.

(5) Demonstrative pronouns are regularly placed in the predicate position.

οὗτος ὁ ἄνθρωπος ἤρξατο οἰκοδομεῖν.

This man began to build. Lk. 14:30.

See also: Jn. 4:53; 2 Cor. 7:8.

DIVISION II

THE VERB

151. The verb is that part of the sentence which affirms action or state of being. The nature of the verb presents two varieties. The action described in the verb may require an object to complete its meaning. Thus merely to say, "He built," creates a sense of suspense: we instinctively wait to learn what he built. When we say, "He built a house," the sense is complete. Such a verb is called a *transitive* verb. Other verbs do not require an object to complete their meaning. Thus, "he ran" makes complete sense. These are called *intransitive* verbs.

Robertson raises timely warning against confusing the nature of a verb with its voice. Transitiveness or intransitiveness belongs to the very character of the verbal idea, while voice is determined by relations to the context, especially the subject. Transitiveness is *discerned* by the relation of the verb to an object, but is *determined* by the nature of the verbal idea. "Transitive verbs belong to any voice, and intransitive verbs to any voice" (R. 330). "That point concerns the verb itself, not the voice" (R. 797). Cf. ἐγείρω in Mt. 10:8 and 26:46. This is not to be construed, however, as meaning that the verb is fixed as transitive or intransitive by its root meaning. Transitiveness consists in the application of the root meaning, its use in a particular expression. Thus βλέπω in Jn. 9:25 is intransitive, τυφλὸς ὢν ἄρτι βλέπω, *though having been blind, now I see;* but in Mk. 8:24 it is transitive, βλέπω τοὺς ἀνθρώπους, *I see men.* Even the character of the verbal idea may be affected by the context, and the change of voice. The distinction to be noted is that transitiveness lies essentially in the character of the verbal idea in a given sense, while voice is determined entirely by the context. Hence transitiveness may change with change of voice, but not necessarily so. Verbs which are transitive in the active voice may be also transitive in the middle, or they may become intransitive. Only transitive verbs are normally used in the passive, though in some instances we find intransitive verbs in the passive (cf. Mk. 10:45; Heb. 11:2). Normally the passive voice makes a verb intransitive, but a verb which takes two objects may retain one of them when used in the passive (cf. Ac. 18:25; Gal. 2:7). Verbs which are ordinarily transitive may sometimes be used intransitively without any change in voice; as ἄγω, *I lead;* present imperative, ἄγε, *go.* This is especially true of ἔχω (*I have*), in certain idiomatic expressions with adverbs; as Mt. 4:24, τοὺς κακῶς ἔχοντας, *those who are ill* (literally, *those having badly*).

I. VOICE, PERSON, AND NUMBER

References: R. 797–820; R–S. 133–135; M. 152–163.

152. Voice is that property of the verbal idea which indicates how the subject is related to the action. We have already seen that it is to be distinguished from the matter of transitiveness, which is discerned by the relation of the verbal idea to the object. A comparison of "he killed" with "he was killed" fixes attention upon a variation with reference to the subject, while "he ran" compared with "he ran a race" fixes attention upon the object. So we see that voice is concerned with the relation of the action to the subject (cf. R. 798).

The variations in use of a particular voice must usually be discerned by examination of the entire context. Thus we find the need of translating συνετέθειντο in Jn. 9:22, *they had agreed among themselves* (reciprocal middle), by inferring from a wide study of the context that the Jews were holding recurrent conferences in their effort to suppress the work of Jesus. It is important for the student to keep in mind that voice is determined, and its varying shades of meaning discerned, by contextual relations. The usage in respect to voice is practically the same in Koiné Greek that it was in the classical Attic.

The Active Voice

153. The active voice describes the subject as *producing the action* or representing the state expressed by the verbal idea. It represents the simplest verb use. The thought of a verb as expressing something acting is obviously the verbal significance which lies at the surface. This does not necessarily mean, however, that the active was the original voice. There are reasons which lead some grammarians to regard the middle as the oldest voice. But as a matter of fact, there is no way of knowing with final certainty.

(1) *The Simple Active.* The ordinary significance of the active voice is to describe the subject as directly performing the act affirmed.

> ὁ δὲ θεὸς γινώσκει τὰς καρδίας ὑμῶν.
> *But God knows your hearts.* Lk. 16:15.
> See also: Lk. 22:54; 1 Cor. 3:6.

Some variations of the simple active are the *active with reflexives* (Mk. 15:30) and the *impersonal active* (1 Pt. 2:6).

(2) *The Causative Active.* The subject is sometimes represented as related to the action through intermediary means.

> τὸν ἥλιον αὐτοῦ ἀνατέλλει.
> *He causes his sun to shine.* Mt. 5:45.
> See also: 1 Cor. 3:6; 8:13.

This idiom is a necessary device of intelligent expression, and is, therefore, in some form common to all languages. In Hebrew we have approximately the same idiom represented in the Hiphil stem. We have it in English in such expressions as "to blow a horn," "to shine a light," "to run a horse," etc. It generally arises from the use of an intransitive verb in a transitive sense.

The Middle Voice

154. Here we approach one of the most distinctive and peculiar phenomena of the Greek language. It is impossible to describe it, adequately or accurately, in terms of English idiom, for English knows no approximate parallel.

It is imperative that the student abandon, as far as possible, the English point of view and comprehend that of the Greek. We can never hope to express exactly the Greek middle voice by an English translation, but must seek to acclimate ourselves to its mental atmosphere, and feel its force, though we cannot express it precisely.

155. The middle voice is that use of the verb which describes the subject as *participating in the results of the action.* Thus βουλεύω means *I counsel,* but βουλεύομαι means *I take counsel:* the subject acting with a view to participation in the outcome. While the active voice emphasizes the action, the middle stresses the agent. It, in some way, relates the action more intimately to the subject. Just how the action is thus related is not indicated by the middle voice, but must be detected from the context or the character of the verbal idea (cf. R. 804).

i. So "the middle is, strictly speaking, never used without some sort of reference to the subject" (Bt. 193). It "refers back the action to the acting subject" (W. 252), or "calls special attention to the subject" (R. 804). "The essence of the middle therefore lies in its calling attention to the agent as in some way clearly concerned with the action" (M. 153). All these opinions represent from various angles the fundamental significance of the middle voice. It is scarcely possible to formulate a single definition of its basal function which could be applied to all its actual occurrences. No single principle can be found to cover all the cases, for "the sphere of the middle was . . . not at all sharply delimited" (M. 158). It is an appropriate warning that Robertson gives in saying that "we must not fall into the error of explaining the force of the middle by the English translation" (R. 804). The importance of the matter in interpretation may be seen by the statement of Blass that "on the whole the conclusion arrived at must be that the New Testament writers were perfectly capable of preserving the distinction between active and middle" (Bl. 186).

ii. "The parent Indogermanic language had two voices—the active and the middle" (Wr. 250). The endings of the middle would suggest that it was the original verb form. Moulton says, "But nothing is more certain than that the parent language of our family possessed no Passive, but only Active and Middle, the latter originally equal with the former in prominence, though unrepresented now in any language, save by forms which have lost all distinction of meaning" (M. 152). The Sanskrit had only active and middle forms, save in the present, where there was a distinctive passive conjugation. The active is termed by Hindu grammarians *parasmai padan*, "word for another"; the middle, *atmane padan*, "word for one's self." This terminology is vividly suggestive of the basal distinction between the two voices.

156. Any analysis of the uses of the middle is of necessity more or less arbitrary. No rigid lines of distinction can in reality be drawn. Distinctions there are, however, and the following analysis is proposed as indicating the main lines of difference. But the student should seek to master the fundamental significance of the middle voice, then interpret each use in the light of its own context and the meaning of the verb.

(1) *The Direct Middle.* The typical use of the middle voice is to refer the results of the action directly to the agent, with a reflexive force.

$$καὶ ἀπελθὼν ἀπήγξατο.^1$$

And having gone forth, he hanged himself. Mt. 27:5.
See also: Mk. 7:4; 1 Cor. 16:16.

"The reflexive sense of the middle is comparatively rare; reflexive pronouns being usually employed with the active" (G. 292). This results from what is termed in comparative philology the "analytic tendency" in language. It has not, however, resulted in obliterating this use of the middle voice, for it still persists in Modern Greek, though sometimes in combination with a reflexive pronoun or its equivalent (T. 114).

(2) *The Indirect Middle.* Sometimes the middle lays stress upon the agent as producing the action rather than participating in its results. This use signifies that the action is closely related to the subject, or is related to the

subject in some special and distinctive sense which the writer wishes to emphasize. The reason for the emphasis is to be inferred from the context.

αἰωνίαν λύτρωσιν εὕρατο.

He himself secured eternal redemption. Heb. 9:12.

See also: 1 Cor. 13:8; 2 Tim. 4:15.

i. This usage is sometimes called the intensive middle, which is suggestive but hardly adequate. It roughly corresponds to the Piel stem in Hebrew, but is more varied and extended in its use. Moulton calls it the "dynamic" middle, and reckons that it "emphasized the part taken by the subject in the action of the verb"— a very pertinent suggestion. He recognizes that the variations of this use are not easy to define, but is surely overestimating the difficulties when he says that "the category will include a number of verbs in which it is useless to exercise our ingenuity on interpreting the middle, for the development never progressed beyond the rudimentary stage" (M. 158). The student should employ all the knowledge he has and all the linguistic sense at his command in seeking an intelligent explanation of any and every occurrence of the middle. It must be admitted, however, that the use of the middle here under consideration is widely varied, and does not submit to definition by fixed and rigid lines of distinction.

ii. The intensive significance of the middle may be seen in 2 Tim. 4:15, ὃν καὶ σὺ φυλάσσου, *of whom do thou also beware.* Here Paul is warning Timothy against Alexander the coppersmith, who had done the Apostle serious damage. The sense of the passage is about this: "Since he has treated me so despitefully, *you* had better take heed for *yourself.*" The Greeks employed the middle where we must resort to italics. A striking and instructive example appears in Ac. 20:24, ἀλλ' οὐδενὸς λόγου ποιοῦμαι τὴν ψυχὴν τιμίαν ἐμαυτῷ, *but I do not make my life of any account as dear to myself.* Here the significance of the middle ποιοῦμαι seems to be, "I do not make, as far as I am personally concerned, my life dear unto myself." Paul does not at all mean to say that he has no interest in living, but means that he considers his divinely appointed ministry as overshadowing any selfish interest which it would be possible for him to have in life. The middle indicates that, however others may regard the matter, this is *his* conclusion. Here the middle is not only intensive, but antithetical in force (cf. αἰτεῖσθαι - αἰτεῖτε - αἰτεῖσθε in Jas. 4:2, 3).

iii. This use of the middle may give to a verb an individualistic or specific application. Thus στρατεύειν means *to conduct a military campaign*, while στρατεύεσθαι means *to be a soldier* (2 Tim. 2:4); πολιτεύειν means *to live in a free state*, while πολιτεύεσθαι means *to take active part in the affairs of a state—to be a citizen* (Phs. 1:27).

iv. This is the most extensive use of the middle, and a use which requires and rewards the closest study. Robertson distinguishes between the indirect middle and the intensive use, of which examples were given above, and employs with Moulton the term "dynamic" for designating a separate variation. This undoubtedly conduces to greater analytic accuracy, but introduces a distinction of which the line of demarcation is vague and confusing to the average student. Since the intensive use unquestionably shares in the basal function of the indirect middle, we conclude that it is best to take care of it by an extension in the definition of the indirect middle, for the "dynamic" middle is admitted to be merely a "drip-pan middle," which is "put at the bottom to catch the drippings of the other uses" (Gildersleeve: *cit.* R. 811). Our policy here is to abandon the drip-pan, and employ the indirect middle to catch the drippings, since we find it so clearly adapted to that purpose.

(3) *The Permissive Middle*. The middle may represent the agent as voluntarily yielding himself to the results of the action, or seeking to secure the results of the action in his own interest.

διὰ τί οὐχὶ μᾶλλον ἀδικεῖσθε;
Why not rather let yourselves be wronged?   1 Cor. 6:7.
See also: Lk. 2:4, 5; 1 Cor. 11:6; Ac. 15:1.

This idiom appears as far back as Homer; e.g., λυσόμενος θύγατρα, *to get his daughter set free*. An example from the papyri may be seen in *Tb. P.* 35, ἑαυτὸν αἰτιάσεται, *he will get himself accused*.

(4) *The Reciprocal Middle*. A middle verb with a plural subject may represent an interchange of effort between the acting agents.

συνετέθειντο οἱ Ἰουδαῖοι.
The Jews had agreed with one another. Jn. 9:22.
See also: Mt. 26:4; Lk. 14:7.

i. Occasionally we find the middle accompanied by a pronoun (Ac. 7:58). Robertson calls this the *redundant middle*. "Gildersleeve sees in this idiom the effort to bring out more clearly the reflexive force of the middle" (R. 811). Since the reflexive came in to aid in the very function performed by the middle, this idiom is not unnatural. The reflexive pronoun and passive voice have gradually encroached upon the middle—the reflexive upon its functions and the passive its forms. But, though the middle in Modern Greek has no distinctive conjugation, yet its functions survive and are expressed in forms identical with the passive. In this way it serves in Modern Greek in deponents, as reflexive, reciprocal, and causative (T. 113–115).

ii. Since the middle and passive have in several tenses forms alike, it is sometimes difficult to distinguish between them. The matter must be determined by the context and the meaning of the verbal idea (cf. Mt. 11:5).

The Passive Voice

157. The passive voice is that use of the verb which denotes the subject as *receiving the action*. Its variations in use are determined by the medium through which the subject receives the action. Upon this basis we may construct the following analysis.

(1) *The Passive With Direct Agent.* When the original agent which produces the action signified in the passive verb is expressed, the regular construction is ὑπό with the ablative.

κατηγορεῖται ὑπὸ τῶν Ἰουδαίων.

He was accused by the Jews. Ac. 22:30.

See also: Mt. 10:22; Rom. 3:21.

Personal agent may also, though rarely, be expressed by the instrumental case (cf. Lk. 23:15). "Yet this use in Greek is by no means so general that we can assume that it can be substituted indifferently in any case and every case for ὑπό with the Genitive" (Bt. 187). It is only where the personal idea is remote and instrumentality is prominent; as above (Lk. 23:15), it is an act of guilt which is contemplated rather than a personal achievement. For use in his Greek composition the student had best adopt the regular construction, ὑπό with the ablative.

(2) *The Passive With Intermediate Agent.* When the agent is the medium through which the original cause has effected the action expressed by the passive verb, the regular construction is διά with the genitive.

πάντα δι' αὐτοῦ ἐγένετο.

All things were made through him. Jn. 1:3.

Here God the Father is thought of as the original cause of creation, and the λόγος as the intermediate agent. See also: Mt. 1:22; Gal. 3:18.

(3) *The Passive With Impersonal Agent.* If the agent through which the action of the passive verb is performed is impersonal, it is ordinarily expressed by the instrumental case, independently or with ἐν.

χάριτί ἐστε σεσωσμένοι.

By grace ye are saved. Eph. 2:8.
See also: Mt. 3:12; Ac. 12:2.

i. Agency is also sometimes expressed by ἀπό (2 Cor. 3:18); ἐκ (Gal. 4:4); and παρά (Jn. 17:7).

ii. The passive arose out of the middle, and the line of demarcation between them was never absolutely fixed. There was a slight margin in which they overlapped and presented a common ground. Thus in Ac. 22:16, βαπτίσαι is middle and means, *get yourself baptized.* But as to practical significance, how much difference is there between that rendering and *be baptized,* the way it is usually rendered? We must beware not to seek a hard and fast English equivalent to be employed persistently in the translation of either of these voices (cf. M. 162). As the passive pressed the middle off the field there remained a common ground of interchanging functions between them. In fact, as we have observed above, the functions of the middle voice still flourish in the Greek language.

iii. When verbs which take two accusatives are put in the passive, and the accusative of the person becomes the subject, the accusative of the thing is ordinarily retained (2 Ths. 2:15). Where the active has a direct object in the accusative and an indirect object in the dative, the dative usually becomes the subject and the direct object is retained as an accusative of reference (Rom. 3:2).

Irregularities in Voice

158. There are two principal ways in which many Greek verbs depart from normal usage in the matter of voice.

(1) *Defective verbs* are those not used in all three voices, or not in every tense of one or more voices. This arose in the natural processes of linguistic development, for the root meaning of a verb would yield itself more readily to usage in one voice than in another, which would cause the less natural forms to become obsolete, and be replaced by another verb root better adapted to use in that voice and tense. Thus ἔρχομαι must have had a primitive active form ἔρχομι, but for some reason the Greek mind found more satisfactory expression in the middle form, so the active was lost. But when they used the aorist, a synonym of ἔρχομι yielded itself better to the desired mode of expression, the verb ἔλθομι, aorist ἦλθον. Thus the present form of this verb became obsolete. By some such process as this the defective verbs probably originated. To this class belong the great majority of what we call the irregular verbs.

(2) *Deponent verbs* are those with middle or passive form, but active meaning. It is obvious that the same verb may be both defective and deponent. The distinctive fact about the deponent verb is that its voice form is different from its voice function. Thus δέχομαι means *I receive,* and not *I receive myself* or *I am received.*

i. It will be found that some grammarians speak of deponents as passive in form, while others call them middle. As a matter of fact, they may be found in either. The difference is to be detected in the aorist. The majority of the deponents have their aorist in the middle;

as ἀσπάζομαι, aorist, ἠσπασάμην; though quite a number have the aorist passive; as, βούλομαι, aorist, ἐβουλήθην. In a few we find the use of both forms; as θεάομαι, aorist, ἐθεασάμην or ἐθεάθην.

ii. Robertson and Moulton both assail the term "deponent" on the ground that it should include both actives without middle form and middles without active form, "if retained for either" (M. 153). Robertson uses the term "dynamic" for this class of verbs, admitting that it is not "much better" (R. 812). The only justification we have to offer for retaining the term here is that there is a phenomenon of the language for which we need a distinct term, and this is the most familiar. While it is truly inappropriate to say that a verb has "lost" (*deponere,* "to lay aside") its active meaning (and indeed, likely contrary to the history of the verb), yet "deponent" has become so thoroughly fixed in grammatical terminology that its inappropriateness is hardly serious enough to require that we seek to displace it—at least, until an obviously better term is found. Perphaps "defective" would cover the whole case, but there should be a distinction between the lack of a voice and the use of one voice with the significance of another. It is, however, likely confusing to go as far as Winer and say, "From middle verbs are to be carefully distinguished Deponent" (W. 258). Deponent is not a voice, but an anomalous variation of voice.

Person and Number

159. In Greek, as in all other languages, person and number are determined by the relation of the speaker or writer to the assertion contained in the verb. If the assertion contains a fact relative to the one asserting, the verb is in the first person. If it presents a fact relative to the one addressed, the verb is in the second person. If it presents a fact relative to someone other than either the one asserting or the one addressed, the verb is in the third person. If the assertion is made concerning more than one, the verb is in the plural (in the Koiné Greek—older Greek had the dual for two). This essential fact of language has given rise to the "rule of concord" that the verb agrees with its subject in person and number.

i. A seeming exception to the above principle of syntax is the fact that a neuter plural subject regularly takes a singular verb (Jn. 9:3). This is doubtless because a neuter plural usually refers to inanimate objects, which are viewed in mass rather than as distinct individuals. Evidence for this explanation is seen in the fact that the verb is generally plural if the neuter plural subject refers to persons (Mt. 12:21), or if it is desired to emphasize the plurality of things (Lk. 24:11). In Jn. 10:27, τὰ πρόβατα τὰ ἐμὰ τῆς φωνῆς μου ἀκούουσιν, *my sheep hear my voice*, Jesus means that each of his disciples individually responds to his command; and further, πρόβατα is a figure of speech referring to persons. Both considerations combine to form a plural verb here.

ii. When two or more subjects are joined together by a conjunction, the verb is regularly plural (Ac. 15:35), though it may agree with the nearest subject (1 Cor. 13:13). When a collective subject is taken in mass, the verb is singular (Mk 5:24), but if the component parts are viewed individually the verb is plural (Mk. 3:7).

II. Mood

References: R. 911–1049; R-S. 128–132; M. 164–201.

160. In the expression of the verbal idea it is necessary to define its relation to reality: that which has, will, or does now exist. For instance, it is impossible to present the thought of a child running without affirming either the *fact* of his running—in present, past, or future, or the *possibility* of his running. To say, "The child runs," places the statement in the first category; to say, "If the child runs," presents the second. This *affirmation of relation to reality* is mood. Whether the verbal idea is objectively a fact or not is not the point: mood represents the way in which the matter is conceived. It represents "an attitude of mind on the part of the speaker" (M. 164). Robertson has aptly defined mood as "the manner of the affirmation" (R. 912).

161. In the strictest analysis of the verb function in language there are but two essential moods. Mood being

the way in which an action is conceived with reference to reality, it presents two viewpoints: that which is actual and that which is possible. The presence of a negative, affirming that a thing is not actual or not possible, does not modify the essential category of thought; it merely negatives these fundamental ideas. The indicative is the mood which denotes the verbal idea as actual. Possible action may employ, in Greek, either of three moods. If it is viewed as contingent upon certain existing and known conditions—being *objectively* possible—the subjunctive is used. If the action is conceived of as possible without reference to existing conditions—being *subjectively* possible—the optative is used. Where the mind purposes the realization of a possible action through the exercise of the will upon an intermediate agent and conditioned upon the agent's response—being *volitionally* possible—the imperative is used. So the two essential moods in language are the *real*—represented in Greek by the indicative; and the *potential*—embracing the subjunctive, optative, and imperative (cf. W. 281). But for simplicity of grammatical analysis it is best that we should present our treatment of moods under the four separate heads, indicative, subjunctive, optative, and imperative.

i. Sheffield's definition of mood as the "speaker's concern with what is said" *(Grammar and Thinking,* p. 120) is pertinent but not adequate, as he himself later concludes *(ibid.,* p. 127). It represents an element in mood but not its totality. One's concern in the assertion of the verb may influence his attitude of mind, but with it there may be associated many other factors, or, on the other hand, the matter of personal interest may be entirely absent from the attitude expressed in the verb. The essence of mood is the way in which the assertion is related to reality.

ii. There has been disagreement among grammarians as to the number of the moods in Greek. Some regard only the subjunctive and optative as being in the strictest sense moods, since they exhibit in the most pronounced manner the attitude of mind expressed in the affirmation; others would include also the imperative, the mood of purpose and, therefore, of mental attitude; but the majority would accept four, because, while it is true that the indicative is the mood of simple assertion of fact, it nevertheless reflects very definitely a mental attitude. The infinitive and participle are not regarded by any as truly moods. Robertson groups infinitives and participles under the general head of "verbal nouns," an entirely justifiable procedure. They cannot appropriately be called moods. We adopt here the prevalent view, which regards as moods the indicative, subjunctive, optative, and imperative.

iii. Some grammarians find evidence for a primitive *injunctive* mood. Robertson decides that because of its close relation to the imperative "it has to be considered in an historical review" (R. 321). Moulton finds in it the origin of the imperative. He thinks that "it represented the bare combination of verbal idea with the ending which supplies the subject." It "was simply an imperfect or aorist indicative without the augment" (M. 165). It is found in actual use in the Sanskrit, where it expresses prohibition.

iv. There is but one mood which has essential temporal relations; viz., the indicative. This is to be normally expected in the indicative, since it asserts actuality, and that which actually occurs or exists is inevitably defined by relations of time. But that which is potential has no definite time relations, its temporal connections being only relative. Hence the time element is entirely absent from the potential moods.

v. The New Testament is fairly accurate in observing the customary distinctions between the Greek moods. "Only it is noticeable that the Optative, as in the later Greek authors who do not aim at classical refinement, is partially set aside . . . and in certain constructions is superseded by the Subjunctive" (W. 282; cf. Bt. 207). The use of the optative after secondary tenses is also discontinued in the Koiné.

vi. "The mode is far and away the most difficult theme in Greek syntax" (R. 912). The greatest difficulty is presented in the overlapping of functions. That is, the same function may be performed by more than one mood. For instance, the subjunctive and imperative are both used in prohibitions. The indicative and imperative are both used for commands, and the indicative and optative for wishes. "The development of the modes was gradual and the differentiation was never absolutely distinct" (R. 924). But the lines of distinction are sufficiently clear to admit of a thorough working analysis.

The Indicative Mood

162. The indicative is the declarative mood, denoting a simple assertion or interrogation. It is the mood of *certainty*. It is significant of a simple fact, stated or inquired about. The thing which distinguishes the indicative is its independence of qualification or condition. It represents the verbal idea from the viewpoint of reality. This is the attitude of mind expressed, whether the assumed reality is an objective fact or not. "The indicative does state a thing as true, but does not *guarantee* the reality of the thing. In the nature of the case only the *statement* is under discussion" (R. 915). It is "primarily the mood of unqualified assertion or simple question of fact" (Br. 73), and hence is by far the most frequently used.

(1) *The Declarative Indicative.* Its basal significance is most clearly seen when the indicative is used in the statement of a simple fact.

ἐν ἀρχῇ ἦν ὁ λόγος.

In the beginning was the word. Jn. 1:1.
See also: Eph. 4:1; 1 Ths. 2:7.

(2) *The Interrogative Indicative.* The viewpoint of reality is implied in a fact inquired about when the indicative is used in asking a simple question.

τί ζητεῖτε;

What do ye seek? Jn. 1:38.
See also: Mt. 16:13; Mk. 1:24.

The interrogative indicative assumes that there is an actual fact which may be stated in answer to the question. Though this essential force of the construction may vary in strength and clearness, it undoubtedly lies at the basis of the usage. Robertson asserts with good reason that there is really no difference between declaration and question, so far as the essential use of the mood is concerned (R. 915). We present them as two distinct uses as a policy of simplification rather than strict scientific analysis. For the negative particles in interrogations, see the section on particles, and for the interrogative pronouns, the section on pronouns.

(3) *The Cohortative Indicative.* The future indicative is sometimes used to express a command.

ἀγαπήσεις τὸν πλησίον σου ὡς σεαυτόν.
Thou shalt love thy neighbor as thyself. Jas. 2:8
See also: Mt. 27:24; Lk. 1:13.

(4) *The Potential Indicative.* Sometimes the idea of contingency accompanies the indicative, being supplied by the use of ἄν, the nature of the verbal idea, or the context. It may be thus used in association with three ideas.

a. The indicative may be used in a claim of *obligation.*

οὓς ἔδει ἐπὶ σοῦ παρεῖναι.
Who ought to be here before thee. Ac. 24:19.
See also: Mt. 25:27; 1 Cor. 4:8.

b. The indicative may be used to express an *impulse.*

ηὐχόμην γὰρ ἀνάθεμα εἶναι.
For I could wish to be accursed. Rom. 9:3.
See also: Ac. 25:22; Gal. 4:20.

c. The indicative is used in certain forms of *condition.*

εἰ ἦς ὧδε οὐκ ἂν ἀπέθανεν.
If thou hadst been here, he would not have died. Jn. 11:21.
See also: Mk. 14:5; Ac. 26:32.

For the indicative in a conditional sentence without ἄν see Gal. 4:15. Let it be kept in mind that the potential use of the indicative is not really an exception to its essential force as the mood of certainty, for the contingent element resides in ἄν, or the context, or the character of the verbal idea.

The Subjunctive Mood

163. The subjunctive is the mood of mild contingency; the mood of *probability*. While the indicative assumes reality, the subjunctive assumes unreality. It is the first step away from that which is actual in the direction of that which is only conceivable, and, therefore, properly leads the list of the potential moods. As the sense departs farther from reality than the subjunctive, it shades off into the optative. When the element of intention or purpose is involved, the potential idea is regularly conveyed by the imperative. These three moods are akin to each other by being related to a common idea, that of potentiality.

i. The close relation of the subjunctive to the imperative is to be seen in the hortatory subjunctive and the subjunctive of prohibition. Its kinship to the optative has been demonstrated by the fact of its having taken over the functions of the optative. It does the full service of the optative in Latin, and is found usurping its functions in the Koiné period of the Greek, pushing it entirely off the field by the time of Modern Greek (T. 115). We might almost say that the subjunctive is the typical potential mood, and that the optative and imperative are but variations of it. The contingent idea is dominant in the optative, and is not at all remote in the imperative. As a matter of fact, action is either real or contingent, and even the slightest variation from the real produces the contingent. Hence the potential moods express varying degrees of contingency.

ii. There is likely close relationship between the subjunctive and the future indicative. "It is quite probable that the future indicative is just a variation of the aorist subjunctive" (R. 924). In the earliest Greek which we have the subjunctive and future indicative are used interchangeably. In the classical literature the distinction is quite rigidly observed, "but in later writers vacillation in the employment of them is again discernible" (Bt. 211). The idea of futurity is almost invariably connected with the subjunctive, but while inevitable in the very nature of the case (for contingency naturally involves relative futurity), it is not the primary and fundamental idea. It is the variation from the real (assumed in thought) which gave rise to the subjunctive and which must remain as its basal idea.

(1) *The Hortatory Subjunctive.* When one exhorts others to participate with him in any act or condition, the subjunctive is used in the first person plural.

κρατῶμεν τῆς ὁμολογίας.

Let us hold fast our confession. Heb. 4:15.

See also: Heb. 12:1; 1 Jn. 4:7.

The first person singular of the subjunctive is sometimes used in a request for permission to do a thing (cf. Mt. 7:4; Lk. 6:42).

(2) *The Subjunctive of Prohibition.* In the expression of a prohibition or a negative entreaty the second person of the aorist subjunctive may be used.

μὴ εἰσενέγκῃς ἡμᾶς εἰς πειρασμόν.

Lead us not into temptation. Mt. 6:13.

See also: Mt. 6:34; Heb. 3:8.

The subjunctive of prohibition may also occur in the third person, especially in dependent clauses of fear or warning, though it may also occur in an independent clause of direct prohibition (1 Cor. 16:11).

(3) *The Deliberative Subjunctive.* When interrogation does not assume an answer in actual fact, but represents deliberation or is employed as a mere rhetorical device, the subjunctive is used.

τί εἴπω ὑμῖν;

What shall I say to you? 1 Cor. 11:22.

See also: Mk. 12:14; Lk. 3:10.

The subjunctive also occurs in indirect deliberative questions (Mt. 6:25). Questions may be classed as real and rhetorical. Real questions are those intended as actual requests for information (Mt. 16:13). Rhetorical questions represent an attitude of mind or an assumption of fact in the form of a question (Rom. 10:14).

(4) *The Subjunctive of Emphatic Negation.* When spe‑ cial stress is placed upon a negative proposition, the sub‑ junctive is used with οὐ μή.

καὶ οὐ μὴ ἐκφύγωσιν.

And they shall not possibly escape. 1 Ths. 5:3.
See also: Mt. 5:20; Lk. 6:37.

(5) *The Potential Subjunctive.* The preceding uses of the subjunctive are confined largely to independent clauses, but it is also widely used in subordinate clauses. These commonly imply future reference, and are qualified by an element of contingency. All uses of the subjunctive in object or conditional clauses are included in this class.

διαμαρτύρομαι ἵνα ταῦτα φυλάξῃς.

I charge thee that thou guard these things. 1 Tim. 5:21.
See also: Mt. 17:20; Lk. 6:34.

The Optative Mood

164. The optative is the mood of strong contingency; the mood of *possibility*. It contains no definite anticipation of realization, but merely presents the action as conceivable. Hence it is one step farther removed from reality than the subjunctive. In fact, it never attained to very pronounced distinction, and was never more than "a sort of weaker subjunctive" (R. 936).

i. Some grammarians describe the optative as expressing "past contingency." This view is determined by the classical use of the mood after secondary tenses—a rather narrow basis of definition. A better definition would be *emphatic contingency,* for this implies the essential force of the mood, and includes independent as well as dependent clauses. The kinship of the optative to the subjunc‑ tive is manifest in both history and function. The probability is that it arose in order to enable the subjunctive to occupy more definite limits of meaning. Its use with secondary tenses was probably one of its earliest functions, since it developed secondary endings in conjugation. Since the optative came in as a helper to the subjunctive, it is not likely that wishing was its original significance, though it was from this idea that it derived its name. But "the name does not signify anything. It 'was invented by grammarians long after the usages of the language were settled'" (R. 936).

ii. In the New Testament the optative is little used in dependent clauses. "The Optative as a dependent mood appears most frequently in the writings of Luke; its use even here, however, is unmistakably on the decrease" (Bt. 215).

iii. In Sanskrit the optative practically displaced the subjunctive, and became the chief potential mood. Whitney tells us that "instead of their being (as in Greek) both maintained in use, and endowed with nicer and more distinctive values, the subjunctive gradually disappears, and the optative assumes alone the office formerly shared by both" (*Sansk. Gr.*, p. 261). In Greek the history of the matter has been exactly opposite. In early and classic Greek the optative is used alongside the subjunctive with about the same frequency. It is rapidly disappearing in the Koiné period, even in the literary language. It was extremely rare in the vernacular, being used only sixty-seven times in the New Testament, and seldom in the papyri and inscriptions. Robertson thinks that "it is doubtful if the optative was ever used much in conversation even in Athens" (R. 325). Indeed, it "was never common in the language of the people, as is shown by its rarity in the Attic inscriptions" (R. 326). Winer appends a very suggestive note on the optative, saying that "it is still a question how far it was used in the popular speech of the ancient Greeks. It is often the case that certain forms and constructions embodying refinements of the literary diction are persistently shunned by the people" (W. 282). The optative is "a literary mood that faded before the march of the subjunctive" (R. 936). In Modern Greek the optative has entirely disappeared (T. 115).

(1) *The Voluntative Optative.* The optative is the ordinary form of the verb used in the expression of a wish. This is its most extensive use in the New Testament.

> ὁ δὲ κύριος κατευθύναι ὑμῶν τὰς καρδίας.
>
> *May the Lord guide your hearts.* 2 Ths. 3:5.
>
> See also: Ac. 8:20; 1 Pt. 1:2.

"The phrase μή γένοιτο is an optative of wishing which strongly deprecates something suggested by a previous question or assertion. Fourteen of the fifteen New Testament instances are in Paul's writings, and in twelve of these it expresses the apostle's abhorrence of an inference which he fears may be (falsely) drawn from his argument" (Br. 79.).

(2) *The Potential Optative.* In several instances in the New Testament the optative serves in a clause which implies a condition. This use is distinguished by the particle ἄν.

τί ἄν θέλοι λέγειν;

What would he wish to say? Ac. 17:18.

See also: Lk. 1:62; Ac. 8:31.

Expressed fully the example would read, *What would he wish to say, if he could say anything?* These optatives occur as the fulfillment of a condition which is implied, and in the great majority of instances we can supply from the context the implied condition.

(3) *The Deliberative Optative.* A few times in the New Testament indirect rhetorical questions are expressed by the optative. In this construction an unusually doubtful attitude of mind is implied.

διελογίζετο ποταπὸς εἴη ὁ ἀσποσμὸς οὗτος.

She was pondering what manner of salutation this might be. Lk. 1:29.

See also: Lk. 22:23; Ac. 17:11.

The Imperative Mood

165. The imperative is the mood of command or entreaty —the mood of *volition*. It is the genius of the imperative to express the appeal of will to will. In ordinary linguistic communication the primary appeal is from intellect to intellect, but in the imperative one will addresses another. It expresses neither probability nor possibility, but only intention, and is, therefore, the furthest removed from reality.

i. There is good reason to suppose that the imperative, which is likely the youngest of the moods, arose in the use of the verb stem as a sort of interjection, for we find it to be the "simplest possible form of the verb" (M. 171). Compare the use of δεῦρο, meaning *hither*, and note that it "only needs the exclamation mark to make it mean *come here*" (M. 172).

ii. The imperative has never been able to secure a field all to itself, as the indicative and subjunctive and even the infinitive and participle (also the optative in Attic Greek) do service in the expression of commands. It has had difficulty in maintaining itself, having survived in Modern Greek only in a bare residuum. However, whatever weakening it may have suffered in the rest of the Koiné does not appear in the New Testament. "The use of the imperative mood in the New Testament preserves all the refinements of the classical language" (Simcox: *Lang. of the N. T.,* p. 114).

(1) *The Imperative of Command.* Where one will makes a direct, positive appeal to another the imperative finds its most characteristic use. The degree of authority involved in the command, and the degree of probability that the one addressed will respond are matters but incidental to the use of the mood. The imperative itself denotes only the appeal of the will.

> ἀγαπᾶτε τοὺς ἐχθροὺς ὑμῶν.
>
> *Love your enemies.* Mt. 5:44.
> See also: Mt. 6:6; 1 Ths. 5:16.

(2) *The Imperative of Prohibition.* The imperative is frequently used to express a negative command.

> ἐγώ εἰμι, μὴ φοβεῖσθε.
>
> *It is I, be not afraid.* Jn. 6:20.
> See also: 1 Cor. 6:9; Lk. 7:14.

For the distinctions in tense, and difference in the force of subjunctive and imperative in commands and prohibitions, see §§288f.

(3) *The Imperative of Entreaty.* Often the imperative does not convey the finality of command, but has the force of urgency or request.

$$\pi\rho\delta\sigma\theta\epsilon\varsigma\ \dot{\eta}\mu\hat{\iota}\nu\ \pi\dot{\iota}\sigma\tau\iota\nu.$$

Increase our faith. Lk. 17:5.
See also: Mk. 9:22; Jn. 17:11.

(4) *The Imperative of Permission.* The command signified by the imperative may be in compliance with an expressed desire or a manifest inclination on the part of the one who is the object of the command, thus involving consent as well as command.

$$\epsilon\dot{\iota}\ \delta\dot{\epsilon}\ \dot{o}\ \ddot{a}\pi\iota\sigma\tau o\varsigma\ \chi\omega\rho\dot{\iota}\zeta\epsilon\tau a\iota,\ \chi\omega\rho\iota\zeta\dot{\epsilon}\sigma\theta\omega.$$

But if the unbeliever depart, let him depart. 1 Cor. 7:15.
See also: Mt. 8:32; 26:45.

Normally the imperative carried with it a very forcible tone of command. This was its characteristic force, though it might shade off into mere permission. The ancient Greeks so regarded it, and hence never employed the imperative in communication with superiors. This fact makes it significant that the imperative is so abundant in the New Testament. The apostles and their associates did not regard it as appropriate to address their readers "with carefully softened commands; and in the imperial edicts of Him who 'taught with authority,' and the ethical exhortations of men who spoke in His name, we find naturally a large proportion of imperatives" (M. 173).

III. Tense

References: R. 821–910; R–S. 136–146; M. 108–151.

166. No element of the Greek language is of more importance to the student of the New Testament than the matter of tense. A variation in meaning exhibited by the use of a particular tense will often dissolve what appears to be an embarrassing difficulty, or reveal a gleam of truth which will thrill the heart with delight and inspiration.

Though it is an intricate and difficult subject, no phase of Greek grammar offers a fuller reward. The benefits are to be reaped only when one has invested sufficient time and diligence to obtain an insight into the idiomatic use of tense in the Greek language and an appreciation of the finer distinctions in force.

The development of tense has reached its highest in Greek, and presents its greatest wealth of meaning. "Among all known ancient languages none distinguishes the manifold temporal (and modal) relations of the verb so accurately as the Greek" (Bt. 194). And "in the use of tenses the New Testament writers are by no means deficient in the requisite skill" (Bt. 195). These considerations should impress the importance of mastering the use of the Greek tenses, yet "probably nothing connected with syntax is so imperfectly understood by the average student as tense" (R. 821). In fact, that the Greeks themselves always observed with conscious accuracy their tense distinctions, Robertson hesitates to conclude (R. 829). It is certainly unsafe, however, to proceed upon any supposition other than that the New Testament writer used the tense which would convey just the idea he wished to express. This is the rule, and all seeming exceptions are to be regarded with doubt.

167. The distinctive function of the verb is to express action. Action as presented in the expression of a verbal idea involves two elements, *time* of action and *kind* of action. That is, the action may be described as occurring at a certain time, and must be described, if intelligible, as performed in a certain manner. Tense deals with these two aspects of verbal expression, kind of action being the chief idea involved, for *time is but a minor consideration in the Greek tenses.*

168. In its temporal relations action may be defined as either past, present, or future. In Greek these distinctions are involved only in the indicative mood, the potential moods being without temporal significance—except that as a rule they are relatively futuristic. Past time is indicated

by augment, which is the only purely temporal element in
the formation of the Greek verb. The distinctive verbal
suffixes of the indicative carry temporal implications, but
associated with other ideas.

169. The important element of tense in Greek is *kind of
action*. This is its fundamental significance. "The chief
function of a Greek tense is thus not to denote time, but
progress" (Br. 6). For this element of tense recent grammarians have adopted the German term *aktionsart*, "kind
of action." The character of an action may be defined
from either of three points of view; it may be continuous,
it may be complete, or it may be regarded simply as occurring, without reference to the question of progress. There
are, therefore, three fundamental tenses in Greek: the
present, representing continuous action; the perfect, representing completed action; and the aorist (*ἀόριστος, without
limits, undefined*), representing indefinite action. "These
three tenses were first developed irrespective of time" (R.
824).

(1) *Action as Continuous.* Here the principal tense is
the *present*, which in the indicative is used primarily of
present time. Continuous action in past time is denoted
by the imperfect tense. For continuous action in future
time the regular future is ordinarily used, though the idea
is best expressed by the periphrastic future.

(2) *Action as Complete.* Here the principal tense is the
perfect, and in the indicative is contemplated from the
viewpoint of present time. Complete action viewed from
a point in past time is expressed by the pluperfect. Complete action viewed from a point in future time is the future
perfect.

(3) *Action as Occurring.* The tense here is the *aorist*.
It has time relations only in the indicative, where it is past
and hence augmented. It has no distinctive form for

present and future time, though the present and future tenses may denote an aoristic force. Modern Greek has developed a separate form for the aoristic future (T. 125). The characteristic significance of the aorist is best seen in the potential moods.

These distinctions are especially vivid in the comparative meanings of the present, perfect, and aorist infinitives; e.g., ποεῖν, to be doing; πεποιηκέναι, to have done; ποιῆσαι, to do (cf. Hadley-Allen: Gr. Grammar, p. 204).

170. There are really two fundamental ways of viewing action. It may be contemplated in single perspective, as a point, which we may call *punctiliar* action (R. 823); or it may be regarded as in progress, as a line, and this we may call *linear* action (M. 109). The perfect tense is a combination of these two ideas: it looks in perspective at the action, and regards the results of the action as continuing to exist; that is, in progress at a given point. Hence the perfect has both elements, linear and punctiliar. The aorist may be represented by a dot (•), the present by a line (————), and the perfect by the combination of the two (•————).

i. The evidence is that there "were originally two verb types, the one denoting durative or linear action, the other momentary or punctiliar action. Hence some verbs have two roots, one linear (durative), like φέρω (fero), the other punctiliar (momentary), like ἤνεγκον (tuli). . . . With other verbs the distinction was not drawn sharply, the root could be used either way (cf. φη-μί, ἔ-φη-ν; λέγ-ω, ἔ-λεγ-ον). All this was before there was any idea of later tense. So ἔ-φαγ-ον is punctiliar, while ἐσθίω is linear or durative" (R. 823). "It is seen that the Aorist has a 'punctiliar' action; that is it regards action as a point. . . . The Present has generally a *durative* action—*linear*, we may call it. . . . The *Perfect* action is a variety by itself, denoting what began in the past and still continues" (M. 109). Thus we see that the present and aorist are the basic tenses in Greek. It is important to keep this fact in mind in all our consideration of the matter of tense, and along with it the fact that neither contains any essential notion of time.

ii. Moulton insists that tense is "a subject on which many of the most crucial questions of exegesis depend," and that "the notion of (present or past) time is not by any means the first thing we must think of in dealing with tenses. For our problem of *aktionsart*, it is a mere accident that φεύγω is (generally) present and ἔφευγον, ἔφυγον, and φυγών past: the main point we must settle is the distinction between φευγ and φυγ which is common to all their moods" (M. 119).

171. In the analysis of the tenses which we offer here we have not sought to be exhaustive, but rather suggestive. To present the Greek tenses in all their variations and distinctions would result in bewildering the student and impairing his appreciation of this important subject. Simplicity and comprehensiveness have been chiefly in view in preparing the following analysis of tense functions. It is hoped and assumed that the student will pursue further a study of the best grammars and an inductive observation of the tenses in their various ramifications of meaning. We can do no more here than introduce and inspire such a line of investigation.

It would doubtless be more strictly scientific to follow Robertson in analyzing our treatment of tense on the basis of the three principal kinds of action, which he denominates punctiliar, durative, and perfected. But it lends to simplicity to take up the tenses in the usual order of their occurrence in the conjugation of the verb, the order with which the average student is most familiar. Since we have primarily in view the average student rather than the scientific scholar, we shall follow that policy. It is true that the imperfect and pluperfect occur only in the indicative, and the future has its chief significance there, but, in view of the great abundance of the indicative in the text of the New Testament, it is well to give it prominence in the treatment of tenses. It is a working knowledge of the Greek verb in the New Testament we seek, and the simplest method of treatment will be most conducive to that end. It is necessary, though, that we give but little place to the time element, even in the indicative,

The Present Tense

172. The fundamental significance of the present tense is the idea of progress. It is the *linear* tense. This is not, however, its exclusive significance. It is a mistake to suppose "that the durative meaning monopolises the present stem" (M. 119). Since there is no aorist tense for present time, the present tense, as used in the indicative, must do service for both linear and punctiliar action. But it is to be borne in mind that the idea of present time is secondary in the force of the tense. The time element belongs to the indicative, where the present tense is really the "imperfect of present time," while what we know as the imperfect tense is the "imperfect of past time." The progressive force of the present tense should always be considered as primary, especially with reference to the potential moods, which in the nature of the case do not need any "present punctiliar" tense. In them the aorist serves the purpose for the punctiliar tense under all circumstances, since they have no temporal significance. In the indicative the linear significance of the present may sometimes be found more or less remote, being modified by other influences. The other elements entering into the resultant import of the present tense are the meaning of the verb itself and the general significance of the context. That is, in dealing with the present tense we must consider not only the fundamental force of the tense, but also the meaning of the verb root, and the significance of the context. As affected by these three factors the present tense exhibits several variations in use.

These same three factors are to be considered in dealing with all the other tenses. Sometimes one, sometimes two, or all three, exert an influence.

Regular Uses of the Present

173. There are three varieties of the present tense in which its fundamental idea of progress is especially patent. To facilitate study we will group these together in a single class as "regular uses."

(1) *The Progressive Present.* This use is manifestly nearest the root idea of the tense. It signifies action in progress, or state in persistence, and may be represented by the graph (————). In the indicative it is related to present time, and because of possible varieties in this relation to present time it may denote three points of view.

a. The present tense may be used in a sense of *description*, to indicate that which is now going on. This use might almost be called the "pictorial present," since its distinctive force is to present to the mind a picture of the events as in process of occurrence.

αἱ λαμπάδες ἡμῶν σβέννυνται.

Our lamps are going out. Mt. 25:8.

See also: Mt. 8:25; Jn. 5:7.

b. The present approaches its kindred tense, the perfect, when used to denote the continuation of *existing results.* Here it refers to a fact which has come to be in the past, but is emphasized as a present reality, as we say, "*I learn* that you have moved" (that is, information has come to me in the past which I now possess).

ἀκούω σχίσματα ἐν ὑμῖν ὑπάρχειν.

I hear that there are divisions among you. 1 Cor. 11:18.

See also: Lk. 15:27; Gal. 1:6.

To say that this use is "present for perfect" (Gildersleeve: *Syntax,* p. 87) is not accurately representing the case. It does approach quite closely the significance of the perfect, but stresses the *continuance* of results through present time in a way which the perfect would not do, for the perfect stresses existence of results but not their continuance.

To say μανθάνω αὐτὸν ἐλθεῖν, *I learn that he has gone*, has a force which is approximated only by μεμάθηκα αὐτὸν ἐλθεῖν, *I have learned that he has gone.*

c. Sometimes the progressive present is retroactive in its application, denoting that which has begun in the past and continues into the present. For the want of a better name, we may call it the present of *duration*. This use is generally associated with an adverb of time, and may best be rendered by the English perfect.

ἀπ' ἀρχῆς μετ' ἐμοῦ ἐστέ.

Ye have been with me from the beginning. Jn. 15:27.

See also: Lk. 13:7; 2 Cor. 12:9.

Gildersleeve appropriately calls this idiom the "present of unity of time" (*op. cit.*, p. 86), and, like most of the grammarians, gives it separate classification. But it conduces to a more accurate comprehension of the construction to treat it as a special application of the progressive present. Here the present tense "gathers up past and present time into one phrase" (M. 119); or in other words, joins them into a single line, in harmony with the essential force of the present. Robertson confines the term "progressive" to this particular idiom, but resorts to this designation as "a poor name in lieu of a better one" (R. 879). The construction is hard to name, as we have confessed above, but "progressive" is too good a name to be hazarded in a doubtful situation, especially when it fits so well as a general designation for this entire class of uses, which lie nearest the "progressive" base of the tense function.

(2) *The Customary Present.* The present tense may be used to denote that which habitually occurs, or may be reasonably expected to occur. In this use the temporal element is remote, even in the indicative, since the act or state is assumed to be true in the past or future, as well as the present.

πᾶς γὰρ οἶκος κατασκευάζεται ὑπό τινος.

For every house is built by some one. Heb. 3:4.

See also: Mt. 7:17; 2 Cor. 9:7.

(3) *The Iterative Present.* The present tense may be used to describe that which recurs at successive intervals, or is conceived of in successive periods. It is sometimes called the present of repeated action.

> καθ' ἡμέραν ἀποθνήσκω.
>
> *I die daily.* 1 Cor. 15:31.
>
> See also: Rom. 8:36; 1 Cor. 11:21.

The difference between the customary and iterative present is not very pronounced. Both can be represented in the graph (......). Robertson treats them under one head as a single usage (R. 880). But a distinction there is, though not always clear. In I Cor. 11:21, ἕκαστος γὰρ τὸ ἴδιον δεῖπνον προλαμβάνει ἐν τῷ φαγεῖν, *for each takes his own supper before the other, when you eat,* the reference is not to a fixed custom, or that which is true in the nature of the case, but to an evil practice which is persistently recurring in the observance of the Lord's Supper by the Corinthian church. It is the recurrent fact which Paul wishes to represent, certainly in the hope that it may *not* become a general custom, or fixed habit. We believe there is here a distinction which deserves notice.

Special Uses of the Present

174. There are several uses of the present tense in which the root idea is not so evidently patent and which are not of so frequent occurrence as the regular uses.

(1) *The Aoristic Present.* Since the indicative has no distinctive tense for expressing the idea of a present fact without reference to progress, that is, punctiliar action in present time, the present tense must be used to perform this function. The aorist indicative is used to convey this idea with reference to past time. The aoristic present sets forth an event as now occurring.

> Αἰνέα, ἰᾶταί σε 'Ιησοῦς Χριστός.
>
> *Aeneas, Jesus Christ heals thee.* Ac. 9:34.
>
> See also: Ac. 16:18; Gal. 1:11.

"This use is a distinct departure from the prevailing use of the present tense to denote action in progress. . . . There being in the indicative no tense which represents an event as a single fact without at the same time assigning it either to the past or the future, the present is used for those instances (rare as compared with the cases of the Progressive Present) in which an action of present time is conceived of without reference to its progress" (Br. 9). The student would do well to note in this observation of Burton's a vivid fore-gleam of the basal significance of the aorist tense.

(2) *The Futuristic Present.* This use of the present tense denotes an event which has not yet occurred, but which is regarded as so certain that in thought it may be contemplated as already coming to pass.

ὁ υἱὸς τοῦ ἀνθρώπου παραδίδοται εἰς τὸ σταυρωθῆναι.

The Son of man is delivered to be crucified. Mt. 26:2.

See also: Lk. 3:9; Jn. 14:3.

While the present is thus used "in appearance for the future," it in reality retains its own temporal and essential force, being employed to denote a future action "either because it is already firmly resolved upon or because it follows because of some unalterable law" (W. 265).

(3) *The Historical Present.* The present tense is thus employed when a past event is viewed with the vividness of a present occurrence.

καὶ ὀψίας γενομένης ἔρχεται μετὰ τῶν δώδεκα.

And when it was evening he comes with the twelve. Mk. 14:17.

See also: Mt. 3:1; Jn. 1:29.

This idiom is possibly a residue from the primitive syntax of the Indo-European language, when, like the Semitic verb, time relations were indicated by the context rather than the inflectional forms. Gildersleeve thinks that it "belongs to the original stock of our family of languages" and "antedates the differentiation into imperfect and aorist" (*op. cit.,* p. 86).

(4) *The Tendential Present.* The present tense may be used of action which is purposed or attempted, though it is not actually taking place. It represents the idea of that which is intended or inclined to occur—that which tends toward realization.

διὰ ποῖον αὐτῶν ἔργον ἐμὲ λιθάζετε;

For which of these works do ye stone me? Jn. 10:32.

See also: Mt. 2:4; Gal. 5:4.

(5) *The Static Present.* The present tense may be used to represent a condition which is assumed as perpetually existing, or to be ever taken for granted as a fact.

πάντα οὕτως διαμένει ἀπ' ἀρχῆς κτίσεως.

All things remain as they were from the beginning of creation.
2 Pt. 3:4.

See also: Jn. 15:27; 1 Jn. 3:8.

While this use is rare, it is nevertheless fully significant of the genius of the tense. The idea of progress in a verb of action finds its natural counterpart in an idea of perpetual state in a verb of being. This use is practically the present of duration applied to a verb of being.

The Imperfect Tense

175. The imperfect may be regarded as a sort of auxiliary to the present tense, functioning for it in the indicative to refer its significance of continuous action to past time. This fact is exhibited even in the form of the imperfect, for it is built on the present stem. The imperfect is "a sort of moving panorama, a 'moving picture show.' . . . The aorist tells the simple story. The imperfect draws the picture. It helps you to see the course of the act. It passes before the eye the flowing stream of history" (R. 883). That is, "it dwells on the course of an event instead of merely stating its occurrence" (Goodwin: *Greek Moods*

and Tenses, p. 12). The time element is more prominent in the imperfect than in the present, owing to the fact that it is exclusively an indicative tense. Since its essential force is identical with that of the present, it follows that its uses should be practically parallel.

Webster quotes from Donaldson the following definition of the imperfect: "The imperfect denotes an incomplete action, one that is in its course, and is not yet brought to its intended accomplishment. It implies that a certain thing was going on at a specified time, but excludes the assertion that the end of the action was attained" (*Syntax and Synon. of the Gr. Test.*, p. 87).

Regular Uses of the Imperfect

176. The regular uses of the imperfect lack but little of being identical with those of the present.

(1) *The Progressive Imperfect.* The imperfect is used to denote action in progress in past time. This is manifestly the most characteristic use of the tense. The thought of process involved in the imperfect may be regarded from two points of view.

a. The process may be vividly represented as actually going on in past time. This use we may define as the progressive imperfect of *description*.

καὶ πολλοὶ πλούσιοι ἔβαλλον πολλά.

And many rich people were casting in much. Mk. 12:41.

See also: Mt. 3:6; Lk. 15:16.

b. The imperfect may contemplate the process as having gone on in past time up to the time denoted by the context, but without any necessary inference as to whether or not the process has been completed. If the writer wished to imply that the process had been completed at a given point in the past, he would normally use the pluperfect. This we may call the imperfect of *duration*. It may sometimes be associated in thought with a concurrent period of time, expressed or implied, or with a parallel event. When thus used, it might be defined as a "simultaneous imperfect." This use of the imperfect may be rendered in English in some instances by the continuous past, in others by the perfect, and in still others by the past perfect. The use of the tense cannot be determined by the English rendering: that matter is to be discerned by a close scrutiny of the context and a discriminating apprehension of the essential force of the tense.

ἐν τῷ μεταξὺ ἠρώτων αὐτὸν οἱ μαθηταί.
In the meantime his disciples had asked him. Jn. 4:31.
See also: Lk. 2:49; 1 Cor. 3:6.

We have been unable to find in the New Testament any example of the imperfect which we could adjudge as really corresponding to the present of existing state. A few instances could possibly be placed in that class, but we consider them as belonging really to the progressive imperfect of duration. The imperfect ἐφίλει in Jn. 11:36 approaches more nearly the idea of existing results than any other example we have found, but even this instance may be interpreted as an imperfect of duration. That the student who desires may go further with the investigation we will list a few additional examples of the imperfects which we regard as belonging to this class: Mt. 14:4; Lk. 23:8; Ac. 9:31; Rom. 15:22; 1 Jn. 2:7.

(2) *The Customary Imperfect.* The imperfect may be used to denote that which has regularly or ordinarily occurred in past time. Here our English expression "used to" is generally a good rendering.

καὶ ἐπηρώτων αὐτὸν οἱ ὄχλοι.
And the multitudes used to ask him questions. Lk. 3:10.
See also: Mk. 15:6; 1 Cor. 10:4.

(3) *The Iterative Imperfect.* The imperfect may be used to describe action as recurring at successive intervals in past time. The vernacular English "kept on" represents

quite well the sense. It may be graphically described by a broken line (--------------).

τὰς πρωτοκλισίας ἐξελέγοντο.

They kept on choosing out the first seats. Lk. 14:7.

See also: Jn. 19:3; Ac. 3:2.

As we observed relative to the present, the customary and iterative uses are very close together, but there is a distinction which needs to be observed in order to the most accurate interpretation.

Special Uses of the Imperfect

177. As the imperfect differs from the aorist in representing a process rather than a simple event, it also differs from the perfect in representing a process and carrying no sense of completion. Hence as a sort of negative function the imperfect fails to imply the attainment of the end toward which progress is made. That is, the imperfect represents process without attainment. Out of this negative aspect of the tense are derived three uses which are very similar, but have a difference in viewpoint which makes it best to distinguish them.

(1) *The Tendential Imperfect.* The lack of a sense of attainment in the imperfect may be emphasized to the point of a positive implication that the end was not attained, but was only attempted, or that action tended toward realization. There are quite a number of these imperfects in the New Testament, and they are one of the most commonly misinterpreted features of the tenses. The student should be carefully on the alert to note any occurrence of this use of the imperfect.

καὶ ἐκάλουν αὐτὸ Ζαχαρίαν.

And they were going to call him Zachariah. Lk. 1:59.

See also: Mt. 3:14; Ac. 7:26.

(2) *The Voluntative Imperfect.* The want of attainment in the imperfect prepares it to submit quite easily to the expression of a desire or disposition, since the statement of a wish itself implies the lack of realization. There are but a few instances of this usage in the New Testament, but adequate grammatical treatment requires that they be recognized as a distinct class.

ἐβουλόμην καὶ αὐτὸς τοῦ ἀνθρώπου ἀκοῦσαι.

Indeed, I myself have been rather wanting to hear the man.
Ac. 25:22.

See also: Rom. 9:3; Gal. 4:20; Phlm. 13.

(3) *The Inceptive Imperfect.* The force of the imperfect may revert to the opposite of realization, and signify the initiation of a process. That is, it may denote the beginning of an action, or that which is upon the point of occurring. This is well represented in our colloquial idiom when we say "one went to doing a thing."

καθίσας ἐδίδασκεν τοὺς ὄχλους.

Having sat down he went to teaching the multitudes. Lk. 5:3.

See also: Mk. 5:32; Ac. 3:8; Heb. 11:17.

i. There is no tense in the New Testament which requires and repays more care in interpretation than the imperfect. The student should get fixed in mind in the very beginning that it *is not identical* with our continuous past, by quite a wide margin. It is also important to distinguish the imperfect from the other past tenses of the Greek indicative.

ii. A splendid example of the distinction between the imperfect and aorist may be found in 1 Cor. 10:4, καὶ πάντες τὸ αὐτὸ πνευματικὸν ἔπιον πόμα, ἔπινον γὰρ ἐκ πνευματικῆς ἀκολουθούσης πέτρας, *and all drank the same spiritual drink, for they were accustomed to drink of the spiritual rock which followed them.* Here the aorist (ἔπιον) states the fact in the history of Israel, while the imperfect (ἔπινον) describes a continuous custom.

iii. It differs from the perfect in that the perfect views a process as complete, with the results remaining, while the imperfect views the process as going on, without implying anything as to its completion. Thus in Mt. 4:10 γέγραπται, *it is written*, refers to the results of a process of divine inspiration whereby the Old Testament Scriptures are in existence, while in the following verse διηκόνουν, *began ministering*, is the inceptive imperfect and refers to the initiation of a process wherein the angels were comforting Jesus after his temptation. The same distinction obtains between the imperfect and pluperfect.

The Future Tense

178. The future is primarily an indicative tense, and hence the element of time is very pronounced. It does, however, signify to a large degree the character of the verbal idea, but instead of presenting progress as the leading idea—as do the present and imperfect—the general significance is indefinite (aoristic or punctiliar). "This is due partly to the nature of the case, since all future events are more or less uncertain" (R-S. 142). The future and aorist are similar, and quite likely kindred, in form. There is evidence in the history of the Greek language that the future arose from the aorist subjunctive. Hence it is but natural that the punctiliar force of the aorist should survive in the future (M. 149). As the aorist indicative narrates an event in past time, so the future indicative expresses anticipation of an event in future time. It is this foretold occurrence of a future event which is its basal significance, and any qualifying idea is derived from the context or the nature of the verbal idea.

i. The periphrastic form of the future consisting of μέλλω with the infinitive, which we quite often meet in the New Testament is different in significance from the regular future. It is more emphatic in force, and contemplates the action as more imminent. Robertson calls it "a sort of half-way station between the futuristic present and the punctiliar future" (R. 870).

ii. Outside the indicative the future is but rarely used in the New Testament. The future optative does not occur at all—in fact, it has disappeared entirely from the Koiné Greek. The fulure infinitive is rare; the future participle more frequent, but not abundant (cf. M. 151).

(1) *The Predictive Future.* The simple, ordinary significance of the future tense is to predict an event which is expected to occur in future time. It is in this use that its aoristic or punctiliar force is most pronounced.

ἐκεῖνος ὑμᾶς διδάξει πάντα.
He will teach you all things. Jn. 14:26.
See also: Rom. 6:14; Phs. 3:21.

(2) *The Progressive Future.* Sometimes the context or nature of the verbal idea requires that the use of the future tense be construed as denoting the idea of progress in future time.

ἐν τούτῳ χαίρω · ἀλλὰ καὶ χαρήσομαι.
In this I rejoice, yea, and will continue to rejoice. Phs. 1:18.
See also: Rom. 6:2; 2 Ths. 3:4.

(3) *The Imperative Future.* The future is sometimes used in the expression of a command. Since a command necessarily involves futurity, this is a very natural idiom.

καὶ καλέσεις τὸ ὄνομα αὐτοῦ Ἰωάνην.
And thou shalt call his name John. Lk. 1:13.
See also: Mt. 1:21; Jas. 2:8.

"This idiom as it occurs in the New Testament shows clearly the influence of the Septuagint. It occurs most frequently in prohibitions, its negative being, as also commonly in classical Greek, not μή, but οὐ" (Br. 35). But we should be careful not to take this idiom as a Hebraism, for it is of frequent occurrence in Attic Greek; e.g., Euripides: *Medea,* 1320,

λὲγ' εἴ τι βούλει · χειρὶ δ' οὐ ψαύσεις ποτέ.

Say whatever you wish; you shall by no means touch my hand. Examples are plentiful (cf. Goodwin: *op. cit.,* p. 19). It is just another case where parallel idioms appear in both languages, it being, therefore, the frequency and not the fact of the idiom in the New Testament which shows Septuagint influence.

(4) *The Deliberative Future.* Questions of uncertainty are occasionally expressed by the future indicative. "Such questions may be real questions asking for information, or rhetorical questions taking the place of a direct assertion" (Br. 36).

κύριε, πρὸς τίνα ἀπελευσόμεθα;
Lord, to whom shall we go? Jn. 6:68.
See also: Rom. 3:6; 10:14.

(5) *The Gnomic Future.* The statement of a fact or performance which may be rightfully expected under normal conditions is expressed by the future tense.

ἕκαστος γὰρ τὸ ἴδιον φορτίον βαστάσει.
For each shall bear his own burden. Gal. 6:5.
See also: Rom. 5:7; Eph. 5:31.

The Aorist Tense

179. We approach now the most prevalent and most important of the Greek tenses. It is also the most peculiar to Greek idiom. The fundamental significance of the aorist is to denote action simply as occurring, without reference to its progress. It is the indefinite tense (ἀόριστος, *unlimited*). It has no essential temporal significance, its time relations being found only in the indicative, where it is used as past and hence augmented. Its true function is best seen in the potential moods, and should be carefully considered in interpretation. The aorist signifies nothing as to completeness, but simply presents the action as attained. It states the *fact* of the action or event without regard to its duration. Thus ἐποίει τοῦτο means *he was doing* or *used to do this;* πεποίηκε τοῦτο, *he has done this;* ἐπεποιήκει τοῦτο,

he had (at some given point in past time) *done this;* but
ἐποίησε τοῦτο means simply *he did this,* without implying
that the action was either durative or perfective.   It presents
the action or event as a "point," and hence is called "punctiliar."

i. The root idea of the aorist has been variously defined by Greek
grammarians. Burton says that "it represents the action denoted
by it indefinitely; i.e., simply as an event" (Br. 16). Quite similar
to this, but not so appropriate, is the definition of Gildersleeve:
"The Aorist states a past action without reference to its duration
simply as a thing attained" (*op. cit.*, p. 103). This definition presents a defect in the emphasis it gives to the time element. Much
more discriminating and accurate is the observation of Goodwin:
"The aorist indicative expresses the simple *occurrence* of an action
in past time." He refers the aorist to past time specifically in the
indicative, and then declares concerning the potential moods: "This
fundamental idea of *simple occurrence* remains the essential characteristic of the aorist through all the dependent moods, however indefinite they may be with regard to time" (*op. cit.*, p. 19). Moulton
presents a happy expression of the root idea as denoting "an event
as a *single whole,* without regarding the time taken in its accomplishment" (*Introd. to Study of N. T. Gr.,* p. 190). Robertson's
definition is quite similar. He regards the aorist as treating "the
act as a single whole irrespective of the parts of time involved"
(R. 832). Green's definition of the aorist as denoting indefinite
action is to the point (G. 296). Webster, likewise, defines the
aorist as indefinite, stating that it represents the action "as simply
acted, without any distinct statement of progress or completion"
(*op. cit.*, p. 80). The observation of Winer that it signifies "occurrence at some former time" (W. 264) applies only to the indicative.
It is strange that Blass should speak of the aorist as the tense
"which denotes completion" (Bl. 193). This definition falls into the
error of making an occasional derived significance fundamental. The
aorist denotes an action simply as an event, without in any sense
defining the manner of its occurrence.

ii. *The Aorist and Present Tense Compared.* A Greek writer in-
stinctively knew what tense to use in expressing an idea accurately.
The more one studies Greek the more this conviction grows upon him.
At times the same verb is repeated in succeeding clauses, but the tense

is changed, because the writer was acutely conscious of the distinctive force of each tense in expressing the state of an action. The play is entirely upon whether the action is punctiliar—viewed as a single whole—or whether it is the opposite, continuous or repeated. A very clear and forceful example of this striking play and interplay between the aorist and present tenses is found in Jn. 10:38: ἵνα γνῶτε καὶ γινώσκητε ὅτι ἐν ἐμοὶ ὁ πατὴρ κἀγὼ ἐν τῷ πατρί, *that you may come to know* (ingressive aorist) *and continue knowing* (progressive present) *that the Father is in me and I in the Father.* Both tenses are again used in this kind of contrast in Heb. 6:10, "For God is not unrighteous to forget your work and the love which you showed toward his name; namely, that you *ministered* (διακονήσαντες) to the saints and *continue ministering* (διακονοῦντες)." On the question of the believer's relation to sin, it is exceedingly important to observe John's use of the present and aorist tenses in his First Epistle. In 1 Jn. 2:1, he uses the aorist tense twice with the verb ἁμαρτάνειν, *to sin*, "My little children, I write these things to you ἵνα μὴ ἁμάρτητε, *in order that you won't even commit an act of sin.* And ἐάν τις ἁμάρτῃ, *if anyone does commit a sin*, we have an advocate with the Father." In 3:9 he uses the present tense with the same verb: "Everyone born of God οὐ ποιεῖ, *does not practice*, or *continue in* sin; because his seed μένει, *is abiding* in him, and he is not able to ἁμαρτάνειν, *continue in sin*, because he γεγένηται, *has been born* of God." Thus the use of tense may often, when clearly understood, illuminate passages which in the translations seem difficult.

Regular Uses of the Aorist

180. While the aorist views an action as a single whole, it may contemplate it from different angles. It may regard the action in its entirety, which we call the *constative* aorist; e.g., ἔζησεν, *he lived.* We might represent the constative aorist in a graph thus: $<\bullet>$. The action may be regarded from the viewpoint of its initiation, which we call the *ingressive* aorist; e.g., ἀπέθανεν, *he died.* The ingressive aorist might be graphically represented thus: $\bullet>$———. When the action is viewed in its results, we call it the *culminative* aorist; e.g., ἀπέκτεινεν, *he killed.* It may be indicated in the graph: ———$<\bullet$. The same verb may, in different contexts, present all three views; e.g., βαλεῖν may mean

throw (constative), or *let fly* (ingressive), or *hit* (culminative).
However, the verbal idea as well as the context usually
affects very decidedly the significance of the aorist (cf. M.
130). These modifications of the fundamental idea present
the regular uses. They appear in all four moods, and also
the infinitive and participle.

(1) *The Constative Aorist.* This use of the aorist contemplates the action in its entirety. It takes an occurrence and, regardless of its extent of duration, gathers it
into a single whole. We have here the basal, unmodified
force of the aorist tense.

> τεσσεράκοντα καὶ ἓξ ἔτεσιν οἰκοδομήθη ὁ ναὸς οὗτος.
>
> *This temple was built in forty-six years.* Jn. 2:20.
>
> See also: Mt. 8:3; Heb. 11:13.

Because of the fact that the constative aorist indicates nothing
relative to duration, this matter may be implied or expressed from
various viewpoints in the context. We may have a constative aorist
referring to a momentary action (Ac. 5:5), a fact or action extended
over a period of time (Eph. 2:4), or a succession of acts or events
(2 Cor. 11:25) (cf. Br. 19f.).

(2) *The Ingressive Aorist.* The action signified by the
aorist may be contemplated in its beginning. This use is
commonly employed with verbs which signify a state or
condition, and denote entrance into that state or condition.

> δι' ὑμᾶς ἐπτώχευσεν.
>
> *For your sakes he became poor.* 2 Cor. 8:9.
>
> See also: Ac. 15:12, 13; 19:26.

(3) *The Culminative Aorist.* The aorist is employed in
this meaning when it is wished to view an event in its entirety, but to regard it from the viewpoint of its existing
results. Here we usually find verbs which signify effort

or process, the aorist denoting the attainment of the end of such effort or process.

ἐγὼ γὰρ ἔμαθον αὐτάρκης εἶναι.

For I have learned to be content. Phs. 4:11.

See also: Lk. 1:1; Ac. 5:4.

This idiom may be best translated by the English perfect when it affects a situation present to the writer, and by the pluperfect when relatively past. "Sometimes the use of an adverb or participle helps the English" (R. 844). As in the case of the ingressive aorist, Robertson thinks that the distinctive idea in this construction belongs to the verb. He calls it the effective aorist, but does not regard this name as "particularly good" (R. 834). Blass thinks that in this use the aorist "has extended its province at the expense of the perfect" (Bl. 199), but in this observation he has in mind the perfect of his own language rather than of the Greek.

Special Uses of the Aorist

181. In addition to the three uses above, which are directly related to the root idea of the tense, there are three other uses in which the force of the aorist is rhetorically applied.

(1) *The Gnomic Aorist.* A generally accepted fact or truth may be regarded as so fixed in its certainty or axiomatic in its character that it is described by the aorist, just as though it were an actual occurrence. For this idiom we commonly employ the general present in English.

ἐν τούτῳ ἐδοξάσθη ὁ πατήρ μου.

In this is my Father glorified. Jn. 15:8.

See also: Lk. 7:35; 1 Pt. 1:24.

i. Sometimes the gnomic aorist is difficult to distinguish from the culminative aorist. For instance, the distinction is rather obscure in Rom. 3:23. It is very plausible to take ἥμαρτον as a gnomic aorist, and construe the passage as meaning, "*As a general rule all sin* and so fell short of the glory of God." This fits exactly into the present of ὑστεροῦνται. But when we consider the larger context, we find that

Paul has been discussing the fact of sin as universal in the human race, and would here stress the fact that past experience stands as evidence that all are condemned under the law, and that all, therefore, fall short of the glory of God. This idea emphasizes the reality of a fact which has taken place, hence should be construed as a culminative aorist and best rendered, *all have sinned.*

ii. A clear case of the gnomic aorist appears in Gal. 5:24, οἱ δὲ τοῦ Χριστοῦ τὴν σάρκα ἐσταύρωσαν, which may be rendered, *it is the normal disposition of those who are Christ's to crucify the flesh.* There is difference of opinion among grammarians as to whether the strict gnomic aorist occurs in the New Testament, but there are unquestionably many instances which must be classified under this head (cf. R. 836f.).

(2) *The Epistolary Aorist.* A Greek writer would some-times place himself at the viewpoint of his reader or readers, and use an aorist indicative in stating an act or event which was present or future to him.

σπουδαιοτέρως οὖν ἔπεμψα αὐτόν.

The more quickly, therefore, I am sending him. Phs. 2:28.
See also: Ac. 23:30; Col. 4:8.

"This idiom is merely a matter of standpoint. The writer looks at his letter as the recipient will" (R. 845). It is a case where the writer "puts himself in the place of his reader and describes as past that which is to himself present, but which will be past to his reader" (Br. 21). The epistolary aorist occurs in Latin, and is of very frequent occurrence in the papyri. "There is therefore no adequate reason for denying its presence in the New Testament" (R. 846).

(3) *The Dramatic Aorist.* The aorist may be used for stating a present reality with the certitude of a past event. This idiom is a device for emphasis. It is commonly used of a state which has just been realized, or a result which has just been accomplished, or is on the point of being accomplished.

νῦν ἐδοξάσθη ὁ υἱὸς τοῦ ἀνθρώπου.

Now is the Son of man glorified. Jn. 13:31.
See also: Mt. 3:17; 1 Cor. 4:18.

i. Moulton thinks that "we have probably to do here with one of the most ancient uses of the aorist" (M. 135), and Robertson agrees describing this idiom as "possibly the oldest use of the tense" (R. 841).

ii. Robertson is undoubtedly correct in his contention that the aorist can never be properly said to be "used for" other tenses. In fact, this whole practice of saying that one idiom of a language is used for another results from the projection of one's own idiom into another language. For instance, a Greek might say that our simple past is equivalent to the aorist, but that the best English writers frequently use the present-perfect for the simple past, because our present-perfect approximates the Greek aorist in certain constructions. Yet, as a matter of fact, no English writer ever uses the present-perfect for anything other than its own function. The same is true of those who used the Greek tenses. Where two or more tenses are grouped together in the same context it but proves "how keen the distinction was felt to be" (R. 838). We sometimes find the aorist and imperfect side by side, but we are not to conclude for that reason that either is used for the other. Each performs its own distinctive function. In such "juxtaposition the aorist lifts the curtain and the imperfect continues the play" (*ibid.*; cf. Mk. 12:41-44). Burton sums the matter up correctly when he observes that the possibility of confusion as to the relation of the aorist to the perfect results "from the difference between the English and Greek idiom" (Br. 24).

iii. It is well to notice particularly the difference between the aorist and present infinitive. The aorist infinitive denotes that which is eventual or particular, while the present infinitive indicates a condition or process. Thus πιστεῦσαι is to exercise faith on a given occasion, while πιστεύειν is to be a believer; δουλεῦσαι is to render a service, while δουλεύειν is to be a slave; ἁμαρτεῖν is to commit a sin, while ἁμαρτάνειν is to be a sinner. These distinctions are typical and basal, though plastic in actual usage.

iv. Robertson calls attention to the difficulty of obtaining an accurate translation of the aorist. To attempt to translate it invariably by the simple past of the English would, in the majority of cases, do violence to the real shade of meaning intended to be conveyed. We should take into consideration the significance of the tense, find its relation to the context, consider the nature of the verbal idea, decide upon the resultant meaning, and select the

English idiom which will most nearly represent that meaning. Probably in no point have translators made more blunders than they have in rendering the aorist. Moulton regards the matter as "so important that no apology is needed for an extended enquiry." He proves his sincerity in this statement by devoting six pages to a discussion of the question (M. 135–140). He gives chief attention to the relation of the aorist to the English simple past and perfect. There are also instances in which the English past-perfect best represents the aorist (cf. Mt. 22:34). No better equipment for interpretation can be secured than an adequate understanding of this tense.

The Perfect Tense

182. The perfect is the tense of complete action. Its basal significance is the progress of an act or state to a point of culmination and the existence of its finished results. That is, it views action as a finished product. Gildersleeve significantly remarks that it "looks at both ends of the action" (*op. cit.*, p. 99). It implies a process, but views that process as having reached its consummation and existing in a finished state. The point of completion is always antecedent to the time implied or stated in connection with the use of the perfect. It might be graphically represented thus: ────•──────

183. In the indicative the perfect signifies action as complete from the point of view of present time. Its exact meaning is often difficult to render, because of a blending of the sense with the English simple past. This makes the impression upon the English student that the line of distinction between aorist and perfect in Greek is not clearly marked, but the confusion arises from the effort to explain the Greek in the terms of our own idiom. It is best to assume that there is a reason for the perfect wherever it occurs.

i. It is easy, under the influence of our English idiom, to confuse the Greek aorist and perfect. But, though it is true that "the line between the aorist and perfect is not always easy to draw" (M. 141), yet it is very necessary that we always assume that the line is there, and do our best to find it. The fact is that the two tenses come very close to each other in actual usage, and in Modern Greek have practically blended, yet to suppose "that the old distinction of aorist and perfect was already obsolete" is "entirely unwarrantable" (*ibid*). The fundamental difference between the perfect and aorist is vividly illustrated in Col. 1:16. We have first the statement, ἐν αὐτῷ ἐκτίσθη τὰ πάντα, *all things were created by him*, which simply notes the *fact* that Christ was the active agent in creation, while the last clause, τὰ πάντα δι' αὐτοῦ καὶ εἰς αὐτὸν ἔκτισται, *all things through him and unto him have been created*, views the universe as a *result* of Christ's creative activity— it is a "Christ-created universe."

ii. We should certainly in fairness take it for granted that the New Testament writer intended the differentiation of meaning which is represented in this distinction, whether we are able to understand fully his reason or not. One who says that "on the whole, then, it seems necessary to admit that the distinction between aorist and perfect is beginning to be obliterated in the New Testament" (Simcox: *op. cit.*, p. 106), is too much influenced by English idiom. It is much more in keeping with a sound linguistic sense when the same writer insists that one "ought, in every case, to *look for* a reason for one tense being used rather than the other" (*ibid.*).

iii. The reason for the confusion of the Greek perfect and aorist by the English student is that these tenses in Greek are not coextensive in their use with the corresponding English tenses. The Greek aorist is much wider in range than the English simple past, while the Greek perfect is more restricted in use than the parallel English tense. An extensive and excellently discriminating discussion of this point may be found in Br. 23–30.

184. The significance of the perfect tense in presenting action as having reached its termination and existing in its finished results lies at the basis of its uses. Emphasis, as indicated by the context or the meaning of the verb root, may be on either the completion of the action or on its finished results. This possible difference in emphasis lies at the basis of the variation in the uses of the perfect tense.

(1) *The Intensive Perfect.* It is most in keeping with the basal significance of the tense to place emphasis upon the existing results, for it is distinctively the tense of the "finished product." When special attention is thus directed to the results of the action, stress upon the existing fact is intensified. This is the emphatic method in Greek of presenting a fact or condition. It is the strong way of saying that a thing *is.* There is no exact equivalent of this idiom in English, consequently there is no way to give it an exact translation. Usually its closest approximation is the English present, but it is important to bear in mind that it is not a mere duplicate of the Greek present. It presents an existing fact more forcibly than either the Greek or English present could possibly do.

> ὁ δὲ διακρινόμενος ἐὰν φάγῃ κατακέκριται.
> *But he who doubts is condemned if he eat.* Rom. 14:23.

i. When fully rendered into English the meaning of this passage is, *but he who doubts has already been condemned, and is then in a state of condemnation if he eat.* And even this circumlocution fails adequately to render the Greek, for it loses the conciseness and pointed emphasis of the original—it spreads the emphasis out, so to speak (see also: Lk. 24:46; Jas. 1:6).

ii. Burton calls this use the "Perfect of Existing State," and says that to it "are to be assigned those instances in which the past is practically dropped from thought, and the attention turned wholly to the existing state" (Br. 38). Burton then employs the term "intensive perfect" in listing a few special verbs the meaning of which yields naturally to this use, but he makes the separate classification with expressed hesitation, and we share in his doubt of its propriety.

(2) *The Consummative Perfect.* The other element in the dual significance of the perfect tense is completed action. In the use of the perfect this is sometimes the phase which is emphasized. Here it is not an existing state, but a consummated process which is presented. However, we are not to suppose that the existing result is entirely

out of sight, for "the writer had in mind both the past act and the present result" (Br. 38). Otherwise he would have used the aorist, which in the culminative sense denotes completed action without reference to existing results. In the consummative perfect it is not merely the process which is denoted, but a consummated process, and consummation implies result.

πεπληρώκατε τὴν Ἰερουσαλὴμ τῆς διδαχῆς ὑμῶν.
Ye have filled Jerusalem with your teachings. Ac. 5:28.
See also: Rom. 5:5; 2 Tim. 4:7.

Whatever difference there is between the consummative perfect and the culminative aorist consists in the reference of the former to the results of the action. The culminative aorist sees the fact that the act has been consummated; the perfect sees the existence of the consummated act. We might make a graphical distinction thus: culminative aorist, presenting the fact that the process has been completed, ──────●; consummative perfect, presenting the completed process, ──────●......... ; intensive perfect, presenting the results of the completed process, ········●_____ . These distinctions are of course theoretical, but they constitute the basis of practice as we find it in the actual text of the Greek. The English student finds difficulty here because all three of these points of view are included in the present-perfect in English.

(3) *The Iterative Perfect.* The process of which the completion is represented in the perfect may have been one of recurrent intervals rather than of continuous progress. This idiom is a perfect of repeated action, but is a true perfect, for it is the fact that the recurrent instances have established a certain result which is denoted by this use of the tense. Its stress is upon completed action, but the character of the action is iterative. It is infrequent in the New Testament.

θεὸν οὐδεὶς ἑώρακεν πώποτε.
No one has seen God at any time. Jn. 1:18.
See also: Jn. 5:37; 2 Cor. 12:17.

(4) *The Dramatic Perfect.* We have here what in former classifications of tense usage we have called a special use, but this single indirect application of the root idea of the tense would hardly justify separate classification. It is a rhetorical application of the perfect tense. Since the perfect represents an existing state, it may be used for the purpose of describing a fact in an unusually vivid and realistic way. The historical present and dramatic aorist are also used in a sense similar to this, but for this purpose the perfect is the most forcible of the three. It is like our vernacular expression when we wish to describe vividly the expedition and ease with which one does a thing, "The first thing you know, he has done it." The Greek would just say, πεποίηκε τοῦτο. Like the intensive perfect, the dramatic perfect emphasizes the results of action. In fact, it is a sort of special rhetorical use of the intensive perfect, for its emphasis is upon the existing state. The New Testament writers used this construction quite frequently.

ἀπελθὼν πέπρακεν πάντα ὅσα εἶχεν.

Having gone out he sold all that he had. Mt. 13:46.

i. This passage is found in the parable of the Pearl of Great Price, and the dramatic perfect as used here stresses the haste and eagerness with which the man sought to secure for himself the rich treasure he had found. In colloquial English we would say, "He goes out, and the first thing you know he's sold everything he has!" See also: Jn. 1:15; Rev. 5:7.

ii. It is probable that the majority of the so-called "aoristic perfects" in the New Testament may be included under this head— if not all of them. Aoristic perfects there may be, for it appears that the idiom is not unknown in earlier Greek, but the scholars are not able to agree on the matter as it affects the New Testament. It is with evident doubt that Moulton admits a bare residuum of "those which have a fair claim to be thus regarded" (M. 145), and even some of these are offered as but "tentative," and "propounded with great hesitation" (M. 238). Burton, though positively maintaining that "the perfect tense was in the New Testament sometimes an aorist in force," yet considers that the usage was "confined within narrow limits," and is found in but "a few forms" (Br. 44). Robertson admits one case (2 Cor. 2:13) as "possible but ' not quite certain," and concludes that "the New Testament writers may be guilty of this idiom, but they have not as yet been proven to be" (R. 901, 902). If there are instances of the aoristic perfect in the New Testament, and possibly there are, the idiom is to be counted as emphasis upon the punctiliar element in the perfect, rather than a use of the perfect "for the aorist." It is quite conceivable that the use of the perfect might stress the performance of an act or the initiation of a state to the extent of a preterite force, but we should regard the idea of finished result as still present, even though we are unable to translate it into English. Since the matter is involved in doubt, we do not give the aoristic perfect as a separate classification. In fact, it is our definite opinion that those so regarded in the New Testament are in reality dramatic perfects.

The Pluperfect Tense

185. Since the pluperfect is but the perfect indicative of past time, the significance and principal uses are the same. It represents action as complete and the results of the action in existence at some point in past time, the point of time being indicated by the context. The temporal force of the pluperfect is incidental, arising from its use in the indicative, but since it is used only in the indicative it never occurs without time significance. That is to say, the essential and invariable temporal reference of the pluperfect indicative arises ultimately from the mood rather than the tense.

(1) *The Intensive Pluperfect.* In the use of the pluperfect, as we saw in the perfect, the emphasis may be upon the existing results. Here stress is laid upon the reality of the fact, which enables it to be presented with more force

than could be done with the aorist, but the only device for construing it in English is the simple past.

> ἄνδρες δύο παριστήκεισαν αὐτοῖς.
> *Two men stood by them.* Ac. 1:10.
> See also: Lk. 4:41; Jn. 18:16.

(2) *The Consummative Pluperfect.* The pluperfect may represent action as a process completed in past time at some point indicated by the context.

> ἤδη γὰρ συνετέθειντο οἱ Ἰουδαῖοι.
> *For the Jews had already agreed.* Jn. 9:22.
> See also: Lk. 8:2; Ac. 9:21.

i. There is but one construction in the New Testament which we can positively conclude is an iterative pluperfect (Lk. 8:29), and this one occurrence does not justify separate treatment. The dramatic pluperfect does not occur at all, since it is the character of action which is the special point in this construction, and for this the perfect entirely serves the purpose.

ii. The future-perfect is rare in the New Testament, and its few occurrences may be interpreted in the light of the basal distinctions which exist in the perfect and pluperfect (cf. R. 906).

The Interpretation of Tense

186. Throughout the foregoing discussion we have persistently reiterated our insistence upon the student's investigating three matters in forming his conclusion as to the significance of a particular use of a tense; viz., the *basal function of the tense,* the *relation to the context,* and the *significance of the verbal idea.* It is not well to leave the consideration of tense without making this matter explicit, for upon the proper apprehension of this process is conditioned the accurate and effective use of whatever knowl-

edge of tense the student may have acquired. As an example observe Rom. 6:12, μὴ οὖν βασιλευέτω ἡ ἁμαρτία, *therefore, let not sin reign.* Here βασιλευέτω is the present active imperative, third person, singular, from βασιλεύω. (1) Note first the tense function. The present signifies continuous action. (2) As to the contextual relation, Paul is here discussing the obligation of the believer to practice pure conduct as the only life commensurate with the significance of his spiritual experience in salvation, wherein he was ushered into a new spiritual state. Hence the prohibition is against the constant domination of sin. (3) This harmonizes exactly with the significance of the verbal idea, for βασιλεύειν means primarily *to be engaged in a process of ruling,* though in the aorist it may mean *to become king.* The present tense here certainly preserves its root idea. Hence in the light of the three cardinal considerations in the exegesis of a verb we may render this passage, "Let not sin *go on reigning* in your mortal body."

i. If Paul had wanted to say here, "Do not let sin *ever reign* in your mortal body," he would normally have used the aorist subjunctive of prohibition, μὴ βασιλεύσῃ. We would, of course, avoid agitating the theological problem which smolders just under the surface here, it being our purpose only to call attention to the linguistic phenomenon. There can be no doubt that the point Paul intended to emphasize here was restraint from the constant practice of sin.

ii. The judgment of tense is one of the realms in which the gravest errors have occurred in the translation and interpretation of the New Testament. Winer is unquestionably just in bringing charge that at this point "New Testament grammarians and expositors have been guilty of the greatest mistakes" (W. 264). This statement, made a hundred years ago, would perhaps need some modification now, in view of the encouraging progress made in the understanding of the Greek tenses since Winer's day, so that "a multitude of absurdities have been removed" (Bt. 195), but certainly it is not yet wholly inapplicable.

iii. Perhaps nothing has been better preserved in Greek than the idiomatic force of the tenses. While it is going too far to say that they "are employed in the New Testament in exactly the same manner as in the Greek authors" (W. 264), yet the wealth of variety in the Greek tenses was by no means an unconscious possession of the New Testament writers. Slight changes of meaning and delicate variations are flashed back and forth in many passages (cf. Mt. 4:11; Rom. 3:23). We have no right whatever to assume that these writers were using such varieties of tense in reckless carelessness. A sufficiently close examination, with the genius of the tense in mind, will generally reveal a significant reason for each variation. Therefore, "whenever our mode of conception departs from the tense employed, it is our business to transfer ourselves to the position of the writer, and take pains in every case to apprehend the temporal relation which corresponds to the tense he used, and, if possible, to reproduce it" (Bt. 195). It should be added to Buttmann's statement that the "temporal relation" is an entirely subordinate matter, for the *aktionsart* of the tense is the preëminent consideration, and the point which the student should diligently seek to understand.

IV. THE INFINITIVE

References: R. 1051-95; R-S. 187-192; M. 202-218.

187. Intelligent expression inevitably occasions at times the naming of an action with substantival relations in a sentence. Here we have noun and verb occupying common ground. This may be sometimes expressed by an ordinary noun of action, but is more forcefully expressed by a verbal substantive. For this function the chief device of language is the infinitive, which doubtless reached its highest known stage of development and variety of usage in the Greek language.

The Origin and Nature of the Greek Infinitive

188. The infinitive is strictly a verbal noun and not a mood. Its significance in Greek can never be appreciated until this fact is recognized. No idiom is more decidedly peculiar to the language than this substantive character of the infinitive. Frequently it occurs in constructions where its idiomatic nature is so fully demonstrated that even the novice cannot fail to discern it. A splendid example may be seen in Heb. 2:15: "Who, because of the fear of death, were subjects of bondage διὰ παντὸς τοῦ ζῆν, *through all their lives.*" Here the infinitive ζῆν is accompanied by a preposition, modified by an adjective, defined by the article, and used in the genitive case: distinctive and essential characteristics of a pure noun. Though this particular example is the most elaborate infinitive construction in the New Testament, yet it is without any doubt typical Greek usage. Plato has διὰ παντὸς τοῦ εἶναι, a striking parallel to the example just cited from Hebrews. In the papyri we find ἅμα τῷ λαβεῖν, *immediately upon receipt,* where the noun characteristics are not so many as above, but quite as pronounced (*P. Tebt.*, 421). The exact translation of such a construction into English is not possible, so the student must learn to sense the force of the Greek idiom.

189. The history of the Greek infinitive shows that it was a noun in its origin. Its earliest appearance in Sanskrit is as a derivative abstract noun, usually in the dative case (Whitney: *Sansk. Gram.*, p. 203). Robertson's thorough review of the matter brings him to the conclusion: "It is then as a substantive that the infinitive makes its start" (R. 1052). Goodwin likewise assumes "that the Greek infinitive was originally developed . . . chiefly from the dative of a primitive verbal noun" (*op. cit.*, p. 297). The very form of the infinitive manifests its substantival nature, for it is a relic of declension rather than of conjugation, representing two primitive noun inflections—the dative and locative. But while these case forms are conclusively evi-

dent, they are not observed in the actual relations of the infinitive, for we find that a form which is clearly dative is used in a nominative or accusative relation (cf. R. 1057). It may be that its assumption of verbal characteristics and functions caused the Greek infinitive to lose its substantive inflection. But this obscuration of its formal significance had no effect upon its essential noun force.

190. The beginning of voice and tense in the infinitive must be consigned to the prehistoric period of the Greek language. Voice of the infinitive is not found in Sanskrit and is found in Homer; consequently it must have been after the origin of the Greek as a distinct language that the infinitive assumed voice distinctions. It is certain that voice and tense are a secondary development, and that substantive form and function are original (cf. R. 1079).

i. Robertson says of the history of the infinitive: "The story is one of the most interesting in the history of language" (R. 1056). The *primitive* Greek infinitive was nothing more than a noun in the dative or locative case, without tense or voice. Other functions later accrued to its use, but the noun force it never lost. In the *Homeric* infinitive the case significance has become very much obscured, and strict verbal elements have appeared, both as to form and function; yet it still retains some of its original case distinction, and the article is not yet used with it. In the *Attic* the infinitive reaches the zenith of its development. It has lost entirely the significance of its dative and locative case forms, but retains in full its noun force and assumes all the case functions (except vocative, if that may be called a case). In this stage we find the article with the infinitive, helping to preserve its substantive character. The *Koiné* infinitive maintains all its classical force and varieties of use, but evidences of decay appear as the period advances. In *Modern* Greek only fragments of the infinitive remain (cf. T. 116). "Outside the Pontic dialect the infinitive is dead, both anarthrous and articular, save with the auxiliary verbs" (R. 1056).

ii. Proper understanding of the Greek infinitive is conditioned upon an adequate apprehension of its dual character. As an aid to that end we will present in parallel columns a list of its noun and verb characteristics.

As a noun:
It has case relations.
It is accompanied by a preposition.
It is used as a subject.
It is used as an object.
It modifies other words.
It takes the article.
It is qualified by adjectives.

As a verb:
It has voice.
It has tense.
It takes an object.
It is qualified by adverbs.

Note that the noun characteristics are in the ascendancy.

The Articular Infinitive

191. Nothing distinguishes the noun force of the infinitive more than its use with the article. Gildersleeve says: "By the substantial loss of its dative force the infinitive became verbalized; by the assumption of the article it was substantivized again with a decided increment of its power" (*Am. Jour. of Phil.* III, p. 195). The articular infinitive was a distinctively Attic idiom, though not exclusively so, for it occurs a few times in other Greek dialects. It appears with relative frequency in the New Testament, and is there true to Attic usage (cf. M. 214). This item is one of the proofs of the general good quality of New Testament Greek, as is clear by comparison with the papyri.

192. The presence of the article with the infinitive has no fixed effect upon its varieties in use. That is, a particular use may occur with or without the article, at the option of the writer, in accordance with his desire to make the expression specific or general (see §146, iii). As to the New Testament, an apparent exception to the above statement is the infinitive with a preposition, which is always articular; but the anarthrous infinitive with a

preposition occurs elsewhere in Biblical Greek, and also in the literary Koiné (cf. Votaw: *Inf. in Bib. Gr.*, p. 5; Allen: *Inf. in Polybius, etc.*, p. 49), hence the absence of this construction from the New Testament must be regarded as incidental. A thorough canvass of the evidence leads to the conclusion that the article made no radical change in the function of the infinitive. It cannot be said, however, that it was without effect. The article influenced the infinitive at two points.

(1) *Historical Significance.* The article "did serve to restore the balance between the substantive and verbal aspects of the infinitive" (R. 1054). We have observed that the infinitive originated as a noun with dative-locative ending. In Homer the significance of this case form has faded to a bare trace, and verbal characteristics are gaining in prominence. The decided direction of development here is toward the loss of the substantive nature. But another line of development in Greek comes in just here to save the noun force of the infinitive. The article is arising from a primitive demonstrative pronoun, and assuming its function of particular designation, and its intimate connection with the substantive. But the fact that in Greek it was not confined in use exclusively to the substantive permitted it to be employed with the infinitive—along with other parts of speech. Henceforth the increase in use of the articular infinitive keeps pace with the growth of the article. There can be no reasonable doubt that this association of the infinitive with the article helped to sustain the substantive force of the infinitive.

(2) *Grammatical Significance.* In some constructions the infinitive appears more natural with the article as an indication of its distinctive case; as, for instance, when it is the object of a verb which takes the genitive (2 Cor.

1:8), or when it is used with a preposition (cf. Mk. 4:6 and Gal. 3:23).

a. The article unquestionably makes the infinitive more adaptable to use with prepositions. This, in fact, is the most prevalent use of the articular infinitive in the New Testament, there being some two hundred occurrences of it, as compared with the entire absence of such a use of the anarthrous infinitive and thirty-three telic uses of the articular infinitive—the next use in order of frequency (cf. Votaw: *op. cit.*, pp. 46, 47). When employed with prepositions, the articular infinitive conforms with regular case usage. For instance, διά with τοῦ means *through* (Heb. 2:15), while with τό it means *because* (Jas. 4:2).

b. Without the preposition we commonly find the articular infinitive in the appropriate case. The infinitive with τό is generally in harmony with the case significance of the article, occurring in nominative and accusative constructions. The infinitive with τοῦ is frequently found modifying a noun in the normal way (Heb. 5:12), or as object of a verb which regularly takes the genitive (Lk. 1:9), or ablative (Rom. 15:22). It is also employed widely in expressions of purpose, occasionally for result, and for various other constructions. It is quite a frequent construction. We find τῷ used with the infinitive without the preposition but once in the entire New Testament, and there it is the instrumental of cause (2 Cor. 2:13). The infinitive with τῷ is almost invariably accompanied by the preposition ἐν.

c. It is to be observed, however, that the conformity of the case of the article with the case relation of the infinitive is not a fixed rule. We may find, for instance, a subject infinitive accompanied by τοῦ (Ac. 27:1).

i. The parallel uses of the anarthrous and articular infinitive may be best exhibited by presenting a brief tabular view of their comparative number of occurrences in a few of the principal infinitive constructions. We get these figures from Votaw (*op. cit.*, pp. 46, 47):—

	Subject	Object	Apposi-tion	Preposi-tional Object	Purpose	Result
Anarth. Inf.....	289	1104	13	....	261	82
Artic. Inf......	27	29	5	200	33	4

ii. Prof. Votaw's work, which was prepared with extreme care by a scholar of extraordinary ability, discloses to us that the infinitive is used 2276 times in the New Testament, of which 1957 occurrences are anarthrous, and 319 articular.

The Uses of the Infinitive

193. There is no other part of speech more widely used in the New Testament than the infinitive. Its dual nature enables it to perform a large number and variety of functions. These functions may be classified under the two phases of its character, verbal and substantival. The two phases are both present in all its uses, but one is naturally more prominent than the other. It is by this comparative prominence that we determine the classification.

Verbal Uses of the Infinitive

194. Here we place those uses in which the relation of the infinitive to its context is defined chiefly by its character as a verb. That is, it functions just as would a finite verb of the appropriate mood in a dependent, or (in one use) in an independent clause.

(1) *Purpose.* The infinitive may be used to express the aim of the action denoted by the finite verb. This is a very common New Testament method for expressing purpose.

> καὶ ἤλθομεν προσκυνῆσαι αὐτῷ.
> *And we have come to worship him.* Mt. 2:2.
> See also: Mt. 5:17; Lk. 1:77.

Purpose may be expressed by the simple infinitive, the infinitive with τοῦ (Ac. 9:15), the infinitive with a preposition (εἰς, 1 Ths. 3:5; πρός, Mt. 6:1), or with ὥστε (Lk. 4:29) or ὡς (Lk. 9:52).

(2) *Result.* There are a few instances in the New Testament (eighty-six according to Votaw, *op. cit.*, pp. 46, 47) where the infinitive is clearly used to signify result. The distinction between purpose and result is far from exact, and in many constructions there is a blending of the two in which it is difficult to decide which should be regarded as the more prominent, but in quite a number of instances the significance of result is perfectly clear.

εὐοδωθήσομαι ἐλθεῖν πρὸς ὑμᾶς.
I shall be prospered to come to you. Rom. 1:10.
See also: Ac. 5:3; Rom. 7:3.

i. Result may be expressed by the simple infinitive (Col. 4:3), the infinitive with τοῦ (Ac. 18:10), and the infinitive with εἰς (Ac. 7:19). Most frequently the infinitive of result is used with ὥστε (Lk. 12:1).

ii. There are three points of view from which result may be expressed by the infinitive. It may represent *actual* result (Mk. 9:26); it may represent *conceived* result, that which follows in the nature of the case, or is assumed as a consequence (1 Cor. 13:2); it may represent *intended* result, when the result is indicated as fulfilling a deliberate aim (Lk. 20:20). The last-mentioned construction is a blending of purpose and result.

(3) *Time.* The infinitive may be used as the equivalent of a temporal clause. But "temporal relations are only vaguely expressed by the infinitive" (R. 1091). It does not have within itself any significance of time, but may derive a temporal meaning from the context and its use with a preposition or particle. Three viewpoints of time are presented by this usage in the New Testament.

a. The infinitive with πρίν or πρίν ἤ is used to express *antecedent* time.

πρὶν ἢ δὶς ἀλέκτορα φωνῆσαι.
Before the cock crow twice. Mk. 14:30.
See also: Jn. 4:49; Ac. 2:20.

b. In the locative construction with ἐν τῷ the infinitive denotes *contemporaneous* time.

καὶ ἐν τῷ σπείρειν αὐτόν.
As he was sowing. Mt. 13:4.
See also: Lk. 1:21; Ac. 9:3.

c. The infinitive with μετὰ τό is used to express *subsequent* time.

μετὰ τὸ ἐγερθῆναί με.
After I have risen. Mt. 26:32
See also: Lk. 12:5; Ac. 1:3.

(4) *Cause.* The accusative infinitive with διά is a very natural construction for the expression of cause.

εὐθέως ἐξανέτειλεν διὰ τὸ μὴ ἔχειν βάθος γῆς.
Immediately it sprang up because it had no depth of earth. Mt. 13:5.
See also: Mk. 5:4; Jas. 4:2.

There is but one instance of the articular infinitive without a preposition being used in the New Testament to express cause (2 Cor. 2:13). In this construction the infinitive is generally accompanied by διὰ τό, though once we find ἕνεκεν τοῦ (2 Cor. 7:12).

(5) *Command.* This is commonly called "the imperative infinitive." It is the only independent use of the Greek infinitive, and is not of very frequent occurrence. "It is of ancient origin, being especially frequent in Homer" (Br. 146). The construction suggests a close kinship between the infinitive and imperative. In fact, "the probability is that imperative forms like δεῖξαι . . . are infinitive in origin" (R. 943). Though this idiom is rare in the New Testament, it is a current Koiné usage, for the papyri contain many occurrences of it. Moulton thinks that its rarity in the New Testament is a "matter for surprise" (M. 180).

εἰς ὃ ἐφθάσαμεν, τῷ αὐτῷ στοιχεῖν
Whereunto we have attained, by this walk. Phs. 3:16.
See also: Rom. 12:15; Tit. 2:2.

i. An example of the imperative infinitive in patristic Greek may be found in the Didaché, 14:3: προσφέρειν μοι θυσίαν καθαράν, *offer to me a pure sacrifice.*

ii. The infinitive in indirect discourse is the practical equivalent of a clause, and may be expressed with a finite verb, for which reason it might be justly included under the present classification. But it is also to be regarded as the object of a verb of saying. It is classified by Votaw as a variety of the infinitive used as a verbal object (*op. cit.*, pp. 8f.). Hence verb force and noun force are quite evenly balanced in this construction. This use of the infinitive will come in for more prominent notice at §285.

Substantival Uses of the Infinitive

195. In some constructions the relation of the infinitive to its context exhibits more clearly its character as a noun. It performs the typical noun functions of subject, object, indirect object, instrument, apposition, and substantive modifier.

(1) *Subject.* The infinitive may function in exactly the same way that a noun would as the subject of a finite verb. We have the same usage in English; for instance, "To prevent the deed was his purpose."

τὸ γὰρ θέλειν παράκειταί μοι.

For to will is present with me. Rom. 7:18.

See also: Mt. 3:15; Eph. 5:12.

(2) *Object.* The substantive character of the infinitive enables it quite readily to serve as the object of a finite verb.

καὶ ἐζήτουν αὐτὸν κρατῆσαι.

And they sought to lay hold on him. Mk. 12:12.

See also: 2 Cor. 8:11; Phs. 2:6.

This use is generally with verbs the meaning of which adapts itself naturally to an infinitive complement. This is in line with the fundamental relationship of the object to its verb, for a substantive object is essentially the complement of the verbal idea.

We would, therefore, include under this head most of the cases of the so-called "complementary infinitive." The complementary infinitive used with nouns or adjectives is really an infinitive modifier, and close scrutiny will always disclose the case relation.

(3) *Indirect Object.* An infinitive may function as the secondary object of a verb, just as would a noun in the dative case. This use of the infinitive conveys a mild telic force, being used to express "that for which or with reference to which the action or state of the governing verb is performed or exists" (Votaw: *op. cit.*, p. 11; cf. Br. 147).

ἡ ἀδελφή μου μόνην με κατέλειπεν διακονεῖν.
My sister has been leaving me to serve alone. Lk. 10:40.
See also: Lk. 7:40; Ac. 7:42.

(4) *Instrument.* The infinitive sometimes functions as a noun in the instrumental case, "to define more closely the content of the action denoted by a previous verb or noun" (Br. 150). Burton classifies this use as a species of the infinitive of conceived result, but its essential function is that of a noun in the instrumental case.

ὁ Χριστὸς οὐχ ἑαυτὸν ἐδόξασεν γενηθῆναι ἀρχιερέα.
Christ glorified not himself by becoming a high priest. Heb. 5:5.

We have here a sort of instrumental of material, used metaphorically to describe more fully the content of the verbal idea. In Ac. 15:10, "Why tempt ye God *by putting* (ἐπιθεῖναι) a yoke upon the neck of the disciples," the infinitive phrase explains more fully what is meant by tempting God. The instrumental of cause is clear in the use of the infinitive in 2 Cor. 2:13, "I had no relief for my spirit *because of not finding* (τῷ μὴ εὑρεῖν) Titus my brother."

(5) *Apposition.* The infinitive is found in apposition with a substantive.

ὁ ἁγιασμὸς ὑμῶν ἀπέχεσθαι ἀπὸ τῆς πορνείας.
Your sanctification is to abstain from fornication. 1 Ths. 4:3.
See also: Ac. 15:28; Jas. 1:27.

(6) *Modifier.* Just as substantives may modify one another in various case relations, so an infinitive may modify a substantive. Many nouns and adjectives have a meaning which is specially adapted to an infinitive construction, such as *authority, need, ability, fitness,* etc.

a. The infinitive may modify a *noun* in a typical substantive relation.

ἔδωκεν αὐτοῖς ἐξουσίαν τέκνα θεοῦ γενέσθαι.

He gave them the right to become children of God. Jn. 1:12.

See also: Mt. 3:14; Rev. 11:18.

b. The infinitive may modify an *adjective* with a regular substantive function.

οὐκ εἰμὶ ἱκανὸς λῦσαι.

I am not worthy to loose. Mk. 1:7.

See also: 1 Cor. 7:39; 1 Pt. 1:5.

i. The substantive force of the infinitive modifier may be seen by substituting in its place a noun in the same case relation. So in Jn. 1:12 we might read, "He gave them the right of a condition as children of God"; while Mk. 1:7 may be changed to, "I am not worthy of the most humble service."

ii. A typical illustration of the idiomatic force of the Greek infinitive may be seen in Heb. 5:11, where it is used in exactly the relation of an adverbial accusative of reference: περὶ οὗ πολὺς ὑμῖν ὁ λόγος καὶ δυσερμήνευτος λέγειν, *concerning whom we have much to say and hard to be explained,* which, literally rendered, would read, *concerning whom we have an important discourse, and one hard of interpretation with reference to its statement* (cf. Gal. 5:3). A descriptive genitive may be found in Rom. 13:11: ὥρα ἤδη ὑμᾶς ἐξ ὕπνου ἐγερθῆναι, *it is high time already for you to be awakened out of sleep;* i.e., *it is already the hour of your awaking out of sleep.* An equivalent of the genitive of apposition occurs in Lk. 2:1: ἐξῆλθεν δόγμα ἀπογράφεσθαι πᾶσαν τὴν οἰκουμένην, *there went out a decree that all the world should be enrolled;* i.e., *a decree of enrollment for the whole world;* likewise in Rom. 1:28: εἰς ἀδόκιμον νοῦν, ποιεῖν τὰ μὴ καθήκοντα, *to a reprobate mind, to do those things which are not becoming;* i.e., *to a mind of unbecoming deeds.* The infinitive thus used with the force of a substantive modifier is frequent in the New Testament. It is hardly possible to emphasize too much the importance of keeping in mind the substantive character of the Greek infinitive.

V. THE PARTICIPLE

References: R. 1095–1141; R–S. 193–198; M. 220–232.

196. There are few languages which have equalled the Greek in the abundance and variety of its use of the participle, and certainly none has surpassed it. The Greek participle is found in all three of the principal tenses, and the future in addition, and in all three voices. There is a wide range in the variation of its "logical force or modal function" (Br. 163); that is, the different modes of expression in which it is employed. This wealth of significance which belonged to the Greek participle at the zenith of its development lies undiminished before the student of the New Testament, and becomes a valuable asset in interpretation when adequately comprehended. The comparatively generous use of the participle in English greatly facilitates the matter of translation. "The English participle is much like the Greek in its freedom and adaptability" (R-S. 193).

The Origin and Nature of the Participle

197. The participle, like the infinitive, is not a mood but a verbal substantive. But while the infinitive maintained itself as a noun, the participle became an adjective. It, therefore, developed inflectionally much more than the infinitive, and came to be declined as an ordinary adjective with variations in form for gender, number, and case. It took on the distinctions of voice and tense very early in its history, exhibiting these characteristics even in the Sanskrit.

i. The participle became an adjective at a very primitive stage of its development, and did not, as the infinitive, lose the significance of its inflectional form. It continued to be in form, as well as function, an adjective. The verbal characteristics of voice and tense and contextual relations, such as subject, object, etc., did not displace the adjectival elements, but were simply added to them. In Sanskrit the participle was superior to the infinitive in development. Whitney tells us that participles are found representing both voices and all the tense stems except the periphrastic future and aorist (*op. cit.*, p. 220). The earlier language had the aorist participle, but it has disappeared from the later Sanskrit. In Homer "the participle occurs as a fully developed part of speech" (R. 1098). It flourishes abundantly in the classical Greek, and is found on the increase in the literary Koiné, but was not popular in vernacular usage, as is witnessed by the papyri. Here again the New Testament as a whole inclines toward literary usage, for in it the participle is extensively used, though not so much as in the strictly literary Koiné. In Modern Greek the participial construction is fading, but still survives and is represented in active, middle, and passive voices (T. 168).

ii. The extent of participial usage in the New Testament varies with different authors, in accordance with their literary training and taste. Luke shows the greatest fondness for the participle, particularly in the book of Acts. Especially noticeable is the frequency in the New Testament of the aorist participle. This is typical Greek usage, for though the aorist participle was lost from the Sanskrit and fails to appear in the Latin, yet it is very abundant in Greek, doubtless due to the fact that Greek is an "aorist-loving language" (Broadus).

The Participle Compared With the Infinitive

198. Because of their intimate relations in nature and function it is not amiss for us to get a comprehensive view of the infinitive and participle compared. There are certain points of similarity, and just as decided points of difference. It will be noticed that the differences exceed considerably the similarities.

(1) *Similarities*. In their general character both belong to the class of verbal substantives, and may be used with or without the article. Both are indefinite in their bearing

upon the limits of action; that is, they are *infinitival* in nature.

(2) *Differences.* The infinitive is an indeclinable noun, which originally had a fixed dative-locative ending, but in historical Greek is used in all the cases, though only in the singular number. On the other hand, the participle has a pronounced adjective function, following the adjective rule of agreement with the noun, and declined in both numbers and in all the genders and cases. The substantive form of the infinitive has lost its significance, while the adjective form of the participle is fully recognized. The infinitive is ordinarily connected closely with the verb, while the participle is more intimately related to the subject or object. The participle generally contemplates action as real, while the infinitive implies the potential. For instance, in Lk. 16:3, *"to beg* I am ashamed," the infinitive ἐπαιτεῖν contemplates an undesirable possibility; while to make the statement represent an actual fact in process of occurrence, the participle would be more adaptable; e.g., ἐπαιτῶν αἰσχύνομαι, *I am ashamed because I am begging.* There is, however, a margin in which they come very near each other in function; as, for instance, in indirect discourse. But their significance in indirect discourse is not to be regarded as identical (cf. R. 1103).

An interesting point of differentiation between the infinitive and participle may be cited from a work belonging to the middle of the nineteenth century:

The use of the infinitive in dependent clauses may be thus distinguished from the use of the participle. The infinitive is used when the *real object* of the governing verb is an *act* or *state*, γνώσουσι τρέφειν τὴν γλῶσσαν ἡσυχώτεραν. The participle is used when the *real object* of the governing verb is a person or thing whose act or state is described by the participle, ὁρῶ ἄνθρωπον ἀποθνήσκοντα. The infinitive is a substantive expressing an act or state; the participle is an adjective expressing an act or state; if, then, the object of a verb is an act or state, the verb is followed by an infinitive, used like a common noun. But when the object of a verb is a person or thing, the participle agrees with the object, and expresses its act or state. (Jacob: *Greek Grammar*, §135.)

To this we may add some observations of Webster, from whose work the above quotation is adopted:

The infinitive is most frequently used as a supplement of other ideas, and especially of verbal ideas. If the idea expressed by a verb is complete, the verb denotes an independent event, or an action finished in itself. If the idea is incomplete, the verb requires a more accurate definition by way of supplement to convey the idea with perfect clearness. . . . Verbs which denote the operation of sensation require only the supplement of the object to which the feeling is directed, and by which it is excited. This is expressed by the participle. Other verbs which express an incomplete idea are supplemented by the epexegetical infinitive, expressive of object, design, purpose (*op. cit.*, p. 108).

The Classification of the Participle

199. This matter has occasioned great diversity of opinion among Greek grammarians. In observation of this fact reference may be had to such standard treatises as Hadley and Allen, Goodwin, Burton, Robertson, etc. Hadley and Allen divide participles into two classes, attributive and predicate, and subdivide the latter into circumstantial and supplementary (*op. cit.*, p. 302). Goodwin offers a threefold classification, attributive, circumstantial, and supplementary, but admits that the "distinction between the second and third of these classes is less clearly marked than that between the first and the two others" (*op. cit.*, p. 329). Burton divides them into three classes, adjective, adverbial, and substantive (Br. 163); and Robertson into two, adjectival and verbal (R. 1103f.). We propose here the twofold classification of *adjectival* and *adverbial* participles,

agreeing with Robertson that "the only way to get sym‑
metry in the treatment of the participle is to follow the
line of its double nature (adjectival and verbal) and discuss
the adjectival functions and verbal functions separately"
(R. 1104). We have tried to offer some improvement in the
direction of simplification.

The Adjectival Participle

200. In keeping with its essential character, the parti‑
ciple may be used directly to limit or qualify a noun.
This qualification may be only a general *ascription* of that
which characterizes, or a clearly marked *restriction* to cer‑
tain facts which define. We have, therefore, two uses of
the adjectival participle.

(1) *The Ascriptive Use.* In this function the participle
ascribes some fact, quality, or characteristic directly to the
substantive, or denotes the substantive as belonging to a
general class. This is its most typical use as an adjective.
It appears in the regular adjective capacities of attributive,
predicate, and substantive.

a. The participle, like the adjective, may modify the
noun in the *attributive* relation. This construction may
occur without the article.

> ἠκρίβωσεν τὸν χρόνον τοῦ φαινομένου ἀστέρος.
> *He ascertained the time of the appearing star.* Mt. 2:7.
> See also: Lk. 1:17; Ac. 10:1.

b. The participle may be used like an adjective in the
predicate, after a verb of being.

> ἤμην δὲ ἀγνοούμενος τῷ προσώπῳ ταῖς ἐκκλησίαις.
> *But I was unknown by face to the churches.* Gal. 1:22.
> See also: Lk. 1:10; Ac. 5:25.

It is important to note a distinction observed by Burton between
three possible uses of the predicate participle. It may be a sub‑

stantive participle which happens to stand in the predicate (Mk. 10:22); or it may be joined in sense to the copula in a periphrastic verb form (Lk. 5:17): or it may function as a pure predicate adjective, just as in the above example (see Br. 168).

c. When the participle is not accompanied by a noun it may function as a *substantive.* This construction may be found with or without the article. It may be used as subject, object, or modifier.

ὁ φοβούμενος αὐτὸν δεκτὸς αὐτῷ ἐστίν.

The one fearing him is acceptable to him. Ac. 10:35.

See also: Jn. 7:32; Heb. 2:9.

Here we have a construction analogous to the substantive adjective. The actor is identified in the action, rather than by a specific term of designation. This idiom also approaches the function of the infinitive.

(2) *The Restrictive Use.* The participle may denote an affirmation that distinguishes the noun which it qualifies as in some way specially defined, or marked out in its particular identity. This use approximates the function of a restrictive relative clause, and may usually be so translated in English. It is to be differentiated from the ascriptive use in that, while the ascriptive participle only assigns a quality or characteristic, the restrictive participle denotes distinctiveness.

οὗτός ἐστιν ὁ ἄρτος ὁ ἐκ τοῦ οὐρανοῦ καταβαίνων.

This is the bread which cometh down from heaven. Jn. 6:50.

See also: Mt. 10:4; Ac. 4:36.

The restrictive participle is not, strictly speaking, a different use from the ascriptive participle, but an extension in use. It is the ascriptive participle used to define in its distinctive identity the word which it modifies. Its force is discerned in the general sense and the context. If the restrictive participle denotes a fact assumed as obvious or already known, it becomes *explanatory* in function (2 Cor. 2:17). A substantive participle may be used in the restrictive sense (Mt. 10:37; Ac. 10:35).

The Adverbial Participle

201. This is the use in which the participle is involved in the relation of the noun which it modifies to the action or state expressed in the main verb, and exhibits predominant verbal characteristics. Robertson treats these uses under the head of "Verbal Aspects of the Participle" (R. 1110ff.). We have adopted Burton's terminology for this class (Br. 169ff.). Though in these uses the sense of the participle may be rendered with a clause, we cannot correctly assume that it is the syntactical equivalent of a clause, for its adjective force is retained and relates it intimately with the noun as well as the verb. It is simply an adjective used to modify a verb, and hence may be appropriately called adverbial. The varieties in adverbial use come, not from alterations in the essential function of the participle, but from variations in the relation of its noun to the main verb and the context. To indicate clearly the significance of the different uses, we translate them below with adverbial clauses, but let the student bear in mind that most frequently that does not preserve the exact significance. Most often the English participle will best render the Greek, for Greek and English are very similar in their use of this idiom.

(1) *The Telic Participle.* Purpose may be denoted by the participle; ordinarily, though not invariably, future. In Ac. 15:27 we find a present participle used to express purpose. This, however, is rare. In fact, the purpose participle is not a frequent occurrence in any form.

ἴδωμεν εἰ ἔρχεται Ἠλείας σώσων αὐτόν.

Let us see if Elijah comes to save him. Mt. 27:49.

See also: Ac. 3:26; Rom. 15:25.

(2) *The Temporal Participle.* The participle is used in

the sense of a temporal clause, where it may be translated in English by *when, after,* or *while.*

ἰδόντες δὲ τὸν ἀστέρα ἐχάρησαν.

And when they saw the star they rejoiced. Mt. 2:10.
See also: Rom. 4:10; 2 Cor. 2:13.

(3) *The Causal Participle.* The participle may denote that which is the ground of action in the main verb. Here it functions in the same general relation as a causal clause introduced by *because* or *since.*

ἐδέξαντο αὐτὸν πάντα ἑωρακότες ὅσα ἐποίησεν.

They received him because they had seen all that he did. Jn. 4:45.
See also: Mt. 3:6; 1 Tim. 4:8.

"Ὡς prefixed to a Participle of Cause implies that the action denoted by the participle is supposed, asserted, or professed by someone, usually the subject of the principal verb, to be the cause of the action of the principal verb. The speaker does not say whether the supposed or alleged cause actually exists"(Br. 170).

(4) *The Conditional Participle.* The participle may function as the protasis of a conditional sentence.

ἐξ ὧν διατηροῦντες ἑαυτοὺς εὖ πράξετε.

From which, if ye keep yourselves, ye will do well. Ac. 15:29.
See also: Lk. 3:11; Heb. 2:3.

(5) *The Concessive Participle.* The participle may denote a sense of concession, being used either with or without the concessive particle.

εἰ γὰρ ἐχθροὶ ὄντες κατηλλάγημεν τῷ θεῷ.

For if, though we were enemies, we were reconciled to God.
Rom. 5:10.
See also: Heb. 5:12; 1 Pt. 1:6.

(6) *The Instrumental Participle*. The participle may indicate the means by which the action of the main verb is accomplished.

> ἐργασίαν πολλὴν παρεῖχεν μαντευομένη.
> *She brought much gain by soothsaying.* Ac. 16:16.
> See also: Mt. 6:27; 1 Tim. 1:12.

(7) *The Modal Participle*. The participle may signify the manner in which the action of the main verb is accomplished. This use of the participle may be accompanied by ὡς.

> παραγίνεται Ἰωάνης ὁ βαπτιστὴς κηρύσσων.
> *John the Baptist appeared preaching.* Mt. 3:1.
> See also: Mt. 19:22; Lk. 1:64.

(8) *The Complementary Participle*. The participle may be used to complete the idea of action expressed in the main verb. When so used, it may modify either the subject or object of the verb and agree with it in case.

> οὐ παύομαι εὐχαριστῶν ὑπὲρ ὑμῶν.
> *I cease not giving thanks for you.* Eph. 1:16.
> See also Mt. 6:16; Heb. 5:12.

In this construction the participle approaches very near the sphere of the infinitive. The participle used in indirect discourse is a variety of the complementary participle (cf. Ac. 8:23).

(9) *The Circumstantial Participle*. A participle may not present in a distinct way any of the above functions, but may merely express an attendant circumstance—an additional fact or thought which is best rendered in English by the conjunction "and" with a finite construction. Here the English participle fails to extend its use sufficiently to take care of the entire force of the Greek participle, and at the same time it is doubtful if a separate clause is an exact

translation. It is one of those idioms which have no exact parallel in English.

ἐκεῖνοι δὲ ἐξελθόντες ἐκήρυξαν πανταχοῦ.

They went forth and preached everywhere. Mk. 16:20.

See also: Lk. 4:15; 2 Tim. 4:11.

(10) *The Participle Used as the Imperative.* Here we have a peculiarity of Koiné Greek, found in the New Testament and the papyri. Only a few examples of it, however, occur in the New Testament. Some have regarded it as a Hebraism, but its use in the papyri contradicts this view (M. 180, 222).

γυναῖκες ὑποτασσόμεναι τοῖς ἰδίοις ἀνδράσιν.

Let wives be in subjection to their own husbands. 1 Pt. 3:1.

See also: Mk. 5:23; Rom. 12:9; 1 Pt. 2:18.

i. Adjectives are also sometimes used in what appears to be an imperative construction, but doubtless in these cases the imperative of the verb *to be* is understood. In this construction it is important that the student bear in mind that the participle "is not technically either indicative, subjunctive, optative or imperative. The context must decide. In itself the participle is non-finite (non-modal) like the infinitive, though it was sometimes drawn out into the modal sphere" (R. 946).

ii. The different uses of the participle are sometimes difficult to distinguish, as, for instance, the attributive and substantive uses, or those of time, cause, and manner. The distinctions may at first seem to the student to be arbitrary in some instances, but a close examination will reveal that the differences, even when remote, are real.

The Tense of the Participle

202. Though the tense of the participle never conveys an independent expression of time, yet its relation to its context usually involves a temporal significance. That is, the

time relations of the participle do not belong to its tense, but to the sense of the context. "Time with the participle is purely relative" (R-S. 197). But as a particular tense may fit better into certain time relations of the context, we ordinarily find that tense used in such a connection in preference to other tenses (cf. Heb. 6:10). It is not to be thought that there are any regulative rules in this matter, but observation of actual practice discloses that the use of tenses in the participle took certain usual directions as to time relations. The significance of tense in the participle, as to kind of action, is the same as in the finite moods.

Time relations of the context with the participle naturally take the following three variations.

(1) *Antecedent action* relative to the main verb is ordinarily expressed by the aorist or perfect. Nevertheless, the aorist frequently expresses contemporaneous (Mt. 22:1) or subsequent action (Heb. 9:12).

τοῦ δὲ πλήθους τῶν πιστευσάντων ἦν καρδία μία.
There was unity in the multitude of those who had believed. Ac. 4:32
See also: Ac. 1:1; Mt. 28:5.

(2) *Simultaneous action* relative to the main verb is ordinarily expressed by the present.

εὐσέβεια ὠφέλιμός ἐστιν, ἐπαγγελίαν ἔχουσα ζωῆς.
Godliness is profitable, having promise of life. 1 Tim. 4:8.
See also: Jn. 11:49; Rom. 12:3.

(3) *Subsequent action* relative to the main verb is regularly expressed by the future.

Μωυσῆς μὲν πιστὸς εἰς μαρτύριον τῶν λαληθησομένων.
Moses was faithful for a testimony of the things which were to be spoken. Heb. 3:5.
See also: Jn. 6:64; 1 Cor. 15:37.

The Periphrastic Use of the Participle

203. The participle is frequently used with a finite verb to constitute a compound tense-form. This mode of expression, common to all languages, is extensively employed in Greek. It occurs in all the voices and tenses, though rare in the aorist. According to Robertson only one periphrastic aorist appears in the New Testament; viz., ἦν βληθείς in Lk. 23:19 (R. 375). Certain tense forms in Greek were expressed exclusively by the periphrastic construction; namely, the perfect middle-passive subjunctive and optative. As the finite verb, εἰμί is generally used, though also γίνομαι and ὑπάρχω, and possibly ἔχω in the perfect (cf. Lk. 14:18; 19:20) and pluperfect (Lk. 13:6). The periphrastic imperfect is the form most common in the New Testament.

This matter can, with perfect propriety, be treated under accidence, but since it is a distinct grammatical use of the participle we prefer to present it here.

(1) *The Periphrastic Present.* This form consists of the present of εἰμί with the present participle. In the present tense the periphrastic construction marks more clearly the durative force, and in view of the fact that the present has no distinctive aoristic (punctiliar) form it offers a very convenient device, which fact makes it a little strange that it is infrequent in the New Testament.

καθὼς καὶ ἐν παντὶ τῷ κόσμῳ ἐστὶν καρποφορούμενον.
Even as also in all the world it is bearing fruit. Col. 1:6.
See also: Mt. 27:33; 2 Cor. 2:17.

(2) *The Periphrastic Imperfect.* Here we have the present participle and the imperfect of εἰμί. This construction is decidedly durative in significance, but was not needed to convey this sense, since the regular imperfect was primarily durative in force, and had the aorist to take care of punctiliar action in past time. Nevertheless the periphrastic

imperfect is widely used in the New Testament, doubtless due to Aramaic influence.

καὶ ἦν διδάσκων τὸ καθ᾽ ἡμέραν ἐν τῷ ἱερῷ.
And he was teaching daily in the Temple. Lk. 19:47.
See also: Mk. 10:32; Gal. 1:22.

(3) *The Periphrastic Future.* This is formed by using the present participle with the future of εἰμί. Since the regular future was chiefly aoristic in significance, the periphrastic form was readily adaptable for expressing durative action in future time.

ἀπὸ τοῦ νῦν ἀνθρώπους ἔσῃ ζωγρῶν.
From henceforth thou shalt be catching men. Lk. 5:10.
See also: Mk. 13:25; Lk. 21:17, 24.

We sometimes find μέλλω with the infinitive in what might be termed a periphrastic future (Rom. 8:18). The infinitive with θέλω occasionally approaches the force of a "volitive future" (R. 878), but the sense of determination is likely preëminent in all the occurrences of θέλω.

(4) *The Periphrastic Perfect.* The perfect participle and the present tense of εἰμί are used in this construction. In function the periphrastic perfect is usually intensive, but there are several clear instances of a consummative force (cf. Br. 40).

εἰ δὲ καὶ ἔστιν κεκαλυμμένον τὸ εὐαγγέλιον ἡμῶν.
But even if our gospel is vailed. 2 Cor. 4:3.
See also: Lk. 20:6; Heb. 4:2.

(5) *The Periphrastic Pluperfect.* This is formed by the imperfect of εἰμί and the perfect participle. As in the case of the perfect, it is generally intensive in force, though quite a number of occurrences are consummative.

καὶ ἦν αὐτῷ κεχρηματισμένον ὑπὸ τοῦ πνεύματος τοῦ ἁγίου.
And it had been revealed to him by the Holy Spirit. Lk. 2:26.
See also: Mt. 26:43; Ac. 21:29.

(6) *The Periphrastic Future Perfect.* This form is made up of the future εἰμί and the perfect participle. It is the regular construction for the future perfect in the New Testament. Exceptions are rare and doubtful.

ἐγὼ ἔσομαι πεποιθὼς ἐπ' αὐτῷ.

I shall have believed on him. Heb. 2:13.

See also: Mt. 18:18; Lk. 12:52.

i. Grammarians see Aramaic influence in the extensive use of the periphrastic construction in the New Testament. It is noteworthy that we find so many examples of it in Luke, and especially in just those passages which were most probably based upon Aramaic sources. But it is also true that periphrastic verb forms are thoroughly Greek, for they are widely used in classical literature and in the extra-Biblical Koiné. "It is only that where Aramaic sources underlie the Greek, there is inordinate frequency of a use which Hellenistic has not conspicuously developed" (M. 226).

ii. *The Participle in Absolute Constructions.* This matter has already been treated under other heads. It is the association of a participle with a noun in the genitive and accusative cases to form clauses which are not grammatically related to the rest of the sentence (cf. §§90 (8), 96 (5)).

iii. *The Verbal Nouns.* There are in the Greek language some verbal substantives which cannot be classed as participles "inasmuch as they have no tense or voice" (R. 1095). They are the verbals in -τος and -τεος. "In the broader sense, however, these verbals are participles, since they partake of both verb and adjective. . . . The verbal in -τος goes back to the original Indo-Germanic time and had a sort of perfect passive idea" (*ibid*). But Robertson goes on to show that these verbals are not to be regarded as really having voice. Perhaps they supplied a primitive function which came to be the province of the passive voice. The passive participle in Latin seems to point to some such use. But "even in Latin a word like *tacitus* illustrates the absence of both tense and voice from the adjective in its primary use" (M. 221). If there was a primitive passive use of this form it was largely conditioned on the root meaning of the word, and disappeared from historical Greek. Thus ἄγνωστος means *not to be known*, while ἄπιστος means *not to believe:* the former passive, the latter active.

VI. THE ADVERB

Reierences: R. 544–552; R–S. 67; G. 136–139.

204. The consideration of the adverb is chiefly a lexical and etymological matter, but its exceedingly important place in the structure of the sentence in general, and in the interpretation of the New Testament in particular, claims for it definite notice in a complete survey of New Testament syntax. The treatment of it, however, may be brief, and will of necessity include etymological as well as syntactical phenomena.

The Nature of the Adverb

205. Adverbs are of great value for defining and stating a matter with exactness, as well as for stimulating the imagination by suggesting graphic, extravagantly painted pictures. Both in form and in function adverbs are closely related to adjectives. For example, καλῶς is different from the adjective καλός only in the matter of the vowel of the final syllable. And like adjectives, adverbs qualify the meaning of words. But adverbs regularly modify the meanings of verbs, adverbs, adjectives, and in rare instances substantives, while adjectives are used almost exclusively with substantives. Adverbs are used to express relationships of time, place, manner, and degree. Thus, they are used for answering such natural questions as *when, where, how, how much,* and sometimes *to what extent;* e. g., νῦν, *now;* ἐκεῖ, *there;* καλῶς, *well;* πόσον, *how much;* τῶν ὑπερλίαν ἀποστόλων, *apostles exceedingly* or *prominent apostles.*

The Scope of the Adverb

206. The term adverb is so general in its scope that it includes a wide range in grammatical usage. In a broad, non-technical sense, all prepositions, conjunctions, particles, and

interjections are adverbs. Giles has well stated, "Between adverbs and prepositions no distinct line can be drawn," and, "The preposition therefore is only an adverb specialized to define the case usage." We have already called attention to this close grammatical relationship in our discussion of prepositions. The conjunctions express adverbial ideas in relation to clauses, whereas adverbs in the narrower sense express such ideas only in relation to words. Thus ὅτε, *when*, is used to introduce a clause; but τότε, *then, at that time*, is used to specify a time relationship pertaining to a word. For example, τότε λέγει αὐτοῖς, *then he says to them;* or, οἱ τότε ἄνθρωποι, *the at that time men.* In the first example *the speaking*, while in the other *the men*, are localized in time. The particles are adverbial in their origin as well as in their usage in the main. They function, however, in a definite field of Greek usage, and so need a separate name. We shall discuss them separately in another chapter. The interjections are frequently just adverbs used in exclamation. Robertson gives the following as "adverbs used in exclamation," ἄγε, δεῦρο, δεῦτε, ἔα, ἴδε, ἰδού, οἴα, ὤ, and mentions others as possibly having similar significance.

The Formation of Adverbs

207. The most common and the simplest way to form an adverb is to take an adjective in the positive degree and in the genitive plural, and substitute *s* for *v* of the ending. The accent remains the same. For example:—

> φίλος, *lovely;* gen. pl., φίλων; adverb, φίλως.
> καλός, *noble;* gen. pl., καλῶν; adverb, καλῶς.
> πᾶς, *all;* gen. pl., πάντων; adverb, πάντως.
> ταχύς, *swift;* gen. pl., ταχέων; adverb, ταχέως.

Adverbs as to form are derived from several parts of speech. Most of them, however, are derived from the fixed case forms of nouns, pronouns, and adjectives.

(1) Adverbs derived from fixed case-forms.

a. The accusative. In the New Testament the accusative case is still used in expressing adverbial relationships. For examples turn to our discussion on the adverbial accusative. But certain words which were frequently so used came to be classed as adverbs; e.g., πέραν, *beyond;* δωρεάν, *freely;* χάριν, *for the sake of.* Adverbs were formed freely by using the neuter accusative, both singular and plural, in the positive, comparative, and even the superlative degrees; e.g., πολύ, *much;* πλησίον, *near;* μᾶλλον, *more;* ὕστερον, *afterwards;* πρῶτον, *first;* μάλιστα, *especially.* A few times the article is combined with a neuter adjective and used as an adverb; e.g., τὸ πρότερον, *formerly;* τὸ λοιπόν, *finally;* τὰ πολλά, *for the most part.*

b. The oblique cases of nouns and pronouns.

(a) The *ablative.* Robertson has registered it as his opinion that all adverbs in -ως were originally ablatives. He thinks καλῶς is from an original καλῶδ and that the ς was substituted for the δ.

(b) The *genitive.* Some of the adverbs with such endings are: αὐτοῦ, *there;* ὁμοῦ, *together;* ὅπου, ποῦ, *where;* τοῦ λοιποῦ (Gal. 6:17), *finally.*

(c) The *locative.* Not many adverbs with such endings occur. In classical Greek ποῖ is frequent, but it does not occur in the New Testament. But we do find ἐκεῖ, *there;* κύκλῳ, *around;* and πρωΐ, *early.*

(d) The *instrumental.* Since this case primarily functions in specifying manner and means, it would naturally contribute to the formation of adverbs. The iota subscript had disappeared early in Greek usage, with a few exceptions. We find the following: ἅμα, *together;* ἄνω, *up;* εἰκῆ, *vainly;* ἔξω, *without;* κρυφῇ, *secretly;* πεζῇ, *by land.*

(e) The *dative.* Grammarians are disagreed as to tracing any adverbs back to this case. Some, however, cite the following as having had such origin: πάλαι, *of old;* σπουδῇ, *zealously;* and χάμαι, *on the ground.*

(2) Adverbs formed by adding suffixes. With a few exceptions these suffixes have significance as follows:—

a. -ι, -σι, -ου denote place where; e.g., ἐκεῖ, *there;* πέρυσι, *last year;* ὅπου, *where.*

b. -θεν denotes place whence; e.g., ἐντεῦθεν, *from this place;* ἄνωθεν, *from above.*

c. -δε, -σε, denote direction whither; e.g., ἐνθάδε, *hither;* ἐκεῖσε, *thither.*

d. -τε denotes time; e.g., ὅτε, *when;* πότε, *at some time;* τότε, *then.*

e. -ως denotes manner; e.g., δικαίως, *justly;* ταχέως, *quickly.*

f. -ις, -κις, denote number; e.g., δίς, *twice;* τρίς, *thrice;* πολλάκις, *many times.*

g. The meaning of other suffixes is no longer clear; e.g., -δην, -δον, -κα, -κας, -τι, -στι.

(3) Adverbs formed from verbs. There are only a few adverbs with such derivation, and all of them were originally imperatives; e.g., ἄγε and δεῦτε, *come;* ἴδε and ἰδού, *behold;* ὄφελον, *would that.*

(4) Adverbs used as prefixes.

a. 'A- and ἀν- (from ἄνευ, *without*), like our English *un,* mean *not* or *without;* e.g., ἄ-γαμος, *un-married;* ἄ-γνωστος, *un-known;* ἀν-άξιος, *un-worthy;* ἄν-υδρος, *without water.*

b. Δυς- expresses difficulty or trouble; e.g., δυσ-βάστακος, *hard to be borne;* δυσ-νόητος, *hard to understand.*

c. Εὐ- means *well* or *good;* e.g., εὐ-γενής, *well born;* εὐ-δοκία, *good thinking* hence *good will;* εὐ-λογία, *good speech* hence *praise.*

The Comparison of Adverbs

208. The comparison of adverbs in Greek follows quite closely the methods employed in the comparison of adjectives. The matter may be presented under three heads.

TABLE OF CORRELATIVE ADVERBS

	Demonstrative	Relative	Indefinite Relative	Indefinite	Interrogative
Time	τότε, then νῦν, now	ὅτε, when ἡνίκα, when	ὅταν, whenever	ποτέ, at some time	πότε; when?
Place	αὐτοῦ, here ὧδε, here	οὗ, where	ὅπου, where	πού, somewhere	ποῦ; where?
	ἐντεῦθεν, hence ἐκεῖθεν, thence	ὅθεν, whence			πόθεν; whence?
	ἐκεῖ, thither ἐνθάδε, hither				
Manner	οὕτως, thus, so	ὡς, as, about	ὅπως, how	πώ(ς), somehow	πῶς; how?

(1) Most of the adverbs which have the endings -ως in the positive have the same endings as adjectives in the comparative and superlative degrees. That is, they have -τερον and -τατα, the neuter accusative adjective endings for the singular and plural, for the comparative and superlative.

Positive	Comparative	Superlative
ἀσφαλῶς, *safely*	ἀσφαλέστερον	ἀσφαλέστατα
δικαίως, *justly*	δικαιότερον	δικαιότατα
ἰσχυρῶς, *strongly*	ἰσχυρότερον	ἰσχυρότατα
φοβερῶς, *fearfully*	φοβερώτερον	φοβερώτατα

(2) Another group of adverbs have -τερω in the comparative and -τατω in the superlative. This is true especially of adverbs with the ending of -ω in the positive.

Positive	Comparative	Superlative
ἄνω, *up*	ἀνωτέρω	ἀνωτάτω
κάτω, *down*	κατωτέρω	κατωτάτω
πόρρω, *far*	πορρωτέρω	πορρωτάτω

(3) The other adverbs are irregular in their comparison. Many, however, end in -ον in the comparative.

Positive	Comparative	Superlative
ταχέως, *quickly*	τάχειον	τάχιστα
ἡδέως, *sweetly*	ἥδιον	ἥδιστα
ἐγγύς, *near*	ἐγγύτερον	ἔγγιστα
μάλα, *very*	μᾶλλον, *more*	μάλιστα, *most*

VII. Conjunctions

209. A conjunction is a word that connects sentences, clauses, phrases, and words. It may be a mere colorless copulative giving no additional meaning to the words preceding or following, as is true of τέ and is usually the case with καί, or it may introduce a new meaning in addition to being a connective, as is true of ἵνα and ὥστε. A correct under-

standing of the uses and meanings of Greek conjunctions
is of fundamental importance for New Testament interpretation. The turning point or direction of a thought is
usually indicated by a conjunction. The meaning of a
sentence following a conjunction, and oftentimes of a whole
paragraph, is suggested or colored by the connective. Then
also, because in Greek, as in Hebrew and Latin, but unlike
the English use, a conjunction may have several meanings,
each requiring separate and careful study.

210. Only the conjunctions that are the most difficult to understand are discussed in this chapter. These are purposely
treated in aphabetic order instead of being classified into
groups, because of their overlapping meanings. The others
are sufficiently treated in lexicons for practical purposes.

Ἀλλά

211. This is a strong adversative conjunction. It usually
has the meaning *but*, as in Mt. 5:17, οὐκ ἦλθον καταλῦσαι
ἀλλὰ πληρῶσαι, *I came not to destroy but to fulfill* (cf. Mk. 5:39;
9:22, 37). It may fittingly be translated *except* in Mk.
4:22, οὐ γάρ ἐστιν κρυπτὸν ἐὰν μὴ ἵνα φανερωθῇ, οὐδὲ ἐγένετο
ἀπόκρυφον, ἀλλ' ἵνα ἔλθῃ εἰς φανερόν, *for there is nothing
hid except that it should be made manifest, nor does it become
hidden except that it should come into manifestation.* Notice
that in the above sentence ἀλλά is translated as equivalent
to ἐὰν μή. "Then there are instances of ἀλλά = *except*" (M.
& M.: *Voc. Gr. Test.;* cf. Mt. 20:23). In Lk. 12:51 and 2
Cor. 1:13 ἀλλὰ ἤ = *except.* But ἀλλά is also clearly emphatic
in several passages. Although it is translated *yea*, this translation is not necessarily the best, even when ἀλλά is confirmatory or emphatic.

And it should be translated as emphatic several times
where it is rendered as adversative in the RV. In 1
Cor. 4:15 *certainly* fits the context very well: "For
though ye have ten thousand tutors in Christ, ye cer-

tainly do not have many fathers." It has the same significance in 1 Cor. 9:2, "If I am not an apostle to others, I most *certainly* am to you." Its emphatic force may be brought out by the words *in fact* in Ac. 19:2, "And they said to him, *In fact* we have not even heard whether there is a Holy Spirit"; likewise in Eph. 5:24, "*In fact*, as the church is subject to Christ, so also let wives be to their husbands"; also in 1 Cor. 3:3, "*In fact* not even now are ye able, for ye are still carnal" (J. R. Mantey: *Expositor* (London), vol. xxiii, p. 376; cf. Jn. 4:23; 7:27; 8:26; 1 Cor. 4:3; 2 Cor. 1:13; 3:15; Phs. 3:8).

Ἄρα

212. This conjunction is a postpositive. It is inferential or illative in function most of the time; i.e., it introduces a conclusive statement. But it seems to be more subjective and indirect than οὖν or διό. In such usages it may be translated *therefore, then, so:* Gal. 3:7, γινώσκετε ἄρα ὅτι οἱ ἐκ πίστεως, οὗτοι υἱοί εἰσιν Ἀβραάμ, *know therefore that they that are of faith, these are sons of Abraham* (cf. Rom. 7:21; 8:1; 10:17). It is uniformly translated as inferential in the RV except in a few instances when it is translated *haply, perchance,* or *perhaps.* The latter translation is really emphatic, for it emphasizes the uncertainty of the statement.

But there is abundant evidence in the New Testament and other Greek literature to establish the fact that this conjunction often has the function of an emphatic particle. And I do not believe there is any real necessity for having the circumflex accent on the word when it begins a question. For, when we give it an emphatic translation in such cases, it throws increased light on that particular sentence and fits the context exactly. Cf. Ac. 8:30, ἀρά γε γινώσκεις ἃ ἀναγινώσκεις; *do you really understand what you are reading?* Herodotus used it as emphatic, as the following sentence proves: ὡς δὲ οὐκ ἔπειθεν ἄρα τὸν ἄνδρα, δεύτερα λέγει ἡ γυνὴ τάδε, *but since she did not really persuade her husband, the woman spoke a second time as follows.* J. Bond and A. S. Walpole translate it *really* in their *Lucian Selections.* And examples from the papyri in which it is emphatic are quoted in the *Vocabulary of the Greek Testament* by Moulton and Milligan. In one of these they translate it *indeed.* Besides the examples they give, there is another in *Papyri Oxyrhynchus*, I, 113:28. In Ac. 12:18, where ἄρα is not translated at all in the RV, it certainly is not inferential, but is effective and helpful at once when considered as intensive or emphatic: "What *really* became of Peter?" There are three words which express fairly well its emphatic uses. They are *indeed, certainly,* and *really,* but the last is perhaps the best. In Mt. 18:1 we can see the value of such a translation: "Who is *really* greatest in the kingdom of Heaven?" Likewise in Lk. 12:42, "And the Lord said, Who is *really* the faithful and wise steward?" Notice particularly 1 Cor. 15:15, εἴπερ ἄρα νεκροὶ οὐκ ἐγείρονται, *if the dead are not really raised.* Other places where it may be emphatic are: Mt. 7:20; Ac. 8:22; 11:18; 2 Cor. 1:17; Heb. 12:8 (J. R. Mantey: *op. cit.* (London), vol. xxiii, pp. 377-378).

Γάρ

213. Kühner has summarized the meanings of this conjunction in the following words: "Γάρ may express: (a) a *ground* or *reason,* (b) an *explanation,* (c) a *confirmation* or *assurance;* and hence it may be translated by (a) *for,* (b) *that is, for example,* (c) *indeed, certainly*" (*Gram. of the Gr. Lang.,* p. 1186). It is a postpositive and a compound of γέ and ἄρα.

(1) It is most frequently used in the *illative* sense introducing a reason. At such times it means *for*. But this translation has been greatly overworked. The lexicons are misleading, and in the RV it is regularly translated *for* with only two exceptions, Ac. 16:36 and Rom. 15:27, where it is properly translated as emphatic. In Rom. 8:18 and in several succeeding verses it introduces reasons; cf. Mt. 1:21, "Thou shalt call his name Jesus *for he shall save his people* ⟨αὐτὸς γὰρ σώσει τὸν λαὸν αὐτοῦ⟩." A close parallel to the above is its function in some sentences where it may properly be translated by the interjectional *why*; Mt. 27:23, ὁ δὲ ἔφη τί γὰρ κακὸν ἐποίησεν, *and he said, Why, what evil thing has he done?* Jn. 9:30, ἐν τούτῳ γὰρ τὸ θαυμαστόν ἐστιν, *Why, in this is the marvel* (cf. Jn. 7:41).

(2) In the following passages the contexts imply that γάρ is *explanatory;* Mt. 9:5, "Why do you think evil in your hearts? *For instance* (γάρ), which is easier, to say, Thy sins are forgiven, etc."; Lk. 14:27, 28, "Whosoever doth not bear his own cross and come after me cannot be my disciple. *For instance* (γάρ), which of you desiring to build a tower, etc." Our word *now* represents its meaning in most passages under this category better than *for instance;* cf. 1 Cor. 11:6, 7, "But if it is a shame to a woman to be shorn, let her be veiled. *Now* (γάρ) a man ought not to have his head veiled, since he is the image and glory of God"; 1 Cor. 10:1, "*Now* I would not, brethren, have you ignorant." So also in Jn. 4:8, 44; Ac. 13:36; 18:3; 19:37; 20:16; 1 Cor. 11:19; 2 Cor. 1:12.

(3) Then there are also unmistakable uses of γάρ as an *emphatic* particle. Liddell and Scott so translate it in a question: ἀλλὰ γάρ, *but really, certainly*. Blass gives "yes, in truth," "indeed" as suggestive equivalents. The RV does not attempt to translate it in Ac. 8:31, where an emphatic word used with the optative mood expresses the utter

hopelessness the eunuch felt with reference to understanding that passage of scripture. In answer to the question whether he understood what he was reading, he responds, "How indeed (γάρ) can I except someone should guide me?" Note Ac. 16:37, "They have beaten us publicly, uncondemned, men that are Romans, and have cast us into prison; and do they now cast us out privily? No indeed! (οὐ γάρ)." Ac. 4:16, "What shall we do to these men? That a very notable miracle indeed (ὅτι μὲν γὰρ γνωστὸν σημεῖον) hath been wrought through them is manifest to all." Ac. 19:35, "Men of Ephesus, who in fact is there who does not know?" (cf. Ac. 4:34; 1 Cor. 5:3; 11:22; 2 Tim. 2:7).

Δέ

214. This is a postpositive conjunction. (1) It is commonly used as an *adversative* particle, when it is translatable *but, however, yet, on the other hand*, etc. Mt. 6:14, ἐὰν δὲ μὴ ἀφῆτε, *but if you do not forgive;* Mt. 5:22, ἐγὼ δὲ λέγω ὑμῖν, *but I say to you* (cf. also Mt. 6:6, 20, 23). (2) It is also common as a *transitional* or *continuative* particle, when it may be translated *and, moreover, then, now*, etc. It is used in this sense thirty-eight times in Matthew's genealogy (cf. Jn. 7:2, "Now (δέ) the feast of the Jews was near"; also Lk. 4:1; Rom. 3:2). (3) Closely akin to this is its *explanatory* usage. Jn. 3:19, "Now (δέ) this is the judgment; namely, that light hath come into the world"; 1 Cor. 1:12, "Now (δὲ) I say this because each one of you says, etc." (cf. Jn. 6:6; 1 Cor. 14:6; Eph. 2:4; 5:32). (4) But this particle has still another use which but very few Greek scholars have expressed; i.e., it is *emphatic* or *intensive* at times, and means the equivalent of *indeed, really, in fact*. The RV translates it *yea* in 2 Cor. 10:2. Notice its effectiveness as emphatic in Ac. 3:24, καὶ πάντες δὲ οἱ προφῆται κατήγγειλαν τὰς ἡμέρας ταύτας, *and in fact all the prophets . . . spoke of these days* (cf. Mt. 23:4; Jn. 8:16; Ac. 13:34; 1 Jn. 2:2).

Διό

215. This is the strongest inferential conjunction. It was formed by uniting a preposition with the neuter relative pronoun δι' ὅ, *on which account, wherefore*. Mt. 27:8, διὸ ἐκλήθη ὁ ἀγρὸς ἐκεῖνος Ἀγρὸς Αἵματος, *wherefore, that field was called Field of Blood* (cf. Lk. 1:35; 7:7; Rom. 1:24). It is translated *therefore*, by Moulton and Milligan (*op. cit.*) in a papyrus quotation (A. D. 108), διὸ ἐπιτελεῖτε ὡς καθήκει, *execute the deed therefore, as is fitting*. The translation *therefore* seems to fit into the meaning of some passages better than *wherefore*, but one would be a stickler for grammatical nicety to insist on one to the exclusion of the other (cf. 2 Cor. 4:13, ἐπίστευσα διὸ ἐλάλησα, *I believed, therefore I have spoken*). A synonym often used is διὰ τοῦτο (cf. Rom. 1:26; 4:16). Διόπερ is twice used (1 Cor. 8:13; 10:14) and it seems slightly stronger than διό, having the significance of *for which very reason*. Another combination is διότι with the meanings *because* and *for* (cf. Lk. 1:13; 2:7; Rom. 1:19, 21). It has stronger causal force than ὅτι.

Ἐάν

216. This is a combination of εἰ plus ἄν. When one knows the function of ἄν (see Particles), which is to indicate uncertainty or indefiniteness, he readily understands why ἐάν is used with the mood for uncertainty—the subjunctive. It introduces a hypothetical condition. Consequently, a statement introduced by ἐάν was not regarded with such certitude as one introduced by εἰ. "The difference between ἐάν and εἰ is considerably lessened in Hellenistic Greek, with the result that ἐάν is found fairly frequently with the indicative—as in Lk. 19:40; Ac. 8:31; 1 Ths. 3:8; 1 Jn. 5:15" (M. & M.: *op. cit.*). The combination εἰ ἄν is frequently spelled ἄν and means *if* just the same as when spelled ἐάν. On the other hand, ἐάν is often used as ἄν, meaning *ever*. It is found frequently with relative pronouns and adverbs, and it indicates indefiniteness or generality; e.g., Mk. 13:11, *whatever*. See further our discussion of ἄν, under Particles. Ἐὰν μή like εἰ μή may be translated *unless* (cf. 1 Cor. 14:6; Rev. 2:22). This idea of uncertainty which ἐάν implies was at times applied to time as well as to fact, and in such instances it is translatable *whenever* (cf. 1 Jn. 3:2, οἴδαμεν ὅτι ἐὰν φανερωθῇ ὅμοιοι αὐτῷ ἐσόμεθα, *we know that whenever he is manifested we shall be like him;* Jn. 8:16, καὶ ἐὰν κρίνω δὲ ἐγώ, ἡ κρίσις ἡ ἐμὴ ἀληθινή ἐστιν, *and whenever I do judge, my judgment is true;* 2 Cor. 13:3, προλέγω . . . ὅτι ἐὰν ἔλθω εἰς τὸ πάλιν οὐ φείσομαι, *I declare in advance that whenever I come again I will not spare*).

Εἰ

217. Its regular meanings are *if* (when it introduces conditions) and *whether* (when it introduces indirect questions). It is found, with only a few exceptions, with the indicative, and implies that there is likelihood that the assumption will be fulfilled, or that there is no hope of fulfillment, as in contrary to fact conditions. When εἰ introduces direct questions it should not be translated (so also with ὅτι when it introduces direct discourse; cf. Lk. 22:49, κύριε, εἰ πατάξομεν ἐν μαχαίρῃ; *Lord, shall we smite with a sword?* See also Mt. 12:10; Lk. 13:23; Ac. 1:6; 19:2). After words denoting wonder it is best translated *that;* as in Mk. 15:44, "Pilate marvelled *that* he was already dead" (cf. also 1 Jn. 3:13; Lk. 12:49). A strange and rare usage is that in which εἰ=μή (μή is substituted for εἰ in Heb. 3:18). This exceptional use of εἰ is due to the fact that the Hebrew conditional particle was also used as a negative occasionally (cf. Mk. 8:12, ἀμὴν, λέγω εἰ δοθήσεται τῇ γενεᾷ ταύτῃ σημεῖον, *verily I say, a sign shall not be given to this generation*). Septuagint examples occur in Gen. 14:23; Num. 14:28 (cf. also Heb. 3:11; 4:3).

This particle is also used in a wide range of combinations. For instance, εἴπερ (1 Cor. 8:5) and εἰ καί (Col. 2:5) mean *although*. But εἴπερ in 1 Cor. 15:15 has a different meaning: ὃν οὐκ ἤγειρεν εἴπερ ἄρα νεκροὶ οὐκ ἐγείρονται, *whom he did not raise, if indeed the dead are not really raised*. And εἰ καί may also be translated *if even* or *if also*. When these words are reversed in order, they mean *even if*. The expression εἰ μή has such meanings as *if not, unless, except* (Mk. 9:29; 1 Cor. 8:4), but in Gal. 1:7 and Rev. 21:27 it means *only*. The similar expression εἰ δὲ μή (Mk. 2:21, 22) means *otherwise*. In Ac. 27:12 and Rom. 1:10 the words εἴ πως seem to mean *if at all possible*. But a special use of εἰ with indefinite pronouns, which is not recognized in translations of the New Testament or in lexicons (Robertson discusses it on page 956), needs explanation. Εἴ τι or εἴ τις is equivalent to ὅ τι or ὅς τις (cf. Xenophon's *Anabasis*, I, 5:1; I, 6:1). Notice the improvement in the translation of Phs. 4:8, "Whatsoever things are of good report; *whatever* is excellent and *whatever* is praiseworthy, think on these things." Paul first particularizes and then generalizes. And Zacchaeus' statement in Lk. 19:8 should read, "*Whatever* I have wrongfully exacted from anyone I will repay four-fold" (cf. also Mt. 18:28; Mk. 4:23; 8:34; Rom. 13:9; 2 Cor. 2:10; 7:14).

Ἐπεί

218. This conjunction is used most frequently in a causal sense with the meanings *since* and *because* (cf. Heb. 5:2, "*Since* he also is compassed with infirmity"; Mt. 18:32, "Thou wicked servant, I forgave you all that debt *because* you besought me"; see also Mt. 21:46; 27:6). In a few sentences it has the significance of *else* or *otherwise;* as in Heb. 9:26, "*Else* must he have often suffered" (cf. also Rom.

11:6, 22). In a question in Rom. 3:6 it is suitably translated *then*, ἐπεὶ πῶς κρινεῖ ὁ θεὸς τὸν κόσμον, *how then will God judge the world?*

῍Η . . . . ἤ

219. These are called correlatives, and are translated *either . . . or* (Mt. 12:33). Sometimes only one ἤ is used (Lk. 20:4). Closely akin to these are εἴτε . . . εἴτε (1 Cor. 3:22), and ἐάν τε . . . ἐάν τε (Rom. 14:8), *whether . . . or.* The negative correlatives *neither . . . nor* occur as follows: οὐκ . . . οὐδέ (Ac. 8:21); οὐδέ . . . οὐδέ (Rev. 9:4); οὐδέ . . . οὔτε (Gal. 1:12); οὔτε . . . οὔτε (Ac. 24:12); μή . . . μηδέ (Jn. 4:15); μηδέ . . . μηδέ (Mt. 10:10); μηδέ . . . μήτε (2 Ths. 2:2); μήτε . . . μήτε (Mt. 5:35).

῍Ινα

220. Its most common occurrence is in purpose or final clauses, and it occurs regularly with the subjunctive mood, there being but few exceptions and those with the optative. Its full translation when final is *in order that*, but what we usually find is simply *that*. The negative μή may be used with ἵνα in stating a purpose negatively; as in Mt. 7:1, ἵνα μὴ κριθῆτε, *in order that you be not judged;* or the simple μή without ἵνα may be used, as in Mk. 13:36, μὴ εὕρῃ ὑμᾶς καθεύδοντας, *in order that he may not find you asleep.* Then ἵνα is also used frequently in a non-final sense in object-clauses in the New Testament. It is simply the equivalent of ὅτι scores of times. At such times the translation *that* suggests its force. It is found after verbs of caring, striving, wishing, saying, asking, etc. (cf. Mk. 7:26, καὶ ἠρώτα αὐτὸν ἵνα τὸ δαιμόνιον ἐκβάλῃ ἐκ τῆς θυγατρὸς αὐτῆς, *and she asked him that he cast the demon out of her daughter*). Or the ἵνα clause can be translated in many cases just as well by an infinitive clause; e.g., "*to cast* the demon out"

(cf. Jn. 4:47). Occasionally ἵνα introduces clauses in apposition; as in 1 Jn. 5:3, αὕτη γάρ ἐστιν ἡ ἀγάπη τοῦ θεοῦ ἵνα τὰς ἐντολὰς αὐτοῦ τηρῶμεν, *for this is the love of God,* (namely) *that we continue keeping his commandments;* Jn. 13:34, ἐντολὴν καινὴν δίδωμι ὑμῖν ἵνα ἀγαπᾶτε ἀλλήλους, *a new commandment I give to you* (namely) *that you love one another.* Again we find ἵνα used in result clauses, when it is translatable *so that,* but this usage is rare and it is a late Koiné development (cf. Jn. 9:2, "Rabbi, who sinned, this man or his parents, *so that* he was born blind?" Rev. 3:9, "Behold I will make them ἵνα ἥξουσιν καὶ προσκυνήσουσιν ἐνώπιον τῶν ποδῶν σου, *so that they will come and worship before thy feet* (see also Gal. 5:17; 1 Jn. 1:9; Rev. 9:20). We agree with Abbott-Smith's statement in his *Lexicon:* "In late writers, ecbatic, denoting result = ὥστε, *that, so that:* Rom. 11:11; 1 Cor. 7:29; 1 Ths. 5:4; al.; so with the formula referring to the fulfillment of prophecy, ἵνα πληρωθῇ; Mt. 1:22; 2:14; 4:14; Jn. 13:8; al." Again, it is used in a strange manner in Mk. 5:23 and 2 Cor. 8:7, where it approaches being inferential in function and may be appropriately translated *so.* And it may even be translated *when* in Jn. 16:32! After a special study of the idiom ἵνα τί in the LXX (cf. Ex. 2:20; 5:4, 15, 22; Ps. 10:1; Isa. 55:2) we are convinced that it simply means *why,* and it should be so translated in Mt. 9:4; Lk. 13:7; 1 Cor. 10:29, and wherever found (cf. Ps. 2:1, ἵνα τί ἐφρύαξαν ἔθνη, *why do the heathen rage?*).

Καί

221. This conjunction is by far the most common in the New Testament. Five pages selected at random from the WH text give us an average use of fourteen times to the page. It should be observed, however, that this average is raised especially by the fact that one of the pages was taken from Mark. where καί is uncommonly frequent, occurring on

an average of more than once to the line. The casual Greek student has difficulty in understanding καί because it has so many diversified uses. For it is often used as a mere mechanical connective (a copulative), and it is left for the reader to determine which possible translation best suits the context. The ordinary Hellenist, as the papyrus records reveal, had but few conjunctions in his vocabulary, and καί was the main one; but he, like the average American, knew how to make those few serve him in numerous ways.

(1) Three generally accepted classifications and meanings for καί are: as transitional or continuative—*and;* as adjunctive—*also;* and as ascensive—*even.* Since these translations are unquestioned we shall not stop to cite examples and references. But in our opinion these translations do not cover all its uses in the New Testament. There ought to be two other classifications; namely, adversative and emphatic.

(2) For its use as adversative we need but call attention to some passages where it is already translated as such in the RV by the words *and yet* (see Jn. 7:19; 16:32; 20:29). The words *however* and *but* are just as good if not better in several passages. Take for instance Ac. 7:5, "And he gave him no inheritance in it; no, not so much as to set his foot on; *but* (καί) he promised that he would give it to him in possession." See also Mk. 4:16, 17, "Who, when they have heard the word, straightway receive it with joy; *but* (καί) they have no root in themselves" (cf. Mt. 7:23; Lk. 10:24; 13:17).

(3) The emphatic use of καί is unquestionable and frequent. In proof of this contention we offer a quotation from J. R. Mantey (*op. cit.* (London), vol. xxiii, p. 381):

> Now, with reference to καί as emphatic. What grammarians call the ascensive use should, in my opinion, be widened in scope and called intensive or empha-

tic, and should be translated by several emphatic words such as *indeed, verily, really, in fact, yea, certainly*, etc., instead of by the one word *even*. The word *even* will not suit every context which is ascensive or emphatic. Why limit the translation to but one stereotyped word? Because the translators were averse to giving any other translation to καί than those current, they did not attempt to translate it a part of the time in the RV. (Neither have Grenfell and Hunt always translated it in their volumes of papyri.) For instance, in Jn. 20:30, Lk. 3:18, and Phs. 3:8, where it is used with emphatic words, it is not translated (cf. also Ac. 22:28; 27:9; 1 Cor. 12:13). But in 2 Cor. 11:1 and Phs. 4:10, in spite of that aversion, we have *indeed*, and in Mt. 10:30 we have *very*. The translators made a good beginning in these places that needs to be carried out to wider applications. In 1 Cor. 14:19 the thought is clearer when this word is considered emphatic: "Howbeit in the church I had rather speak five words with my understanding, that I might *really* (καί) instruct others, than ten thousand words in a tongue." Col. 4:4, "To speak the mystery of Christ for which *in fact* (καί) I am in bonds" (cf. 1 Ths. 2:13, 19; Phs. 4:15; Col. 3:8; Ac. 22:28), in which καί seems to have the effect of intensifying the personal pronoun (cf. also Lk. 3:9, 18; 10:29; 11:18; 2 Cor. 4:3, 10, 11).

The combination of καί γάρ has long been considered as emphatic in some of its occurrences in classical Greek as well as in the New Testament. And in M. & M., *op. cit.*, this example and translation occur: καί γάρ ἐγὼ ὅλος διαπονοῦμαι εἰ Ἑλενος χαλκοὺς ἀπόλεσεν, *I am quite upset at Helenos' loss of the money*. And in the RV these conjunctions are translated either *for indeed* or *for verily* in Ac. 19:40; 2 Cor. 3:10; 5:2, 4; 1 Ths. 3:4:

4:10. But the words *in fact* seem to suit most contexts even better (cf. also Lk. 22:37; 1 Cor. 12:13; 14:8; 2 Cor. 7:5).

Ὅτι

222. This conjunction in form is simply the neuter indefinite relative pronoun ὅ τι. (1) It is very common as a causal particle meaning *because* or *for*. In this sense it occurs in each one of the beatitudes (cf. Jn. 1:30, "After me comes a man who existed before me, ὅτι πρῶτός μου ἦν, *because he was before me*"; Lk. 6:20; Ac. 1:5). (2) Again, ὅτι is very common as a conjunction introducing an objective clause after verbs of knowing, saying, seeing, feeling, etc. (cf. Mk. 3:28, "Verily I say to you *that* (ὅτι) all things shall be forgiven, etc." (cf. Mt. 3:9; 6:32; 11:25; Lk. 2:49). (3) Then with direct discourse, just as εἰ with direct questions, ὅτι does not need translation, for it is practically equivalent to our quotation marks. Mt. 7:23, καὶ τότε ὁμολογήσω αὐτοῖς ὅτι οὐδέποτε ἔγνων ὑμᾶς, *and then I will profess unto them, I never knew you* (see also Mk. 2:16; Lk. 1:61; Jn. 1:20). (4) Professor Milligan (*op. cit.*) calls attention to two unusual uses of ὅτι: "In Mk. 9:11, 28 the AV rightly makes ὅτι=τί, *why;* for this use of ὅτι in indirect interrogation see the examples in *Field Notes*, p. 33 . . . . In 2 Cor. 5:19, al., ὡς ὅτι is taken by Blass, *Grammar*, p. 321f., as equal to Attic ὡς c. genitive absolute (Vg. *quasi*), but in papyri of late date ὡς ὅτι often means merely *that*."

Οὖν

223. Because this conjunction is treated as having only inferential meanings by the Greek New Testament lexicographers, by most Greek grammarians (Robertson excepted), and by practically all commentators, and in as much as J. R. Mantey wrote his doctor's thesis on *The Meaning of Οὖν in John's Writings*, and published the results of his findings

in the *Expositor* (London) under the title "Newly Discovered Meanings for Οὖν," we are giving an extended discussion of this word, setting forth these newly established meanings.

(1) This word occurs four hundred and ninety-six times in the WH text. It should be translated as inferential only about two hundred times, by such words as *therefore, so, consequently, then* (cf. Jn. 3:23; 4:5, 12, 33, 40). When οὖν is inferential, that inference is expressed by the main verb in the sentence and not by a verb in a subordinate clause nor by an infinitive nor a participle. It is woefully mistranslated scores of times both in the AV and the RV because it was rendered only as inferential (cf. Jn. 18:24; 20:30; Lk. 14:34; Ac. 8:25).

(2) Οὖν should be translated as *then* and *now* about one hundred and seventy times. This usage is variously termed as transitional, or continuative, or resumptive. It predominates in John's Gospel. The word *then* indicates a succession of either time or events under this classification, but it may also be used in stating a conclusion, so it properly belongs also under the classification termed inferential. The word *now* indicates the continuation of a subject from one thought to another, the introduction of a new phase of thought, or of an explanation. Under this classification οὖν is a synonym for such words as γάρ, δέ, καί, and even τότε. Following are two extracts from the papyri: (a) B. G. U. iv, 1079:6 (41 A. D.), "I sent you two letters, one by Nedymus and one by Cronius, the swordbearer. *Then* (οὖν) at last I received the letter from the Arab and I read it and was grieved." (b) B. G. U. ii, 423:11 (2c. A. D.), καλῶς μοί ἐστιν ἐρωτῶ σε οὖν, κύριέ μου πατήρ, γράψον μοι ἐπιστόλιον, *I am well. Now I beg you, my lord father, write me a little letter.* Some other references illustrating this usage in the papyri are B. G. U. i, 48:4; 73:10; 322:9; iv, 1024:7; 1078:6; 1097:8. Plato used οὖν in this sense frequently; e.g., *Phaedo,*

"After waiting so long time he came and ordered us to go in. *Now* when we went in we found Socrates already bathed."

In spite of their training and prejudice against this sort of translation the revisers translated οὖν *now* in Ac. 1:18; 1 Cor. 9:25; Heb. 7:11; 8:4; 9:1. The following quotations illustrate the advantage and fitness of such a translation: Jn. 3:24, "For John had not yet been cast into prison. *Now* there was a controversy among the disciples of John with a Jew"; Jn. 4:6, "And the well of Jacob was there. *Now* Jesus having been wearied by the journey, etc."; Jn. 4:27, 28, "Yet no man said, What seekest thou? or, Why speakest thou with her? *Then* the woman left her waterpot"; Jn. 18:23, 24, "If I have spoken evil, bear witness of the evil; but if well, why do ye strike me? *Then* Annas sent him bound to Caiaphas, the high priest (cf. also Jn. 9:17, 20, 21, 32, 38, 56; 12:1, 2, 3, 9, 17, 21, 29; Ac. 8:25; 9:19, 31; 10:29, 32).

(3) Hartung in his *Lehre von den Partikeln der Griechischen Sprache* has a classification for οὖν in some of its uses that he terms *responsive*, and he cites several examples from classical Greek to prove such a usage. In Ex. 8:10 we have a good example of this: ὁ δὲ εἶπεν, Εἰς αὔριον. εἶπεν οὖν, Ὡς εἴρηκας ἵνα ἴδῃς ὅτι οὐκ, *And he said, Tomorrow. In reply he said, As you have spoken, that you may know that there is not another except the Lord.* In the New Testament οὖν should be translated as responsive about thirty times, and all these occurrences are in John's Gospel. When it is responsive, it may fittingly be translated *in reply, in response,* or *in turn* (cf. Jn. 4:8, 9, "Jesus said to her, Give me a drink . . . . *In response* the Samaritan woman said, etc."; Jn. 4:47, 48, "He asked that he come down and heal his son. . . . *In response* Jesus said to him, etc."; Jn. 6:52, 53, "How is this one able to give us his flesh to eat? *In response* Jesus said to them, etc." (cf. also Jn. 7:6, 16, 28, 47: 8:13, 19, 25, 57; 9:10, 16, 20, 25, 26).

(4) There is extensive and convincing evidence in the papyri and much in the New Testament that οὖν was frequently used also as an emphatic or intensive particle. This discovery came as the result of studying οὖν first in postscripts. Observe P. Fay. 110:34 (A. D. 94), μὴ οὖν ἄλλως ποιήσῃς; B.G.U. iii, 824:17 (A. D. 56), μὴ οὖν ἄλλως ποιῇς; both of which may be translated, *Be sure that you do not do otherwise.* An unmistakable example of this usage is found in Brit. M. P. i. 28 (B. c. 162), "Apollonius to Sarapion his brother: greeting. καλῶς οὖν ποιήσῃς φρότισαί μοι σιτάριον, *please be sure to look after the grain for me*" (cf. also P. Tebt. i, 33; P. Oxy. ii, 281:9; 282:6; 294:14, 25; x, 12,937; xii, 1493:9). There are some unusually peculiar uses of οὖν in the papyri in which it occurs in the body of a sentence in a relative clause, and its function seems to be to intensify the indefiniteness of the pronoun, very much as ἄν does. The following examples illustrate this usage: ὃν δή ποτε οὖν τρόπον (P. Amh. ii, 86:9); ἢ ὅστις οὖν (Brit. M. P. iii, 1171:8); ὅσα ποτὲ οὖν (P. Ryl. iii, 243:9); ὅστις ποτ' οὖν (P. Par. 574:1240).

In Phs. 3:8 we have ἀλλὰ μὲν οὖν γε καί and in 1 Cor. 6:7, ἤδη μὲν οὖν ὅλως. The presence of so many particles in these places is clearly for the purpose of emphasis. There are at least three words in each example that are emphatic. What depth of feeling is here expressed! Paul's inmost soul cries out through these expressive particles. The revisers did not attempt to translate οὖν in either place. The context in each case should suggest what emphatic English word or phrase is most suitable. Some suggestive translations are *be sure, to be sure, surely, by all means, indeed, very, really, above all, certainly, in fact.* It seems to be emphatic in the following passages: Jn. 20:30, "*To be sure* Jesus also performed many other signs"; Lk. 14:34, "Salt *to be sure* is good, etc."; Rev. 3:3, "*By all means* remember how thou hast received and didst hear"; Mt. 10:32; 12:12; Lk. 14:33; 21:7; Ac. 2:33; 10:33; 25:11; Rom. 4:10; 5:9, al. The following is a quotation from Professor Milligan (*op. cit.*): "Οὖν is also used with an intensive force in exhortations, etc. . . . In drawing attention to this usage, Mantey (*Exp.* VII, xxii, p. 210f.) thinks that this emphatic sense might be given οὖν in about 65 places in the NT: e.g., Mt. 3:8, 10, '*By all means* produce fruit worthy of acceptance. . . . Every tree, *rest assured*, that does not produce good fruits. . . .'"

(5) That οὖν may also be translated as an adversative, we were led to conclude from a study chiefly of the following two extracts from the papyri: P. Oxy. 1609:12 (98–138 A. D.), "And it seems to appear there. For it is not seen on that mirror, but the reflection to the one seeing. *However* (οὖν), concerning these things mention has been made in the discussion on Timaeus." P. Tebt. ii, 315:16 (2c. A. D.), "Know that an inspector of finance in the temples has arrived and intends also to go into your district. But do not be at all disturbed, for I will deliver you. *However* (οὖν), if you really have time write up your books and come up to me." Hartung classified οὖν as an adversative particle and likened it to ὁμῶς in meaning at times. We quote Professor Milligan again (*op. cit.*): "From this is developed a slightly adversative sense in such passages as P. Tebt. 37:15 (B. C. 73), ἐγὼ οὖν περισπώμενος περὶ ἀναγκαίων γέγραφά σοι ἵνα ἱκανὸς γένῃ, *howbeit as I am occupied with urgent affairs, I have written to you, in order that you may undertake the matter* (cf. Ac. 25:4; 28:5, and Mantey *op. cit.*, p. 207f.)." It should be translated *however* in the following passages: Ac. 25:22, "For this cause the Jews seized me in the Temple and tried to kill me. *However* (οὖν), having obtained help from God, I stand even to this day witnessing to small and great"; 1 Cor. 11:20, "*However*, when ye as-

	Temporal	Causal	Purpose	Result	Inferential	Conditional	Continuative	Adversative	Explanatory	Emphatic
ἀλλά								however		certainly
ἄρα					therefore					really
ἄχρι(s)	until									
γάρ		for							now	
δέ							and, now	but	now	indeed
διό					wherefore					
διότι		because								
ἐάν						if				ever
εἰ						if				
ἐπεί	when	since				otherwise				
ἐπειδή	when	since								
ἵνα			in order that	so that			that			
καί							and	but		even
μέντοι								however		indeed
ὅπως			in order that							
ὅτε	when									
ὅτι		because					that			
οὖν					therefore		then, now	however	now	really
πλήν								nevertheless		
πρίν	before									
τε							and			
τοίνυν					therefore					
ὡς	when, as	since	in order that							
ὥστε				so that	therefore					

257

semble together, it is not possible to eat the Lord's Supper, for each one in his eating takes in advance his own supper"; Jn. 8:38, "What I have seen with the Father I speak. *However*, do you also do what you have heard from the Father?" (cf. also Mt. 10:26; Lk. 21:14; Jn. 2:22; 4:45; 6:19; 9:18; 11:6; 12:29; 18:11, 27; Rom. 2:21; 10:14; 11:1, al.) In all there are about thirty such usages in the New Testament.

VIII. PARTICLES

224. The term *particle* has undefined limits among Greek grammarians. To some it includes nearly all parts of speech except verbs, nouns, and pronouns; namely, adverbs, conjunctions, prepositions, and interjections. The word *particle* is derived from a Latin word which means a *small part*. It is a suitable word to head a classification which deals with the "odds and ends" in Greek grammar. We have chosen to limit it chiefly to those words which do not properly belong to the regular classifications, such as conjunctions, adverbs, prepositions, etc. The abundant and diversified uses of particles by the Greeks is one of the most unique and distinctive characteristics of their unparalleled language. However, in contrast with classical Greek we find comparatively few particles in the papyri and the New Testament.

225. The fact that they are seldom used makes their use all the more significant, for it is evident that each occurrence of a particle was necessary to help express the writer's ideas. In them lurk hidden meanings and delicate shades of thought that intensify and clarify the thought of the sentence. Unless one learns to understand and appreciate their significance, he will miss getting the author's full thought and fail to realize the benefit of the niceties of Greek.

The Emphatic or Intensive Particles

References: R. 1144–1154; M. 165–169, 200f.

226. The emphatic particles are inserted in the sentence either to emphasize some word in it or the thought of the sentence as a whole. And it is not always easy to decide by which word, if by any, the force of the particle should be expressed in translation. The same particle may be translated by different emphatic words in different contexts. As in the case with prepositions and conjunctions, so with particles—the context is the final court of appeal in determining the most suitable translation.

Ἀμήν

227. This particle is a transliteration of the Hebrew verbal adjective אָמֵן, *to be firm*, which is rendered ἀληθινός (Isa. 65:16) and ἀληθῶς (Jer. 35:28) in the LXX. It is used in the Gospels for introducing solemnly significant statements of our Lord in the sense of *truly, verily* (cf. Jn. 3:3, ἀμὴν ἀμὴν λέγω σοι, ἐὰν μή τις γεννηθῇ ἄνωθεν, *verily, verily I say unto you, if one is not born again, etc.*) Then it is also used to express assent to prayers or praise (cf. 1 Cor. 14:16, πῶς ἐρεῖ τὸ ἀμὴν ἐπὶ τῇ σῇ εὐχαριστίᾳ, *how will he say So be it to your giving of thanks?* Rom. 15:33, ὁ δὲ θεὸς τῆς εἰρήνης μετὰ πάντων ὑμῶν · ἀμήν, *and the God of peace be with you. So be it (amen).*

Ἄν

228. "We have no English word which corresponds to ἄν. The most that can be said is that it implies vagueness or uncertainty in the sentences where it occurs" (Nunn: *Syn. of N. T. Gr.*, p. 128). And ἐάν occurs more frequently that ἄν, but functions as the particle ἄν as well as a conditional conjunction. It is merely a matter of spelling. "Two originally connected uses are now sharply distinguished. In one, ἄν stands with the optative or indicative, and imparts to the verb a contingent meaning, depending on an *if* clause, expressed or understood, in the context. In the other the ἄν (in the NT period more often written ἐάν) has formed a close contact with a conjunction or a relative, to which it generally imparts the meaning *-soever:* of course this exaggerates the differentia in most cases" (M. 166). At any rate we term it an emphatic particle.

(1) In most of its occurrences our word *ever* suggests the force of ἄν. For instance, ὅταν, ἐπειδάν, *whenever;* ὅπου ἐάν, *wherever;* ὅς ἄν, *whoever.* Ac. 8:19, ἵνα ᾧ ἐὰν ἐπιθῶ τὰς χεῖρας, *that upon whomever I place my hands.* It is of interest that the indefinite relative clause in the New Testament is introduced but rarely by ὅστις (which in some contexts functions as an emphatic relative), but very often by ὅς ἄν or ὅς ἐάν (Mt. 11:6; Mk. 10:43). In Mt. 12:50 and Gal. 5:10 ἄν is used with ὅστις to intensify, apparently, the generalization.

(2) Since ἄν implies vagueness and uncertainty it is very fitting that it should be used with the subjunctive and optative moods, which affirm things with varying degrees of uncertainty; and its use is also significant with the indicative in contrary to fact conditions, because they deal with obvious unrealities.

Γέ

229. It emphasizes usually the word with which it is used and may be translated *at least, indeed, even, in fact* (cf. Rom. 8:32, ὅς γε τοῦ ἰδίου οὐκ ἐφείσατο, *who in fact did not spare his own son*). It is found most frequently with other emphatic particles, such as ἀλλά, ἄρα, δέ. A good example is found in Mt. 7:20, ἄρα γε ἀπὸ τῶν καρπῶν αὐτῶν ἐπιγνώσεσθε αὐτούς, *you shall really know them by their fruits.* When it is used with ἀλλά, it expresses strong emphasis: *yea even.*

Δή

230. Robertson says aptly concerning this particle: "It is climacteric and indicates that the point is now at last clear and may be assumed as true" (R. 1149). It is used only seven times in the New Testament. In Lk. 2:15; Ac. 6:3; 13:2; 15:36; and 1 Cor. 6:20 the emphatic phrase *by all means* suggests its force. In Mt. 13:23 and Heb. 2:16 it means *really* (cf. Mt. 13:23, *Who really bears fruit;* i.e., is a genuine Christian).

Εἰ μήν

231. This expression is very rare in the New Testament. In Heb. 6:14 its emphatic meaning stands out clearly, "*Assuredly* (or *Above all*) blessing I will bless thee."

Μέν

232. Its most common usage is to help differentiate the word or clause with which it occurs from that which follows (cf. Mt. 3:11, ἐγὼ μέν . . . ὁ δέ, *I in fact . . . but he;* Lk. 3:16, ὃς μέν . . . ὃς δέ, *one . . . another*). When it is used with the article, the expression may be translated as a pronoun; (cf. Jn. 7:12, οἱ μὲν ἔλεγον, *some were saying—* just as ὁ δέ may be translated *he*). At other times it is purely emphatic, but is usually associated with other emphatic particles when it is (cf. Ac. 4:16, ὅτι μὲν γὰρ γνωστὸν σημεῖον, *that a really notable miracle;* see also Ac. 9:31; Rom. 1:8; 3:2; Phs. 3:8). At such times the translation *in fact* is about as good as any. In Lk. 11:28, where it is used with οὖν, the expression contains both contrast and emphasis, with the significance of *in fact, rather*. Μέντοι, as often in the papyri, is emphatic in Jas. 2:8 and Jude 8, ὁμοίως μέντοι καὶ οὗτοι, *likewise these also in fact;* but it seems adversative in the other passages.

Νή, ναί

233. The former is used only in 1 Cor. 15:31 in its characteristic and exclusive use, which is only in oaths, νὴ τὴν ὑμέτεραν καύχησιν, *I affirm by your boasting.* The following extracts from the papyri illustrate its use effectively: P. Par. 49:30 (164–158 B. C.) ἐγὼ γὰρ νὴ τοὺς θεοὺς ἀγωνιῶ, μήποτε ἀρρωστεῖ τὸ παιδάριον, *for I swear by the gods that I am worrying lest the lad is not well;* P. Oxy. vi, 939:20 (4c. A. D.), νὴ γὰρ τὴν σὴν σωτηρίαν, κύριέ μου, ἧς μάλιστά μοι μέλει, *for I swear by your salvation, my lord, which is of special care to me.*

234. Ναί is a strong emphatic particle, confirmatory of a preceding statement, with the significance of our *yes* or *yea* (cf. Mt. 13:51, λέγουσιν αὐτῷ, ναί, *they say to him, Yes;* Jn. 11:27, λέγει αὐτῷ, ναὶ κύριε, *he says to him, Yes, Lord;* see also 2 Cor. 1:17, 18, 19, 20).

Πέρ

235. According to the WH text, this particle does not occur except as a part of another word. It emphasizes the meaning of the word to which it is affixed, and has such meanings as *indeed, really, completely,* etc. (cf. Rom. 8:17, εἴπερ συνπάσχομεν, *if we really suffer together;* see also Heb. 3:14; 5:4, 8).

Ποτέ

236. This is an enclitic particle which occurs frequently. (1) In several passages our word *ever* suggests its force better than any other word (cf. Heb. 1:5, τίνι γὰρ εἶπέν ποτε τῶν ἀγγέλων, *for to whom of the angels did he ever say, etc.?* Eph. 5:29, οὐδεὶς γάρ ποτε τὴν ἑαυτοῦ σάρκα ἐμίσησεν, *for no one ever hated his own flesh;* see also 2 Pt. 1:10, 21). (2) It is often used with temporal significance and may be translated *at that time* (notice the relationship to the interrogative particle πότε, *at what time?*), *at length, once, formerly*

(cf. Eph. 2:2, ἐν αἷς ποτε περιεπατήσατε, *in which you at that time walked;* Phs. 4:10, ὅτι ἤδη ποτὲ ἀνεθάλετε τὸ ὑπὲρ ἐμοῦ φρονεῖν, *that now at length you have revived your thinking about me;* see also Eph. 2:3, 11, 13; Lk. 22:32).

Πού, πώς

237. These are also enclitic, emphatic particles, but are rarely used in the New Testament. The former may be translated *somehow* and *about* in Ac. 27:29 and Rom. 4:19. It seems to mean *at all* in Heb. 2:16. Πώς is translatable *by any means* in Rom. 11:14. It is so translated in Xenophon's *Anabasis* by Goodwin and White (ii, 5:2).

Τοί

238. This particle does not occur except as affixed to another word and is clearly emphatic in function, but it is rather difficult to translate that emphasis (cf. Jas. 2:8).

The Negative Particles

References: R. 1155-1175; M. 169-171, 187-194.

239. There are two chief negative particles in Greek, οὐ and μή. The distinction between them is real and clear, but it has not always been observed. Modifications in use came with the advancing history of the language. Very much modified in form and function, and reinforced by the addition of δέ (ν), these negatives persist in Modern Greek (T. 199f.). It is not to be questioned, however, that they had in the Koiné period a pronounced distinction, and that the New Testament writers were aware of this distinction.

Οὐ

240. This negative particle is spelled οὐ before words beginning with consonants, οὐκ before words beginning

with vowels which have a smooth breathing, οὐχ before words beginning with vowels which have a rough breathing.

(1) Οὐ is the particle used in *summary negation*. It is the stronger of the two negatives, and "the proper negative for the statement of a downright fact" (M. 232). "Οὐ denies the reality of an alleged fact. It is the clear-cut, point-blank negative, objective, final" (R. 1156). When John the Baptist was asked if he was "the prophet" he simply replied, οὔ (see Jn. 1:21, ὁ προφήτης εἶ σύ; καὶ ἀπεκρίθη· οὔ). Since οὐ is the stronger negative we would naturally expect to find it used most frequently with the indicative mood, which is the mood for stating facts positively and forcefully. And this is the case. But Blass has overstated the facts in attempting to bring the differences between οὐ and μή under a single rule. "All instances." he states, "may practically be brought under the single rule, that οὐ negatives the indicative, μή, the other modes, including the infinitive and participle" (B. 253). That is true of the majority of uses, but there are numerous exceptions. Whenever a Greek wanted to make a denial or state a prohibition emphatically, he was not fenced in by grammatical conventions from using οὐ with any of the moods. He simply used whatever mood best expressed the idea he had in mind and accompanied it with the proper negative. Οὐ is found with the subjunctive (1 Pt. 3:3), the infinitive (Heb. 7:11), and with the participle (Jn. 10:12), but its predominant use is with the indicative. "In addition to its regular use with the indicative οὐ is frequently found in the papyri with the participle, apparently for the reason that it is the proper negative for a statement of fact" (Milligan in *Voc. Gr. Test.*; cf. P. Oxy. iv, 726:10 (A. D. 135): οὐ δυνάμενος δι' ἀσθενείαν πλεῦσαι, *since he is unable on account of sickness to make the voyage*).

(2) When οὐ (or οὐχί) is used in a *question* its use always implies that the expected answer is "yes." In this regard

it is the equivalent of the Latin *nonne* (cf. Mt. 13:55, οὐχ οὗτός ἐστιν ὁ τοῦ τέκτονος υἱός; οὐχ ἡ μήτηρ αὐτοῦ λέγεται Μαριάμ, *this is the carpenter's son, is it not? His mother is called Mary, is she not?*

Μή

241. This is the weaker, milder negative, denying subjectively and with hesitancy. "In a word, μή is just the negative to use when one does not wish to be too positive. Μή leaves the question open for further remarks or entreaty. Οὐ closes the door abruptly" (R. 1156).

(1) Then μή is the particle of *qualified negation*. Since the subjunctive and optative moods imply uncertainty, it is but natural that μή, which denies hypothetically and with reserve, should predominate with these moods. It also predominates with imperatives, infinitives, and participles, but it is used sparingly with the indicative. The student should remember that this is true not because of any fixed rule, but due to the fact of the inherent meaning of the moods and the negatives.

Professor Milligan (*op. cit.*) summarizes the occurrences of μή with the indicative in the papyri thus: "(a) in relative clauses . . . (b) in cautious assertions (as in Lk. 11:35; Gal. 4:11; Col. 2:18)."

(2) In *questions* μή (or μήτι) implies that the expected answer is "no." Notice how Judas asked the memorable question, μήτι ἐγώ εἰμι; *It is not I, is it?* (Mt. 26:25). The difference in meaning in questions between the two negatives is clearly apparent in Lk. 6:39, μήτι δύναται τυφλὸς τυφλὸν ὁδηγεῖν; οὐχὶ ἀμφότερος εἰς βόθυνον ἐμπεσοῦνται; *a blind man is not able to guide a blind man, is he? They will both fall into a ditch, will they not?* (cf. Mk. 4:21; Jn. 4:29.)

The differences between these negatives in other sentences besides the interrogative may be summarized as follows: "The general distinction between οὐ and μή is that οὐ is *objective*, dealing only with facts, while μή is *subjective*, involving will and thought. . . . In the NT οὐ is almost entirely confined to the indicative, while μή monopolises the other moods" (*Voc. Gr. Test.*) Or, according to Dr. C. B. Williams (Union University, Jackson, Tenn.), "Οὐ expresses a definite, emphatic negation; μή an indefinite, doubtful negation. If a negation was to be asserted unequivocally, οὐ was always used; if hypothetically, μή was invariably used" (unpublished *Grammar Notes*). An illuminating comment may be quoted from Webster: "Οὐ conveys a direct and absolute denial; μή conveys a subjective and conditional denial. In a conditional proposition, μή belongs to the protasis, οὐ to the apodosis. Μή negatives a supposition; it prohibits, or forbids. Οὐ negatives an affirmation, affirming that it is not so. Οὐ is used when an object is regarded independently in itself; μή when it is regarded as depending on some thought, wish, purpose. Οὐ negat rem ipsam; μή, cogitationem rei. Οὐ implies non-existence simply; but μή implies non-existence, when existence was probable or possible. Οὐ is negative; μή is privative" (*op. cit.*, p. 138). The relative difference between these negatives is evident in 1 Pt. 1:8, ὃν οὐκ ἰδόντες ἀγαπᾶτε, εἰς ὃν ἄρτι μὴ ὁρῶντες πιστεύοντες δὲ ἀγαλλιᾶτε χαρᾷ ἀνεκλαλήτῳ, *whom having never seen you continue loving; upon whom, though not looking you continue trusting, and you are rejoicing with unspeakable joy.* In the above sentence οὐκ, used with the aorist participle, states positively that they had not seen Jesus, while μή in a milder way, with the present participle, states that they are not now seeing him. Dr. A. T. Robertson has the happy way of illustrating to his students the difference in meaning between these negatives by picturing graphically a young man proposing to his lady friend. If she answers him, μή, it may only mean that she wants to be coaxed a little longer, or that she is still in a state of uncertainty; but if she responds, οὐ, he may as well get his hat and leave at once.

Οὐ μή

242. In the WH. text the combination οὐ μή occurs ninety-six times. With the light that the papyri have thrown upon this doubling of the negatives we can now say unreservedly that the negatives were doubled for the purpose of stating denials or prohibitions emphatically. "Οὐ μή is rare, and very emphatic in the non-literary papyri" (M. 188). The following papyrus quotation from a boy's letter to his father illustrates the papyri occurrences very effectively: P. Oxy.

i, 119:5, 14f. [(2c.–3c. A. D.), ἢ οὐ θέλις ἀπενέκκειν μετ'
ἐσοῦ εἰς Ἀλεξανδρίαν, οὐ μὴ γράψω σε ἐπιστολήν . . .
ἄμ (=ἐάν) μὴ πέμψῃς, οὐ μὴ φάγω, οὐ μὴ πείνω, *if you
refuse to take me along with you to Alexandria, I positively will
not write you a letter. . . . If you do not send (for me) I
will not eat; I will not drink.* The above illustrates how people used the doubling of the negatives for making categorical
and emphatic denials (cf. Mt. 5:20, οὐ μὴ εἰσέλθητε εἰς τὴν
βασιλείαν τῶν οὐρανῶν, *ye shall by no means enter into
the kingdom of heaven;* 1 Cor. 8:13, οὐ μὴ φάγω κρέα εἰς τὸν
αἰῶνα, *I will never at all eat meat again* (cf. also Lk. 22:16, 18,
67, 68).

Οὐ is found in composition frequently in the following combinations:
οὐδαμῶς, *by no means;* οὐδέ, *not even, neither;* οὐδείς, οὐθείς, *no one;*
οὐδέποτε, *never* (not even ever); οὐδέπω, *not yet;* οὐκέτι, *no longer, no
more;* οὔπω, *not yet;* οὔτε, *neither.* When a less positive denial was
desired, the same suffixes were attached to μή. The suffixes -χι on οὐ,
and -τι on μή have the force of strengthening and intensifying these
negatives (Mt. 13:27; 26:25; Lk. 1:60).

DIVISION III

CLAUSES

243. Regardless of what kind of comparisons are made in the study of languages, the Greek language, with scarcely an exception, proves to be the most accurate, euphonious, and expressive. And it keeps up its high average in the realm of clauses. There is an ample number of different types of clauses, and each type is exquisitely developed, so as to be the most suitable vehicle for expressing with ease and grace any elusive thought.

244. Not many grammars have a separate treatment of clauses. This is no doubt due to the fact that the clause does not represent a separate part of speech. It is essentially interwoven with other parts of speech which call for specific treatment in a descriptive grammar. Consequently, whenever all the parts of speech have been discussed, the clauses have already been considered. To devote to them a separate discussion might, therefore, seem to necessitate either the omission of important matters pertaining to the parts of speech involved in clauses, or useless duplication in treating each clause a second time. That there is some truth in this objection cannot be denied, but the objection is offset by the fact that the clause is a unique element of syntactical structure and cannot be adequately comprehended until all its phenomena are presented in a single systematic view. There will also appear duplication between different groups of clauses. This is especially true of the relative clauses, which occur under various classifications. But in such repetition we venture to sacrifice rhetorical propriety to pedagogical efficiency.

245. As to their general character, clauses gather about the two pivotal points of syntax, the noun and the verb. They present a triple character—substantival, adjectival, and adverbial (cf. R. 952). To treat them in three groups under this classification according to character would conduce to scientific accuracy, but would sacrifice simplicity and clearness. We employ in our grouping here the more obvious basis of their sense in relation to the context. For a fuller analysis of clauses on the basis of their character see Br. 82.

246. As to the use of moods in subordinate clauses, this general rule applies; viz., that the moods used in coördinate clauses have exactly the same force in subordinate clauses. "There is no essential difference in meaning of the modes in subordinate clauses from their significance in independent sentences" (R. 950).

I. THE STRUCTURAL RELATION OF CLAUSES

247. When two or more clauses are connected in a coördinate relation, they constitute what is known as a *compound* sentence. The distinctive feature of the compound sentence is that in its structure no clause is subordinate to another, but all are in coördinate or *paratactic* relation (παρατακτός: *arranged alongside*). When one clause is subordinate to another, the relation is called *hypotactic* (ὑποτακτός: *arranged under*), and the technical name for the sentence is *complex*. The common practice of the Greek language was that each clause be connected with the preceding by some connective word. The term for the lack of such a connective is *asyndeton* (ἀσύνδετος: *not bound together*). Many examples of asyndeton are found in the New Testament. It occurs most frequently in John's Gospel and First Epistle.

248. A clause is simply the employment of a circumlocution by which we convey a meaning that we cannot readily

express with a single word or phrase. Thus to say, "I saw the man going home," is modified and expanded in meaning by saying, "I saw the man who was going home." In this modifying function the clause presents a threefold relation to the principal sentence of (cf. §245).

(1) A clause may sustain the relation of a *substantive*, and be used as subject or object of a verb.

οὐκ ἔχω ὃ παραθήσω αὐτῷ.

I do not have that which I may place before him. Lk. 11:6.
See also: Jn. 12:10; 1 Cor. 4:2.

(2) A clause may have the function of an *adjective*, and be used to modify a noun.

τῷ σπέρματί σου, ὅς ἐστιν Χριστός.

To thy seed, who is Christ. Gal. 3:16.
See also: Jn. 4:34; 15:12.

(3) A clause may serve as an *adverb*.

ἀκολουθήσω σοι ὅπου ἐὰν ἀπέρχῃ.

I will follow you wherever you go. Lk. 9:57.
See also: Jn. 3:16; 1 Cor. 14:12.

i. The student will find interesting variation and unmeasured possibilities of expression in the Greek use of clauses.

ii. In the treatment of clauses it is easiest on the whole to denominate them according to the connectives that introduce them, having first classified the clauses according to the ideas they are used to express. However, with a few exceptions, as far as clarity is concerned, only the subordinate clauses need separate discussion.

II. RELATIVE CLAUSES

References: R. 953–962; R–S. 168–170.

249. The relative is used to indicate clauses of various types. This variety in the nature of relative clauses does not, of course, arise from the character of the relative itself, but is determined by the nature and relations of the clause. For instance, a relative pronoun has the same essential

character in a causal clause that it does in a purpose clause. But while the character of the relative is not the determining factor, it does affect the clause in the matter of definiteness or indefiniteness.

Nature of the Relative

250. A relative is a word by means of which the complete expression of one idea is connected in sense with the complete expression of another. Thus, "The man lives" is a complete thought, and "The pastures are green" is a complete thought. These two sentences may become principal and subordinate clauses in a single sentence by the insertion of the relative adverb *where:* "The man lives *where* the pastures are green." In this construction the first sentence becomes the principal clause and the second the subordinate clause. Relatives may be pronouns; e.g., ὅς and ὅστις; or adverbs, e.g., ἕως and ὡς.

Uses of the Relative

251. The relative pronoun has no invariable effect as to mood. That is determined by the general relation of the clause to its context. So we need not be surprised to find relative clauses embracing two moods, indicative and subjunctive. It is true, however, that the definite relative accords more naturally with the indicative, while the indefinite relative suits the subjunctive better. This fact is in line with the fundamental character of the two moods. The indicative assumes the actual existence of the event or thing denoted by the relative, while the subjunctive contemplates it as hypothetical.

The Indicative with Relative Clauses

252. In by far the greater number of relative clauses, both as to frequency of occurrence and variety in use,

we find the indicative used. It appears in five types of clauses.

(1) *Adjectival Clauses.* Sometimes a relative clause is used to directly limit or define a substantive, performing a pure adjective function.

μνημονεύετε τοῦ λόγου οὗ ἐγὼ εἶπον ὑμῖν.

Remember the word which I spoke to you. Jn. 15:20.
See also: Jn. 6:37; Gal. 3:16.

(2) *Causal Clauses.* The relative clause may denote the grounds for the assertion in the main clause.

οἵτινες ἀπεθάνομεν τῇ ἁμαρτίᾳ πῶς ἔτι ζήσομεν ἐν αὐτῇ;

We who died to sin, how shall we longer live therein? Rom. 6:2.
See also: Ac. 10:41; Gal. 5:4.

(3) *Concessive Clauses.* A relative clause may imply the idea of concession.

οἱ λέγοντες αὔριον κερδήσομεν,
οἵτινες οὐκ ἐπίστασθε τῆς αὔριον.

Some say, "Tomorrow we will get gain," who know nothing about tomorrow. Jas. 4:13, 14.

(4) *Simple Condition.* The relative clause may supply the protasis of a simple condition.

ὅσοι γὰρ ἀνόμως ἥμαρτον, ἀνόμως καὶ ἀπολοῦνται.

For as many as sin without law also perish without law. Rom. 2:12.
See also: Mk. 10:43; 2 Cor. 2:10.

(5) *Purpose Clauses.* The relative clause may express purpose.

τὸν ἀμπελῶνα ἐκδώσεται ἄλλοις γεωργοῖς, οἵτινες ἀποδώσουσιν αὐτῷ τοὺς καρπούς.

He will let the vineyard to other husbandmen, who will render to him the fruits. Mt. 21:41.
See also: Mk. 1:2; 1 Cor. 4:17.

The Subjunctive With Relative Clauses

253. Where the contingent or indefinite idea is supplied by the context, or the context and the nature of the relative, the subjunctive is used.

(1) *More Probable Condition.* The protasis of a more probable future condition may be expressed by the use of a relative pronoun with ἄν.

ὃς δ'ἂν ποιήσῃ καὶ διδάξῃ, οὗτος μέγας κληθήσεται.

Whosoever shall do and teach them, he shall be called great. Mt. 5:19.

See also: Mk. 10:43; Jas. 2:10.

This construction is sometimes found in the future indicative without ἄν (cf. Mt. 10:32). In the New Testament we sometimes find ἐάν instead of ἄν. This was current Koiné usage, as is abundantly evidenced by the papyri.

(2) *Voluntative Result Clauses.* A relative clause may express a result which the context shows was intended or contemplated.

ὅθεν ἀναγκαῖον ἔχειν τι καὶ τοῦτον ὃ προσενέγκῃ.

Wherefore, this one must have something which he may offer. Heb. 8:3.

See also: Mk. 14:14; Lk. 7:4.

i. We have in this construction a blending of purpose and result, and it is often difficult to determine which is the more prominent. Where the voluntative force is but slightly felt the future indicative is used, instead of the subjunctive as in the above case (Phs. 2:20).

ii. *Some Correlative and Interrogative Pronouns Illustrated.* We find ὅσος, *as much as,* used frequently with τοσοῦτος, *so much as;* e.g., Heb. 1:4, τοσούτῳ . . . ὅσῳ, *by so much as.* Similarly οἷος, *what kind of,* occurs in connection with τοιοῦτος, *such kind of;* e.g., 1 Cor. 15:48, οἷος ὁ χοϊκός, τοιοῦτοι, *as is the earthy, such also are those who are earthy.* There is no difference in meaning between ποῖος, *of what sort,* and ὁποῖος, *of what sort.* The former is an interrogative pronoun, so the difference is one of function (cf. Lk. 24:19; 1 Cor. 3:13). The use of πόσος, *how great, how much* (Mt. 6:23), is closely akin to that of ἡλίκος, *how great, how large* (Jas. 3:5). The latter seems to have reference more to size, while the former deals rather with quantity or number.

III. Causal Clauses

References: R. 962–966; Nunn 115.

254. A causal clause is one which states the ground or reason for the assertion contained in another.

Coördinate Causal Clauses

255. The inferential particle γάρ is the regular connective for two coördinate clauses which bear to each other some relation of cause and effect, or reason and conclusion. These coördinate sentences joined by γάρ do not in the strictest sense belong to clauses.

μάρτυς γάρ μού ἐστιν ὁ θεός.

For God is my witness. Rom. 1:9.

i. In the preceding statement Paul has expressed his profound interest in the Roman church and his appreciation of it, and here he adds an evidence in proof of his claim (see also: 1 Cor. 8:5; Gal. 4:15; *et innum.*).

ii. It is sometimes difficult to decide whether a clause is coördinate or subordinate. When the particle is γάρ, that usually fixes it as coördinate. If it is ὅτι, the clause is regularly subordinate, although there are a few apparent exceptions (cf. 1 Cor. 1:25; 10:17).

Subordinate Causal Clauses

256. Four chief methods of expression are exhibited in the construction of subordinate causal clauses.

(1) *By a Subordinating Conjunction.* The particles used are, ὅτι, διότι, καθότι, ἐπεί, ἐπειδή, ὅθεν; also the phrases, ἐφ' ᾧ, ἐφ' ὅσον, ἀνθ' ὧν, οὗ χάριν.

ὅτι ἐγὼ ζῶ καὶ ὑμεῖς ζήσετε.

Because I live, you also shall live. Jn. 14:19.

ἐφ' ὅσον ἐποιήσατε ἐνὶ τούτων.

Since you did it to one of these. Mt. 25:40.

See also: Rom. 1:21: 1 Cor. 1:22; Heb. 3:1.

(2) *By* διά *with the Articular Infinitive.*

διὰ τὸ εἶναι αὐτὸν ἐξ οἴκου Δαυείδ.

Because he was of the house of David. **Lk. 2:4.**
See also: **Lk. 8:9; Jn. 2:24.**

(3) *By the Participle.* The participle may express cause either when it is in agreement with some word in the principal clause, or in the genitive absolute.

μὴ θέλων αὐτὴν δειγματίσαι.

Because he did not wish to make her a public example. **Mt. 1:19.**

μὴ ἔχοντος δὲ αὐτοῦ ἀποδοῦναι.

And since he did not have anything to pay. **Mt. 18:25.**
See also: **Lk. 16:1; Ac. 12:3.**

The use of ὡς with a causal participle implies that the action denoted by the participle is the supposed or alleged cause of the action of the principal verb.

(4) *By the Relative Pronoun.*

προσέχετε ἀπὸ τῶν ψευδοπροφητῶν, οἵτινες ἔρχονται πρὸς ὑμᾶς ἐν ἐνδύμασιν προβάτων.

Beware of false prophets who come to you in sheep's clothing.
Mt. 7:15.
See also: **Rom. 6:2; Heb. 12:6.**

IV. COMPARATIVE CLAUSES

References: R. 966–968; R–S. 175–176.

257. A comparative clause introduces an analogous thought for the purpose of elucidating or emphasizing the thought expressed in the principal clause. To say, "The believer is baptized as the Savior was," is to *describe* the believer's baptism; while to say, "The believer shall be raised even as Christ was raised," is to *emphasize* the certainty of the resurrection. Description or emphasis will be found to be the function of nearly all comparative clauses, which are of frequent occurrence in the New Testament.

The Particles Used

258. It is well that the student should become easily familiar with the various connective particles which are used to introduce comparative clauses.

(1) Those used most are ὡς and καθώς.

οὕτως ἡμᾶς λογιζέσθω ἄνθρωπος ὡς ὑπηρέτας Χριστοῦ.

In this way let a man think of us, as servants of Christ. 1 Cor. 4:1

ἵνα πάντες τιμῶσι τὸν υἱὸν καθὼς τιμῶσι τὸν πατέρα.

In order that all will honor the Son as they honor the Father. Jn. 5:23.

(2) Compounds of κατά; viz., καθό (Rom. 8:26), καθότι (Ac. 2:45), καθώσπερ (Heb. 5:4), καθάπερ (Rom. 3:4).

ἐσμὲν εὐηγγελισμένοι καθάπερ κἀκεῖνοι.

We have been evangelized even as also they. Heb. 4:2.

(3) Compounds of ὡς; viz., ὡσεί (Mt. 9:36), ὥσπερ (Mt. 6:2), ὡσπερεί (1 Cor. 15:8), ὡσαύτως (Mt. 20:5).

καταβαῖνον ὡσεὶ περιστεράν.

Descending as a dove. Mt. 3:16.

(4) The correlative pronoun ὅσος. In the comparative sense it is found only four times, each of which is in Hebrews.

ὅσῳ διαφορώτερον παρ᾽ αὐτοὺς κεκληρονόμηκεν ὄνομα.

By how much he has inherited a more excellent name than they. Heb. 1:4.

(5) The comparative particle ἤ, *than.* It occurs most frequently with single words, but now and then also with a clause.

εὐκοπώτερόν ἐστιν κάμηλον διὰ τρήματος ῥαφίδος εἰσελθεῖν ἢ πλούσιον εἰς τὴν βασιλείαν τοῦ θεοῦ.

It is easier for a camel to go through a needle's eye than for a rich man to enter into the kingdom of God. Mt. 19:24.

(6) The use of the phrase ὃν τρόπον, *as, just as.* It is frequent in 2 Clement with this meaning (cf. 8, 9, 12).

ποσάκις ἠθέλησα ἐπισυναγαγεῖν τὰ τέκνα σου, ὃν τρόπον
ὄρνις ἐπισυνάγει τὰ νοσσία αὐτῆς.

*How often would I have gathered together thy children just as
a hen gathers together her little ones!* Mt. 23:37
See also: Lk. 13:34; Ac. 1:11.

The Moods Used

259. It is not the meaning of the particles or the significance of the comparison *per se* which causes the variation in mood, but the implications of the context. The fundamental ideas of actuality and potentiality determine the matter, as is always the case with mood.

(1) Regularly we find the indicative.

ἔσεσθε ὑμεῖς τέλειοι ὡς ὁ πατὴρ ὑμῶν τέλειός ἐστιν.

Ye shall be perfect as your Father is perfect. Mt. 5:48.
See also: Rom. 3:4; 8:26.

(2) Where the element of contingency is introduced, the subjunctive is used.

ὡς καιρὸν ἔχωμεν, ἐργαζώμεθα τὸν ἀγαθόν.

As we have opportunity, let us do good. Gal 6:10.
See also: Mk. 4:26; 2 Cor. 8:12.

V. LOCAL CLAUSES

References: R. 969–970; Nunn 114.

260. A local clause is one which is introduced by a relative adverb of place.

The Particles Used

261. These clauses are introduced in the New Testament by three local adverbs.

(1) By ὅπου.

καὶ ἄλλο ἔπεσεν ἐπὶ τὸ πετρῶδες ὅπου οὐκ εἶχεν γῆν πολλήν.
And other fell upon stony soil where it had not much ground.
Mk. 4:5.

(2) By οὗ.

ἀνοίξας τὸ βιβλίον εὗρεν τὸν τόπον οὗ ἦν γεγραμμένον.
Having opened the book he found the place where it was written.
Lk. 4:17.

(3) By ὅθεν.

εἰς τὸν οἶκόν μου ἐπιστρέψω ὅθεν ἐξῆλθον.
I will return to my house whence I came out. Mt. 12:44.

The Moods Used

262. The same general principles operate here which affect moods elsewhere.

(1) The indicative only is used when the local clause is *definite*.

θησαυροὺς ἐπὶ τῆς γῆς, ὅπου σὴς καὶ βρῶσις ἀφανίζει.
Treasures upon earth, where moth and rust consume. Mt. 6:19.
See also: Mt. 2:9; Mk. 2:4.

(2) The indicative is used in *indefinite* local clauses when the action took place prior to the writing, but the subjunctive occurs when the action is expected to take place in the future. In such constructions ἄν or ἐάν occurs with the local adverb.

ὅπου ἂν εἰσπορεύετο εἰς κώμας.
Wherever he entered into villages. Mk. 6:56.

ἀκολουθήσω σοι ὅπου ἐὰν ἀπέρχῃ.
I will follow thee wherever thou goest. Lk. 9:57.
See also: Mt. 24:28; Mk. 6:10.

VI. Temporal Clauses

References: R. 970–979; R–S. 171–174.

263. There are in the Greek language several particles, derived from relative adverbs, which are used to introduce clauses that define a thought by means of its temporal relations. Some temporal particles are also used as prepositions, introducing a phrase rather than a clause (cf. Mt. 24:38; Lk. 16:16; Heb. 12:4).

The Character of Temporal Clauses

264. The function of a temporal clause is to limit the action of the verb in the principal clause by the introduction of a relation of time. The quality of such a clause may be defined from two points of view.

The Relation of the Time Limit

(1) *Antecedent Time.* The time limit may be described as prior to the action of the principal verb, in which case the clause is generally introduced by πρίν, *before.*

(2) *Contemporaneous Time.* The time limit may be the continuance of an action which is described as parallel with the action of the principal verb, the clause being introduced by ἕως, *while,* or ὅτε, ὡς, *when.*

(3) *Subsequent Time.* The time limit may be described as the terminus of the action of the principal verb, the clause being introduced by ἕως, *until.*

The Nature of the Temporal Idea

(1) *Definite.* The time limit may be indicated as a specific point or period, corresponding in meaning to "when," by the use of the indicative mood.

(2) *Indefinite.* The time limit may be stated as a con-

tingency, carrying a conditional element, and corresponding in meaning to "whenever." The indicative with ἄν is generally used in such clauses for past time, and the subjunctive with ἄν for future time.

The prevalence of relative adverbs among the temporal particles quite naturally makes the grammarians disposed to class them with relative clauses. So Burton gives as his classification of this group, "Relative Clauses Introduced by Words Meaning Until, While and Before" (Br. 128). Blass describes them as "only a special class of relative sentences," which "exhibit the same constructions" (Bl. 218). But Robertson takes issue with this opinion, and contends for the temporal clause as a distinct construction. He does admit, however, their kinship to relative clauses, as exhibited in their character as definite or indefinite. Indefiniteness is based upon "futurity, frequency and duration." He calls attention to one place in the New Testament where the optative occurs in a temporal clause (Ac. 25:16), but is "due to indirect discourse." The presence or absence of ἄν in temporal clauses varies in accordance with the conjunction and context (cf. R. 970).

The Constructions in Temporal Clauses

265. We may distinguish five constructions in the use of the temporal clause in the New Testament.

(1) *With the Indicative.* Where the temporal limitation is stated as definite, or assumed as real, the indicative is regularly used.

a. Introduced by ὅτε, ἐπειδή, ὁπότε, ὡς, meaning *when.*

ὅτε ἐτέλεσεν ὁ Ἰησοῦς τοὺς λόγους τούτους, μετῆρεν.

When Jesus had finished these words, he departed. Mt. 19:1.
See also: Mt. 7:28; 21:1; Lk. 7:1; 11:1.

b. Introduced by ὅταν, meaning *whenever.*

ὅταν στήκετε προσευχόμενοι, ἀφίετε.

Whenever ye stand praying, forgive. Mk. 11:25.
See also: Mk. 3:11; Rev. 4:9.

c. Introduced by ἕως, ἕως οὗ, ἕως ὅτου, ἄχρι οὗ, ἐφ' ὅσον, meaning *while.*

ἠνάγκασεν τοὺς μαθητὰς ἐμβῆναι, ἕως ἀπολύει τὸν ὄχλον.

He constrained the disciples to embark, while he dismissed the multitude. Mk. 6:45.

See also: Jn. 9:4; 1 Tim. 4:13; Heb. 3:13; Lk. 12:58.

d. Introduced by ἕως, ἄχρι, ἄχρι οὗ, meaning *until.*

ὁ ἀστὴρ προῆγεν αὐτούς, ἕως ἐστάθη ἐπάνω οὗ ἦν τὸ παιδίον.

The star went before them until it stood over where the child was. Mt. 2:9.

See also: Ac. 7:18; Rev. 17:17.

e. Introduced by ὡς, ἀφ' οὗ, meaning *since.*

πόσος χρόνος ἐστὶν ὡς τοῦτο γέγονεν αὐτῷ;

How long is it since this happened to him? Mk. 9:21.

See also: Lk. 13:7.

(2) *With the Subjunctive.* The subjunctive is used where the temporal clause is conceived as an indefinite possibility, and its use implies uncertainty as to realization.

a. Introduced by ὅταν, ἐπάν, ἡνίκα, meaning *whenever.*

ὅταν δὲ εἰσφέρωσιν ὑμᾶς ἐπὶ τὰς συναγωγάς, μὴ μεριμνήσετε τί εἴπητε.

And whenever they bring you into synagogues, be not anxious what ye may say. Lk. 12:11.

See also: Mt. 24:33; Mk. 13:11; Lk. 11:34; 2 Cor. 3:15.

b. Introduced by ἕως, ἄχρι, ἄχρι οὗ, μέχρι, μέχρι οὗ, meaning *until.*

ἐκεῖ μένετε ἕως ἂν ἐξέλθητε ἐκεῖθεν.

There abide until ye depart thence. Mk. 6:10.

See also: Lk. 21:24; Rev. 15:8; Eph. 4:13; Mk. 13:30.

When the temporal clause has an actual future reference, ἄν is often used (Lk. 15:4). When the principal clause is past, and the temporal clause presents a future reference relative to the principal clause, ἄν is omitted (Mk. 18:30).

(3) *With the Infinitive.* For antecedent time the regular construction is the infinitive with πρίν or πρὶν ἤ, meaning *before.*

εἴρηκα ὑμῖν πρὶν γενέσθαι.

I have told you before it comes to pass. Jn. 14:29.
See also: Mt. 1:18; 26:34.

i. The infinitive is also used with πρὸ τοῦ to mean *before* (Gal. 2:12), with ἐν τῷ to mean *while* (Mt. 13:25) or *when* (Ac. 8:6), and with μετὰ τό to mean *after* (Ac. 1:3; cf. (3) above).

ii. Where the principal clause is negative, πρὶν ἤ is followed by the indicative (cf. Lk. 2:26).

(4) *With a Relative Phrase.* A relative pronoun with a preposition may express a temporal idea.

ἐν ᾧ ὁ νυμφίος μετ' αὐτῶν ἐστίν.

While the bridegroom is with them. Mk. 2:19.
See also: Mt. 9:15; 13:25.

(5) *With the Participle.* One of the regular uses of the participle is as the equivalent of a temporal clause.

καὶ ἐξελθὼν εἶδεν πολὺν ὄχλον.

And when he came forth, he saw a great multitude. Mt. 14:14.
See also: Mt. 14:32; Heb. 11:21.

VII. Purpose Clauses

References: R. 981–991; R–S. 152–154.

266. The variety and distinctiveness of the constructions for expressing purpose in Greek make it important that close attention be given to the matter. The student will do well to tarry with this section until he has mastered it.

The Character of Purpose Clauses

267. The function of a purpose clause is to express the aim of the action denoted by the main verb. This aim may be of the nature of a deliberate design, it may be a matter

of general direction, or merely of contemplated results. Thus to say, "Paul went to Berea to preach the gospel," could mean that Paul went in accordance with an actual plan, or that he went so that he could preach. So purpose clauses may exhibit various shades of meaning, ranging from deliberate design to mere tendency or result. They may be divided into two classes.

(1) *Pure Final Clauses* are those which express a distinct purpose conceived as the aim of the action indicated in the principal verb.

(2) *Semi-Final Clauses* are those which denote a direction of the action in the main verb toward a given result, which result is sought or anticipated.

The Constructions in Purpose Clauses

268. Purpose may be expressed in six ways according to New Testament usage.

(1) By ἵνα and ὅπως, meaning *that, in order that;* or, a negative purpose, by ἵνα μή and μή, *that not, lest.* The subjunctive occurs regularly, and the future indicative occasionally.

> ἦλθεν ἵνα μαρτυρήσῃ περὶ τοῦ φωτός.

He came that he might bear witness concerning the light. Jn. 1:7.

> δέδωκεν ἡμῖν διάνοιαν ἵνα γινώσκομεν τὸν ἀληθινόν.

He has given us a mind that we know the truth. 1 Jn. 5:20.

> μὴ κρίνετε ἵνα μὴ κριθῆτε.

Judge not that you be not judged. Mt. 7:1.

> μὴ τίς με δόξῃ ἄφρονα εἶναι.

Lest anyone think me a fool. 2 Cor. 11:16.

> ὅπως φανῶσιν τοῖς ἀνθρώποις.

That they may be seen by men. Mt. 6:5.

See also: Lk. 20:10; 22:11.

(2) By the simple infinitive.

μὴ νομίσητε ὅτι ἦλθον καταλῦσαι τὸν νόμον.

Think not that I came to destroy the law. Mt. 5:17.

See also: Mt. 11:8; 22:3.

(3) By the infinitive with τοῦ.

μέλλει γὰρ Ἡρῴδης ζητεῖν τὸ παιδίον τοῦ ἀπολέσαι αὐτό.

For Herod will seek the child to destroy him. Mt. 2:13.

See also: Ac. 26:18; Phs. 3:10.

(4) By the accusative of the articular infinitive with εἰς and πρός; and very rarely also by ὡς and ὥστε without the article.

εἰς τὸ στηριχθῆναι ὑμᾶς.

To the end that ye may be established. Rom. 1:11.

πᾶς ὁ βλέπων γυναῖκα πρὸς τὸ ἐπιθυμῆσαι.

Every one that looks on a woman for the purpose of lust. Mt. 5:28.

συμβούλιον ἔλαβον ὥστε θανατῶσαι αὐτόν.

They took counsel in order to put him to death. Mt. 27:1.

εἰσῆλθον εἰς κώμην Σαμαρειτῶν, ὡς ἑτοιμάσαι αὐτῷ.

They entered a village of the Samaritans to make ready for him.
Lk. 9:52.

See also: Mt. 6:1; Lk. 4:29; Heb. 7:9.

(5) By the relative with the future indicative or the subjunctive.

ὃς κατασκευάσει τὴν ὁδόν.

That he may prepare thy way. Mk. 1:2.

ἀναγκαῖον ἔχειν τι καὶ τοῦτον ὃ προσενέγκῃ.

It is necessary that this one really have something to offer. Heb. 8:3.

See also: Ac. 6:3; 21:16.

(6) By the future and, rarely, the present participle.

ἀπέστειλεν αὐτὸν εὐλογοῦντα ὑμᾶς.

He sent him to bless you. Ac. 3:26.

ἐληλύθει προσκυνήσων εἰς Ἰερουσαλήμ.

He had come to Jerusalem to worship. Ac. 8:27.
See also: Mk. 3:31; Mt. 27:49.

VIII. RESULT CLAUSES

References: R. 997–1003; R–S. 155–156.

Definition

269. A result clause states that which is consequent upon or issues from the action of the main verb. As indicated under Purpose Clauses (§267) it is often difficult to determine whether a clause should be translated as denoting result or purpose.

The Constructions in Result Clauses

270. Result may be introduced in the following ways:

(1) By far the most common way of expressing result is the use of ὥστε followed by the infinitive.

κἂν ἔχω πᾶσαν τὴν πίστιν ὥστε ὄρη μεθιστάνειν.

And if I have all faith, so as to remove mountains. 1 Cor. 13:2
See also: Mk. 1:27; 2:12.

(2) By the simple infinitive.

τὰ δὲ ἔθνη ὑπὲρ ἐλέους δοξάσαι τὸν θεόν.

So that the Gentiles might glorify God for His mercy. Rom. 15:9.
See also: Lk. 1:54; Ac. 5:3.

(3) Rarely by the infinitive with τοῦ.

ἐλευθέρα ἐστὶν ἀπὸ τοῦ νόμου, τοῦ μὴ εἶναι αὐτὴν μοιχαλίδα.

She is free from the law, so that she is not an adulteress. Rom. 7:3.
See also: Ac. 18:10; 20:3; 27:1.

(4) By the infinitive with εἰς τό, which is also rare.

εἰς τὸ εἶναι αὐτοὺς ἀναπολογήτους.

So that they are without excuse. Rom. 1:20.
See also: Phs. 1:10; Heb. 11:3; Jas. 1:19.

(5) By the indicative with ὅτι and ὥστε, also rare.

ποῦ οὗτος μέλλει πορεύεσθαι ὅτι οὐχ εὑρήσομεν αὐτόν;

Where is this man about to go so that we shall not find him?
Jn. 7:35.

ὥστε τὸν υἱὸν τὸν μονογενῆ ἔδωκεν.

So that he gave his only begotten son. Jn. 3:16.
See also: Mk. 4:41; Gal. 3:13; Heb. 2:6.

With the infinitive ὥστε expresses conceived or intended result, but with the indicative (only two occurrences in the New Testament) it expresses actual result. But actual result may also be expressed by the infinitive with ὥστε (Mt. 8:24; 12:22; Lk. 5:7).

(6) By the subjunctive with ἵνα. Grammarians have been reluctant to admit this use for ἵνα. But J. H. Moulton and A. T. Robertson, who at first stood against admitting the consecutive force of ἵνα, came to do so later (R. 997). See our discussion of ἵνα in the section on conjunctions (§220).

λέγω οὖν, ἔπταισαν ἵνα πέσωσιν;

I say then, did they stumble so that they fell? Rom. 11:11.
See also: Gal. 5:17; Lk. 1:43; Jn. 6:7.

IX. CONDITIONAL CLAUSES

References: R. 1004–1129; R–S. 161–167.

The Character of Conditional Clauses

271. A conditional clause is the statement of a supposition, the fulfillment of which is assumed to secure the realization of a potential fact expressed in a companion clause. The clause containing the supposition is called the

protasis. The clause containing the statement based on the supposition is called the *apodosis*. Conditional clauses may be classified on the basis of the attitude they express with reference to reality.

(1) *Supposition from the Viewpoint of Reality.* The protasis of a condition may present one fact as conditioning another. In one form of condition there is nothing implied as to whether or not this fact actually exists. This we call the *simple condition*. In another form of condition it is implied that this fact has not been realized, and therefore does not exist. This we call the *contrary to fact condition*.

(2) *Supposition from the Viewpoint of Probability.* The protasis may imply that the fact suggested as a condition is a probability. Sometimes it is implied that there is considerable probability of its fulfillment. This we call the *more probable future condition*. Again, the protasis may not contain any special implication of the fulfillment of the condition, viewing it merely as a possibility. This we call the *less probable future condition*. Thus we find that there are four classes of conditional sentences.

272. The primary thing in understanding conditional sentences is to keep in mind what kind of affirmation each mood expresses. As has already been stated in the chapter on mood, the indicative states a thing as a fact, the subjunctive with a degree of uncertainty, and the optative with a greater degree of uncertainty. Hence, on the basis of mood, the four kinds of conditional sentences can be conveniently grouped into two types. First, there are the two that have the indicative mood, which assume that the premise is either true or untrue. The speaker takes for granted that what he assumes is true, as in the simple condition; or that it is known not to be true, as is the case in the contrary to fact condition. The indicative, being the mood for reality, is regularly used in this type of sentence.

It would be contrary to the genius of the Greek moods if it were otherwise. Second, the other two conditional sentences composing the second type do not have the indicative mood, but rather the subjunctive and optative, which are used to express varying degrees of uncertainty or doubt. Inasmuch as the optative has vanished almost entirely from the New Testament, we see in it but traces of the fourth class of conditional sentences. But the subjunctive in conditions is very common.

273. Another thing that lends light toward a thorough understanding of conditional sentences is the particle ἄν that is used in all but the first-class condition. The third-class condition begins with εἰ+ἄν or ἐάν, or sometimes ἄν. In the apodosis of sentences in the second and fourth classes ἄν occurs most of the time, but it is not necessary according to Koiné usage. As we have pointed out in our discussion of ἄν in the section on particles, it implies doubt or indefiniteness. Its very presence in a sentence indicates lack of certainty on the part of the one using it. It warns us not to take at full face value what the other words may imply. If we but remember that this word which implies uncertainty is used with the moods for uncertainty, we are far advanced in a proper understanding of it.

274. If the indicative is used in a conditional clause, naturally the negative is οὐ. Whenever any other mood is used, the regular negative is μή. In a few cases this rule is not followed absolutely, the contrary to fact condition being a notable exception, where μή, the weaker negative and the one for expressing doubt, is used regularly with but two exceptions in the New Testament.

Robertson has termed these four kinds of conditional sentences as follows: (1) *reality;* (2) *unreality;* (3) *probability;* (4) *possibility.* And he makes a very pertinent statement, the substance of which needs to be remembered: "The point about all the four classes to note is that the form of the condition has to do only with the *statement,* not with the absolute truth or certainty of the matter. . . . We must distinguish always therefore between the fact and the *statement* of the fact. The conditional sentence deals only with the statement" (R. 1005).

The Constructions in Conditional Sentences

275. We have developed in the above discussion that there are two general types of conditional sentences, of two varieties each, thus requiring four different constructions for expression.

(1) *The Simple Condition.* This condition was used when one wished to assume or to seem to assume the reality of his premise. Εἰ occurs regularly in the protasis, with any tense of the indicative. There is no fixed form for the apodosis—any mood or tense may occur.

εἰ δὲ πνεύματι ἄγεσθε, οὐκ ἐστὲ ὑπὸ νόμον.

But if you are led by the Spirit, you are not under law. Gal. 5:18.

See also: Mk. 4:23; Rev. 20:15.

(2) *The Contrary to Fact Condition.* The premise is assumed to be contrary to fact in this class, and only the past tenses of the indicative are used. As suggested above, this condition states a thing as if it were untrue or unreal, although in actual fact it may be true, as the first example below shows. The protasis is introduced by εἰ, and ἄν usually occurs in the apodosis. Exceptions are found in Mt. 26:24; Ac. 26:32; 2 Cor. 2:2.

a. A contrary to fact condition dealing with *present time* has the imperfect tense in both protasis and apodosis.

οὗτος εἰ ἦν προφήτης ἐγίνωσκεν ἂν τίς καὶ ποταπὴ ἡ γυνή.

If this man were a prophet, he would know who and what sort of woman this is. Lk. 7:39.

See also: Jn. 15:19, 22; Gal. 1:10.

b. A contrary to fact condition dealing with *past time* has the aorist or pluperfect tense in both protasis and apodosis.

εἰ ἦς ὧδε οὐκ ἂν ἀπέθανεν ὁ ἀδελφός.

If you had been here, my brother would not have died. Jn. 11:32.
See also: Mt. 11:21; Mk. 13:20.

(3) *The More Probable Future Condition.* Because the subjunctive is used in the protasis, uncertainty is implied. The protasis is introduced by ἐάν, and almost any form of the verb may occur in the apodosis, but the thought always has to do with the future.

καὶ τοῦτο ποιήσομεν ἐὰν ἐπιτρέπῃ ὁ θεός.

And this we will do, if God permit. Heb. 6:3.
See also: Mt. 9:21; Rom. 7:2.

(4) *The Less Probable Future Condition.* This condition is expressed by εἰ with the optative in the protasis and ἄν with the optative in the apodosis.

ἀλλ' εἰ καὶ πάσχοιτε διὰ δικαιοσύνην, μακάριοι.

But even if ye should suffer for righteousness sake, happy are ye.
1 Pt. 3:14.
See also: 1 Cor. 14:10; 15:37.

i. No example of this condition complete in both protasis and apodosis is to be found in the New Testament. Indeed, Robertson denies that a complete example occurs in the LXX or papyri "so far as examined." . . . "It is an ornament of the cultured class and was little used by the masses save in a few set phrases" (R. 1020).

ii. Of these four forms of condition, the New Testament uses the first two with great frequency, the third occurs quite often, but the fourth is used but rarely and never in full form. The contrary to fact condition could not occur in anything but its full form, for the simple reason that "an alteration of it would have caused ambiguity, and have disturbed at once the character of the hypothetical statement" (Bt. 224).

Irregular Forms of Condition

276. It was inevitable that in actual practice speakers and writers would not confine themselves to fixed forms of hypothetical expression. Variations are found which cannot be reduced to logical analysis, but can be grouped only according to their distinctive aspect of irregularity. (1) There occur a good many *mixed conditions;* that is, conditions one member of which belongs to one class, while the other belongs to a different class (Lk. 17:6). (2) There are also *implied conditions,* in which the apodosis is expressed and the protasis implied in a participle (1 Tim. 4:4), imperative (Mk. 1:17), or question (Mt. 26:15). (3) An *elliptical condition* is one from which one member has been entirely omitted, and must be supplied from the context (Lk. 13:9).

X. CONCESSIVE CLAUSES

References: R. 1026–1027; R–S. 166–167.

Character

277. Concessive clauses are in their essential nature conditional clauses, but differ from the latter in that with the condition the apodosis attains reality by reason of the protasis, while in the concessive clause realization is secured in spite of the protasis.

There is manifest reason for Robertson's contention that concessive clauses are at bottom a type of conditional sentence. For this reason he treats them as a subhead under conditional sentences (cf. R. 1026). In this position he is in agreement with Blass, who declares that "there is no real distinction between them and conditional sentences" (Bl. 215). We can but feel, though, that the distinctive phenomena are sufficient to call for a separate treatment of concessive clauses, though we would not be so positive as Burton in holding that "the force of a concessive sentence is thus very different from that of a conditional sentence" (Br. 112). They are in the last analysis really not "very different" from conditional sentences.

Classification

278. It is difficult to maintain with final consistency any analysis of concessive clauses in the New Testament, but it is not wholly arbitrary to divide them into three classes.

(1) *Logical Concession.* This is where the concession is assumed to be a fact. The clause is introduced by εἰ καί followed by the indicative.

εἰ καὶ ἐλύπησα ὑμᾶς ἐν τῇ ἐπιστολῇ, οὐ μεταμέλομαι.

Though I grieved you by my letter, I do not regret it. 2 Cor. 7:8.
See also: Lk. 11:8; Phs. 2:17.

(2) *Doubtful Concession.* We find this type proposing the concession as a possibility. It is introduced by ἐὰν καί followed by the subjunctive.

ἐὰν καὶ προλημφθῇ ἄνθρωπος ἔν τινι παραπτώματι, καταρτίζετε τὸν τοιοῦτον.

Even though a man be overtaken in a fault, restore such a one.
Gal. 6:1.

(3) *Emphatic Concession.* This type of clause expresses concession with the added thought that the supposed assumption has no likelihood of fulfillment. Such a clause is introduced by καὶ ἐάν with the subjunctive or καὶ εἰ with the indicative.

καὶ ἐὰν κρίνω δὲ ἐγώ, ἡ κρίσις ἡ ἐμὴ ἀληθινή ἐστιν.
But if I should judge, my judgment is true. Jn. 8:16.

καὶ εἰ θέλετε δέξασθαι, αὐτός ἐστιν Ἡλείας.
And if you will receive it, this is Elijah. Mt. 11:14.
See also: Lk. 6:32; Gal. 1:8.

279. Concession may also be expressed by the use of the participle. Five times καίπερ is used with the participle expressing concession, but the participle by itself is often so used.

καίπερ ὢν υἱός, ἔμαθεν ὑπακοήν.

Although he was a son, he learned obedience. Heb. 5:8.

εἰ γὰρ ἐχθροὶ ὄντες κατηλλάγημεν τῷ θεῷ.

For even though we were enemies we were reconciled to God.
Rom. 5:10.
See also: Heb. 5:12; 11:4.

XI. SUBSTANTIVAL CLAUSES

Definition

280. A substantival clause (often called noun clause) is one that is so related to the main verb in the sentence that it functions in the capacity of a noun. Such clauses are abundant in the New Testament, and they exhibit the characteristics of a noun as subjective, as objective, and as appositive.

Constructions

281. There are three general divisions under which these clauses naturally fall. It is of interest to note also that there were three optional ways open to a Greek to make a statement regardless of whether the clause was subjective, objective, or appositive. He could use the infinitive, or he could introduce the clause with ἵνα, or ὅτι.

(1) *Subjective Clauses.*

a. With the infinitive.

τὰ αὐτὰ γράφειν ὑμῖν ἐμοὶ μὲν οὐκ ὀκνηρόν.

To write the same things to you is not irksome to me. Phs. 3:1.
See also: Heb. 4:6; 9:27.

b. With ὅτι.

οὐ μέλει σοι ὅτι ἀπολλύμεθα;

Is it not of care to thee that we are perishing? Mk. 4:38.
See also: 1 Jn. 5:9.

c. With ἵνα.

ἐμὸν βρῶμά ἐστιν ἵνα ποιήσω τὸ θέλημα τοῦ πέμψαντός με.

My meat is to do the will of him that sent me. Jn. 4:34.
See also: Mt. 18:14; 1 Cor. 4:3.

(2) *Objective Clauses.*

a. With the infinitive.

βούλομαι οὖν προσεύχεσθαι τοὺς ἄνδρας.

I desire, therefore, that men pray. 1 Tim. 2:8.
See also: Phs. 2:6; 4:11.

b. With ὅτι.

ἰδὼν αὐτὸν ὅτι νουνεχῶς ἀπεκρίθη.

Seeing that he answered wisely. Mk. 12:34.
See also: Jn. 10:36; 11:27.

c. With ἵνα and ὅπως after verbs of saying, asking, exhorting, wishing, caring, striving, etc.

ἠρώτα ἵνα καταβῇ καὶ ἰάσηται αὐτοῦ τὸν υἱόν.

He asked that he come down and heal his son. Jn. 4:47.

δεήθητε οὖν τοῦ κυρίου τοῦ θερισμοῦ ὅπως ἐκβάλῃ ἐργάτας.

*Pray ye, therefore, the Lord of the harvest that he send forth
laborers.* Mt. 9:38.
See also: Mt. 4:3; Lk. 4:2; 7:3.

d. With μή after verbs of fearing, warning, caution, etc.

βλέπετε μή τις ὑμᾶς πλανήσῃ.

Beware lest anyone lead you astray. Mt. 24:4.
See also: Mk. 13:5; Col. 2:8.

e. Without a conjunction (asyndeton).

λέγει αὐτῷ, ὅρα μηδενὶ μηδὲν εἴπῃς.
He says to him, See that you tell nobody anything. Mk. 1:44.
See also: Mt. 9:30; Mk. 12:34.

(3) *Appositive Clauses.*

a. With the infinitive.

θρησκεία καθαρὰ αὕτη ἐστίν, ἐπισκέπτεσθαι ὀρφανοὺς
καὶ χήρας.
Pure religion is this, to visit orphans and widows. Jas. 1:27.
See also: Eph. 3:6, 8; 4:17.

b. With ὅτι.

αὕτη δέ ἐστιν ἡ κρίσις, ὅτι τὸ φῶς ἐλήλυθεν εἰς τὸν κόσμον.
And this is the judgment, that light has come into the world.
Jn. 3:19.
See also: 2 Cor. 1:18, 23; 11:10.

c. With ἵνα.

τίς οὖν μού ἐστιν ὁ μισθός; ἵνα εὐαγγελιζόμενος ἀδάπανον
θήσω τὸ εὐαγγέλιον.

*What then is my reward? That I while preaching will give them
the gospel without cost.* 1 Cor. 9:18.
See also: Lk. 1:43; Jn. 15:8, 12.

The Moods Used

282. The indicative is always found with ὅτι; the sub-junctive is predominant with ἵνα at a ratio of thirty-two to one: there being twenty-six occurrences with the indicative, seventeen of which occur in the Johannine writings; the subjunctive is dominant with ὅπως and μή, there being only one occurrence of ὅπως with the indicative (Lk. 24:20), and only four of μή (as conjunction) with the indicative.

XII. Indirect Discourse

References: R. 1027–1043; R–S. 181–186.

283. There is not a great deal of indirect discourse in the New Testament. This is true also of other Koiné writings. Direct quotations are characteristic of vernacular speech. Such language is simpler and more picturesque. The indirect discourse found in the New Testament is in full accord with the general Greek rules and may be readily analyzed.

Verb Forms in Indirect Discourse

284. Striking differences from the English idiom make this a matter which requires close attention from the student.

(1) *Tense.* It was a regular thing that the same tense used by the original speaker was also used by the one quoting the statement indirectly. This is an important fact for the student to grasp. For instance, if Jesus said, βλέπω, *I see,* Luke in putting the statement into indirect discourse would say, Ἰησοῦς εἶπεν ὅτι βλέπει (or βλέπειν). Although the statement was made in the past, the present tense is used in recording it, because *the original statement occurred in the present tense.* There are, however, a few examples where the imperfect in indirect discourse seems to represent a present tense in the original statement (cf. Jn. 2:25). If the original writer or speaker used an aorist or future tense, the same tense was observed in indirect discourse. Our English idiom differs widely here from Greek usage. While we would say, "He said he was going home," changing the tense from present to past, in Greek it would be εἶπεν ὅτι πορεύεται εἰς τὸν οἶκον, preserving the present tense (cf. Lk. 24:23; Jn. 9:9).

(2) *Mood.* The mood like the tense, barring a few exceptions, is preserved regularly when the statement is put

into indirect discourse. In classical Greek the indicative and subjunctive were often changed to the optative in indirect discourse. Only Luke of the New Testament writers ever does this, and he only a few times (cf. Lk. 3:15; 22:23; Ac. 25:16). When we find the subjunctive or indicative in indirect discourse, we are to infer that the original speaker used that particular mood in making his statement. The infinitive is often used in indirect discourse to represent the indicative in the direct, but it is, strictly speaking, not a mood but a verbal noun.

(3) *Person.* The person of the verb in indirect discourse is determined by the relation of the speaker to the quoted statement. If the speaker is quoting his own statement, the person remains unchanged; if he is quoting the statement of another, the third person is used; if he is quoting it to the one who made the original statement, it is in the second person. This is practically the same as English usage. For example, note Mk. 9:6, οὐ γὰρ ἤδει τί ἀποκριθῇ, *for he knew not what he might answer*, where the original statement was, τί ἀποκριθῶ.

We are not to suppose that indirect discourse can be introduced only by verbs of saying or thinking: a wide variety of verbs may take this construction (cf. R. 1035). Any verb which introduces a definite idea that would of itself permit independent expression may take a clause of indirect discourse.

Types of Indirect Discourse

285. There are three types of indirect discourse: indirect declarations, indirect questions, and indirect commands. These each take their own distinct constructions, and therefore must be treated separately.

(1) *Indirect Declarations.* These are expressed in three ways.

a. By ὅτι with the indicative.

> ἐγὼ πεπίστευκα ὅτι σὺ εἶ ὁ Χριστός.
> *I believe that thou art the Christ.* Jn. 11:27.
> See also: Ac. 10:34; Gal. 2:14.

b. By the infinitive.

> οἳ λέγουσιν αὐτὸν ζῆν.
> *Who say that he lives.* Lk. 24:23.
> See also: Rom. 2:19; Phs. 2:13.

c. By the participle.

> ἀκούομεν γάρ τινας περιπατοῦντας ἐν ὑμῖν ἀτάκτως.
> *For we hear that some among you walk disorderly.* 2 Ths. 3:11.
> See also: Ac. 7:12; 8:22.

(2) *Indirect Questions.* These are regularly introduced by τίς or τί, though a relative pronoun or adverb may be used. In Ac. 9:6 we find ὅτι in an indirect question. The original mood is generally retained, though Luke sometimes uses the optative (cf. Lk. 18:36).

> καὶ ἦλθον ἰδεῖν τί ἐστιν τὸ γεγονός.
> *And they came to see what had happened.* Mk. 5:14.
> See also: Mk. 15:44.

(3) *Indirect Commands.* Indirect commands present three modes of expression.

a. By the infinitive.

> οἵτινες τῷ Παύλῳ ἔλεγον μὴ ἐπιβαίνειν εἰς Ἱεροσόλυμα.
> *Who were telling Paul to not go to Jerusalem.* Ac. 21:4.
> See also: Ac. 21:21; 26:20.

b. By ἵνα and ὅπως with the subjunctive.

> παρήγγειλεν αὐτοῖς ἵνα μηδὲν αἴρωσιν εἰς ὁδόν.
> *He commanded them to take nothing for the journey.* Mk. 6:8.
> See also: Ac. 25:3.

c. An indirect deliberative question may imply an original command.

ὑποδείξω δὲ ὑμῖν τίνα φοβηθῆτε.
But I will warn you whom ye should fear. Lk. 12:5.

XIII. COMMANDS AND PROHIBITIONS

References: R. 851, 855, 890, 908, 942–950; M. 122–126.

286. It is very uncommon to find this class of sentences treated separately in Greek grammars. But the average student never fully appreciates the important distinctions involved for the simple reason that he never sees them in a single comprehensive view. Therefore, the purpose of this book requires that we treat commands and prohibitions in a separate group. It is most practical to classify them under the three tenses used.

In the Future Tense

287. Occasionally the future indicative is used in the sense of a command. This usage occurs frequently in the LXX, each of the ten commandments being given this way.

ἀγαπήσεις τὸν πλησίον σου καὶ μισήσεις τὸν ἐχθρόν σου.
Thou shalt love thy neighbor and hate thy enemy. Mt. 5:43.
See also: Mt. 6:5; 27:4; Lk. 13:9.

In the Aorist Tense

288. The essential force of the aorist tense is very clearly exhibited in commands and prohibitions.

(1) *Prohibitions with the Aorist Subjunctive.* The main idea of the aorist tense, as has been indicated, is to express punctiliar action. When a prohibition, which is a negative command, is expressed in the aorist it means to forbid in advance whatever may be contemplated. The only way a prohibition *in the second person* and in the aorist tense is

expressed in the New Testament is by the use of the subjunctive mood. But *in the third person* either the subjunctive or imperative is used.

καὶ μηδένα κατὰ τὴν ὁδόν ἀσπάσησθε.

And salute nobody along the way. Lk. 10:4.

See also: Mt. 10:9; Ac. 7:60.

(2) *The Aorist Imperative in Commands.* When the aorist imperative is used it denotes *summary* action—"an action that is either transient or instantaneous, . . . or to be undertaken at once" (W. 313).

ἀράτω τὸν σταυρὸν αὐτοῦ καὶ ἀκολουθείτω μοι.

Let him take up his cross (at once, aor.) *and follow me* (continually, pres.). Mt. 16:24.

See also: Jn. 5:8; Mk. 2:11.

The aorist imperative predominates in the New Testament, which fact "is characteristic of the κοινή generally" (R. 855). The distinction between the present and aorist imperative sometimes seems to be ignored. But we are safest when we assume that the author had a reason in his mind for using one rather than the other. Indeed, Winer says that "in many cases it depends on the writer whether or not he will represent the action as occurring, in a point of time and momentary, or as only commencing, or likewise continuing" (W. 314). Why does it not in every case depend upon the writer? As a matter of fact, it does.

In the Present Tense

289. In the present tense the imperative is used for both commands and prohibitions.

(1) *The Present Imperative in Commands.* When the present imperative is used, it denotes *continuous* or *repeated* action. Every time Jesus asked a person to follow him he used the verb ἀκολουθέω in the present imperative.

καὶ λέγει αὐτῷ, ἀκολούθει μοι.

And he says to him, Follow me. Mt. 9:9.

That is, begin now to follow me, and continue doing so.

As a climax to Jesus' parable about the man who persisted in asking for three loaves until he got them, we find, αἰτεῖτε . . . ζητεῖτε . . . κρούετε, *keep on asking; keep on seeking; keep on knocking* (Lk. 11:9). And Luke reports that Jesus answered the man who asked help to get part of an inheritance, ὁρᾶτε καὶ φυλάσσεσθε ἀπὸ πάσης πλεονεξίας, *be constantly alert in guarding yourselves from every form of greed* (Lk. 12:15).

(2) *The Present Imperative in Prohibitions.* The present tense is properly used for expressing continued action. A prohibition in the present imperative demands that action then in progress be stopped.

μὴ κρίνετε, ἵνα μὴ κριθῆτε.
Stop judging, lest ye be judged. Mt. 7:1.

ἐγὼ ἔκλαιον . . . λέγει μοι, Μὴ κλαῖε.
I was weeping; he says to me, Stop weeping. Rev. 5:4, 5.
See also: Lk. 10:7; Jas. 3:1.

The Aorist Subjunctive and Present Imperative in Prohibitions Contrasted

290. The purpose of a prohibition, when expressed by the aorist subjunctive, is to forbid a thing *before it has begun;* i.e., it commands to never do a thing. But a prohibition in the present imperative means to forbid the *continuance* of an act; it commands to quit doing a thing. There should be nothing confusing about understanding the force of these negative commands as they occur in these tenses. As we learned in the study of tense, the present tense in any of its moods means linear or durative action, whereas the aorist tense in any of its moods means the converse of linear or durative action, it means punctiliar or summary action.

(1) Thus a prohibition expressed with the *present tense*

demands the cessation of some act that is already in progress.

μὴ κλαίετε ἐπ᾽ ἐμέ.

Do not continue (i.e., stop) *weeping for me.* Lk. 23:28.
See also: Jn. 2:16; 20:17.

Moulton tells how his friend Davidson learned the difference in meaning between the present and aorist in prohibition by hearing a Greek command his dog to stop barking by using μή with the present imperative. With that as a clue he found the distinction carefully observed throughout the history of the Greek language, from the classical Attic literature to the Greek which is spoken today (M. 122).

(2) A prohibition expressed in the *aorist tense* is a warning or exhortation against doing a thing not yet begun.

μὴ εἰσενέγκῃς ἡμᾶς εἰς πειρασμόν.

Do not (ever) lead us into temptation. Lk. 11:4.
See also: Lk. 14:8; Jn. 19:24.

i. There are a few occurrences in the New Testament of prohibitions in the aorist tense in which the general rule is disregarded. In Jn. 3:7 we find μὴ θαυμάσῃς addressed to Nicodemus who was already marveling, and in Mt. 1:20 μὴ φοβηθῇς παραλαβεῖν Μαριάν is addressed to Joseph who is then planning to break his engagement with Mary. "But, as a rule, it is the ingressive aorist subjunctive used in prohibitions to forbid a thing not yet done, or the durative present imperative to forbid the continuance of an act" (R. 852).

ii. The subjunctive with ἵνα may be used in passionate exhortation or entreaty with the approximate force of a command. Thus in Mk. 5:23 the petition of Jairus to Jesus, ἵνα ἐλθὼν ἐπιθῇς τὰς χείρας αυτῇ, might be rendered, *Oh, that thou wouldst come and lay thy hands on her!*

iii. Buttmann's description of the aorist subjunctive in prohibition as a "substitute" for the imperative is scarcely accurate (Bt. 211). While it is true that the subjunctive fills the office of the aorist imperative, yet the genius of the subjunctive is present. Thus μὴ ποίει τινὰ means *quit doing a thing*, while μὴ ποιήσῃς τινὰ carries both authority and expediency and is more nearly equivalent to our, *you had better not do it.* It is hardly to be taken for granted that any mood loses its own significance when filling an office ordinarily supplied by another.

iv. Moulton finds in the New Testament one hundred and thirty-four examples of the present imperative in prohibitions, while there are only eighty-four of the aorist subjunctive. This probably arises from the immediate ethical application involved in the viewpoint of the New Testament writers. It is to be noticed in this connection that aorist prohibitions are expressed in the New Testament almost exclusively by the subjunctive, the aorist imperative occurring only a few times in the second person. This arises from the sense of ethical restraint in the aorist subjunctive. The emphatic sense of the aorist subjunctive is evident from the fact that it is the construction most used with the double negative, only the future indicative dividing the usage with it, and that in a ratio of eighty-six to fourteen (cf. R. 854).

APPENDIX

PARADIGMS

PARADIGM 1   FIRST DECLENSION

TERMINATIONS

Singular

	Feminine			Masculine	
N..............	ᾱ	ᾰ	η	ης	ᾱς
G. (Ab.)........	ᾱς	ης	ης	ου	ου
D. (L. I.).......	ᾳ	ῃ	ῃ	ῃ	ᾳ
Ac..............	ᾱν	ᾰν	ην	ην	ᾱν
V..............	ᾱ	ᾰ	η	ᾰ	ᾱ

Plural

N. (V.)...................	αι
G. (Ab.).................	ων
D. (L. I.)................	αις
Ac.......................	ας

FEMININE NOUNS

	ἡμέρα: day	δόξα: glory	ἀρχή: beginning
	Singular		
N. (V.).....	ἡμέρα	δόξα	ἀρχή
G. (Ab.)....	ἡμέρας	δόξης	ἀρχῆς
D. (L. I.)...	ἡμέρᾳ	δόξῃ	ἀρχῇ
Ac.........	ἡμέραν	δόξαν	ἀρχήν
	Plural		
N. (V.).....	ἡμέραι	δόξαι	ἀρχαί
G. (Ab.)....	ἡμερῶν	δοξῶν	ἀρχῶν
D. (L. I.)...	ἡμέραις	δόξαις	ἀρχαῖς
Ac.........	ἡμέρας	δόξας	ἀρχάς

MASCULINE NOUNS

	προφήτης: prophet	νεανίας: young man
	Singular	
N............	προφήτης	νεανίας
G. (Ab.)......	προφήτου	νεανίου
D. (L. I.).....	προφήτῃ	νεανίᾳ
Ac...........	προφήτην	νεανίαν
V............	προφῆτα	νεανία
	Plural	
N. (V.).......	προφῆται	νεανίας
G. (Ab.).....	προφητῶν	νεανιῶν
D. (L. I.).....	προφήταις	νεανίαις
Ac...........	προφήτας	νεανίας

PARADIGM 2　　　　　　　　　　**SECOND DECLENSION**

TERMINATIONS

	Singular			Plural		
	Mas. Fem.		Neut.	Mas. Fem.		Neut.
N............	ος		ον	οι		α
G. (Ab.)......		ου			ων	
D. (L. I.).....		ῳ			οις	
Ac...........		ον		ους		α
V............	ε		ον	οι		α

Masculine (and Feminine)　　Neuter

	λόγος: word	ἔργον: work
	Singular	
N............	λόγος	ἔργον
G. (Ab.)......	λόγου	ἔργου
D. (L. I.).....	λόγῳ	ἔργῳ
Ac...........	λόγον	ἔργον
V.	λόγε	ἔργον

Plural

N. (V.)......	λόγοι	ἔργα
G. (Ab.)......	λόγων	ἔργων
D. (L. I.).....	λόγοις	ἔργοις
Ac..........	λόγους	ἔργα

PARADIGM 3   THIRD DECLENSION

TERMINATIONS

	Singular		Plural	
	Mas. Fem.	Neut.	Mas. Fem.	Neut.
N............	s	—	ες	α
G. (Ab.)......	ος		ων	
D. (L. I.).....	ι		σι	
Ac..........	ν or α	—	ας	α
V.	—	—	ες	α

MASCULINE AND FEMININE NOUNS

χάρις, ἡ: αἰών, ὁ: ἄρχων, ὁ: ἀνήρ, ὁ:

grace   age   ruler   man

Singular

N............	χάρις	αἰών	ἄρχων	ἀνήρ
G. (Ab.)......	χάριτος	αἰῶνος	ἄρχοντος	ἀνδρός
D. (L. I.).....	χάριτι	αἰῶνι	ἄρχοντι	ἀνδρί
Ac..........	χάριν	αἰῶνα	ἄρχοντα	ἄνδρα
V............	χάρις	αἰών	ἄρχον	ἄνερ

Plural

N. (V.).......	χάριτες	αἰῶνες	ἄρχοντες	ἄνδρες
G. (Ab.)......	χαρίτων	αἰώνων	ἀρχόντων	ἀνδρῶν
D. (L. I.).....	χάρισι	αἰῶσι	ἄρχουσι	ἀνδράσι
Ac..........	χάριτας	αἰῶνας	ἄρχοντας	ἄνδρας

Singular

	γονεύς, ὁ:	πόλις, ἡ:	ἰχθύς, ὁ:
	parent	*city*	*fish*
N..........	γονεύς	πόλις	ἰχθύς
G. (Ab.)....	γονέως	πόλεως	ἰχθύος
D. (L. I.)...	γονεῖ	πόλει	ἰχθύι
Ac.........	γονέα	πόλιν	ἰχθύν
V..........	γονεῦ	πόλι	ἰχθύ

Plural

N. (V.).....	γονεῖς	πόλεις	ἰχθύες
G. (Ab.)....	γονέων	πόλεων	ἰχθύων
D. (L. I.)...	γονεῦσι	πόλεσι	ἰχθύσι
Ac.........	γονεῖς	πόλεις	ἰχθύας (ἰχθῦς)

NEUTER NOUNS

σῶμα: *body*   γένος: *race*

Singular

N. (V.).......	σῶμα	γένος
G. (Ab.)......	σώματος	γένους
D. (L. I.).....	σώματι	γένει
Ac..........	σῶμα	γένος

Plural

N. (V.).......	σώματα	γένη
G. (Ab.)......	σωμάτων	γενῶν
D. (L. I.).....	σώμασι	γένεσι
Ac..........	σώματα	γένη

PARADIGM 4   IRREGULAR NOUNS

βοῦς, ὁ: *ox*   νοῦς, ὁ (νόος): *mind*

	Singular	Plural	Singular	Plural
N.............	βοῦς	βόες	νοῦς	νοῖ
G. (Ab.)......	βοός	βοῶν	νοῦ	νῶν
D. (L.I.)	βοΐ	βουσί	νῷ	νοῖς
Acc..........	βοῦν	βοῦς(βόας)	νοῦν	νοῦς
V............	βοῦ	βόες	νοῦ	νοῖ

Like *νοῦς* are declined several contracted nouns of the second declension, such as διπλοῦς, ὀστοῦν, χρυσοῦς. Other irregular forms of declension deserving of special notice are:

αἰδώς (f.), gen. αἰδοῦς (from αἰδόσος), dat. αἰδοῖ, acc. αἰδῶ.

ἅλων (f.), gen. ἅλω, dat. ἅλῳ, acc. ἅλων.

βορρᾶς (m.), gen. βορρᾶ.

γάλα (n.), gen. γάλακτος, etc.

γῆρας (n.), gen. γήρως (from γήραος), dat. γήρει.

γόνυ (n.), gen. γόνατος, etc.

γυνή (f.), gen. γυναικός, dat. γυναικί, acc. γυναῖκα, voc. γύναι.

ἔρις (f.), gen. ἔριδος, acc. ἔριν; nom. pl. ἔρεις or ἔριδες.

Ζεύς (m.), gen. Διός, dat. Διί, acc. Δία, voc. Ζεῦ.

ἥμισυ (n.), gen. ἡμίσους, dat. ἡμίσει; nom. and acc. pl. ἡμίσια.

θρίξ (f.), gen. τριχός, etc.; dat. pl. θριξί.

Ἰησοῦς (m.), gen. Ἰησοῦ, dat. Ἰησοῦ, acc. Ἰησοῦν, voc. Ἰησοῦ.

ἱμάς (m.), gen. ἱμάντος, etc.; dat. pl. ἱμᾶσι.

κλείς (f.), gen. κλειδός, dat. κλειδί, acc. κλεῖν and κλεῖδα; acc. pl. κλεῖς and κλεῖδας.

Κλήμης (m.), gen. Κλήμεντος, etc.

κρέας (n.), gen. κρέατος, etc.; acc. pl. κρέα.

κύων (m.), gen. κυνός, etc.; dat. pl. κυσί.

μάρτυς (m.), gen. μάρτυρος, etc.; dat. pl. μάρτυσι.

ναῦς (f.), sing. νεώς, νηί, ναῦν; pl. νῆες, νεῶν, ναυσί, ναῦς.

ὀδούς (m.), gen. ὀδόντος, etc.

οὖς, (n.), gen. ὠτός, etc.; dat. pl. ὠσί.

πούς (m.), gen. ποδός, etc.; dat. pl. ποσί.

πῦρ (n.), gen. πυρός, etc.

ὕδωρ (n.), gen. ὕδατος, etc.

χείρ (f.), gen. χειρός, etc.; dat. pl. χερσί.

ὠδίν (f.), gen. ὠδῖνος, etc.

PARADIGM 5   THE ARTICLE

	Singular			Plural		
	Mas.	Fem.	Neut.	Mas.	Fem.	Neut.
N.........	ὁ	ἡ	τό	οἱ	αἱ	τά
G. (Ab.).....	τοῦ	τῆς	τοῦ	τῶν	τῶν	τῶν
D. (L. I.).....	τῷ	τῇ	τῷ	τοῖς	ταῖς	τοῖς
Acc.........	τόν	τήν	τό	τούς	τάς	τά

PARADIGM 6   DECLENSION OF ADJECTIVES

καλός: beautiful

	Singular			Plural		
	Mas.	Fem.	Neut.	Mas.	Fem.	Neut.
N........καλός	καλή	καλόν	καλοί	καλαί	καλά
G. (Ab.)..καλοῦ	καλῆς	καλοῦ	καλῶν	καλῶν	καλῶν
D. (L. I.).καλῷ	καλῇ	καλῷ	καλοῖς	καλαῖς	καλοῖς
Acc......καλόν	καλήν	καλόν	καλούς	καλάς	καλά
V........καλέ	καλή	καλόν	καλοί	καλαί	καλά

ἑκών: willing

	Singular		
	Mas.	Fem.	Neut.
N. (V.)..........	ἑκών	ἑκοῦσα	ἑκόν
G. (Ab.)..........	ἑκόντος	ἑκούσης	ἑκόντος
D. (L. I.)........	ἑκόντι	ἑκούσῃ	ἑκόντι
Acc.............	ἑκόντα	ἑκοῦσαν	ἑκόν

	Plural		
N. (V.)..........	Mas.	Fem.	Neut.
N. (V.).........	ἑκόντες	ἑκοῦσαι	ἑκόντα
G. (Ab.)..........	ἑκόντων	ἑκουσῶν	ἑκόντων
D. (L. I.)........	ἑκοῦσι	ἑκούσαις	ἑκοῦσι
Acc.. ·.........	ἑκόντας	ἑκούσας	ἑκόντα

ἄδικος: unjust

	Singular			Plural		
	Mas. Fem.	Neut.		Mas. Fem.	Neut.	
N.	ἄδικος	ἄδικον		ἄδικοι	ἄδικα	
G. (Ab.)	ἀδίκου	ἀδίκου		ἀδίκων	ἀδίκων	
D. (L. I.)	ἀδίκῳ	ἀδίκῳ		ἀδίκοις	ἀδίκοις	
Acc.	ἄδικον	ἄδικον		ἀδίκους	ἄδικα	
V.	ἄδικε	ὄδικον		ἄδικοι	ἄδικα	

ἀληθής: true

	Singular			Plural		
	Mas. Fem.	Neut.		Mas. Fem.	Neut.	
N.	ἀληθής	ἀληθές		ἀληθείς	ἀληθῆ	
G. (Ab.)	ἀληθοῦς	ἀληθοῦς		ἀληθῶν	ἀληθῶν	
D. (L. I.)	ἀληθεῖ	ἀληθεῖ		ἀληθέσι	ἀληθέσι	
Ac.	ἀληθῆ	ἀληθές		ἀληθεῖς	ἀληθῆ	
V.	ἀληθές	ἀληθές		ἀληθεῖς	ἀληθῆ	

σώφρων: sane

	Singular			Plural		
	Mas. Fem.	Neut.		Mas. Fem.	Neut.	
N.	σώφρων	σῶφρον		σώφρονες	σώφρονα	
G. (Ab.)	σώφρονος	σώφρονος		σωφρόνων	σωφρόνων	
D. (L. I.)	σώφρονι	σώφρονι		σώφροσι	σώφροσι	
Ac.	σώφρονα	σῶφρον		σώφρονας	σώφρονα	
V.	σῶφρον	σῶφρον		σώφρονες	σώφρονα	

ταχύς: swift

	Singular		
	Mas.	Fem.	Neut.
N.	ταχύς	ταχεῖα	ταχύ
G. (Ab.)	ταχέος	ταχείας	ταχέος
D. (L. I.)	ταχεῖ	ταχείᾳ	ταχεῖ
Ac.	ταχύν	ταχεῖαν	ταχύ
V.	ταχύ	ταχεῖα	ταχύ

Plural

	Mas.	Fem.	Neut.
N...............	ταχεῖς	ταχεῖαι	ταχέα
G. (Ab.)..........	ταχέων	ταχειῶν	ταχέων
D. (L. I.)........	ταχέσι	ταχείαις	ταχέσι
Ac...............	ταχεῖς	ταχείας	ταχέα
V...............	ταχεῖς	ταχεῖαι	ταχέα

πᾶς: all

Singular

	Mas.	Fem.	Neut.
N. (V.)...........	πᾶς	πᾶσα	πᾶν
G. (Ab.)..........	παντός	πάσης	παντός
D. (L. I.)........	παντί	πάσῃ	παντί
Ac...............	πάντα	πᾶσαν	πᾶν

Plural

	Mas.	Fem.	Neut.
N. (V.)..........	πάντες	πᾶσαι	πάντα
G. (Ab.)..........	πάντων	πασῶν	πάντων
D. (L. I.)........	πᾶσι	πάσαις	πᾶσι
Ac...............	πάντας	πάσας	πάντα

μέγας: great

Singular

	Mas.	Fem.	Neut.
N. (V.)...........	μέγας	μεγάλη	μέγα
G. (Ab.)..........	μεγάλου	μεγάλης	μεγάλου
D. (L. I.)........	μεγάλῳ	μεγάλῃ	μεγάλῳ
Ac...............	μέγαν	μεγάλην	μέγα

Plural

	Mas.	Fem.	Neut.
N. (V.)	μεγάλοι	μεγάλαι	μεγάλα
G. (Ab.)	μεγάλων	μεγαλῶν	μεγάλων
D. (L. I.)	μεγάλοις	μεγάλαις	μεγάλοις
Ac.	μεγάλους	μεγάλας	μεγάλα

πολύs: *much*

Singular

	Mas.	Fem.	Neut.
N. (V.)	πολύς	πολλή	πολύ
G. (Ab.)	πολλοῦ	πολλῆς	πολλοῦ
D. (L. I.)	πολλῷ	πολλῇ	πολλῷ
Ac.	πολύν	πολλήν	πολύ

Plural

	Masc.	Fem.	Neut.
N. (V.)	πολλοί	πολλαί	πολλά
G. (Ab.)	πολλῶν	πολλῶν	πολλῶν
D. (L. I.)	πολλοῖς	πολλαῖς	πολλοῖς
Ac.	πολλούς	πολλάς	πολλά

Declension of the forms of comparison: - τερος, - τατος, and -ιστος are declined like καλός; -ιων is declined like σώφρων.

The following are a few of the principal irregular comparatives and superlatives.

ἀγαθός	βελτίων	βέλτιστος
	κρείσσων	κράτιστος
κακός	κακίων	κάκιστος
	χείρων	χείριστος
μικρός	ἐλάσσων	ἐλάχιστος
	ἥσσων	ἥκιστος
πολύς	πλείων or πλέων	πλεῖστος

These are the comparative and superlative forms of primi‑tive roots whose positive form had become obsolete.

PARADIGM 7   DECLENSION OF PRONOUNS

ἐγώ: I   ἡμεῖs: we   σύ: thou   ὑμεῖs: ye

N..........	.ἐγώ	ἡμεῖs	σύ	ὑμεῖs
G. (Ab.)......	.ἐμοῦ, μου	ἡμῶν	σοῦ	ὑμῶν
D. (L. I.)....	.ἐμοί, μοι	ἡμῖν	σοί	ὑμῖν
Ac..........	.ἐμέ, με	ἡμᾶs	σέ	ὑμᾶs

αὐτόs: he (she, it)

	Singular			Plural		
	Mas.	Fem.	Neut.	Mas.	Fem.	Neut.
N..........	αὐτόs	αὐτή	αὐτό	αὐτοί	αὐταί	αὐτά
G. (Ab.)....	αὐτοῦ	αὐτῆs	αὐτοῦ	αὐτῶν	αὐτῶν	αὐτῶν
D. (L. I.)...	αὐτῷ	αὐτῇ	αὐτῷ	αὐτοῖs	αὐταῖs	αὐτοῖs
Ac........	αὐτόν	αὐτήν	αὐτό	αὐτούs	αὐτάs	αὐτά

οὗτοs: this

Singular

	Mas.	Fem.	Neut.
N...............	οὗτοs	αὕτη	τοῦτο
G. (Ab.).........	τούτου	ταύτηs	τούτου
D. (L. I.)........	τούτῳ	ταύτῃ	τούτῳ
Ac..............	τοῦτον	ταύτην	τοῦτο

Plural

	Mas.	Fem.	Neut.
N...............	οὗτοι	αὗται	ταῦτα
G. (Ab.).........	τούτων	τούτων	τούτων
D. (L. I.).......	τούτοιs	ταύταιs	τούτοιs
Ac..............	τούτουs	ταύταs	ταῦτα

ἐκεῖνος: *that*

Singular

	Mas.	Fem.	Neut.
N..............	ἐκεῖνος	ἐκείνη	ἐκεῖνο
G. (Ab.)..........	ἐκείνου	ἐκείνης	ἐκείνου
D. (L. I.).........	ἐκείνῳ	ἐκείνῃ	ἐκείνῳ
Ac..............	ἐκεῖνον	ἐκείνην	ἐκεῖνο

	Mas.	Fem.	Neut.
N..............	ἐκεῖνοι	ἐκεῖναι	ἐκεῖνα
G. (Ab.)..........	ἐκείνων	ἐκείνων	ἐκείνων
D. (L. I.).........	ἐκείνοις	ἐκείναις	ἐκείνοις
Ac..............	ἐκείνους	ἐκείνας	ἐκεῖνα

ὅς: *who*

	Singular			Plural		
	Mas.	Fem.	Neut.	Mas.	Fem.	Neut.
N..........	ὅς	ἥ	ὅ	οἵ	αἵ	ἅ
G. (Ab.).....	οὗ	ἧς	οὗ	ὧν	ὧν	ὧν
D. (L. I.)....	ᾧ	ᾗ	ᾧ	οἷς	αἷς	οἷς
Ac.........	ὅν	ἥν	ὅ	οὕς	ἅς	ἅ

τίς: *who? (what?)*

	Singular		Plural	
	Mas. Fem.	Neut.	Mas. Fem.	Neut.
N............	τίς	τί	τίνες	τίνα
G. (Ab.)......	τίνος	τίνος	τίνων	τίνων
D. (L. I.).....	τίνι	τίνι	τίσι	τίσι
Ac..........	τίνα	τί	τίνας	τίνα

The indefinite pronoun τὶς, τὶ, is declined like the above, except for accent, being an enclitic.

ἐμός: my

| | Singular | | | Plural | | |
	Mas.	Fem.	Neut.	Mas.	Fem.	Neut.
N.............	ἐμός	ἐμή	ἐμόν	ἐμοί	ἐμαί	ἐμά
G. (Ab.).....	ἐμοῦ	ἐμῆς	ἐμοῦ	ἐμῶν	ἐμῶν	ἐμῶν
D. (L. I.)....	ἐμῷ	ἐμῇ	ἐμῷ	ἐμοῖς	ἐμαῖς	ἐμοῖς
Ac............	ἐμόν	ἐμήν	ἐμόν	ἐμούς	ἐμάς	ἐμά

Like the above are declined σός, thy; ἡμέτερος, our; ὑμέτερος, your.

PARADIGM 8   DECLENSION OF PARTICIPLES

Singular

	Mas.	Fem.	Neut.
N................	λύων	λύουσα	λῦον
G. (Ab.)..........	λύοντος	λυούσης	λύοντος
D. (L. I.)........	λύοντι	λυούσῃ	λύοντι
Ac...............	λύοντα	λύουσαν	λῦον

Plural

	Mas.	Fem.	Neut.
N................	λύοντες	λύουσαι	λύοντα
G. (Ab.)..........	λυόντων	λυουσῶν	λυόντων
D. (L. I.)........	λύουσι	λυούσαις	λύουσι
Ac...............	λύοντας	λυούσας	λύοντα

Singular

	Mas.	Fenn.	Neut.
N................	λύσας	λύσασα	λῦσαν
G. (Ab.)..........	λύσαντος	λυσάσης	λύσαντος
D. (L. I.)........	λύσαντι	λυσάσῃ	λύσαντι
Ac...............	λύσαντα	λύσασαν	λῦσαν

Plural

	Mas.	Fem.	Neut.
N.	λύσαντες	λύσασαι	λύσαντα
G. (Ab.).	λυσάντων	λυσασῶν	λυσάντων
D. (L. I.).	λύσασι	λυσάσαις	λύσασι
Ac.	λύσαντος	λυσάσας	λύσαντα

Singular

	Mas.	Fem.	Neut.
N.	λελυκώς	λελυκυῖα	λελυκός
G. (Ab.).	λελυκότος	λελυκυίας	λελυκότο:
D. (L. I.).	λελυκότι	λελυκυίᾳ	λελυκότι
Ac.	λελυκότα	λελυκυῖαν	λελυκός

Plural

	Mas.	Fem.	Neut.
N.	λελυκότες	λελυκυῖαι	λελυκότα
G. (Ab.).	λελυκότων	λελυκυιῶν	λελυκότω:
D. (L. I.).	λελυκόσι	λελυκυίαις	λελυκόσι
Ac.	λελυκότας	λελυκυίας	λελυκότα

Singular

	Mas.	Fem.	Neut.
N.	λυθείς	λυθεῖσα	λυθέν
G. (Ab.).	λυθέντος	λυθείσης	λυθέντος
D. (L. I.).	λυθέντι	λυθείσῃ	λυθέντι
Ac.	λυθέντα	λυθεῖσαν	λυθέν

Plural

	Mas.	Fem.	Neut.
N.	λυθέντες	λυθεῖσαι	λυθέντα
G. (Ab.).	λυθέντων	λυθεισῶν	λυθέντων
D. (L. I.).	λυθεῖσι	λυθείσαις	λυθεῖσι
Ac.	λυθέντας	λυθείσας	λυθέντα

Singular

	Mas.	Fem.	Neut.
N.	λυόμενος	λυομένη	λυόμενον
G. (Ab.)	λυομένου	λυομένης	λυομένου
D. (L. I.)	λυομένῳ	λυομένῃ	λυομένῳ
Ac.	λυόμενον	λυομένην	λυόμενον

Plural

	Mas.	Fem.	Neut.
N.	λυόμενοι	λυόμεναι	λυόμενα
G. (Ab.)	λυομένων	λυομένων	λυομένων
D. (L. I.)	λυομένοις	λυομέναις	λυομένοις
Ac.	λυομένους	λυομένας	λυόμενα

PARADIGM 9   DECLENSION OF NUMERALS

CARDINALS

	Mas.	Fem.	Neut.	M. F. & N.	Mas. Fem.	Neut.
N.	εἷς	μία	ἕν	δύο	τρεῖς	τρία
G. (Ab.)	ἑνός	μιᾶς	ἑνός	δύο	τριῶν	τριῶν
D. (L. I.)	ἑνί	μιᾷ	ἑνί	δυσί	τρισί	τρισί
Ac.	ἕνα	μίαν	ἕν	δύο	τρεῖς	τρία

	Mas. Fem.	Neut.
N.	τέσσαρες	τέσσαρα
G. (Ab.)	τεσσάρων	τεσσάρων
D. (L. I.	τέσσαρσι	τέσσαρσι
Ac.	τέσσαρας	τέσσαρα

	Mas.	Fem.	Neut.
N.	χίλιοι	χίλιαι	χίλια
G. (Ab.)	χιλίων	χιλιῶν	χιλίων
D. (L. I.)	χιλίοις	χιλίαις	χιλίοις
Ac.	χιλίους	χιλίας	χίλια

Following are other forms found in the New Testament.

Future pass. 3 p. sing. ἀφεθήσεται.

Pres. ind. middle 3 p. sing. ἀφίεται, pl. ἀφίενται and ἀφίουσιν.

Aor. pass. ind. 3 p. pl. ἀφέθησαν; subj. 3 p. sing. ἀφεθῇ.

The aor. active ind. ἀφῆκα is conjugated like ἔθηκα, and the aor. subj. ἀφῶ is conjugated like λύω.

Aor. imper. active 2 p. sing. ἄφες, pl. ἄφετε.

Aor. active inf. ἀφεῖναι.

Aor. active part. ἀφείς, - εῖσα, -έν.

Pf. middle ind. 3 p. pi. ἀφέωνται.

Οἶδα, *know*, which is second perfect in form, is conjugated as follows:

Second Perfect

Indicative	Subjunctive	Optative	Imperative
οἶδα	εἰδῶ	εἰδείην	
οἶδας, οἶσθα	εἰδῇς	εἰδείης	ἴσθι
οἶδε	εἰδῇ	εἰδείη	ἴστω
ἴσμεν	εἰδῶμεν	εἰδείημεν	
ἴστε	εἰδῆτε	εἰδείητε	ἴστε
ἴσασι	εἰδῶσι	εἰδείησαν	ἴστωσαν

Infinitive	Participle
εἰδέναι	εἰδώς, εἰδυῖα, εἰδός

Second Pluperfect	Future		
ᾔδειν	εἴσομαι	or	εἰδήσω
ᾔδεις	εἴσῃ		εἰδήσεις
ᾔδει	εἴσεται		εἰδήσει
ᾔδειμεν	εἰσόμεθα		εἰδήσομεν
ᾔδειτε	εἴσεσθε		εἰδήσετε
ᾔδεισαν·	εἴσονται		εἰδήσουσι

The Second Aorist of γινώσκω, know

Indic.	Impv.	Subj. γνῶ, inflected like δῶ
ἔγνων		Inf. γνῶναι
ἔγνως	γνῶθι	Part. γνούς, γνοῦσα, γνόν
ἔγνω	γνώτω	
ἔγνωμεν		
ἔγνωτε	γνῶτε	
ἔγνωσαν	γνώτωσαν	

The Second Aorist of βαίνω, go

Indic	Imp.	Subj. βῶ, inflected like δῶ
ἔβην		
ἔβης	βῆθι	Inf. βῆναι
ἔβη	βήτω	Part. βάς, βᾶσα, βάν
ἔβημεν		
ἔβητε	βῆτε	
ἔβησαν	βάντων	

Future and Aorist of βάλλω, throw

In forming the future one λ is dropped and ε is substituted for it. We have as a result the following contract forms:

In forming the aorist the stem is shortened by dropping one λ, thereby leaving the simple verb stem.

βαλῶ	βαλῶμεν	ἔβαλον	ἐβάλομεν
βαλεῖς	βαλεῖτε	ἔβαλες	ἐβάλετε
βαλεῖ	βαλῶσι	ἔβαλε	ἔβαλον

Other forms are the pf. ind. active and middle βέβληκα, βέβλημαι; 1 aor. ind. pass. ἐβλήθην. These are conjugated like the corresponding forms of λύω.

PRINCIPAL PARTS OF IRREGULAR VERBS

To give an exhaustive list of the irregular verbs would carry us far beyond the prescribed limits of this volume. We present here some of the most difficult and most frequently used, with the recommendation that they be thoroughly mastered by the student. A more extended list may be found in R–S. 48–56, 241–244, or M–II. 224–266.

Present	Future	Aorist	Perfect Act.	Per. Mid.	Aor. Pas.
ἀγγέλλω	ἀγγελῶ	ἤγγειλα		ἤγγελμαι	ἠγγέλην
ἄγω	ἄξω	ἤγαγον		ἤγμαι	ἤχθην
αἱρέω	αἱρήσομαι	εἷλον		ᾕρημαι	ᾑρέθην
αἴρω	ἀρῶ	ἦρα	ἦρκα	ἦρμαι	ἤρθην
ἀκούω	ἀκούσω	ἤκουσα	ἀκήκοα		ἠκούσθην
ἁμαρτάνω	ἁμαρτήσω	ἥμαρτον ἡμάρτησα	ἡμάρτηκα		
ἀνοίγω	ἀνοίξω	ἠνέῳξα ἀνέῳξα ἤνοιξα	ἀνέῳγα	ἠνέῳγμαι ἀνέῳγμαι ἤνοιγμαι	ἠνεῴχθην ἀνεῴχθην ἠνοίχθην
ἀποκτείνω	-κτενῶ	-έκτεινα			-ἐκτάνθην
ἀπόλλυμι	ἀπολέσω	ἀπώλεσα	ἀπώλωλα		
ἀρέσκω	ἀρέσω	ἤρεσα			
ἀρνέομαι	ἀρνήσομαι	ἠρνησάμην		ἤρνημαι	ἠρνήθην
ἄρχω	ἄρξομαι	ἠρξάμην			
ἀφίημι	-ήσω	-ῆκα	-εἷκα	-έωμαι	-έθην
βαίνω	βήσομαι	ἔβην	βέβηκα		
βάλλω	βαλῶ	ἔβαλον	βέβληκα	βέβλημαι	ἐβλήθην
γαμέω	γαμήσω	ἔγημα	γεγάμηκα		ἐγαμήθην
γίνομαι	γενήσομαι	ἐγενόμην	γέγονα	γεγένημαι	ἐγενήθην
γινώσκω	γνώσομαι	ἔγνων	ἔγνωκα	ἔγνωσμαι	ἐγνώσθην
γράφω	γράψω	ἔγραψα	γέγραφα	γέγραμμαι	ἐγράφην
δείκνυμι	δείξω	ἔδειξα		δέδειγμαι	ἐδείχθην
δέχομαι	δέξομαι	ἐδεξάμην		δέδεγμαι	ἐδέχθην

Present	Future	Aorist	Perfect Act.	Per. Mid.	Aor. Pas.
διδάσκω	διδάξω	ἐδίδαξα			ἐδιδάχθην
δίδωμι	δώσω	ἔδωκα	δέδωκα	δέδομαι	ἐδόθην
διώκω	διώξω	ἐδίωξα		δεδίωγμαι	ἐδιώχθην
δύναμαι	δυνήσομαι	ἐδυνάμην			ἠδυνήθην
		ἠδυνάμην			ἠδυνάσθην
ἐγγίζω	ἐγγίσω	ἤγγισα	ἤγγικα		
	ἐγγιῶ				
εἰμί	ἔσομαι	ἤμην (impf.)			
ἐλπίζω	ἐλπιῶ	ἤλπισα	ἤλπικα,		
ἐργάζομαι		ἠργασάμην		εἴργασμαι	εἰργάσθην
ἔρχομαι	ἐλεύσομαι	ἦλθον	ἐλήλυθα		
ἐσθίω	φάγομαι	ἔφαγον			
εὐαγγελίζω		εὐηγγέλισα		εὐηγγέλισμαι	
					εὐηγγελίσθην
		εὐηγγελισάμην			
εὑρίσκω	εὑρήσω	εὗρον	εὕρηκα		εὑρέθην
εὔχομαι	εὔξομαι	εὐξάμην			
ἔχω	ἔξω	ἔσχον	ἔσχηκα		
θέλω	θελήσω	ἠθέλησα			
θνήσκω	θανοῦμαι	ἔθανον	τέθνηκα		
ἵστημι	στήσω	ἔστησα	ἔστηκα		ἐστάθην
καίω	καύσω	ἔκαυσα		κέκαυμαι	ἐκαύθην
καλέω	καλέσω	ἐκάλεσα	κέκληκα	κέκλημαι	ἐκλήθην
κλίνω	κλινῶ	ἔκλινα	κέκλικα		ἐκλίθην
κρίνω	κρινῶ	ἔκρινα	κέκρικα	κέκριμαι	ἐκρίθην
λαμβάνω	λήψομαι	ἔλαβον	εἴληφα	εἴλημμαι	ἐλήφθην
λείπω	λείψω	ἔλιπον	λέλοιπα	λέλειμμαι	ἐλείφην
μανθάνω		ἔμαθον	μεμάθηκα		
μέλλω	μελλήσω	ἤμελλον			
		ἔμελλον			
μένω	μενῶ	ἔμεινα	μεμένηκα		
μιμνήσκω	μνήσω	ἔμνησα		μέμνημαι	ἐμνήσθην

Present	Future	Aorist	Perfect Act.	Per. Mid.	Aor. Pas.
ὁράω	ὄψομαι	εἶδον	ἑόρακα		
			ἑώρακα		ὤφθην
πάσχω		ἔπαθον	πέπονθα		
πείθω	πείσω	ἔπεισα	πέποιθα	πέπεισμαι	ἐπείσθην
πίνω	πίομαι	ἔπιον	πέπωκα		ἐπόθην
πίπτω	πεσοῦμαι	ἔπεσον	πέπτωκα		
στέλλω	στελῶ	ἔστειλα	ἔσταλκα	ἔσταλμαι	ἐστάλην
στρέφω	στρέψω	ἔστρεψα		ἔστραμμαι	ἐστράφην
σώζω	σώσω	ἔσωσα	σέσωκα	σέσωσμαι	ἐσώθην
τελέω	τελῶ	ἐτέλεσα	τετέλεκα	τετέλεσμαι	ἐτελέσθην
τίθημι	θήσω	ἔθηκα	τέθεικα	τέθειμαι	ἐτέθην
τρέχω		ἔδραμον			
φαίνω	φανοῦμαι	ἔφανα			ἐφάνην
φέρω	οἴσω	ἤνεγκα	ἐνήνοχα		ἠνέχθην
φεύγω	φεύξομαι	ἔφυγον	πέφευγα		
φθείρω	φθερῶ	ἔφθειρα		ἔφθαρμαι	ἐφθάρην

Note:—A few forms not occurring in the New Testament have been given in order that the student may become familiar with the variations in verb stems.

EXERCISES FOR COMPOSITION IN GREEK NEW TESTAMENT

Orthography

1. Paul saluted the church at Gaius' house. 2. On account of him some blasphemed the name of God. 3. Thus he shall do for all. 4. He brought the fruit of the Olive. 5. God is righteous and I am evil. 6. They crucified my Savior, and he died for you and me. 7. Christ is the Lord of my life.

Declension

8. The man sent his brother to the master. 9. The gifts of the servants are pleasing to the kings. 10. The priests will bring the coats for the children. 11. The man wrote the epistle to his brother. 12. The shepherds came in the night. 13. The children of the king are running through the temple.

Conjugation

14. The lambs are playing in the fields. 15. The birds were eating the wheat. 16. The teacher will call his disciples. 17. The angels sang, praising God. 18. The enemies have crucified the Redeemer. 19. Many had determined not to believe the word of Jesus.

Nominative and Vocative Cases

20. Thanksgiving ascended to the throne of God. 21. The gospel is the hope of all men. 22. Oh, vain works of sinful flesh! 23. O God, hear the prayer of thy people.

Genitive and Ablative Cases

24. The message of life came from Heaven. 25. The journey of Paul was the salvation of the people. 26. Three of the disciples heard the message. 27. Jesus having been crucified, the soldiers parted his garments. 28. The message of the woman was worthy of praise. 29. John gave the people the revelation from Christ.

Dative, Locative, and Instrumental Cases

30. The Jews made trouble for them. 31. Those who trust the Savior are pleasing to Him. 32. It seemed best to them to go away. 33. The fishermen left in the boats. 34. On that same night Judas betrayed him. 35. The believer should be a child in spirit. 36. He calmed the sea with a word. 37. The believer enjoys fellowship with his brethren. 38. They proclaimed the gospel with zeal. 39. He came earlier by five days.

Accusative Case

40. Paul remained in Ephesus three years. 41. They served in the same way. 42. He was mighty in the ministry of the word. 43. Barnabas lived a good life. 44. The publicans asked him many questions.

Prepositions

45. The teacher went through the cities and up to the sea. 46. Jesus came from the Father and died for sinners. 47. Paul suffered on account of his love for the cross. 48. John went out of the city and into the country and preached in the wilderness. 49. He went down to the river with the disciples. 50. The women remained by the altar and prayed for their sons. 51. The multitudes journeyed before Christ to the city. 52. The Savior died under the curse for sin.

Adjectives

53. He spoke a good word to the idle boy. 54. The heart of the saint was pure. 55. The evil one is not able to do good. 56. He first gave commandment to the twelve. 57. Christ was greater than the law.

Pronouns

58. I am not the Christ, but thou art the Christ. 59. He is grieved on account of my sin. 60. Stephen, who was stoned for the faith, died without fear. 61. This boy is the son of that woman. 62. The jailer himself was baptized on the same night. 63. Certain said unto him, Who is this who forgives sins?

Article

64. Atonement is the work of Christ; grace belongs to God. 65. James was killed by Herod; but the church prayed for Peter. 66. Nations are in the bondage of sin. 67. This Jesus is not only man; he is God.

Voice and Mood

68. They took counsel to slay him. 69. The uproar was silenced by the officers with a word. 70. What was the Master teaching? 71. Thou shalt hear the words of truth. 72. Let us ask the Master what we shall teach. 73. Do not disobey God. 74. Let us love God. 75. Shall sin conquer us? May it never be! 76. Yield yourself to the entreaties of the Spirit.

Tense

77. Their enemies are making war upon the city. 78. Saints submit to the providence of God. 79. The priest was praying in the Temple. 80. They were waiting to slay him, and began crying out for his blood. 81. The redeemed in

heaven shall rejoice. 82. The multitude cried out against Jesus. 83. Peter became penitent. 84. The prophets wrote concerning the Messiah. 85. We have believed their message. 86. The council had condemned the Lord of glory.

Infinitive

87. Paul went to Macedonia to preach the gospel. 88. The women prayed while they worked. 89. The Pharisees ceased persecuting because they feared the people. 90. To work righteousness is becoming to the people. 91. Herod feared to keep his oath. 92. To win souls to Christ is the believer's joy. 93. They were not worthy to receive the gospel.

Participle

94. The saints were waiting for the coming kingdom. 95. The one keeping his commandments loves him. 96. The people having assembled, the disciples proclaimed the message. 97. The priests were afraid because they had crucified Jesus. 98. By sitting in the boat he was able to teach the multitude. 99. When the Sabbath came the scribes ceased working.

Adverbs

100. Finally, they were there. 101. They ran thither quickly. 102. He spoke more friendly and came nearer. 103. He ran farthest and quickest. 104. God loves most and always.

Conjunctions and Particles

105. In fact, he loved his father, but he was covetous. 106. They lived, for they obeyed the vision. 107. Whenever we preach the gospel somebody will believe. 108. Wherefore, we must give glory to God. 109. Now, the believer

prays in order that he may receive a blessing. 110. The Passover was indeed a great feast. 111. Yea, our flesh is weak through sin. 112. One is under the law, while another is under grace. 113. How shall we return his love, if indeed he died for us? 114. Above all, do good.

Relative and Causal Clauses

115. John baptized those who repented of their sins. 116. God, who loves us, will not forget His children. 117. He who lives in sin does not have true faith. 118. We trust our souls to Christ, who will save them. 119. Paul rebuked Peter because Peter was wrong (write in four ways).

Comparative, Local, and Temporal Clauses

120. We will suffer for our Lord as he suffered for us. 121. The believer prays as the Spirit guides him. 122. Whenever a man sins and wherever he sins, he grieves the Holy Spirit. 123. Let us work until Jesus comes. 124. Paul was to wait at Troas until Titus came. 125. Paul waited at Philippi until Titus came. 126. Before the leper departed he asked to be healed. 127. While we wait, we must not be idle.

Purpose, Result, and Substantival Clauses

128. John was preaching near the Jordan in order that he might baptize the people. 129. Paul went with Luke to preach the gospel in Philippi. 130. The Greeks came to inquire concerning Christ. 131. The way is so plain that the poor may understand it. 132. He left by night so that his enemies did not see him. 133. That he may please his Master is the Christian's desire. 134. There came no one who really cared for him. 135. It seemed best to him to go to the feast. 136. They feared to seize him.

Conditional and Concessive Clauses

137. If Paul preached the gospel in Bithynia, men believed. 138. If Paul had preached the gospel in Bithynia, men would have believed. 139. If Paul preaches the gospel in Bithynia, men will believe. 140. If Paul should preach the gospel in Bithynia, men would believe. 141. Even though Christ died on the cross, he was not a sinner. 142. Though the heavens should fall, the word of God will not fail.

Indirect Discourse, Commands, and Prohibitions

143. Jesus said that John was least in the kingdom of heaven. 144. The Spirit informed Paul what he would encounter at Jerusalem. 145. Paul instructed Titus to ordain bishops in every city. 146. Receive the message of truth and preach it to the world. 147. Do not cease keeping the commandment of the Lord. 148. Stop sinning. 149. Do not sin.

ENGLISH-GREEK VOCABULARY

(This vocabulary is designed especially for the aid of students in preparing English-Greek composition. Instructors will find it adequate for a large variety of exercises. The exercises offered above may be used, or the teacher may give exercises of his own. For the preparation of this vocabulary we are principally indebted to Mr. John W. Patterson.)

Key to Abbreviations

1 a.: first aorist; abl.: ablative; acc.: accusative; act.: active; adj.: adjective; adv.: adverb; ai.: from the bottom; a. ps.: aorist passive; Aram.: Aramaic; AS: Abbott-Smith's *Manual Greek Lexicon;* Att.: Attic Greek; cf.: compare; cl. and cl. Gr.: classical Greek; conj.: conjunction; cons.: consonant; contra.: contraction; D.: Davis' *Beginner's Grammar of the Greek New Testament;* decl.: declension; dubl.: double; emph.: emphatic; f.: future; fem.: feminine; fm.: from; ftn.: footnote; G.: Green's: *Handbook and Vocabulary of the Greek New Testament;* Ger.: German; impf.: imperfect; imv.: imperative; inc.: including; indel.: indeclinable; indef.: indefinite; inf.: infinitive; instru.: instrumental; inter.: interrogative; Lat.: Latin; l. i. d.: locative, instrumental, dative; lit.: literally; LS.: Liddell and Scott; Man.: *Manual Grammar of the Greek New Testament,* Dana and Mantey; mid.: middle; MM.: Moulton and Milligan's *Vocabulary of the Greek Testament;* mngs.: meanings; N.: Nestle's *Greek New Testament;* nom.: nominative; obj.: object; obs.: obsolete; opp.: opposite; pl.: plural; poss.: possessive; pred.: predicate; ps.: passive; ptc.: participle; sts.: sometimes; subst.:

substantive; t.: times; T.: Tischendorf's Greek Text; Th.:
Thayer's *New Testament Greek Lexicon;* T.R.: Text Re-
ceived; Tr.: Tregelles' Greek Text; WH.: Westcott and
Hort's Greek Text; Vulg.: Vulgate.

A, an, expressed by the absence of the definite article. The
    absence of the article also denotes quality.
able, to be, δύναμαι.
above all, οὖν, εἰ μήν (Man.).
according to, κατά with acc. (Man.).
afraid, be, φοβέομαι (τρέμω, tremble, be afraid).
against, εἰς, acc. only (into); κατά (down), w. gen.; πρός
    (toward), w. acc. (Man.).
all, πᾶς, πᾶσα, πᾶν.
altar, θυσιαστήριον, -ου, τό (βωμός, -οῦ, ὁ, elevated place
    altar; Ac. 17:23).
always, πάντοτε.
am, εἰμί (be).
and, καί (also); δέ, in the next place, and, but, on the other
    hand.
angel, ἄγγελος, -ου, ὁ (messenger).
appoint, καθίστημι, a. subj. καταστήσω, pres. inf. καθιστάναι·
arrive, καταπλέω, 1 a. κατέπλευσα (παραβάλλω, place
    beside; mid. arrive).
as, ὡς; καθώς (according as, even as).
ascend, ἀναβαίνω (come up, go up).
ask, αἰτέω (ask for something); ἐρωτάω (ask a question).
assemble, συνέρχομαι (convene, come together, go with), 2
    a. -ῆλθον, 2 pf. -ελήλυθα, 2 pf. ptc. -εληλυθός; 2 a. act. ptc.
    -ελθών; συγκαλέω, convoke, call together, assemble; 1 a.
    συνεκάλεσα; συνάγω, gather together, collect; 1 a.
    συνῆξα, 2 a. συνήγαγον, pf. συνῆχα, or συναγάγοχα,
    1 a. ptc. συνάξας (LS.), pf. ptc. mid. συνηγμένος.
at, ἐν (in, loc.,); ἐπί, upon (loc. or gen.).
atonement. καταλλαγή, -ῆς, ἡ (reconciliation).

baptize, βαπτίζω, f. βαπτίσω, 1 a. ἐβάπτισα, pf. ptc. βεβαπτισμένος.

Barnabas, Βαρνάβας, -α, ὁ.

be, εἰμί (exist); γίνομαι (begin to be, become); 2 a. ἐγενόμην.

because, ὅτι; διά, because, or prep. with acc.

become, γίνομαι, begin to be, come into being; 2 a. ἐγενόμην.

becoming, εὐσχήμων, -ον (well-shaped, 1 Cor. 8:35); ἄξιος, -α, -ον, worthy, becoming.

before, πρό (prep. w. abl.); ἔμπροσθεν, in front of, w. abl. (L. ante); both are used in cl. Gr. of time and place; but in NT, chiefly time; ἔμπροσθεν, place only; πρίν, before (formerly, L. prius).

begin, ἄρχομαι, 1 a. ἠρξάμην.

believe, πιστεύω, f. πιστεύσω.

believers, οἱ πιστοί (the trusty, the faithful); believer, ὁ πιστεύων.

belong, εἰμί with the dative case (cf. Man. under dat. case).

best, κρείττων, -ονος (κρείσσων, -ονος); πρῶτος, -η, -ον.

betray, παραδίδωμι, impf. ind. 3 sg. παρεδίδου, f. παραδώσω, 1 a. παρέδωκα.

bird, πετεινόν, -ου, τό (flying or winged animals, fm. πετεινός, -ή, -όν, flying).

bishop, ἐπίσκοπος, -ου, ὁ.

Bithynia, βιθυνία, -ας, ἡ.

blaspheme, βλασφημέω.

blessing, εὐλογία, -ας, ἡ.

blood, αἷμα, αἵματος, τό.

both . . . and, τέ . . . τέ; καί . . . καί.

bondage, δουλεύω, το be a slave, to be in bondage; (κατα) -δουλόω, to enslave.

boy, παῖς, παιδός, ὁ (ἡ, girl); παιδίσκος, -ου, ὁ, young boy.

bring, ἄγω; φέρω, bear, carry.

brother, ἀδελφός, -οῦ, ὁ.

but, ἀλλά; δέ (cf. Man.).

by, ὑπό (abl. of agent, w. pass); παρά, beside (w. loc. abl. acc.; cf. Man.).

call, καλέω, f. καλέσω, 1 a. ἐκάλεσα (καλέω denotes to cry out for a purpose (for help). βοάω (Lat. *boo*), to cry out as a manifestation of feeling, sensibility; κράζω, croak, cry out harshly, instinctively; κραυγάζω, shout coarsely.

calm, to, καταστέλλω (to quiet); φράσσω, fence up, stop.

calm, to be, ἡσυχάζω, be or keep quiet, silent; σιγάω, keep silent (mental); σιωπάω (physical).

care, n.; ἐπιμέλεια, -ας, ἡ, attention; σπουδή, -ης, ἡ, diligence; μέριμνα, -ης, ἡ, anxiety, distraction.

cease, παύομαι (fm. παύω, stop), f. παύσομαι, 1 a. ἐπαυσάμην, pf. πέπαυμαι.

certain (one), τὶς, τὶ (any one, anything).

child, τέκνον, -ου, τό; βρέφος, -ους, τό, infant; παῖς, -δός, ὁ, ἡ (boy or girl).

Christ, Χριστός, -οῦ, ὁ (the annointed one, fm. χριστός, -η, -ον, verbal adj. of χρίω, *annoint*).

Christian, Χριστιανός, -οῦ, ὁ (a follower of Christ).

church, ἐκκλησία, -ας, ἡ.

city, πόλις, -εως, ἡ.

coat, χιτών, -ῶνος, ὁ (tunic).

come, ἔρχομαι, 2 a. ἦλθον, come, go; -βαίνω, 2 a. -έβην, go, come (in NT only in comp).

commandment, ἐντολή, -ῆς, ἡ.

concerning, περί with gen. or acc.; εἰς, κατά with acc.; ὑπέρ w. abl.

condemn, κατακρίνω.

conscience, συνείδησις, -εως, ἡ.

conquer, νικάω, f. νικήσω, 1 a. ἐνίκησα, pf. νενίκηκα.

council, συνέδριον, -ου, τό (Sanhedrin).

counsel (noun), βουλή, -ῆς, ἡ; συμβούλιον, -ου, τό; (vb.) συμβουλεύω, to give counsel, συμβουλεύομαι, to take counsel (together); βουλεύομαι (to give one's self counsel), to take counsel.

country, χώρα, -as, ἡ (place, region, field); ἀγρός, -οῦ, ὁ, field (cf. L. *ager*, G. *Acker*, Eng. acre), farm (cf. MM); πατρίς, -ίδος, ἡ, fatherland.

covetous, πλεονέκτης, -ου, ὁ, a covetous person (πλέον, more + ἔχω, have), greedy (Th.); avaricious (G.); φιλάργυρος, -ον.

cross, σταυρός, -οῦ, ὁ.

crucify, σταυρόω, f. σταυρώσω, 1 a. ἐσταύρωσα, pf. ἐσταύρωμαι (on improper reduplication, i.e., "like the augment"; cf. Man.).

cry out, κράζω, f. κράξω, 1 a. ἔκραξα, 2 a, ἔκραγον, pf. κέκραγα; κραυγάζω, cry coarsely, in contempt; intensive (see sub. call).

curse (n.), κατάρα, -as, ἡ (judicial sentence, קְלָלָה); ἀνάθεμα, -τος, τό, set up, laid by (Th.); vb. ἀναθεματίζω, to curse.

day, ἡμέρα, -as, ἡ.

depart, ἀφίστημι, 1 a. ἀπέστησα, 2a. ἀπέστην; ἀπέρχομαι, 2 a. ἀπῆλθον, go away.

desire, ἐπιθυμία, -as, ἡ, active or evil desire; πάθος, -ους, τό, passionate or ungovernable desire (passive side of vice in NT; in cl. Gr., good or evil).

determine, κρίνω, f. κρινῶ, 1 a. ἔκρινα; pf. κέκρικα; ὁρίζω, determine, appoint, designate, settle, 1 a. ὥρισα.

die, ἀποθνήσκω, f. ἀποθανοῦμαι, 2 a. ἀπέθανον.

disciple, m., μαθητής, -οῦ, ὁ (used also for fem. exc. Ac. 9:36. μαθήτρια, -as, ἡ).

disobey, ἀπειθέω.

do, ποιέω, make, cause to be; πράσσω (root, πραγ-), carry out, practice.

early (adv.), πρωί.

early (adj.), πρώιος, -η, -ον.

eat, ἐσθίω, impf. ἤσθιον, f. φάγομαι, 2 a. ἔφαγον.

encounter, συμβάλλω, 2 a. συνέβαλον.

enemy, ἐχθρός, -οῦ, ὁ (subst. fm. ἐχθρός, -ά, -όν, hated).

enjoy, ἔχω ἀπόλαυσιν with gen., ἔχω εἰς ἀπόλαυσιν with acc.

entreaty, παράκλησις, -εως, ἡ (exhortation, consolation); αἴτημα, -ατος, τό (request).

Ephesus, Ἔφεσος, -ου, ἡ.

epistle, ἐπιστολή, -ῆς, ἡ.

even, καί, and, also (copulative coördinating conj.).

even though, καὶ εἰ.

every, πᾶς, πᾶσα, πᾶν.

evil, κακός, -ή, -όν (bad); πονηρός, -ά, -όν (πονηρός, -οῦ, ὁ, the evil one).

fail, ἐκλείπω (leave out; eclipse, LS.).

faith, πίστις, -εως, ἡ (fidelity, loyalty, Gal. 5:22; Titus 2:10).

fall, πίπτω.

farthest, see Man. on Adverbs.

father, πατήρ, πατρός, ὁ.

fear, φόβος, -ου, ὁ; εὐλάβεια, -ας, ἡ, reverence, pious fear.

feast, δεῖπνον, -ου, τό supper, δοχή, -ῆς, ἡ banquet.

fellowship, μετοχή, -ῆς, ἡ (sharing, Vulg. participatio); κοινωνία, -ας, ἡ, communion, partnership.

field, ἀγρός, -οῦ, ὁ (χωρίον of papyri, MM).

finally, τὸ λοιπόν.

first, πρῶτος, -η, -ον; adv. πρῶτον, πρώτως; τὸ πρῶτον = at first.

fisherman, ἀλεεύς, -εως, ὁ (T. WH. N.) = ἁλιεύς, εως, ὁ, (T. R. cl.).

five, πέντε, οἱ, αἱ, τά (indeclinable).

for, γάρ (causal conjunction).

for (prep), διά w. acc., for the sake of; ὑπέρ w. abl., for the sake of; "for" is a meaning of the dat. without any prep.; ἀντί w. abl. in the sense of "instead of"; εἰς, into, may acquire the resultant mng. "for" after vbs. of

"ethical direction (one's advantage or disadvantage)" or "of purpose" (Th.).

forget, to, ἐπιλανθάνομαι, 2 a. ἐπελαθόμην.

forgive, to, ἀφίημι, f. ἀφήσω, 1 a. ἀφῆκα, pf. ἀφεῖκα, a. ps. ἀφέθην.

forsake, καταλείπω, f. καταλείψω, 2 a. κατέλιπον, 1 a. κατέλειψα.

friendly, see Man. on Adverbs.

from, ἀπό, off, away from (L. a, ab, abs; Ger. von., ab, weg); ἐκ (ἐξ) out of (abl.) (L. e, ex); παρά, from beside (Man., Th.)

fruit, καρπός, -οῦ, ὁ.

Gaius, Γάϊος, -ου, ὁ (so Nestle uniformly; WH in 3 Jn. 1, but elsewhere Γαῖος).

garment, ἱμάτιον, -ου, τό, cloak, mantle; χιτών, -ῶνος, ὁ, tunic, (under) garment, coat.

gift, δῶρον, -ου, τό, present; δωρεά, -ᾶς, ἡ (free) gift.

give, δίδωμι, f. δώσω, 1 a. ἔδωκα, pf. δέδωκα, 1 a. ps. ἐδόθην.

glory, δόξα, -ης, ἡ.

go, πορεύομαι, proceed, advance; ἔρχομαι, go, come; ἄγομαι, lead one's self, proceed; -βαίνω, go, walk.

go away, ἀπέρχομαι.

go down, καταβαίνω.

God, θεός, -οῦ, ὁ

good, ἀγαθός, -ή, -όν (in inner nature); καλός, beautiful (outwardly); δίκαιος, -α, -ον, right.

gospel, εὐαγγέλιον, -ου, τό (good news).

grace, χάρις, χάριτος, ἡ; εὐπρέπεια, -ας, ἡ, beauty, comeliness.

great, μέγας, μεγάλη, μέγα.

Greek, n., Ἕλλην, -ηνος, ὁ; adj. Ἑλληνικός, -ή, -όν, Grecian.

grieve, to, λυπέω.

guide, ὁδηγέω.

have, ἔχω, impf. εἶχον; durative. f. ἕξω; punctiliar f. σχήσω; 2 a. ἔσχον; pf. ἔσχηκα.

he, expressed by vb. endings; emph. "he," αὐτός, -ή, -όν.

heal, ἰάομαι, f. ἰάσομαι, 1 a. ἰασάμην; pf. ἴαμαι, 1 a. ps.
    ἰάθην; θεραπεύω, cure.

hear, ἀκούω.

heart, καρδία, -ας, ἡ.

heaven, οὐρανός, -οῦ, ὁ (never used in pl. in cl. Gr. (LS)).

Herod, Ἡρῴδης, -ου, ὁ.

himself, αὐτός, -ή, -ό.

his, αὐτοῦ; ἴδιος, -α, ον, his own.

holy, ἅγιος, -α, -ον; ἱερός, -ά, -όν, sacred; ὅσιος, -α, -ον, pious.

hope, ἐλπίς, -ίδος, ἡ.

house, οἰκία, -ας, ἡ (the dwelling); οἶκος, -ου, ὁ, house(hold),
    οἰκητήριον, -ου, τό, habitation.

how? πῶς (interrogative adv.); ὅπως (adv. of manner).

I, indicated by vb. end'g; emphatic I, ἐγώ.

idle, ἀργός, -ή, όν (inactive) βραδύς, -εῖα, -ύ, slack, slow;
    νωθρός, -ά, -όν, slothful, sluggish.

idle, to be, ἀργέω.

if, εἰ (also "whether," usually w. ind.); ἐάν (w. subj. or
    fut. ind.).

in, ἐν w. loc. only; εἰς w. acc., into.

in fact, καὶ γάρ (etenim, namque, for truly), καί, γάρ, δέ, ἀλλά
    (Man)

in order that, ἵνα.

indeed, μέν, δέ, οὖν, γάρ, all postpositive particles (Man.).

inform, κατηχέω, instruct; ἐμβανίζω, manifest, exhibit.

inquire, πυνθάνομαι; ζητέω, seek (for); ἐρωτάω, ask (for).

instruct, κατηχέω, 1 a. κατηχήσα; παιδεύω, teach, correct.

into, εἰς, always w. acc.

is, be, am, εἰμί, γίνομαι (γίγνομαι, Att.), begin to be.

jailer (jailor), δεσμοφύλαξ, -ακος, ὁ.

James, Ἰάκωβος, -ου, ὁ; cf. Ἰακώβ, ὁ (indeclinable), Jacob
    Isaac's son.

Jerusalem, Ἰεροσόλυμα, -ων, τα (N., Th., G.); Ἰερουσαλήμ (Th., N., G.), ἡ.

Jesus, Ἰησοῦς, -οῦ, ὁ.

Jew, Ἰουδαῖος, -ου, ὁ (subst. of Ἰουδαῖος, -α, -ον, Jewish).

John, Ἰωάνης, -ου, ὁ.

Jordan, Ἰορδάνης, -ου, ὁ.

journey (n.), ὁδός, -οῦ, ἡ, way, road; journeying, ὁδοιπορία, -ας, ἡ.

journey, to, ὁδεύω, travel; πορεύομαι, go, pass; ὁδοιπορέω, go on a journey.

joy, χαρά, -ᾶς, ἡ.

Judas, Ἰούδας, gen. abl. -α, l. i. d. -ᾳ, acc. -αν, ὁ.

keep, τηρέω (referring to the result); φυλάσσω, guard (refers to the means).

kill, ἀποκτείνω.

king, βασιλεύς, -έως, ὁ

kingdom, βασιλεία, -ας, ἡ (cf. βασίλεια, ἡ, queen (LS), royal palace (LXX)).

lamb, ἀμνός, -οῦ, ὁ (used 4 t. of Christ); ἀρνίον, -ου, τό, (little) lamb (used only in Jn. 21:15 and Rev.).

Law, νόμος, -ου, ὁ.

least, ἐλάχιστος, -η, -ον (smallest: superlative fr. ἐλαχύς).

leave, λείπω.

leper, λεπρός, -οῦ, ὁ.

let, ἐάω (allow, permit); ἀφίημι, omit, let go, let be.

life, ζωή, -ῆς, ἡ; βίος, -ου, ὁ; βίος is naturally (classically) used of men, but NT usage exalts the feminine word ζωή, and so tends to debase the masculine word βίος (G.). "ζωή is the nobler word" (Trench. NT Syn. 90).

live, ζάω (really live, from ζωή above); βιόω, exist ("live . . . in flesh," 1 Pt. 4:2).

lodge, pass the night (in open), αὐλίζομαι; entertain strangers, ξενίζω.

lord, sir, κύριος, -ου, ὁ.

love (noun), ἀγάπη, -ης, ἡ, esteem plus the expression of it.

love, ἀγαπάω (voluntary, rational); φιλέω (emotional).

Luke, Λουκᾶς, Λουκᾶ, ὁ (declined like βορρᾶς, -ᾶ, -ό).

Macedonia, Μακεδονία, -ας, ἡ.

make, create, cause to be, do, ποιέω; make war, πολεμέω.

man (male or female, L. *homo*, human being), ἄνθρωπος, ου,
   ὁ. ἀνήρ, ἀνδρός, ὁ, man (in the sense of male, husband,
   gentleman, L. *vir*, hero).

many, use the plural of πολύς, πολλή, πολύ.

master, ἐπιστάτης, -ου, ὁ (superintendent, overseer);
   δεσπότης, ου, ὁ, lord.

may, as Engl. auxiliary, Gr. subj. or ind.; ἰσχύω, be strong;
   ἔξεστι, is permitted.

message, ἀγγελία, -ας, ἡ; ἐπαγγελία, -ας, ἡ, promise, an-
   nouncement.

Messiah, Μεσσίας, -ου, ὁ (only in Jn: 1:41 and 4:25).

mighty, κραταιός, -ά, -όν; δυνατός, -ή, -όν, powerful; ἰσχυρός,
   -ά, -όν, strong.

ministry, διακονία, -ας, ἡ; λειτουργία, -ας, ἡ, public religious
   and social service.

most, see Man. on Adverbs.

multitude, πλῆθος, -ους, τό; ὄχλος, -ου, ὁ, crowd, throng,
   mixed multitude, common people.

must (it is necessary), δεῖ, is meet morally; χρή, meet cir-
   cumstantially (both are impersonal vbs. followed by inf).

my (adj.), ἐμός, -ή, -όν (my own, mine); ἐμοῦ (emphatic);
   μοῦ (unemph.), my, mine.

name, ὄνομα, ὀνόματος, τό.

nation, ἔθνος, ἔθνους, τό; γένος, γένους, τό, race.

near, ἐγγύς.

near (at), by, πρός w. loc. (w. acc., toward, to; w. abl. for).

necessary, is (Gr. idiom for Eng. "must"), δεῖ indicates
divine obligation; and χρή indicates circumstantial
necessity (followed by inf.).

never, οὐδέποτε, μηδέποτε (οὐ μὴ πώποτε, Jn. 6:35; οὐ μὴ
εἰς τὸν αἰῶνα, Jn. 10:28).

night, νύξ, νυκτός, ἡ (Ger. *Nacht*, L. *nox, noctis,* fem.).

no one, none, οὐδείς, μηδείς.

not, οὐ (with ind. only, denies positively; negates a single
word). Written οὐ before consonants; οὐκ before a
smooth breathing; οὐχ before rough breathing; written
οὔ only when final (end of clauses) or emphatic. μή (w.
subj., opt., inf., impv., ptc. and sts. ind. conditions and
when denial is a matter of thought, not fact; G. §401).
Indicates a hesitating denial, or "according to the
judgment, opinion, will, purpose, preference, of some
one," in distinction from οὐ; which "denies the thing
itself (simply, absolutely, directly, categorically, objectively)."

O (as sign of Voc.), ὦ, 2 Cor. 12:21, Rom. 11:33.

oath, pledge, ὅρκος, -ου, ὁ (ὀρκωμοσία, -ας, ἡ, taking an oath).

obey, ὑπακούω; πειθαρχέω, obey God (rulers), 1 a. πειθήρ-
χησα.

of, denoted in Gr. by gen.; when denoting source or separation by ἐκ (ἐξ) w. abl.

officer, Synag. or Sanh., attendant, ὑπηρέτης, -ου, ὁ; πράκτωρ,
-ορος, ὁ, court officer.

olive (tree and fruit), ἐλαία, -ας, ἡ.

on, upon, ἐπί, w. gen., loc., and acc. in sense of onto (on,
i.e., in, ἐν w. loc).

on account of, διά, w. acc.

one, εἷς, μία, ἕν; one . . . another, ὁ μὲν . . . ὁ δέ,
ὅς μὲν . . . ὅς δέ; μόνος, μόνη, μόνον, alone.

ordain, διατάσσω, ὁρίζω.

our, ἡμέτερος, -α, -ον; ἡμῶν.

out of, ἐκ (ἐξ), w. abl. only, from within, out of; ἀπό, w. abl., away from (exterior).

part (vb.), διαμερίζω, 1 a. διεμέρισα.

Passover, πάσχα (indecl.), τό.

Paul, Παῦλος, -ου, ὁ.

people, λαός, -οῦ, ὁ.

persecute, διώκω.

Peter, Πέτρος, -ου, ὁ.

Pharisee, Φαρισαῖος, -ου, ὁ.

Philippi, Φίλιπποι, -ων, οἱ.

plain, δῆλος, -η, -ον, evident; φανερός, -ά, -όν, visible.

play, παίζω (1 Cor. 10:7, quoted from the Septuagint).

please, ἀρέσκω, f. ἀρέσω, 1 a. ἤρεσα; used w. dat.

plot against, ἐπιβουλεύω.

poor, πτωχός, -ή, -όν (beggar); πένης, -ητος, ὁ (penniless worker, 2 Cor. 9:9).

praise (noun), ἔπαινος, -ου, ὁ; (vb.), αἰνέω (w. dat. and acc. of person).

pray, προσεύχομαι, 1 a. προσηυξάμην.

prayer, προσευχή, -ῆς, ἡ.

preach, proclaim, κηρύσσω, 1 a. ἐκήρυξα, pf. κεκήρυχα.

preach the gospel, εὐαγγελίζομαι, 1 a., εὐηγγελισάμην.

preaching, κήρυγμα, -τος, τό (proclamation, MM. announce, ment).

present, to (vb.), παρίστημι, -ιστάνω.

priest, ἱερεύς, -έως, ὁ.

prophet, προφήτης, -ου, ὁ.

providence, πρόνοια, -ας, ἡ.

publican, τελώνης, -ου, ὁ (tax collector).

pure, καθαρός, -ά, -όν (clean, free); ἁγνός, -ή, -όν (holy).

question, ζήτημα, -ατος, τό (inquiry); ζήτησις, -εως, ἡ (questioning).

quickly, ταχέως, ταχύ. (See Man. on Adv. for superlative.)

really, ὄντως (actually); γάρ (for); δή (indeed); -περ (indeed)
ἄρα (then, therefore).

rebuke, ἐπιτιμάω (award a penalty).

receive, δέχομαι; ἀποδέχομαι, accept; παραλαμβάνω, or
λαμβάνω, take, receive.

redeem, λυτρόω.

redeemer, λυτρωτής, -οῦ, ὁ.

rejoice, χαίρω, f. χαρήσομαι (punct. stem for earlier χαι-
ρήσω) w. instr.

remain, (ἐπι) μένω, abide (stay), f. (ἐπι) μενῶ; 1 a. (ἐπ) ἔμεινα.

repent, μετανοέω (change of mind, purpose, life); μεταμέλομαι
(change of feeling).

return, ὑποστρέφω (turn back); ἀποδίδωμι (give back, return, render).

revelation, ἀποκάλυψις, -εως, ἡ.

righteous, just, ἔνδικος, -ον; δίκαιος, -α, -ον, just.

righteousness, δικαιοσύνη, -ης, ἡ.

river, ποταμός, -οῦ, ὁ.

run, τρέχω (cf. Engl. trek), 2 a. ἔδραμον (fr. obs. δράμω).

sabbath, σάββατα, -ων, τά; σάββατον, -ου, τό.

saint, ἅγιος, -ου, ὁ (subts. fr. ἅγιος, -α, -ον; holy).

salute, to, ἀσπάζομαι (greet, bid farewell), 1 a. ἠσπασάμην.

salvation, σωτηρία, -ας, ἡ; σωτήριον, -ου, τό.

same, (adj.), very, self, he, she, it, αὐτός, -ή, -ό.

Savior, σωτήρ, σωτῆρος, ὁ.

save, σώζω.

say, φημί (declare); λέγω, say, speak, tell; λαλέω, speak
out (in cl. Gr., chat, babble, prattle).

scribe, γραμματεύς, -έως, ὁ.

sea, θάλασσα, -ης, ἡ; πέλαγος, -ους, τό, high sea, deep.

see, to, ὁράω, f. ὄψομαι, 2 a. εἶδον, Alexandrian 2 a. εἶδα (fr.
obs. pres. εἴδω); βλέπω, physically look, behold.

seem, seem best (lit. seem good), δοκέω; commonly used in
impersonal construction.

seize, ἐπιλαμβάνομαι, 2 a. ἐπελαβόμην; κατέχω, hold back, possess.

send, πέμπω; ἀποστέλλω.

servant, διάκονος, -ου, ὁ, ἡ, minister; δοῦλος, slave.

serve, δουλεύω.

service, διακονία, -ας, ἡ, ministry; λειτουργία, -ας, ἡ, social or religious service.

shepherd, ποιμήν, -ένος, ὁ.

should (it is necessary), δεῖ w. inf.

silence, to, φιμόω.

sin (noun), ἁμαρτία, -ας, ἡ; to sin (vb.), ἁμαρτάνω, f. ἁμαρτήσω, 2 a. ἥμαρτον.

sinful, sinner, ἁμαρτωλός, -όν.

sing, ᾄδω; 1 a. ᾖσα; ψάλλω, sing to a harp, sing psalms; ὑμνέω, sing a hymn.

sit, κάθημαι (G. §367); (παρα)καθίζω, make to sit down, set, sit.

slay, σφάζω (Attic σφάττω), slaughter; ἀποκτείνω, f. -ενῶ, 1 a. ἀπέκτεινα, 1 a. ps. ἀπεκτάνθην.

so, γέ; so that, ὥστε, consequence, result; w. inf. and in NT twice with the ind.

soldier, στρατιώτης, -ου, ὁ.

some (one), τὶς, τὶ (note grave accent, indicating enclitic and distinguishing this word, an indefinite pronoun, fr. the interrog. τίς, τί).

some, others, ἄλλοι . . . ἄλλοι.

son, υἱός, -οῦ, ὁ.

soul, ψυχή, -ῆς, ἡ.

speak, λαλέω, speak out, talk, chat, babble, prattle; λέγω, consecutive expression.

spirit, πνεῦμα, -τος, τό (wind, Jn. 3:8; breath, 2 Th. 2:8, Rev. 11:1).

Stephen, Στέφανος, -ου, ὁ.

stone, to, λιθάζω.

stop, φράσσω (fence in); παύω (in mid., cease).

submit, ὑπείκω (yield); ὑποτάσσω (subject); ὑποτίθημι, lay down; submit.

suffer, πάσχω, f. πείσομαι, 2 a. ἔπαθον.

take, λαμβάνω; αἱρέω, grasp, choose (in NT only mid., αἱρέομαι).

take counsel, συμβουλεύομαι.

teach, διδάσκω (παιδεύω, correct, teach; κατηχέω, instruct.)

teacher, διδάσκαλος, -ου, ὁ.

temple, ἱερόν, -οῦ, τό; ναός, -οῦ, ὁ, sanctuary.

teaching, διδαχή, -ῆς, ἡ.

thanksgiving, εὐχαριστία, -ας, ἡ.

that, ἐκεῖνος, -η, -ο, that one (demonstr.); ὅς, ἥ, ὅ, who, which (rel.); ἵνα, conj. followed by subj. of purpose; ὅτι (expletive.)

the, ὁ, ἡ, τό.

therefore, ἄρα, accordingly; differs from οὖν, then, in "denoting subjective impression, rather than a positive conclusion"; ἄρα οὖν, so then; τοιγαροῦν, wherefore then; τοίνυν, accordingly.

this (one), οὗτος, αὕτη, τοῦτο.

thither, ἐκεῖσε.

thou, σύ.

though, καίπερ; ἐὰν καί, if even (see "even though").

three, τρεῖς, τρία.

throne, θρόνος, -ου, ὁ ("official seat, chair of state"—MM).

through, διά, w. gen. (mediate agent).

thus, οὕτως (186 times, WH), οὕτω (10, WH, all before consonants).

thine, σός, σή, σόν.

Titus, Τίτος, -ου, ὁ.

to, dat. without prep., acc. w. πρός, toward: εἰς, into (acc. only), παρά w. acc.

together, ἅμα.

Troas, Τρωάs, -άδοs, ἡ.

trouble, τάραχοs, -ου, ὁ.

true, ἀληθήs, -έs (truthful, L. *verax*); ἀληθινόs, -ή, -όν, real, genuine (Eng. adjective "very").

trust, πιστεύω, have faith in, believe, entrust; w. dat.

truth, ἀλήθεια, -αs, ἡ.

twelve, δώδεκα, οἱ, αἱ, τά (indecl. numeral).

under, ὑπό w. acc.

understand, συνίημι, f. συνήσω, 1 a. συνῆκα.

until, till, ἕωs.

unto, until, ἕωs (prep. w. gen, R. 643), as far as (place and time); πρόs, to, toward.

upon, ἐπί, w. gen., loc., and acc.

uproar, θόρυβοs, -ου, ὁ.

vain, μάταιοs, -α, -ον; κενόs, -ή, όν, empty.

vision, ὅραμα, -τοs, τό, sight, ὀπτασία, -αs, ἡ, act of exhibiting; ὅρασιs, -εωs, ἡ, seeing.

wait, ἐκδέχομαι; περιμένω, wait for, await.

want, ὑστερέω (be in want, lack); θέλω, wish, will.

war, πόλεμοs, -ου, ὁ.

way, road, ὁδόs, -οῦ, ὁ, journey; πάροδοs, -ου, ἡ; πορεία, -αs, ἡ, journey, going.

we, ἡμεῖs.

weak, ἀσθενήs, -έs, infirm, feeble; ἀδύνατοs, -ον, impossible.

what? τίs; τί (simple interrogative pron.), preserves its acute unchanged to distinguish it from indefinite pron., τὶs, τὶ, any one, an enclitic.

what? of what kind? ποῖοs, ποία, ποῖον (inter. pron. of quality; L. *qualis*).

what kind of? ὁποῖοs, ὁποῖα, ὁποῖον (indefinite rel. pron.; L. *qualis*, what sort of).

wheat, σῖτοs, -ου, ὁ.

whenever, ὅταν (ὅτε + ἄν) (Ger. *dann wann, wann irgend*); ἡνίκα ἄν, whensoever.

wherefore, διό.

while, until, ἕως.

who, which, ὅς, ἥ, ὅ.

who? τίς; which? what? τί; (inter. pron.).

wilderness, desert, ἔρημος, -ου, ἡ.

wilderness, waste place, ἐρημία, -ας, ἡ.

win, gain, κερδαίνω.

with, instr. case without prep. or associational instr. w. σύν.

without, ἄνευ (opp. to σύν) w. abl.; ἄτερ, without, apart from; χωρίς, apart from.

woman, γυνή, γυναικός, ἡ (wife).

word, λόγος, -ου, ὁ (word, reason, *sermo, ratio*) ῥῆμα, ῥήματος, τό, word, speech.

work, ἔργον, -ου, τό. ἐργασία, -ας, ἡ, work, working, business.

work, to, ἐργάζομαι.

world, κόσμος, -ου, ὁ; οἰκουμένη, -ης, ἡ, inhabited land.

worthy, ἄξιος, ἀξία, ἄξιον.

write, γράφω.

wrong, to, to do wrong, ἀδικέω.

yea, ναί.

year, ἔτος, ἔτους, τό.

yield, ὑπείκω.

you, sg. σύ, thou; pl. ὑμεῖς, ye; or second per. pl. vb. endings

zeal, ζῆλος, -ου, ὁ.

ENGLISH INDEX

354 A MANUAL GRAMMAR

GREEK INDEX

INDEX OF SCRIPTURE REFERENCES

355